Fundamentals of Predictive Analytics with JMP®

Third Edition

Ron Klimberg

sas.com/books

The correct bibliographic citation for this manual is as follows: Klimberg, Ron. 2023. *Fundamentals of Predictive Analytics with JMP®, Third Edition*. Cary, NC: SAS Institute Inc.

Fundamentals of Predictive Analytics with JMP®, Third Edition

Copyright © 2023, SAS Institute Inc., Cary, NC, USA

ISBN 978-1-68580-003-1 (Hardcover)
ISBN 978-1-68580-027-7 (Paperback)
ISBN 978-1-68580-000-0 (Web PDF)
ISBN 978-1-68580-001-7 (EPUB)
ISBN 978-1-68580-002-4 (Kindle)

SAS Institute Inc., SAS Campus Drive, Cary, NC 27513-2414

April 2023

SAS® and all other SAS Institute Inc. product or service names are registered trademarks or trademarks of SAS Institute Inc. in the USA and other countries. ® indicates USA registration.

Other brand and product names are trademarks of their respective companies.

SAS software may be provided with certain third-party software, including but not limited to open-source software, which is licensed under its applicable third-party software license agreement. For license information about third-party software distributed with SAS software, refer to https://support.sas.com/en/technical-support/license-assistance.html.

Contents

About This Book

What Does This Book Cover?

This book focuses on the business statistics intelligence component of business analytics. It covers processes to perform a statistical study that might include data mining or predictive analytics techniques. Some real-world business examples of using these techniques are as follows:

- target marketing
- customer relation management
- market basket analysis
- cross-selling
- forecasting
- market segmentation
- customer retention
- improved underwriting
- quality control
- competitive analysis
- fraud detection and management
- churn analysis

Specific applications can be found at https://www.jmp.com/en_my/customer-stories/customer-listing/featured.html. The bottom line, as reported by the KDNuggets poll (2008), is this: The median return on investment for data mining projects is in the 125–150% range. (See http://www.kdnuggets.com/polls/2008/roi-data-mining.htm.)

This book is *not* an introductory statistics book, although it does introduce basic data analysis, data visualization, and analysis of multivariate data. For the most part, your introductory statistics course has not completely prepared you to move on to real-world statistical analysis. The primary objective of this book is, therefore, to provide a bridge from your introductory statistics course to practical statistical analysis. This book is also not a highly technical book that dives deeply into the theory or algorithms, but it will provide insight into the "black box" of the methods covered. Analytics techniques covered by this book include the following:

- regression
- ANOVA
- logistic regression
- principal component analysis

- LASSO and Elastic Net
- cluster analysis
- decision trees
- *k*-nearest neighbors
- neural networks
- bootstrap forests and boosted trees
- text mining
- time series forecasting
- association rules

Is This Book for You?

This book is designed for the student who wants to prepare for his or her professional career and who recognizes the need to understand both the concepts and the mechanics of predominant analytic modeling tools for solving real-world business problems. This book is designed also for the practitioner who wants to obtain a hands-on understanding of business analytics to make better decisions from data and models, and to apply these concepts and tools to business analytics projects.

This book is for you if you want to explore the use of analytics for making better business decisions and have been either intimidated by books that focus on the technical details, or discouraged by books that focus on the high-level importance of using data without including the how-to of the methods and analysis.

Although not required, your completion of a basic course in statistics will prove helpful. Experience with the book's software, JMP Pro 17, is not required.

What's New in This Edition?

This third edition includes one new chapter on time series forecasting. All the old chapters from the second edition are updated to JMP 17. In addition, about 60% more end-of-chapter exercises are provided.

What Should You Know about the Examples?

This book includes tutorials for you to follow to gain hands-on experience with JMP.

Software Used to Develop the Book's Content

JMP Pro 17 is the software used throughout this book.

Example Code and Data

You can access the example code and data for this book by linking to its author page at http://support.sas.com/klimberg. Some resources, such as instructor resources and add-ins used in the book, can be found on the JMP User Community file exchange at https://community.jmp.com.

Where Are the Exercise Solutions?

We strongly believe that for you to obtain maximum benefit from this book you need to complete the examples in each chapter. At the end of each chapter are suggested exercises so that you can practice what has been discussed in the chapter. Professors and instructors can obtain the exercise solutions by requesting them through the author's SAS Press webpage at http://support.sas.com/klimberg.

We Want to Hear from You

SAS Press books are written *by* SAS Users *for* SAS Users. We welcome your participation in their development and your feedback on SAS Press books that you are using. Please visit sas.com/books.

About The Author

Ron Klimberg, PhD, is a professor at the Haub School of Business at Saint Joseph's University in Philadelphia, PA. Before joining the faculty in 1997, he was a professor at Boston University, an operations research analyst at the U.S. Food and Drug Administration, and an independent consultant. His current primary interests include multiple criteria decision making, data envelopment analysis, data visualization, data mining, and modeling in general. Klimberg was the 2007 recipient of the Tengelmann Award for excellence in scholarship, teaching, and research. He received his PhD from Johns Hopkins University and his MS from George Washington University.

Learn more about the author by visiting his author page, where you can download free book excerpts, access example code and data, read the latest reviews, get updates, and more: http://support.sas.com/klimberg.

Acknowledgments

I would like to thank Catherine Connolly and Suzanne Morgen of SAS Press for providing editorial project support from start to finish.

I want to thank Mia Stephens, Dan Obermiller, Adam Morris, Sue Walsh, and Sarah Mikol, as well as Russell Lavery, Majid Nabavi, and Donald N. Stengel, for their detailed reviews on previous editions, which improved the final product. I would like to thank Daniel Valente and Christopher Gotwalt of SAS Institute for their guidance and insight in writing the text mining chapter. Thank you also to Peng Liu and Jian Cao for their review of the time series forecasting chapter.

Dedication

This third edition of the book is dedicated to B. D. (Bruce) McCullough. Bruce and I wrote the first two editions of this book. Bruce sadly passed away September 2020 of complications from cancer. Bruce was a good colleague, friend, husband, and father.

Chapter 1: Introduction

Historical Perspective

In 1981, Bill Gates made his infamous statement that "640KB ought to be enough for anybody" (Lai, 2008).

Looking back even further, about 10 to 15 years before Bill Gates's statement, we were in the middle of the Vietnam War era. State-of-the-art computer technology for both commercial and scientific areas at that time was the mainframe computer. A typical mainframe computer weighed tons, took an entire floor of a building, had to be air-conditioned, and cost about $3 million. Mainframe memory was approximately 512 KB with disk space of about 352 MB and speed up to 1 MIPS (million instructions per second).

In 2016, only 45 years later, an iPhone 6 with 32-GB memory has about 9300% more memory than the mainframe and can fit in a hand. A laptop with the Intel Core i7 processor has speeds up to 238,310 MIPS, about 240,000 times faster than the old mainframe, and weighs less than 4 pounds. Further, an iPhone or a laptop cost significantly less than $3 million. As Ray Kurzweil, an author, inventor, and futurist has stated (Lomas, 2008): "The computer in your cell phone today is a million times cheaper and a thousand times more powerful and about a hundred thousand times smaller (than the one computer at MIT in 1965) and so that's a billion-fold increase in capability per dollar or per euro that we've actually seen in the last 40 years." Technology has certainly changed!

Then in 2019, the Covid-19 pandemic turned our world upside down. The two major keys to many companies' survival have been the ability to embrace technology and analytics, perhaps quicker than planned, and the ability to think outside the box. Before the Covid-19 pandemic, the statement was "we will see more change in the next five years than there have been in the last 50 years." The pandemic has accelerated this change such that many of these changes will now occur in the next two to three years. Companies that take full advantage of new technology and analytics and find their distinct capability will have a competitive advantage to succeed.

Two Questions Organizations Need to Ask

Many organizations have realized or are just now starting to realize the importance of using analytics. One of the first strides an organization should take toward becoming an analytical competitor is to ask themselves the following two questions:

- With the huge investment in collecting data, do organizations get a decent return on investment (ROI)?
- What are your organization's two most important assets?

Return on Investment

With this new and ever-improving technology, most organizations (and even small organizations) are collecting an enormous amount of data. Each department has one or more computer systems. Many organizations are now integrating these department-level systems with organization systems, such as an enterprise resource planning (ERP) system. Newer systems are being deployed that store all these historical enterprise data in what is called a data warehouse. The IT budget for most organizations is a significant percentage of the organization's overall budget and is growing. The question is as follows:

With the huge investment in collecting this data, do organizations get a decent return on investment (ROI)?

The answer: mixed. No matter if the organization is large or small, only a limited number of organizations (yet growing in number) are using their data extensively. Meanwhile, most organizations are drowning in their data and struggling to gain some knowledge from it.

Cultural Change

How would managers respond to this question:

What are your organization's two most important assets?

Most managers would answer with their employees and the product or service that the organization provides (they might alternate which is first or second).

The follow-up question is more challenging: Given the first two most important assets of most organizations, what is the third most important asset of most organizations?

The actual answer is "the organization's data!" But to most managers, regardless of the size of their organizations, this answer would be a surprise. However, consider the vast amount of knowledge that's contained in customer or internal data. For many organizations, realizing and accepting that their data is the third most important asset would require a significant cultural change.

Rushing to the rescue in many organizations is the development of business intelligence (BI) and business analytics (BA) departments and initiatives. What is BI? What is BA? The answers seem to vary greatly depending on your background.

Business Intelligence and Business Analytics

Business intelligence (BI) and business analytics (BA) are considered by most people as providing information technology systems, such as dashboards and online analytical processing (OLAP) reports, to improve business decision-making. An expanded definition of BI is that it is a "broad category of applications and technologies for gathering, storing, analyzing, and providing access to data to help enterprise users make better business decisions. BI applications include the activities of decision support systems, query and reporting, online analytical processing (OLAP), statistical analysis, forecasting, and data mining" (Rahman, 2009).

The scope of BI and its growing applications have revitalized an old term: *business analytics* (BA). Davenport (Davenport and Harris, 2007) views BA as "the extensive use of data, statistical and quantitative analysis, explanatory and predictive models, and fact-based management to drive decisions and actions." Davenport further elaborates that organizations should develop an analytics competency as a "distinctive business capability" that would provide the organization with a competitive advantage.

In 2007, BA was viewed as a subset of BI. However, in recent years, this view has changed. Today, BA is viewed as including BI's core functions of reporting, OLAP and descriptive statistics, as well as the advanced analytics of data mining, forecasting, simulation, and optimization. Figure 1.1 presents a framework (adapted from Klimberg and Miori, 2010) that embraces this

Figure 1.1: A Framework of Business Analytics

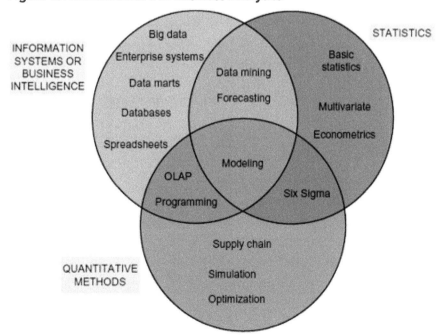

expanded definition of BA (or simply analytics) and shows the relationship of its three disciplines (Information Systems/Business Intelligence, Statistics, and Operations Research) (Gorman and Klimberg, 2014). The Institute of Operations Research and Management Science (INFORMS), one of the largest professional and academic organizations in the field of analytics, breaks analytics into three categories:

- Descriptive analytics: provides insights into the past by using tools such as queries, reports, and descriptive statistics,
- Predictive analytics: understand the future by using predictive modeling, forecasting, and simulation,
- Prescriptive analytics: provide advice on future decisions using optimization.

The buzzword in this area of analytics for about the last 25 years has been *data mining*. Data mining is the process of finding patterns in data, usually using some advanced statistical techniques. The current buzzwords are *predictive analytics* and *predictive modeling*. What is the difference in these three terms? As discussed, with the many and evolving definitions of business intelligence, these terms seem to have many different yet quite similar definitions. Chapter 18 briefly discusses their different definitions. This text, however, generally will not distinguish between *data mining*, *predictive analytics*, and *predictive modeling* and will use them interchangeably to mean or imply the same thing.

Most of the terms mentioned here include the adjective *business* (as in *business intelligence* and *business analytics*). Even so, the application of the techniques and tools can be applied outside the business world and are used in the public and social sectors. In general, wherever data is collected, these tools and techniques can be applied.

Introductory Statistics Courses

Most introductory statistics courses (outside the mathematics department) cover the following topics:

- descriptive statistics
- probability
- probability distributions (discrete and continuous)
- sampling distribution of the mean
- confidence intervals
- one-sample hypothesis testing

They might also cover the following:

- two-sample hypothesis testing
- simple linear regression
- multiple linear regression
- analysis of variance (ANOVA)

Yes, multiple linear regression and ANOVA are multivariate techniques. But the complexity of the multivariate nature is for the most part not addressed in the introduction to statistics course. One main reason—not enough time!

Nearly all the topics, problems, and examples in the course are directed toward univariate (one variable) or bivariate (two variables) analysis. Univariate analysis includes techniques to summarize the variable and make statistical inferences from the data to a population parameter. Bivariate analysis examines the relationship between two variables (for example, the relationship between age and weight).

A typical student's understanding of the components of a statistical study is shown in Figure 1.2. If the data are not available, a survey is performed or the data are purchased. Once the data are obtained, all at one time, the statistical analyses are done—using Excel or a statistical package, drawing the appropriate graphs and tables, performing all the necessary statistical tests, and writing up or otherwise presenting the results. And then you are done. With such a perspective, many students simply look at this statistics course as another math course and might not realize the importance and consequences of the material.

Figure 1.2: A Student's View of a Statistical Study from a Basic Statistics Course

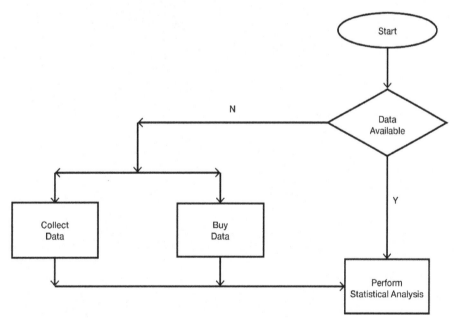

The Problem of Dirty Data

Although these first statistics courses provide a good foundation in introductory statistics, they provide a rather weak foundation for performing practical statistical studies. First, most real-world data are "dirty." *Dirty data* are erroneous data, missing values, incomplete records, and the like. For example, suppose a data field or variable that represents gender is supposed to be coded as either M or F. If you find the letter N in the field or even a blank instead, then you have dirty data. Learning to identify dirty data and to determine corrective action are fundamental skills needed to analyze real-world data. Chapter 3 will discuss dirty data in detail.

Added Complexities in Multivariate Analysis

Second, most practical statistical studies have data sets that include more than two variables, called multivariate data. Multivariate analysis uses some of the same techniques and tools used in univariate and bivariate analysis as covered in the introductory statistics courses, but in an expanded and much more complex manner. Also, when performing multivariate analysis, you are exploring the relationships among several variables. There are several multivariate statistical techniques and tools to consider that are not covered in a basic applied statistics course.

Before jumping into multivariate techniques and tools, students need to learn the univariate and bivariate techniques and tools that are taught in the basic first statistics course. However, in some programs this basic introductory statistics class might be the last data analysis course required or offered. In many other programs that do offer or require a second statistics course, these courses are just a continuation of the first course, which might or might not cover ANOVA and multiple linear regression. (Although ANOVA and multiple linear regression are multivariate, this reference is to a second statistics course beyond these topics.) In either case, the students are ill-prepared to apply statistics tools to real-world multivariate data. Perhaps, with some minor adjustments, real-world statistical analysis can be introduced into these programs.

On the other hand, with the growing interest in BI, BA, and predictive analytics, more programs are offering and sometimes even requiring a subsequent statistics course in predictive analytics. So, most students jump from univariate/bivariate statistical analysis to statistical predictive analytics techniques, which include numerous variables and records. These statistical predictive analytics techniques require the student to understand the fundamental principles of multivariate statistical analysis and, more so, to understand the process of a statistical study. In this situation, many students are lost, which simply reinforces the students' view that the course is just another math course.

Practical Statistical Study

Even with these ill-prepared multivariate shortcomings, there is still a more significant concern to address: the idea that most students view statistical analysis as a straightforward exercise in which you sit down once in front of your computer and just perform the necessary statistical techniques and tools, as in Figure 1.2. How boring! With such a viewpoint, this would be like telling someone that reading a book can simply be done by reading the book cover. The practical statistical study process of uncovering the *story* behind the data is what makes the work exciting.

Obtaining and Cleaning the Data

The prologue to a practical statistical study is determining the proper data needed, obtaining the data, and if necessary, cleaning the data (the dotted area in Figure 1.3). Answering the questions "Who is it for?" and "How will it be used?" will identify the suitable variables required and the

Figure 1.3: The Flow of a Real-World Statistical Study

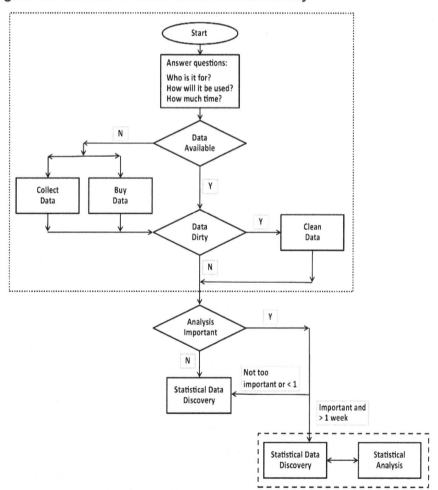

appropriate level of detail. Who will use the results and how they will use them determine which variables are necessary and the level of granularity. If there is enough time and the essential data is not available, then the data might have to be obtained by a survey, purchasing it, through an experiment, compiled from different systems or databases, or other possible sources. Once the data is available, most likely the data will first have to be cleaned—in essence, eliminating erroneous data as much as possible. Various manipulations will prepare the data for analysis, such as creating new derived variables, data transformations, and changing the units of measuring. Also, the data might need to be aggregated or compiled in various ways. These preliminary steps account for about 75% of the time of a statistical study and are discussed further in Chapter 18.

As shown in Figure 1.3, the importance placed on the statistical study by the decision-makers/ users and the amount of time allotted for the study will determine whether the study will be only a *statistical data discovery* or a more complete *statistical analysis*. *Statistical data discovery* is the discovery of significant and insignificant relationships among the variables and the observations in the data set.

Understanding the Statistical Study as a Story

The *statistical analysis* (the enclosed dashed-line area in Figure 1.3) should be read like a book— the data should tell a story. The first part of the story and continuing throughout the study is the *statistical data discovery*.

The story develops further as many different statistical techniques and tools are tried. Some will be helpful, some will not. With each iteration of applying the statistical techniques and tools, the story develops and is substantially further advanced when you relate the statistical results to the actual problem situation. As a result, your understanding of the problem and how it relates to the organization is improved. By doing the statistical analysis, you will make better decisions (most of the time). Furthermore, these decisions will be more informed so that you will be more confident in your decision. Finally, uncovering and telling this statistical story is fun!

The Plan-Perform-Analyze-Reflect Cycle

The development of the statistical story follows a process that is called here the *plan-perform-analyze-reflect* (PPAR) cycle, as shown in Figure 1.4. The PPAR cycle is an iterative progression.

The first step is to plan which statistical techniques or tools are to be applied. You are combining your statistical knowledge and your understanding of the business problem being addressed. You are asking pointed, directed questions to answer the business question by identifying a particular statistical tool or technique to use.

The second step is to perform the statistical analysis, using statistical software such as JMP.

Figure 1.4: The PPAR Cycle

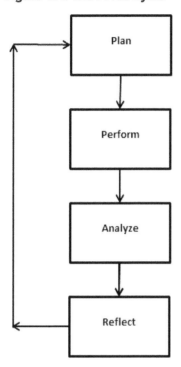

The third step is to analyze the results using appropriate statistical tests and other relevant criteria to evaluate the results. The fourth step is to reflect on the statistical results. Ask questions like what do the statistical results mean in terms of the problem situation? What insights have I gained? Can you draw any conclusions? Sometimes the results are extremely useful, sometimes meaningless, and sometimes in the middle—a potential significant relationship.

Then, it is back to the first step to plan what to do next. Each progressive iteration provides a little more to the story of the problem situation. This cycle continues until you feel you have exhausted all possible statistical techniques or tools (visualization, univariate, bivariate, and multivariate statistical techniques) to apply, or you have results sufficient to consider the story completed.

Using Powerful Software

The software used in many initial statistics courses is Microsoft Excel, which is easily accessible and provides some basic statistical capabilities. However, as you advance through the course, because of Excel's statistical limitations, you might also use some nonprofessional, textbook-specific statistical software or perhaps some professional statistical software. Excel is not a professional statistics software application; it is a spreadsheet.

The statistical software application used in this book is the JMP statistical software application. JMP has the advanced statistical techniques and the associated, professionally proven, high-quality algorithms of the topics and techniques covered in this book. Nonetheless, some of the early examples in the textbook use Excel. The main reasons for using Excel are twofold: (1) to give you a good foundation before you move on to more advanced statistical topics, and (2) JMP can be easily accessed through Excel as an Excel add-in, which is an approach many will take.

Framework and Chapter Sequence

In this book, you first review basic statistics in Chapter 2 and expand on some of these concepts to *statistical data discovery* techniques in Chapter 4. Because most data sets in the real world are dirty, in Chapter 3, you discuss ways of cleaning data. Subsequently, you examine several multivariate techniques:

- regression and ANOVA (Chapter 5)
- logistic regression (Chapter 6)
- principal components (Chapter 7)
- cluster analysis Chapter 9)

The framework for statistical and visual methods in this book is shown in Figure 1.5. Each technique is introduced with a basic statistical foundation to help you understand when to use the technique and how to evaluate and interpret the results. Also, step-by-step directions are provided to guide you through an analysis using the technique.

Figure 1.5: A Framework for Multivariate Analysis

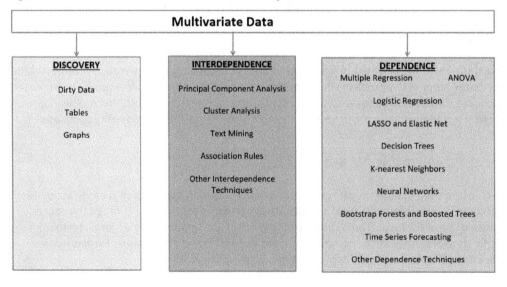

The second half of the book introduces several more multivariate and predictive techniques and provides an introduction to the predictive analytics process:

- LASSO and Elastic Net (Chapter 8),
- decision trees (Chapter 10),
- *k*-nearest neighbor (Chapter 11),
- neural networks (Chapter 12)
- bootstrap forests and boosted trees (Chapter 13)
- model comparison (Chapter 14)
- text mining (Chapter 15)
- association rules (Chapter 16),
- time series forecasting (Chapter 17), and
- data mining process (Chapter 18).

The discussion of these predictive analytics techniques uses the same approach as with the multivariate techniques—understand when to use it, evaluate and interpret the results, and follow step-by-step instructions.

When you are performing predictive analytics, you will most likely find that more than one model will be applicable. Chapter 14 examines procedures to compare these different models.

The overall objectives of the book are to not only introduce you to multivariate techniques and predictive analytics, but also provide a bridge from univariate statistics to practical statistical analysis by instilling the PPAR cycle.

Chapter 2: Statistics Review

Introduction

Regardless of the academic field of study—business, psychology, or sociology—the first applied statistics course introduces the following statistical foundation topics:

- descriptive statistics
- probability
- probability distributions (discrete and continuous)
- sampling distribution of the mean
- confidence intervals
- one-sample hypothesis testing and perhaps two-sample hypothesis testing
- simple linear regression
- multiple linear regression
- ANOVA

Not considering the mechanics or processes of performing these statistical techniques, what fundamental concepts should you remember? We believe there are six fundamental concepts:

- FC1: Always take a random and representative sample.
- FC2: Statistics is not an exact science.
- FC3: Understand a *z*-score.
- FC4: Understand the central limit theorem (not every distribution has to be bell-shaped).
- FC5: Understand one-sample hypothesis testing and *p*-values.
- FC6: Few approaches are correct and many are wrong.

Let's examine each concept further.

Fundamental Concepts 1 and 2

The first fundamental concept explains why we take a random and representative sample. The second fundamental concept is that sample statistics are estimates that vary from sample to sample.

FC1: Always Take a Random and Representative Sample

What is a random and representative sample (called a 2R sample)? Here, *representative* means representative of the population of interest. A good example is state election polling. You do not want to sample everyone in the state. First, an individual must be old enough and registered to vote. You cannot vote if you are not registered. Next, not everyone who is registered votes, so, does a given registered voter plan to vote? You are not interested in individuals who do not plan to vote. You don't care about their voting preferences because they will not affect the election. Thus, the population of interest is those individuals who are registered to vote and plan to vote.

From this representative population of registered voters who plan to vote, you want to choose a random sample. *Random* means that each individual has an equal chance of being selected. Suppose that there is a huge container with balls that represent each individual who is identified as registered and planning to vote. From this container, you choose a certain number of balls (without replacing the ball). In such a case, each individual has an equal chance of being drawn.

You want the sample to be a 2R sample, but why? For two related reasons. First, if the sample is a 2R sample, then the sample distribution of observations will follow a pattern resembling that of the population. Suppose that the population distribution of interest is the weights of sumo wrestlers and horse jockeys (sort of a ridiculous distribution of interest, but that should help you remember why it is important). What does the shape of the population distribution of weights of sumo wrestlers and jockeys look like? Probably somewhat like the distribution in Figure 2.1. That is, it's bimodal, or two-humped.

If you take a 2R sample, the distribution of sampled weights will look somewhat like the population distribution in Figure 2.2, where the solid line is the population distribution and the dashed line is the sample distribution.

Figure 2.1: Population Distribution of the Weights of Sumo Wrestlers and Jockeys

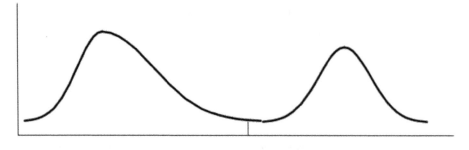

μ

Figure 2.2: Population and a Sample Distribution of the Weights of Sumo Wrestlers and Jockeys

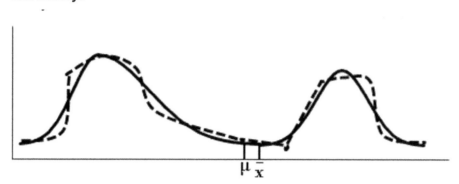

Why not exactly the same? Because it is a sample, not the entire population. It can differ, but just slightly. If the sample was of the entire population, then it would look exactly the same. Again, so what? Why is this so important?

The population parameters (such as the population mean, μ, the population variance, σ^2, or the population standard deviation, σ) are the true values of the population. These are the values that you are interested in knowing. In most situations, you would not know these values exactly only if you were to sample the entire population (or census) of interest. In most real-world situations, this would be a prohibitively large number (costing too much and taking too much time).

Because the sample is a 2R sample, the sample distribution of observations is very similar to the population distribution of observations. Therefore, the sample statistics, calculated from the sample, are good estimates of their corresponding population parameters. That is, statistically they will be relatively close to their population parameters because you took a 2R sample. For these reasons, you take a 2R sample.

FC2: Remember That Statistics Is Not an Exact Science

The sample statistics (such as the sample mean, sample variance, and sample standard deviation) are estimates of their corresponding population parameters. It is highly unlikely that they will equal their corresponding population parameter. It is more likely that they will be slightly below or slightly above the actual population parameter, as shown in Figure 2.2.

Further, if another 2R sample is taken, most likely the sample statistics from the second sample will be different from the first sample. They will be slightly less or more than the actual population parameter.

For example, suppose that a company's union is on the verge of striking. You take a 2R sample of 2,000 union workers. Assume that this sample size is statistically large. Out of the 2,000, 1,040 of them say that they are going to strike. First, 1,040 out of 2,000 is 52%, which is greater than 50%. Can you therefore conclude that they will go on strike? Given that 52% is an estimate of the percentage of the total number of union workers who are willing to strike, you know that another 2R sample will provide another percentage. But another sample could produce a percentage perhaps higher and perhaps lower and perhaps even less than 50%. By using statistical techniques, you can test the likelihood of the population parameter being greater than 50%. (You can construct a confidence interval, and if the lower confidence level is greater than 50%, you can be highly confident that the true population proportion is greater than 50%. Or you can conduct a hypothesis test to measure the likelihood that the proportion is greater than 50%.)

Bottom line: When you take a 2R sample, your sample statistics will be good (statistically relatively close, that is, not too far away) estimates of their corresponding population parameters. And you must realize that these sample statistics are estimates, in that, if other 2R samples are taken, they will produce different estimates.

Fundamental Concept 3: Understand a Z-Score

Suppose that you are sitting in on a marketing meeting. The marketing manager is presenting the past performance of one product over the past several years. Some of the statistical information that the manager provides is the average monthly sales and standard deviation. (More than likely, the manager would not present the standard deviation, but, a quick conservative estimate of the standard deviation is the (Max − Min)/4; the manager most likely would give the minimum and maximum values.)

Suppose that the average monthly sales are $500 million, and the standard deviation is $10 million. The marketing manager starts to present a new advertising campaign which he or she claims would increase sales to $570 million per month. And suppose that the new advertising looks promising. What is the likelihood of this happening? Calculate the z-score as follows:

$$Z = \frac{x - \mu}{\sigma} = \frac{570 - 500}{10} = 7$$

The z-score (and the t-score) is not just a number. The z-score is how many standard deviations away that a value, like the 570, is from the mean of 500. The z-score can provide you some guidance, regardless of the shape of the distribution. A z-score greater than (absolute value) 3 is considered an outlier and highly unlikely. In the example, if the new marketing campaign is as effective as suggested, the likelihood of increasing monthly sales by 7 standard deviations is extremely low.

On the other hand, what if you calculated the standard deviation and it was $50 million? The z-score is now 1.4 standard deviations. As you might expect, this can occur. Depending on how much you like the new advertising campaign, you would believe it could occur. So the number $570 million can be far away, or it could be close to the mean of $500 million. It depends on the spread of the data, which is measured by the standard deviation.

In general, the *z*-score is like a traffic light. If it is greater than the absolute value of 3 (denoted |3|), the light is red; this is an extreme value. If the *z*-score is between |1.65| and |3|, the light is yellow; this value is borderline. If the *z*-score is less than |1.65|, the light is green, and the value is just considered random variation. (The cutpoints of 3 and 1.65 might vary slightly depending on the situation.)

Fundamental Concept 4

This concept is where most students become lost in their first statistics class. They complete their statistics course thinking every distribution is normal or bell-shaped, but that is not true. However, if the FC1 assumption is not violated and the central limit theorem holds, then something called the sampling distribution of the sample means will be bell-shaped. And this sampling distribution is used for inferential statistics; that is, it is applied in constructing confidence intervals and performing hypothesis tests.

FC4: Understand the Central Limit Theorem

If you take a 2R sample, the histogram of the sample distribution of observations will be close to the histogram of the population distribution of observations (FC1). You also know that the sample mean from sample to sample will vary (FC2).

Suppose that you actually know the value of the population mean and you took every combination of sample size *n* (and let *n* be any number greater than 30), and you calculated the sample mean for each sample. Given all these sample means, you then produce a frequency distribution and corresponding histogram of sample means. You call this distribution the sampling distribution of sample means. A good number of sample means will be slightly less and more, and fewer will be farther away (above and below), with equal chance of being greater than or less than the population mean. If you try to visualize this, the distribution of all these sample means would be bell-shaped, as in Figure 2.3. This should make intuitive sense.

Nevertheless, there is one major problem. To get this distribution of sample means, you said that every combination of sample size n needs to be collected and analyzed. That, in most cases, is an enormous number of samples and would be prohibitive. Also, in the real world, you take only **one** 2R sample.

This is where the central limit theorem (CLT) comes to our rescue. The CLT holds regardless of the shape of the population distribution of observations—whether it is normal, bimodal (like the sumo wrestlers and jockeys), or whatever shape, as long as a 2R sample is taken and the sample size is greater than 30. Then, the sampling distribution of sample means will be approximately normal, with a mean of $\bar{x}$ and a standard deviation of ($s / \sqrt{n}$) (which is called the standard error).

What does this mean in terms of performing statistical inferences of the population? You do not have to take an enormous number of samples. You need to take only one 2R sample with a

Figure 2.3: Population Distribution and Sample Distribution of Observations and Sampling Distribution of the Means for the Weights of Sumo Wrestlers and Jockeys

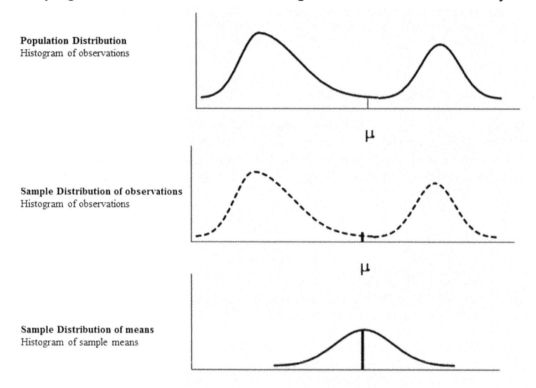

sample size greater than 30. In most situations, this will not be a problem. (If it is an issue, you should use nonparametric statistical techniques.) If you have a 2R sample greater than 30, you can approximate the sampling distribution of sample means by using the sample's $\bar{x}$ and standard error, $s / \sqrt{n}$. If you collect a 2R sample greater than 30, the CLT holds. As a result, you can use inferential statistics. That is, you can construct confidence intervals and perform hypothesis tests. The fact that you can approximate the sample distribution of the sample means by taking only one 2R sample greater than 30 is rather remarkable and is why the CLT theorem is known as the "cornerstone of statistics."

Learn from an Example

The implications of the CLT can be further illustrated with an empirical example. The example that you will use is the population of the weights of sumo wrestlers and jockeys.

Open the Excel file called SumowrestlersJockeysnew.xls and go to the first worksheet called "data." In column A, you see that the generated population of 5,000 sumo wrestlers' and jockeys' weights with 30% of them being sumo wrestlers.

First, you need the Excel Data Analysis add-in. (If you have loaded it already, you can jump to the next paragraph). To upload the Data Analysis add-in:

1. Click **File** from the list of options at the top of window. A box of options will appear.
2. On the left side toward the bottom, click **Options**. A dialog box will appear with a list of options on the left.
3. Click **Add-Ins**. The right side of this dialog box will now list Add-Ins. Toward the bottom of the dialog box there will appear the following:

4. Click **Go**. A new dialog box will appear listing the Add-Ins available with a check box on the left. Click the check boxes for **Analysis ToolPak** and **Analysis ToolPak—VBA**. Then click **OK**.

Now, you can generate the population distribution of weights:

1. Click **Data** on the list of options at the top of the window. Then click **Data Analysis.** A new dialog box will appear with an alphabetically ordered list of Analysis tools.
2. Click **Histogram** and **OK**.
3. In the Histogram dialog box, for the **Input Range**, enter **$A$2:$A$5001**; for the **Bin Range**, enter **$H$2:$H$37**; for the **Output range**, enter **$K$1**. Then click the options **Cumulative Percentage** and **Chart Output** and click **OK**, as in Figure 2.4.

Figure 2.4: Excel Data Analysis Tool Histogram Dialog Box

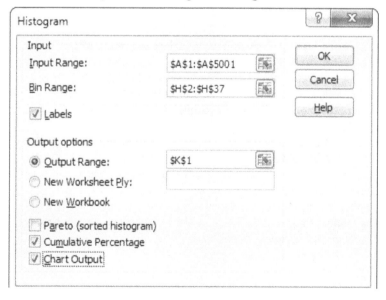

Figure 2.5: Results of the Histogram Data Analysis Tool

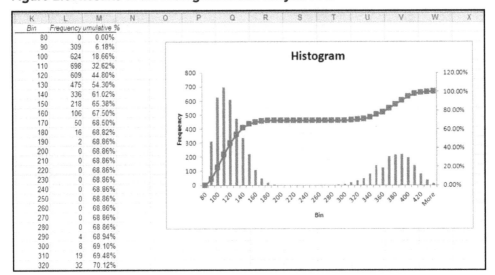

A frequency distribution and histogram similar to Figure 2.5 will be generated.

Given the population distribution of sumo wrestlers and jockeys, you will generate a random sample of 30 and a corresponding dynamic frequency distribution and histogram (you will understand the term *dynamic* shortly):

1. Select the **1 random sample** worksheet. In columns C and D, you will find percentages that are based on the cumulative percentages in column M of the worksheet **data**. Also, in column E, you will find the average (or midpoint) of that particular range.
2. In cell **K2**, enter **=rand()**. Copy and paste K2 into cells **K3** to **K31**.
3. In cell **L2**, enter **=VLOOKUP(K2,$C$2:$E$37,3)**. Copy and paste L2 into cells **L3** to **L31**. (In this case, the VLOOKUP function finds the row in $C$2:$D$37 that matches K2 and returns the value found in the third column (column E) in that row.)
4. You have now generated a random sample of 30. If you press **F9**, the random sample will change.
5. To produce the corresponding frequency distribution (and *be careful!*), highlight the cells **P2** to **P37**. In cell **P2**, enter the following: =frequency(L2:L31,O2:O37). Before pressing **Enter,** *simultaneously* hold down and press **Ctrl, Shift,** and **Enter**. The frequency function finds the frequency for each bin, O2:O37, and for the cells L2:L31. Also, when you simultaneously hold down the keys, an array is created. Again, as you press the **F9** key, the random sample and corresponding frequency distribution changes. (Hence, it is called a *dynamic frequency distribution*.)

a. To produce the corresponding dynamic histogram, highlight the cells **P2** to **P37**. Click **Insert** from the top list of options. Click the Chart type **Column** icon. An icon menu of column graphs is displayed. Click under the left icon that is under the 2-D Columns. A histogram of your frequency distribution is produced, similar to Figure 2.6.

b. To add the axis labels, under the group of Chart Tools at the top of the screen (remember to click on the graph), click **Layout.** A menu of options appears below. Select **Axis Titles ▶ Primary Horizontal Axis Title ▶ Title Below Axis**. Type Weights and press **Enter**. For the vertical axis, select **Axis Titles ▶ Primary Vertical Axis Title ▶ Vertical title.** Type **Frequency** and press **Enter**.

c. If you press **F9**, the random sample changes, the frequency distribution changes, and the histogram changes. As you can see, the histogram is definitely not bell-shaped and does look somewhat like the population distribution in Figure 2.5.

Now, go to the sampling distribution worksheet. Much in the way you generated a random sample in the random sample worksheet, 50 random samples were generated, each of size 30, in columns L to BI. Below each random sample, the average of that sample is calculated in row 33. Further in column BL is the dynamic frequency distribution, and there is a corresponding histogram of the 50 sample means. If you press F9, the 50 random samples, averages, frequency distribution, and histogram change. The histogram of the sampling distribution of sample means (which is based on only 50 samples—not on every combination) is not bimodal, but is generally bell-shaped.

Figure 2.6: Histogram of a Random Sample of 30 Sumo Wrestler and Jockeys Weights

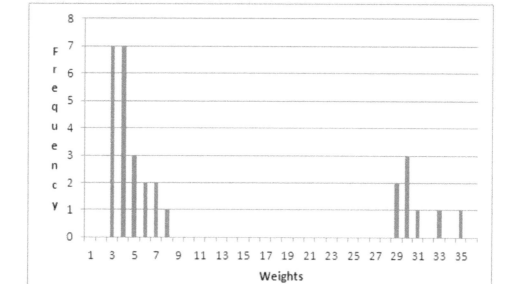

Fundamental Concept 5

One of the inferential statistical techniques that you can apply, thanks to the CLT, is one-sample hypothesis testing of the mean.

Understand One-Sample Hypothesis Testing

Generally speaking, hypothesis testing consists of two hypotheses, the null hypothesis, called H_0, and the opposite to H_0—the alternative hypothesis, called H_1 or H_a. The null hypothesis for one-sample hypothesis testing of the mean tests whether the population mean is equal to, less than or equal to, or greater than or equal to a particular constant, $\mu = k$, $\mu \leq k$, or $\mu \geq k$. An excellent analogy for hypothesis testing is the judicial system. The null hypothesis, H_0, is that you are innocent, and the alternative hypothesis, H_1, is that you are guilty.

Once the hypotheses are identified, the statistical test statistic is calculated. For simplicity's sake, in our discussion here assume only the z test will be discussed, although most of what is presented is pertinent to other statistical tests—such as t, F, and χ^2. This calculated statistical test statistic is called Z_{calc}. This Z_{calc} is compared to what here will be called the critical z, $Z_{critical}$. The $Z_{critical}$ value is based on what is called a level of significance, called α, which is usually equal to 0.10, 0.05, or 0.01. The level of significance can be viewed as the probability of making an error (or mistake), given that the H_0 is correct. Relating this to the judicial system, this is the probability of wrongly determining someone is guilty when in reality they are innocent. So you want to keep the level of significance rather small. Remember that statistics is not an exact science. You are dealing with estimates of the actual values. (The only way that you can be completely certain is if you use the entire population.) So, you want to keep the likelihood of making an error relatively small.

There are two possible statistical decisions and conclusions that are based on comparing the two z-values, Z_{calc} and $Z_{critical}$. If $|Z_{calc}| > |Z_{critical}|$, you reject H_0. When you reject H_0, there is enough statistical evidence to support H_1. That is, in terms of the judicial system, there is overwhelming evidence to conclude that the individual is guilty. On the other hand, you do fail to reject H_0 when $|Z_{calc}| \leq |Z_{critical}|$, and you conclude that there is *not* enough statistical evidence to support H_1. The judicial system would then say that the person is innocent, but, in reality, this is not necessarily true. You just did not have enough evidence to say that the person is guilty.

As discussed under FC3, "Understand a Z-Score," the $|Z_{calc}|$ is not simply a number. It represents the number of standard deviations away from the mean that a value is. In this case, it is the number of standard deviations away from the hypothesized value used in H_0. So, you reject H_0 when you have a relatively large $|Z_{calc}|$; that is, $|Z_{calc}| > |Z_{critical}|$. In this situation, you reject H_0 when the value is a relatively large number of standard deviations away from the hypothesized value. Conversely, when you have a relatively small $|Z_{calc}|$ (that is, $|Z_{calc}| \leq |Z_{critical}|$), you fail to reject H_0. That is, the $|Z_{calc}|$ value is relatively near the hypothesized value and could be simply due to random variation.

Consider *p*-Values

Instead of comparing the two *z*-values, Z_{calc} and $Z_{critical}$, another more generalizable approach that can also be used with other hypothesis tests (such as *t*, *F*, χ^2) is a concept known as the *p*-value. The *p*-value is the probability of rejecting H_0. Thus, in terms of the one-sample hypothesis test using the *Z*, the *p*-value is the probability that is associated with Z_{calc}. So, as shown in Table 2.1, a relatively large $|Z_{calc}|$ results in rejecting H_0 and has a relatively small *p*-value. Alternatively, a relatively small $|Z_{calc}|$ results in not rejecting H_0 and has a relatively large *p*-value. The *p*-values and $|Z_{calc}|$ have an inverse relationship: Relatively large $|Z_{calc}|$ values are associated with relatively small *p*-values, and, vice versa, relatively small $|Z_{calc}|$ values have relatively large *p*-values.

Table 2.1: Decisions and Conclusions to Hypothesis Tests in Relationship to the *p*-Value

Critical Value	*p*-value	Statistical Decision	Conclusion
$|Z_{Calc}| > |Z_{Critical}|$	*p*-value < α	Reject H_0	There is enough evidence to say that H_1 is true.
$|Z_{Calc}| \leq |Z_{Critical}|$	*p*-value ≥ α	Do Not Reject H_0	There is not enough evidence to say that H_1 is true.

General interpretation of a *p*-value is as follows:

- Less than 1%: There is overwhelming evidence that supports the alternative hypothesis.
- Between 1% and 5%. There is strong evidence that supports the alternative hypothesis.
- Between 5% and 10%. There is weak evidence that supports the alternative hypothesis.
- Greater than 10%: There is little to no evidence that supports the alternative hypothesis.

An excellent real-world example of *p*-values is the criterion that the U.S. Food and Drug Administration (FDA) uses to approve new drugs. A new drug is said to be effective if it has a *p*-value less than .05 (and the FDA does not change the threshold of .05). So, a new drug is approved only if there is strong evidence that it is effective.

Fundamental Concept 6

In your first statistics course, many and perhaps an overwhelming number of approaches and techniques were presented. When do you use them? Do you remember why you use them? Some approaches and techniques should not even be considered with some data. Two major questions should be asked when considering the use of a statistical approach or technique:

- Is it statistically appropriate?
- What will it possibly tell you?

Understand That Few Approaches and Techniques Are Correct–Many Are Wrong

An important factor to consider in deciding which technique to use is whether one or more of the variables is categorical or continuous. Categorical data can be nominal data such as gender, or it might be ordinal such as the Likert scale. Continuous data can have decimals (or no decimals, in which the datum is an integer), and you can measure the distance between values. But with categorical data, you cannot measure distance. Simply in terms of graphing, you would use bar and pie charts for categorical data but not for continuous data. On the other hand, graphing a continuous variable requires a histogram or box plot. When summarizing data, descriptive statistics are insightful for continuous variables. A frequency distribution is much more useful for categorical data.

Illustration 1

To illustrate, use the data in Table 2.2 and found in the file Countif.xls in worksheet **rawdata**. The data consists of survey data from 20 students, asking them how useful their statistics class was (column C), where 1 represents extremely not useful and 5 represents extremely useful, along with some individual descriptors of major (Business or Arts and Sciences (A&S)), gender, current salary, GPA, and years since graduating. Major and gender (and correspondingly gender code) are examples of nominal data. The Likert scale of usefulness is an example of ordinal data. Salary, GPA, and years are examples of continuous data.

Some descriptive statistics, derived from some Excel functions, are found in rows 25 to 29 in the **stats** worksheet. These descriptive statistics are valuable in understanding the continuous data—An example would be the fact that since the average is somewhat less than the median the salary data could be considered to be slightly left-skewed and with a minimum of $31,235 and a maximum of $65,437. Descriptive statistics for the categorical data are not very helpful. For example, for the usefulness variable, an average of 3.35 was calculated, slightly above the middle value of 3. A frequency distribution would give much more insight.

Next examine this data in JMP. First, however, you must read the data from Excel.

Ways JMP Can Access Data in Excel

There are three ways that you can open an Excel file. One way is similar to opening any file in JMP; another way is directly from inside Excel (when JMP has been added to Excel as an Add-in). Lastly, the third way is accomplished by copying and pasting the data from Excel:

1. To open the file in JMP, first open JMP. From the top menu, click **File ▶ Open**. Locate the Countif.xls Excel file on your computer and click on it in the selection window. The Excel Import Wizard box will appear as shown in Figure 2.7. In the upper right corner, click the worksheet called **rawdata**, as shown in Figure 2.7. Click **Import.** The data table should then appear.

Table 2.2: Data and Descriptive Statistics in Countif.xls file and Worksheet Statistics

	A	B	C	D	E	F	G
1	Major	Gender	Usefulness	Salary	Gender code	GPA	Years
2	Business	Male	3	52125	0	3.53	4.40
3	Business	Female	1	52325	1	2.58	4.18
4	Business	Male	4	63042	0	3.52	5.30
5	A&S	Male	3	54928	0	3	4.49
6	Business	Male	4	50599	0	3.22	4.06
7	A&S	Female	2	42036	1	3.06	3.87
8	A&S	Female	3	46427	1	2.35	4.64
9	A&S	Male	3	51865	0	3.22	5.08
10	A&S	Female		33263	1	2.86	2.03
11	Business	Female	5	58434	1	3.6	5.76
12	Business	Male	4	61551	0	3	5.38
13	A&S	Male	5	31235	0	3.11	1.38
14	Business	Male	2	58730	0	3.43	4.83
15	A&S	Female	4	35830	1	3.31	2.91
16	Business	Male		53267	0	2.62	4.87
17	Business	Male	5	65437	0	3.28	5.54
18	A&S	Female	4	47591	1	2.68	3.76
19	A&S	Female	4	42659	1	3.16	3.27
20	Business	Male	3	50996	0	3.84	4.33
21	A&S	Male	2	40185	0	3.29	3.02
22	A&S	Male	5	33155	0	3.69	2.32
23	Business	Female	1	52695	1	2.54	3.38
24							
25	min		1	31235	0	2.35	1.38
26	max		5	65437	1	3.84	5.76
27	average		3.35	49017.05	0.409090909	3.131364	4.036364
28	median		3.5	51430.5	0	3.19	4.255
29	stdev		1.2680279	9937.653	0.50323628	0.400705	1.18139

2. If you want to open JMP from within Excel (and you are in Worksheet rawdata), on the top Excel menu click **JMP**. (Note: The first time you use this approach, select **Preferences**. Check the box for **Use the first rows as column names**. Click **OK**. Subsequent use of this approach does not require you to click Preferences.) Highlight cells **A1:G23**. Click **Data Table**. JMP should open and the data table will appear.
3. In Excel, copy the data including column names. In JMP, with a new data table, click **File ▶ New**. Click **Edit** in the new data table and select **Paste with Column Names**. (We prefer this approach.)

Now that you have the data in the worksheet rawdata from the Excel file Countif.xls in JMP, let's examine it.

In JMP, as illustrated in Figure 2.8, move your cursor to the Columns panel on top of the red bar chart symbol to the left of the variable Gender. The cursor should change and look like a hand.

Figure 2.7: Excel Import Wizard Dialog Box

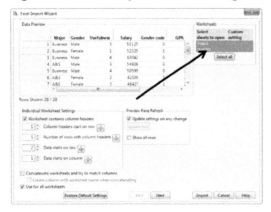

Figure 2.8: Modeling Types of Gender

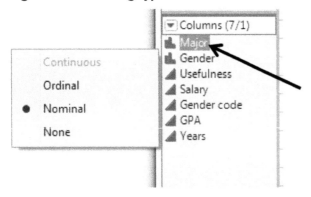

Right-click. You will get three rows of options: continuous (which is grayed out), ordinal, and nominal. Next to Nominal will be a dark colored marker, which indicates the JMP software's best guess of what type of data the column Gender is: Nominal.

If you move your cursor over the blue triangle beside Usefulness, you will see the dark colored marker next to Continuous. But actually the data is ordinal. So, click **Ordinal**. JMP now considers that column as ordinal (note that the blue triangle changed to a green bar chart).

Following the same process, change the column Gender code to nominal (the blue triangle now changes to a red bar chart). The data table should look like Figure 2.9. To save the file as a JMP file, first, in the Table panel, right-click Notes and select Delete. At the top menu, click **File ▶ Save As**, enter the file name **Countif**, and click **OK**.

Figure 2.9: The Data Table for Countif.jmp after Modeling Type Changes

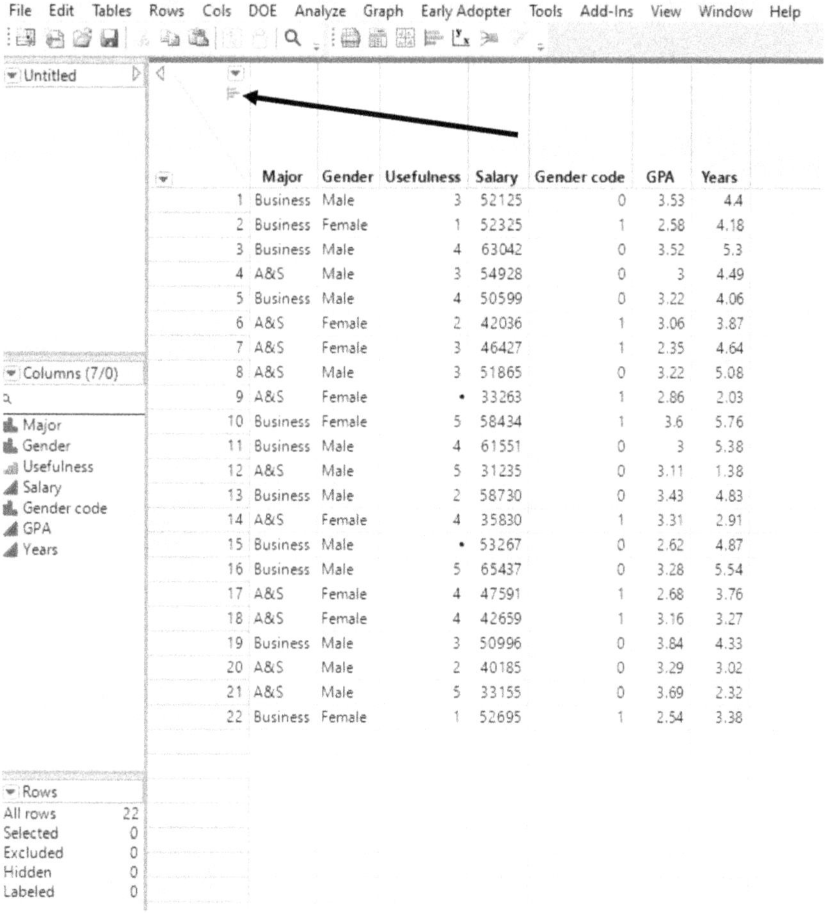

	Major	Gender	Usefulness	Salary	Gender code	GPA	Years
1	Business	Male	3	52125	0	3.53	4.4
2	Business	Female	1	52325	1	2.58	4.18
3	Business	Male	4	63042	0	3.52	5.3
4	A&S	Male	3	54928	0	3	4.49
5	Business	Male	4	50599	0	3.22	4.06
6	A&S	Female	2	42036	1	3.06	3.87
7	A&S	Female	3	46427	1	2.35	4.64
8	A&S	Male	3	51865	0	3.22	5.08
9	A&S	Female	•	33263	1	2.86	2.03
10	Business	Female	5	58434	1	3.6	5.76
11	Business	Male	4	61551	0	3	5.38
12	A&S	Male	5	31235	0	3.11	1.38
13	Business	Male	2	58730	0	3.43	4.83
14	A&S	Female	4	35830	1	3.31	2.91
15	Business	Male	•	53267	0	2.62	4.87
16	Business	Male	5	65437	0	3.28	5.54
17	A&S	Female	4	47591	1	2.68	3.76
18	A&S	Female	4	42659	1	3.16	3.27
19	Business	Male	3	50996	0	3.84	4.33
20	A&S	Male	2	40185	0	3.29	3.02
21	A&S	Male	5	33155	0	3.69	2.32
22	Business	Female	1	52695	1	2.54	3.38

At the top menu in JMP, select **Analyze ▶ Distribution**. The **Distribution** dialog box will appear. In this new dialog box, click **Major**, hold down the Shift key, click **Years**, and release. All the variables should be highlighted, as in Figure 2.10.

Click **Y, Columns**, and all the variables should be transferred to the box to the right. Click **OK,** and a new window will appear. Examine Figure 2.11 and your Distribution window in JMP. All the categorical variables (**Major, Gender, Usefulness,** and **Gender code**), whether they are nominal or ordinal, have frequency numbers and a histogram, and no descriptive statistics. But the continuous variables have descriptive statistics and a histogram.

As shown in Figure 2.11, click the area/bar of the Major histogram for Business. You can immediately see the distribution of Business students within each variable; they are highlighted in each of the histograms.

Figure 2.10: The JMP Distribution Dialog Box

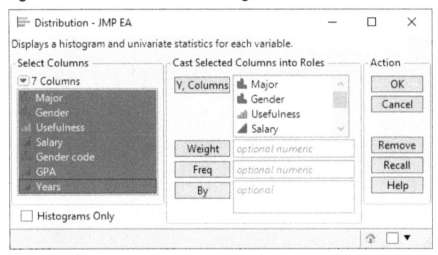

Figure 2.11: Distribution Output for Countif.jmp Data

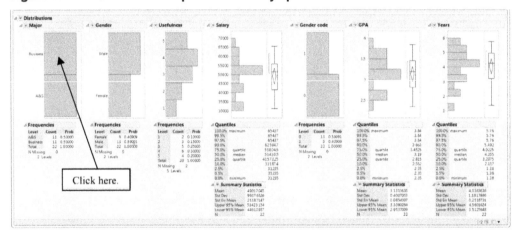

Most of the time in JMP, if you are looking for some more information to display or statistical options, they can be usually found by clicking the red triangle. For example, notice in Figure 2.11, just to the left of each variable's name, there is a red triangle. Click any one of these red triangles, and you will see a list of options. For example, click **Histogram Options** and deselect **Vertical**. Here's another example: click the red triangle next to Summary Statistics (note that summary statistics are listed for continuous variables only), and click **Customize Summary Statistics**. Click the check box, or check boxes, on the summary statistics that you want displayed, such as **Median**, **Minimum** or **Maximum**; and then click **OK**.

Figure 2.12: Fit Y by X Dialog Box

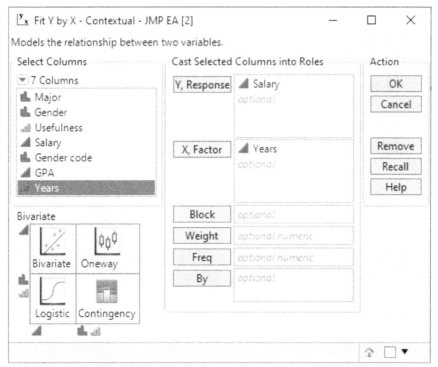

A quick way to see the histogram of all the variables is to click on the grayish histogram at the top of the data table—where the arrow is pointing in Figure 2.9. At the top of each column, below the column name will appear an overall histogram.

Illustration 2

What if you want to further examine the relationship between Business and these other variables or the relationship between any two of these variables (in essence, perform some bivariate analysis)? You can click any of the bars in the histograms to see the corresponding data in the other histograms. You could possibly look at every combination, but what is the right approach? JMP provides excellent direction. The bivariate diagram in the lower left of the new window, the Y/X tool table as shown in Figure 2.12, provides guidance on which technique is appropriate—for example, as follows:

1. Select **Analyze ▶ Fit Y by X**.
2. Drag **Salary** to the white box to the right of **Y, Response** (or click **Salary** and then click **Y, Response**).

3. Similarly, click **Years**, hold down the left mouse button, and drag it to the white box to the right of **X, Factor**. The **Fit Y by X** dialog box should look like Figure 2.12. According to the Y/X tool table in Figure 2.12, bivariate analysis will be performed.
4. Click **OK**.

In the new Fit Y by X output, click the red triangle to the left of Bivariate Fit of Salary by Years, and click **Fit Line**. The output will look like Figure 2.13. The positive coefficient of 7743.7163

Figure 2.13: Bivariate Analysis of Salary by Years

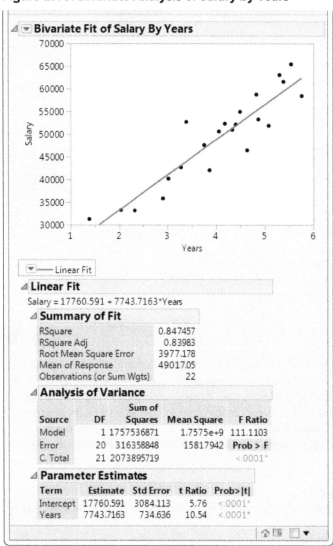

demonstrates a strong positive relationship. A positive value implies that as Years increases, Salary also increases, or the slope is positive. In contrast, a negative relationship has a negative slope. So, as the *X* variable increases, the *Y* variable decreases. The RSquare value or the coefficient of determination is 0.847457, which also shows a strong relationship.

RSquare values can range from 0 (no relationship) to 1 (exact/perfect relationship). You take the square root of the RSquare and multiply it as follows:

- by 1 if it has a positive slope (as it is for this illustration), or
- by −1 if it has a negative slope.

This calculation results in what is called the *correlation* of the variables **Salary** and **Years**. Correlation values near −1 or 1 show strong linear associations. (A negative correlation implies a negative linear relationship, and a positive correlation implies a positive linear relationship.) Correlation values near 0 imply no linear relationship. In this example, **Salary** and **Years** have a very strong correlation of .920574 = 1* √(0.847457).

On the other hand, what if you drag **Major** and **Gender** to the **Y**, **Response** and **X**, **Factor**, respectively in the Fit Y by X dialog box (Figure 2.12) and click **OK**? The Y/X tool table, that is, the bivariate analysis diagram on the lower left in Figure 2.12, would suggest a Contingency analysis. The contingency analysis output is shown in Figure 2.14.

The Mosaic Plot graphs the percentages from the contingency table. As shown in Figure 2.14, the Mosaic plot visually shows what appears to be a significant difference in **Gender** by **Major**. However, looking at the χ^2 test of independence results, the *p*-value, or Prob>ChiSq, is 0.1933. The χ^2 test assesses whether the row variable is significantly related to the column variable. That is, in this case, is **Gender** related to **Major** and vice versa? With a *p*-value of 0.1993, you would fail to reject H$_0$ and conclude that there is not a significant relationship between **Major** and **Gender**.

In general, using the χ^2 test of independence when one or more of the expected values are less than 5 is not advisable. In this case, if you click the red triangle next to Contingency Table and click **Expected**, you will see in the last row of each cell the expected value, as seen in Figure 2.14. (You can observe that for both A&S and Business in the Female row that the expected value is 4.5. So, in this circumstance, the χ^2 test of independence and its results should be ignored.)

As illustrated, JMP, in the bivariate analysis diagram in the lower left of the Fit Y by X dialog box, that is the Y/X tool table, as shown in Figure 2.15, helps the analyst select the proper statistical method to use. The *Y* variable is usually considered to be a dependent variable and is the vertical axis. The X variable, or independent variable is the horizontal axis. For example, if the Y variable is categorical and the X variable is continuous, then the Y/X tool table would suggest logistic regression should be used. This will be discussed in Chapter 6. Finally, in the last scenario, with the *X* variable as categorical and the *Y* variable as continuous, JMP will suggest One-way ANOVA,

Figure 2.14: Contingency Analysis of Major by Gender

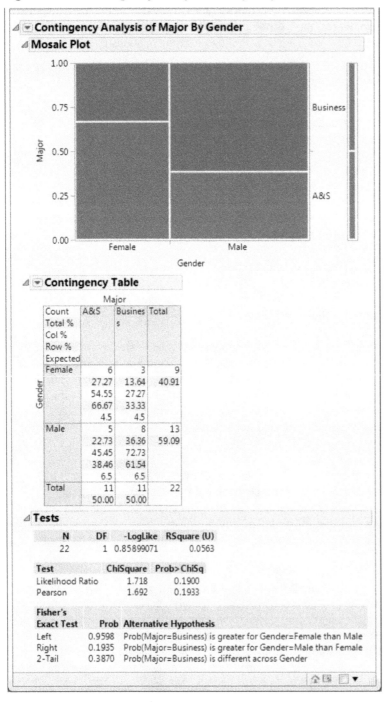

Figure 2.15: The Y/X tool Table

which will be discussed in Chapter 5. If two (or more variables) have no dependency, that is, they are interdependent, as you will learn in this book, there are other techniques to use.

Three Possible Outcomes When You Choose a Technique

Depending on the type of data, some techniques are appropriate and some are not. As you can see, one of the major factors is the type of data being considered—either continuous or categorical. Although JMP is a great help, just because an approach or technique appears appropriate, before running it, you need to step back and ask yourself what the results could provide. Part of that answer requires understanding and having knowledge of the actual problem situation being solved or examined. For example, you could be considering the bivariate analysis of GPA and Years. But logically they are not related, and if a relationship is demonstrated, it would most likely be a spurious one. What would it mean?

So, you might decide that you have an appropriate approach or technique, and it could provide some meaningful insight. However, you cannot guarantee that you will get the results that you expect or anticipate. You are not sure how it will work out. Yes, the approach or technique is appropriate. But depending on the theoretical and actual relationship that underlies the data, it might or might not be helpful.

When using a certain technique, three possible outcomes could occur:

- The technique is not appropriate to use with the data and should not be used.
- The technique is appropriate to use with the data. However, the results are not meaningful.
- The technique is appropriate to use with the data and, the results are meaningful.

This process of exploration is all part of developing and telling the statistical story behind the data.

Exercises

1. Use the hmeq.jmp file and the variable Loan. Are there any outliers on the high or lower end?

2. Use the hmeq.jmp file and the variable Mortgage. Are there any outliers on the high or lower end?

3. Using the hmeq.jmp file, show the relationship between Mortgage and Loan. Discuss it.

4. Using the hmeq.jmp file, show the relationship between Mortgage and Reason. Discuss it.

5. Using the hmeq.jmp file, show the relationship between Default and Reason. Discuss it.

6. Use the Promotion_new.jmp file and the variable Combine. Are there any outliers on the high or lower end?

7. Using the Promotion_new.jmp file, show the relationship between Race and Position. Discuss it.

8. Using the Promotion_new.jmp file, show the relationship between Race and Combine. Discuss it.

9. Using the Promotion_new.jmp file, show the relationship between Oral, Written, and Combine. Discuss it.

Chapter 3: Dirty Data

Introduction

Dirty data refers to fields or variables within a data set that are erroneous. Possible errors could range from spelling mistakes, incorrect values associated with fields or variables, or simply missing or blank values. Most real-world data sets have some degree of dirty data. As shown in Figure 3.1, dealing with dirty data is one of the multivariate data discovery steps.

In some situations (for example, when the original data source can be obtained), you can be 100% certain of the proper value for the variable. Typically, you cannot be 100% certain, so you must put the data through various programmed "cleaning" processes in which you do the best you can to make sure that the values are correct or at least reasonable.

Realize that the best, most unbiased solution to dirty data is not to have any bad data in the first place. So, starting at the initial stages of data input, every measure possible should be taken to guarantee quality of data. However, many times this guarantee of quality is out of your control. For example, you might obtain the data from some outside source. Nonetheless, the goal should

Figure 3.1: A Framework to Multivariate Analysis

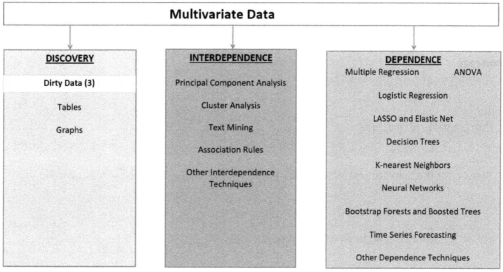

be that the data over which you have control should be as clean as possible—it will save you money in the long run!

Cleaning the data, manipulating the data, creating and deriving variables (as mentioned in Chapter 1 and discussed to a certain degree further in Chapter 18), and arranging the data in a suitable format for building models takes about 75% of the time. The entire data cleaning or scrubbing process, also known as ETL (extraction, transformation, loading), is very data set dependent and is beyond the scope of this book.

This chapter focuses on the major steps that you can take to clean the data when you do not have access to the raw data. The first part of the chapter addresses how JMP can assist you with descriptive statistics and data visualization methods in detecting and removing major errors, inconsistencies, and outliers. If these values remain in the data set, parameter estimates from statistical models might be biased and possibly produce significantly biased results. The remainder of the chapter addresses missing values. Missing values can be a serious problem since most standard statistical methods presume complete information (no blank fields) for all the variables in the analysis. If one or more fields are missing, the observation is not used by the statistical technique.

Data Set

To provide context to our discussion of these topics, you will use the data set file **hmeq.jmp.**[1] The data set contains 5,960 records of bank customers that have received a home equity loan and whether they have defaulted on the loan and some of their attributes. The variables included are as follows:

Default
   Loan status (1 = defaulted on loan; 0 = paid loan in full)

Loan
   Amount of loan requested

Mortgage
   Amount due on existing mortgage

Value
   Current value of property

Reason
   Reason for the loan request (HomeImp = home improvement; DebtCon = debt consolidation)

---

[1] Thanks to Tom Bohannon of SAS for providing the data set.

Job
Six occupational categories

YOJ
Years at present job

Derogatories
Number of major derogatory reports

Delinquencies
Number of delinquent credit lines

CLAge
Age of oldest credit line in months

Inquiries
Number of recent credit inquiries

CLNo
Number of existing credit lines

DEBTINC
Debt-to-income ratio

Error Detection

When you are given a new data set, one of the first steps is to perform descriptive statistics on most of the variables. You have two major goals during this exploratory process: (1) to check on the quality of the data, and (2) to start to get a basic understanding of the data set.

First, examine the data set's categorical variables, **Default**, **Reason,** and **Job**:

1. Select **Analyze ▶ Distribution**.
2. In the **Distribution** dialog box (Figure 3.2), select **Default**, **Reason**, and **Job**. Then click **Y, Columns**. (If you want to bring all three variables over at one time, hold down the **Ctrl** key and click each variable).
3. Click **OK**.

Figure 3.3 displays the distribution results for these three categorical variables. The data set contains 5,960 records. You can see that there are no missing values for **Default** (look toward the bottom of the output, where it says "N Missing 0"). On the other hand, the variable **Reason** has

Figure 3.2: Distribution Dialog Box

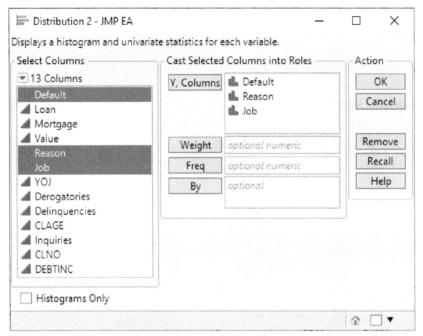

252 missing values, and **Job** has 279 missing values. You will return to address these missing values later in the chapter in the discussion about missing values. For now, just note this occurrence.

Besides the 279 missing values, the variable **Job** looks fine. However, it appears that the variable **Reason** has a few typographical errors—Debtcon, DebtConn, and Homeimp. One way to change these errors is to scan through the data table to find each of them. Because there are few typographical errors in this case, you could use this approach. But, with a large data set and many errors, this approach would be very tedious. A more general and very powerful approach is to use the JMP Recode tool:

1. Click on the column heading **Reason**, as shown in Figure 3.4.
2. Select **Cols ▶ Recode...**. The Recode dialog box (Figure 3.5) will appear.
3. Highlight **Debtcon, DebtCon,** and **DebtConn** by clicking **Debtcon,** holding down the **Shift** key, and clicking **DebtConn**.
4. Right-click to open the option list and select **Group To DebtCon**. This groups the variable names together.
5. Similarly, group **Homeimp** and **HomeImp** to **HomeImp**.
6. You can have your changes replace the values for that column/variable or create a new column/variable with the changes. Let's not create a new variable and change the

Figure 3.3: Distribution Output for Variables Default, Reason, and Job

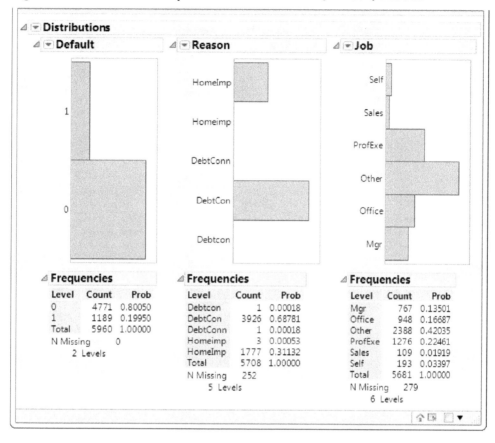

current variable by clicking the down arrow in the box in the upper left labeled **New Column**.[2] Click **In Place**.

7. At the bottom, click **Recode**.
8. To check your changes, rerun the distribution function to see that the typographical errors have been corrected. You have two categories of **Reason—DebtCon** and **HomeImp**.

Outlier Detection

Here are two approaches to identifying *outliers*.

---

[2] Although it is generally considered bad practice to change the raw data, you might want to do a **Save As.** If you do change the raw data, consider documenting your changes.

Figure 3.4: Data Table for hmeq.jmp

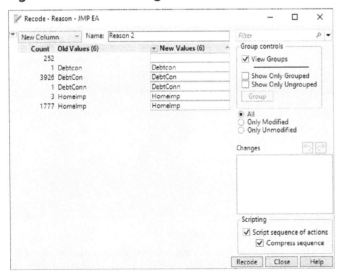

	Default	Loan	Mortgage	Value	Reason	Job
1	1	1100	25860	39025	HomeImp	Other
2	1	1300	70053	68400	HomeImp	Other
3	1	1500	13500	16700	HomeImp	Other
4	1	1500	•	•		
5	0	1700	97800	112000	HomeImp	Office
6	1	1700	30548	40320	HomeImp	Other
7	1	1800	48649	57037	HomeImp	Other
8	1	1800	28502	43034	HomeImp	Other
9	1	2000	32700	46740	HomeImp	Other
10	1	2000	•	62250	HomeImp	Sales
11	1	2000	22608	•		
12	1				HomeImp	Office
13	1				HomeImp	Other
14	0	2000	64536	87400		Mgr
15	1	2100	71000	83850	HomeImp	Other
16	1	2200	24280	34687	HomeImp	Other
17	1	2200	90957	102600	HomeImp	Mgr
18	1	2200	23030	•		
19	1	2300	28192	40150	HomeImp	Other
20	0	2300	102370	120953	HomeImp	Office
21	1	2300	37626	46200	HomeImp	Other
22	1	2400	50000	73395	HomeImp	ProfExe
23	1	2400	28000	40800	HomeImp	Mgr
24	1	2400	18000	•	HomeImp	Mgr
25	1	2400	•	17180	HomeImp	Other
26	1	2400	34863	47471	HomeImp	Mgr

Click either place.

hmeqa

Columns (13/1)
- Default
- Loan
- Mortgage
- Value
- Reason
- Job
- YOJ
- Derogatories
- Delinquencies
- CLAGE
- Inquiries
- CLNO
- DEBTINC

Figure 3.5: Recode Dialog Box

Recode - Reason - JMP EA   —   □   ×

New Column   Name: Reason 2   Filter

Count	Old Values (6)	New Values (6)
252		
1	Debtcon	Debtcon
3926	DebtCon	DebtCon
1	DebtConn	DebtConn
3	Homeimp	Homeimp
1777	HomeImp	HomeImp

Group controls
☑ View Groups

☐ Show Only Grouped
☐ Show Only Ungrouped
Group

◉ All
○ Only Modified
○ Only Unmodified

Changes

Scripting
☑ Script sequence of actions
☑ Compress sequence

Recode   Close   Help

Approach 1

Examine the continuous variables, **Loan**, **Mortgage**, and **Value**:

1. Select **Analyze ▶ Distribution**.
2. In the Distribution dialog box, select **Loan**, **Mortgage**, and **Value**. Then select **Y, Columns**. (Since all three variables are listed consecutively, click **Loan** first, hold down the **Shift** key, and click **Value**. As a result, all three should be highlighted).
3. Click **OK**.

Figure 3.6 displays the distribution results for these three variables.

If you want more statistics or to customize what summary statistics are displayed, click the red triangle next to Summary Statistics:

Figure 3.6: Distribution Output for Variables Loan, Mortgage, and Value

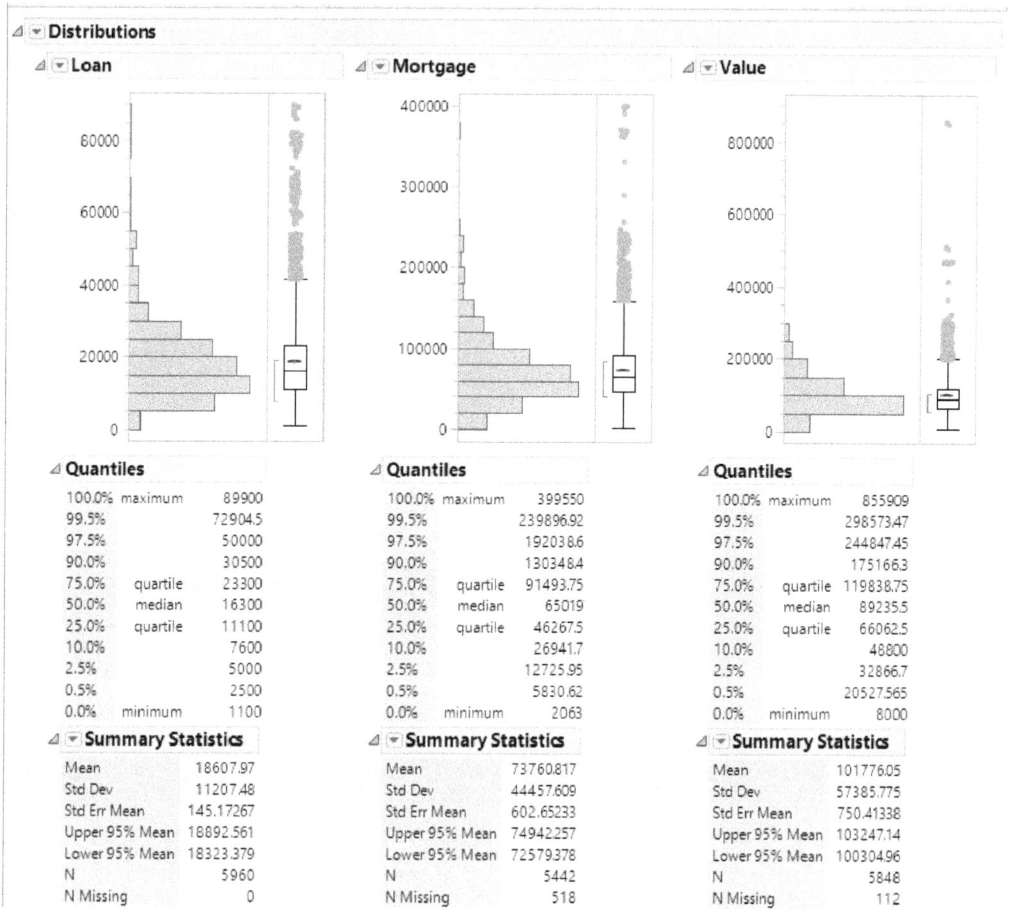

1. Click **Customize Summary Statistics**.
2. Click the check boxes for the summary statistics that you want displayed.
3. Click **OK**.

Examining the summary statistics and histograms in Figure 3.6, you will see that they look plausible. All three distributions are right-skewed. However, notice that the variable **Value** seems to have around the value of 850,000 several rather large observations (called *outliers*). You are not sure how many observations are out there. Complete the following steps:

1. Hold down the left mouse key and draw a rectangle around these large values. The Data Table window in the Rows panel should have four Selected. That is, four **Value** observations have large numbers.
2. In the Rows panel, click **Selected**.
3. Right-click the mouse to open the list of options and click **Data View**.

A new data table similar to Figure 3.7 will appear with the four outlier observations. The variable Value represents the current variable of the property. Suppose you happen to know that the values of the homes in the bank's region are not greater than $600,000. So you that know these four values of $850,000, $854,112, $854,114, and $855,909 are not possible. You will change these outlier values later after you look at another approach to identifying *outliers*. Close this new data table and return to the hmeq data table.

Figure 3.7: Data Table of Outliers for Variable Value

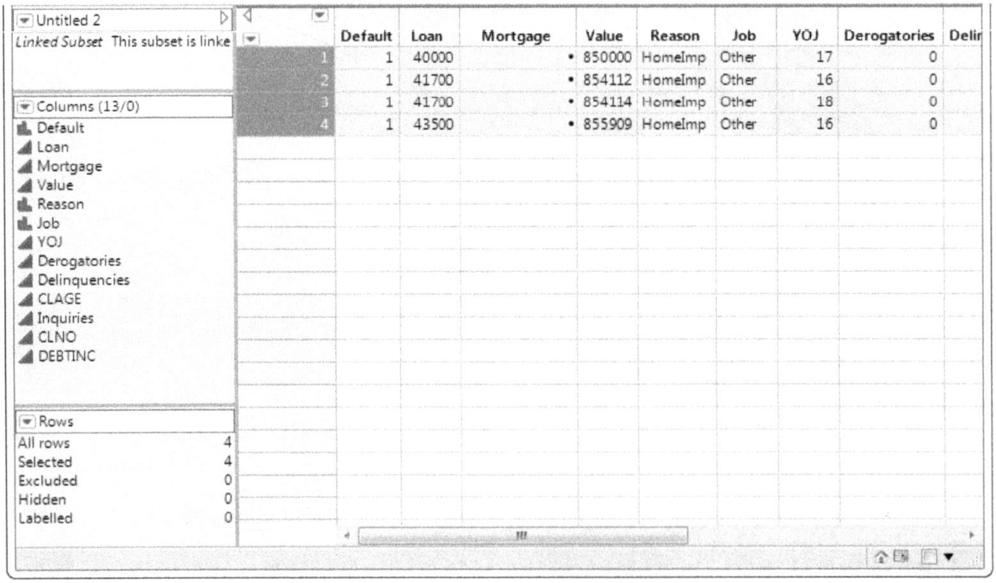

Approach 2

Another useful approach in identifying extreme values, as well as discovering missing values or error codes in the data, is to use the Quantile Range Outliers report. You produce this report by doing the following:

1. Select **Analyze ▶ Screening ▶ Explore Outliers**. The Explore Outliers dialog box will appear.
2. Under Select Columns, click **Value** and then click **Y, Columns**.
3. Click **OK**. The Explore Outliers dialog box will appear.
4. Click **Quantile Range Outliers**.

The Quantile Range Outlier report will appear as shown in Figure 3.8.

Quantiles divide the data into 10 equal parts. That is, each quantile has 10% of the observations. Quantiles are similar to quartiles that divide the data into four equal parts. To obtain the values at which each quantile occurs, you must first sort the data in ascending order. The 1st quantile value, or the lower 10% value, is the value that is greater than the lowest 10% of values for that variable. Conversely, the 9th quantile is the value where 90% of the values are less than are equal to this value. Only 10% of the values are above this 9th quantile value.

Figure 3.8: Quantile Range Outliers Report for Variable Value

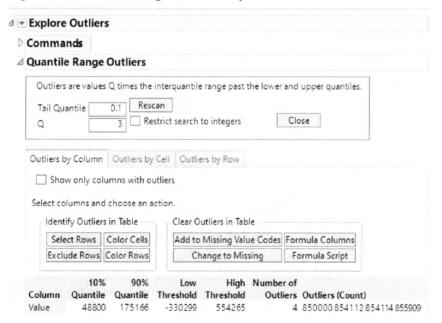

Column	10% Quantile	90% Quantile	Low Threshold	High Threshold	Number of Outliers	Outliers (Count)
Value	48800	175166	-330299	554265	4	850000 854112 854114 855909

The Tail Quantile probability (Figure 3.8), whose default value is 0.1, defines the interquantile range, which is from the Tail Quantile probability to (1 – Tail Quantile probability). So with a Tail Quantile probability equal to .1, the interquantile range is between the 0.1 and 0.9 quantiles. Corresponding quantile values for this data set are 48,800 and 175,166, respectively (Figure 3.8). The interquantile range (or the difference) is 175,166 – 48,800 = 126,366.

Q is a multiplier used to determine outliers for the chosen variable, or variables (Figure 3.8). Its default value is 3. Outliers are defined as values Q times the interquantile range below or above the lower and upper Tail quantile value. So, with this data and for the variable **Value**, as shown in Figure 3.8, you observe the following:

- Q * Interquantile range = 3 * 126,366 = 379,098.
- So, the Low Threshold = 10% Quantile – 3Q = 48,800 – 379,098 = – 330,298.
- And the High Threshold = 175,166 + 379,098 = 554,264. (Both numbers are off by one, due to rounding.)

Looking at the Quantile Range Outlier report (Figure 3.8), you can see that your four outliers were identified. Now complete the following steps:

1. At the bottom of the Quantile Range Outlier report click the **Value** variable. The row in the report should now be highlighted.
2. Just above in the Quantile Range Outlier report, click the **Select Rows** tab.
3. Go back to the data table. In the Rows panel, the value selected is equal to 4.
4. As discussed earlier, you can click **Selected**, right-click the mouse, and then click **Data View** to look at the same four outlier observations.

Now, what do you do, given that you have identified these observations as *outliers*? One of two situations could be true:

- The actual value of the outlier is correct. If so, you might want to examine this observation further to try to understand why such a large value occurred.
- Or the value is incorrect. If possible, go and find out what the actual value is. If you cannot find out the what the actual value should be, you could consider excluding that observation.

With this data set, it is not possible to verify these values. Yet, you know they are incorrect because you know (you assumed earlier in the chapter) that the largest value for Value must be less than 600,000.

However, look closely at these four outlier values in Table 3.1. They have repeated numbers. You assume that whoever entered these values happened to accidentally press a key a few more times than was correct. So, you want to make the changes shown in Table 3.1.

Table 3.1: Outlier Values for Variable Value and the Suggested Corrections

Current	Corrected
850,000	85,000
854,112	85,412
854,114	85,414
855,909	85,909

One way to make these changes is to search through the data table until you find them. However, even with this small data set of 5,960 records, that would take time. Another approach would be to sort the data by descending values of **Value**:

1. Click the column heading **Value**.
2. Right-click and select **Sort ▶ Descending**. The four outliers should be the first four observations.

Another approach would be to use the Recode tool.

Missing Values

The remainder of this chapter covers observations that have missing values. Many statistical techniques will ignore, delete, or not use an observation if any values are missing. If your data set has many variables and each variable has a small percentage of missing values, the number of usable observations can drop drastically. If you are using 10 variables in your model, for example, and each has 5% missing values (assume independently distributed), then you will be able to use only about 60% of the observations in the data set (.95^10 = 0.5987). It seems a shame to "throw away" an observation with 9 good pieces of information because you are missing 1 value out of 10. If you can "fix" the missing values, in a reasonable way, then you can use more observations.

Data fields or variables with missing values are a rather common occurrence when you are dealing with real-world data sets. Consequently, a given technique's results can be misleading or biased. The problem of missing values and approaches for dealing with them have only been addressed and developed since the late 1970s.

The reason for the missing values might or might not be logically justifiable. An example of a frequent, logically justifiable, and legitimate reason for missing data occurs with surveys. Suppose in a survey there is a question about whether you own a house. Subsequent questions might concern details about your homeownership, such as whether you have a mortgage, the amount of the mortgage, the amount of yearly real estate taxes, and so on. If you do not own a house, those data fields should be blank or missing. Justifiable missing values can also occur with government data sets. For example, suppose the data set contains information about census tracts, and there are data fields pertaining to land use. Census tract observations

Table 3.2: An Example of Patterns of Missingness for 100 Observations (0 Implies Missing)

Y	x1	x2	N
1	1	1	60
1	1	0	20
0	1	1	15
0	0	1	5

that happen to be in urban areas would most likely contain blank fields for data pertaining to agricultural use, and, equally likely, rural census tract areas could have blank fields for commercial use.

Care should be taken in making adjustments to variables with justifiable missing values if any of those values will be used as a denominator in a later calculation. For example, referring back to the homeownership survey, if you plan on reporting the percentage of people who own homes, the denominator should be the total number sampled. However, if the question is what percentage of homeowners have mortgages, the denominator should be the number of respondents that own a house.

When examining possibly unjustifiable missing values, you would like know why the data is missing. The underlying mechanisms for the missing values can range from being completely random to purposeful patterns of missingness. For example, people often underreport socially unacceptable behaviors, such as drug use, or many high income people do not report salary information.

You cannot be 100% certain about the probability of causes of missing values since you do not actually know the values of the missing values and cannot establish their true relationships. As a second-best solution, you look at the pattern of missingness. To illustrate, Table 3.2 shows an example of the patterns of missingness for 100 observations. From the patterns of missingness, you can see the following: 60% of the observations were complete and had no missing values; 20% had the Y variable missing, and 15 of those observations had only Y missing, while 5 observations had Y and X1 missing, and so on.

Statistical Assumptions of Patterns of Missing

There are three important statistical assumptions that you can make about the reason that data are missing (called the *missing data mechanism*) and their possible impact on statistical analysis: missing completely at random (MCAR), missing at random (MAR), and missing not at random (MNAR).

Missing Completely at Random

A variable *Y* is considered to be missing completely at random (MCAR) if the probability of its being missing does not depend on the values of *Y* or *X*. In essence, $P(Y \text{ is missing} | X, Y) = P(Y \text{ is missing})$.

MCAR implies that data are missing independently of both observed and unobserved data. That is, some values were deleted randomly. MCAR's only effect is that the sample size is smaller. It does not introduce any biases to the results. However, many times in practice, this is an unrealistically strong assumption.

A violation of MCAR would be if the people who did not provide their mortgage were on average older than people who did report it.

Missing at Random

The missing at random (MAR) assumption is a weaker assumption of MCAR. For example, suppose some data are missing for *Y*. The data for *Y* that are missing are considered MAR if the probability that *Y* is missing does not depend on Y after controlling for other variables in the analysis. That is, $P(Y \text{ is missing} | X, Y) = P(Y \text{ is missing} | X)$.

MAR implies, *given* the observed data, that data are missing independently of unobserved data. The missingness is not random but systematic. That is, it is conditional (on itself or on other variables). The MAR assumption is satisfied if the probability of missing data on *Y* (mortgage) depended on an individual's age. But within age groups, the probability of missing mortgage was not related to mortgage. However, you cannot test whether missingness on *Y* (mortgage) depends on *Y*. That is, you cannot compare the *Y* values of those with and without missing data to see whether they systematically differ on *Y* since you do not know the *Y* values of the missing data.

The underlying reason for the missing values of MAR data might or might not be important in understanding the relationships of the data.

Missing Not at Random

When the data are assumed to be neither MCAR nor MAR, then the data are classified as MNAR. Suppose some data are missing for *Y*. *Y* is considered to be MNAR if the probability that *Y* is missing does depend on the values of *Y*. MNAR implies that the missing values are related to the true value of the variable. In this situation, the amount of a mortgage is more likely to be missing with certain age groups. The fact that the data are missing contains information about the response. The observed data is a biased sample, and missing data cannot be ignored. In this case, the missing data mechanism should be modeled as part of the estimation process.

If the MAR assumption is satisfied (that is, MCAR or MAR), then the missing data mechanism is said to be ignorable, which implies that there is no need to model the missing data mechanism as part of the analysis. Most commercial statistical software, including JMP, handles missing data as if the missing data were based on this assumption of ignorability.

If the MAR assumption is not satisfied (that is, if the missing data mechanism is assumed MNAR), the missing value issue must be addressed and corrected to produce correct estimates of the parameters of interest. Both of the model-based methods (discussed later in this chapter) can produce valid estimates in the MNAR case if a model for the missing data mechanism is correctly specified.

Conventional Correction Methods

The four primary methods used for dealing with missing values are as follows:

- **Listwise deletion method**. Remove rows with missing values.
- **Variable removal method**. Eliminate any column/variable with missing values.
- **Conventional estimate values methods**. Replace missing values using typical statistical methods to estimated values.
- **Model-based methods**. Impute missing values by using model-based correction methods.

The first two methods remove or discard information (either a row or a column) while the last two methods estimate the missing values. A concern is, if the missing values are ignored, that later when you are using a predictive model you won't be able to score a new observation with missing values. (Another option is to use a predictive modeling technique such as decision trees or regression trees that can handle missing values. See Chapter 10.)

Listwise Deletion Method

The most common method for handling missing values (and the default of many statistical techniques) is merely to refrain from using any observations when one or more of the X and Y variables used in the analysis has a missing value. This method is called listwise deletion (or complete case analysis). Advantages of the listwise deletion method are that it is simple (usually requires the analyst to do nothing) and that the analyses across statistical techniques are comparable in that they use the same observations.

On the other hand, not including these observations can produce biased estimates (if the data are not MCAR). Also, by reducing the number of observations being used, the statistical power of the statistical test is reduced. The listwise deletion method often works well, particularly if the number of rows with any missing data is limited to a small (less than 5%) number of observations. In this case, any biases or loss of statistical power is likely inconsequential.

Table 3.3: A Small Example of Missing Data

Observation	Gender	Mortgage	Equity Loan
1	M	450,000	
2	F		9,900
3	M	550,000	8,600
4	M	285,000	8,800
5	M	280,000	5,700
6		381,000	28,000
7	F	475,000	8,000
8	M	395,000	
9	M	286,000	9,000
10	F	570,000	7,500
11	F	485,000	

A special case of the listwise deletion method is the pairwise deletion (or available case analysis) method. This method keeps as many observations as possible for each analysis. For example, using the small example in Table 3.2, Observations 2 and 6 would not be used in analyzing Gender and Mortgage. And Observations 1, 6, 8, and 11 would not be used in analyzing Gender and Equity Loan. The pairwise deletion method does use all the information possible for each analysis. However, you cannot compare the analyses because there is a different sample for each model.

Variable Removal Method

A similar approach might be taken in dropping some variables or fields from the model if a substantial proportion of observations has missing values. For example, in a survey, a great deal of missing values in one variable might be the result of a poorly worded question. A non-survey example could be problems in collecting or reporting the data for those variables. If it is believed that the variables with a large proportion of missing values have insignificant effect on Y, there is no great loss in not including them.

Conventional Estimate Value Methods

The following subsections give the methods that historically have been used to estimate missing values.

Mean, Median, or Mode Substitution

The idea with this method is that without any data, the mean, median, or mode would provide the best estimate to replace the missing value. This approach results in artificially reducing the variance of the variable and could yield lower covariance and correlation estimates.

Dummy Variable

Similar to the above mean, median, or mode substitution method, the missing values are estimated to a constant such as a mean, median, or mode. In addition, a dummy or indicator variable is created (1 = value is missing; 0 = otherwise). If the missing values are legitimately not there, the estimates from this method are unbiased. However, if the missing values are not legitimately missing, this method produces biased estimates.

Regression Imputation

Also known as *conditional mean imputation*, this method models the missing value based on the other variables. Suppose that you are examining a regression model with multiple independent X variables. Further suppose that one independent variable, Xi, has missing values. You select all those observations with complete information, use Xi as the dependent variable (also called regress Xi), and use all the other Xs as independent variables to predict the missing values of Xi. This method reduces the variance of Xi and could produce higher covariance between the X variables and increase correlation values.

In general, the major limitations of the regression imputation methods are that they lead to underestimates of the variance and can produce biased test statistics. These issues are caused by the fact that the imputed values are determined by the observed data (hence, they contain no error).

Model-Based Methods

Model-based methods to imputing missing values explicitly model the missingness of the data and provide confidence intervals of the parameter estimates. These methods provide a significant improvement over the conventional correction methods. As a result, the model-based methods are today the most common approaches to handling missing data. The two major model-based methods are maximum likelihood (ML) and multiple imputation (MI). Both of these approaches assume the joint distribution of data is multivariate normal and the missing data mechanism is ignorable (MCAR or MAR). The major advantage of the multivariate normal distribution assumption is that any independent variable follows a normal distribution conditional on all the other variables including the dependent and outcome variable.[3]

Maximum Likelihood Methods

The prominent ML method uses an expectation-maximization (EM) algorithm. The EM algorithm produces maximum likelihood estimates through an iterative process. This iterative process has two steps:

---

[3] This multivariate normal distribution assumption is different from the assumption used in linear regression. In linear regression, you assume that the dependent variable is univariate normal conditional on the values of the fixed independent variables.

- **Expectation Step**. If all the values are present, the sums, the sums of squares, and sums of cross-products are incremented. Otherwise, if one or more of the data fields are missing, the missing value(s) is (are) estimated using regression with all the variables. This estimated value(s) is (are) added to the sums. If only one value is missing, the sums of squares and cross-products are incremented. If more than one value is missing, a random correction error (from a multivariate normal distribution) is added to the sums of squares and cross-products. This step assumes that you have an estimate of the population mean and variance/covariance matrix, so you have a specification of the population distribution. From this population distribution, you can compute the expected value of sums.
- **Maximization Step**. Based on the current expected sums, you estimate the sums of squares and sums of cross-products and produce population mean and variance/covariance matrix. Using this variance/covariance matrix, new regression equations are calculated for each variable using all the other variables. These new regression equations are then used to update the best guess for the missing values during the Expectation Stage of the next iteration.

This two-stage process continues back and forth until the estimates do not change substantially. A disadvantage of this EM algorithm is that it does not provide standard errors (used to generate confidence intervals or perform hypothesis testing). So, an additional step such as a bootstrapping procedure is necessary to produce the standard errors.

Multiple Imputation Methods

The MI methods use a simulation-based approach. Unlike the ML method, the goal of the MI methods is to obtain estimates of the missing values rather than the expected values.

The MI methods also have a two-stage process:

- **Impute Estimates Stage**. A set of possible values for the missing observations are generated based on the multivariate normal distribution. Estimates of the missing values are produced by simulating random draws from the distribution of missing values given the observed values.
- **Generate Complete Data Sets Stage**. Repeat the Impute Estimates Stage *m* times to produce m complete data sets.

Averages and standard errors of the parameter estimates are produced from the m complete data sets. The resulting parameter estimates and confidence intervals have been shown to provide more robust estimates than the conventional methods.

The JMP Approach

When there is a high percentage of missing data, no method can reliably estimate the parameters. Even in the case of a high rate of missingness, the estimates from using one of the model-based methods provide reasonable results. In general, a model-based method is the best approach to handling missing data. Both model-based methods, ML and MI, have been shown to produce parameter estimates superior to those produced by conventional methods. The ML method has been shown to provide more robust parameter estimates than the MI methods. However, due to the extra step of estimating standard errors, the MI methods have been found to be easier to implement, and those are the methods most often found in commercial statistical software applications.

JMP provides two MI methods: multivariate normal imputation and multivariate singular value decomposition (SVD) imputation. The multivariate normal imputation replaces the missing values based on a multivariate normal distribution and provides an option to improve the estimation of the covariance matrix with a shrinkage estimator. The multivariate SVD method is the suggested method to use with wide data sets—that is, data sets with a large number of columns/variables (100s or 1000s of variables).

The two MI methods provided in JMP and model-based methods do not work with categorical data, because of the multivariate normal distribution assumption. Historically, the popular approach to replacing missing categorical data was to generate and replace the missing categorical values with a new category called *Missing*. Recently, studies have shown this approach can produce biased estimates. An alternative approach has been to change the data type of the dummy variables to continuous variables. This approach can produce imputed values outside the range of 0 to 1. If the categorical variables are being used as predictor variables in, for example, a regression model, the imputed values are used.

Example Using JMP

Now return to the hmeq.jmp data set that you were using earlier in this chapter.

To get a high-level value of the degree of missingness in the data set, complete the following steps:

1. At the top menu, select **Tables ▶ Missing Data Pattern**. The Missing Data Pattern dialog box will appear, as in Figure 3.9.
2. Select all the columns, from **Default** to **DEBTINC** and click **Add Columns**.
3. Click **OK**.

A Missing Data Pattern data table will appear (Figure 3.10). This new data table contains all the different patterns of missingness.

As you can see in Figure 3.10, there are 117 rows, so there are 117 different patterns of missingness. Each row represents a particular pattern of missingness. Notice in the first row that the count is 3,364, and the number of columns missing is 0. So, out of the original 5,960 rows, 3,364 have complete data. In the Missing Data Pattern window, in the upper-leftmost panel, click the green triangle next to Treemap. Do the same for **Cell Plot**. In each case, you get a visualization of the patterns of missingness in the data set.

Figure 3.9: Missing Data Pattern Dialog Box

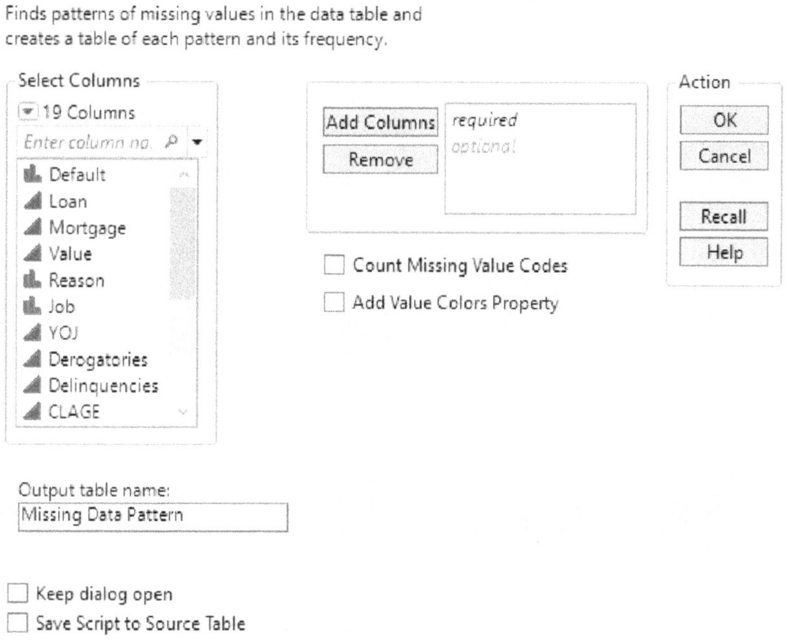

Finds patterns of missing values in the data table and
creates a table of each pattern and its frequency.

Select Columns
☑ 19 Columns
Enter column no. 🔍 ▼
🔹 Default
🔺 Loan
🔺 Mortgage
🔺 Value
🔹 Reason
🔹 Job
🔺 YOJ
🔺 Derogatories
🔺 Delinquencies
🔺 CLAGE

Add Columns   *required*
Remove   *optional*

☐ Count Missing Value Codes
☐ Add Value Colors Property

Action
OK
Cancel

Recall
Help

Output table name:
Missing Data Pattern

☐ Keep dialog open
☐ Save Script to Source Table

In the Missing Data Pattern data table, look at the categorical variables **Default**, **Reason**, and **Job** by examining their distributions (use **Analyze ▶ Distributions**). As shown earlier in the chapter in Figure 3.3, **Default** does not have any missing values, but **Reason** and **Job** have 252 and 279 missing values, respectively.

Complete the following steps:

1. Go back to the hmeg.jmp data table. In the Columns panel, select **Reason** and **Job**. Then from the top menu, select **Cols ▶ Utilities ▶ Make Indicator Columns**.
2. In the new dialog box, click the **Append Column Name** box.
3. Click **OK**.

The data table will change as shown in Figure 3.11. This procedure created an indicator variable for each level of a categorical variable. For example, for the variable **Reason**, you now have two indicator variables: **Reason_DebtCon** and **Reason_HomeImp**.

If there are missing values for the categorical variable, such as Reason, you now want these new indicator variables to show missing values. As shown in Figure 3.11, you first want to sort the column:

Figure 3.10: Missing Data Pattern

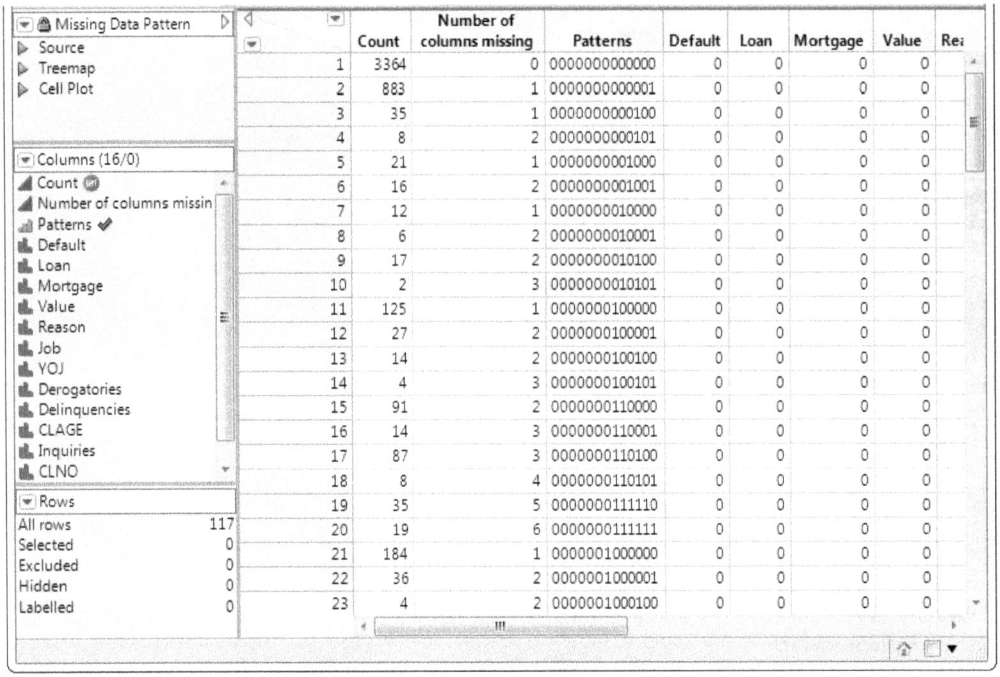

	Count	Number of columns missing	Patterns	Default	Loan	Mortgage	Value	Rea
1	3364	0	0000000000000	0	0	0	0	
2	883	1	0000000000001	0	0	0	0	
3	35	1	0000000000100	0	0	0	0	
4	8	2	0000000000101	0	0	0	0	
5	21	1	0000000001000	0	0	0	0	
6	16	2	0000000001001	0	0	0	0	
7	12	1	0000000010000	0	0	0	0	
8	6	2	0000000010001	0	0	0	0	
9	17	2	0000000010100	0	0	0	0	
10	2	3	0000000010101	0	0	0	0	
11	125	1	0000000100000	0	0	0	0	
12	27	2	0000000100001	0	0	0	0	
13	14	2	0000000100100	0	0	0	0	
14	4	3	0000000100101	0	0	0	0	
15	91	2	0000000110000	0	0	0	0	
16	14	3	0000000110001	0	0	0	0	
17	87	3	0000000110100	0	0	0	0	
18	8	4	0000000110101	0	0	0	0	
19	35	5	0000000111110	0	0	0	0	
20	19	6	0000000111111	0	0	0	0	
21	184	1	0000001000000	0	0	0	0	
22	36	2	0000001000001	0	0	0	0	
23	4	2	0000001000100	0	0	0	0	

Sidebar panel (left):
- Missing Data Pattern
  - Source
  - Treemap
  - Cell Plot
- Columns (16/0)
  - Count
  - Number of columns missin
  - Patterns ✔
  - Default
  - Loan
  - Mortgage
  - Value
  - Reason
  - Job
  - YOJ
  - Derogatories
  - Delinquencies
  - CLAGE
  - Inquiries
  - CLNO
- Rows
  - All rows 117
  - Selected 0
  - Excluded 0
  - Hidden 0
  - Labelled 0

1. Click on the column name **Reason**. Make sure that the entire column is highlighted. With your cursor still on the column heading, right-click and select **Sort ▶ Ascending**. The first 252 rows should now be blank for the Reason column and there should be zeros in cells **Reason_DebtCon** and **Reason_HomeImp**.
2. You would like all those zeros in the first 252 records for **Reason_DebtCon** and **Reason_ HomeImp** to be missing. To accomplish this, first highlight all the data in **Reason_ DebtCon** and **Reason_HomeImp** for the first 252 records in the data table. Then press **Delete** on your keyboard. Now, all those zeros have a dot, indicating *missing*.

Similarly, follow this entire process of sorting the data table to delete zeros to **Job** and its indicator variables.

Another approach to examining the missingness in the data set is to do as follows:

1. On the top menu, select **Analyze ▶ Screening ▶ Explore Missing Values**. The Explore Missing Values dialog box will appear.
2. +
3. Click **OK**.

The Explore Missing Values report box will appear as shown in Figure 3.12. The report lists by variable the number of missing observations; for example, **DEBTINC** is missing in 1267 rows.

Figure 3.11: New Data Table after Creating Indicator Columns

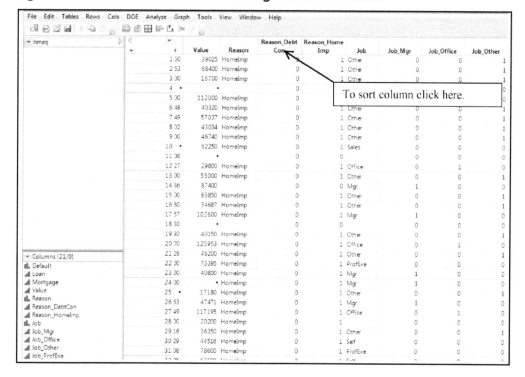

Two visualization tools are provided. Just click their respective boxes to examine the pattern of missingness of the data:

- **Missing Value Clustering**. This tool provides a hierarchical clustering tree of the missing values within rows and also within columns (notice the hierarchical tree at the bottom). Missing values are shown in red, and nonmissing values are shown in blue. You can explore to see which variables or observations tend to be missing together (click anywhere on the tree).
- **Missing Value Snapshot**. This tool shows the missing data for each observation. Exploring the snapshot patterns could help identify patterns of missing values.

Notice that none of the categorical variables, **Default**, **Reason**, and **Job**, are listed, but the indicator variables for **Reason** and **Job** are listed because they are now continuous.

Now go back and select **Analyze ▶ Screening ▶ Explore Missing Values**. This time, do not highlight all the variables. Instead, highlight all the continuous variables. A new Explore Missing Values report box will appear as shown in Figure 3.13.

In Figure 3.13, you can see that you have four imputation options. You will use the first one:

Figure 3.12: Explore Missing Values Report

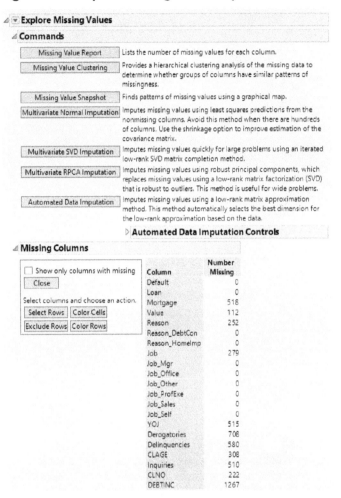

1. Click the **Multivariate Normal Imputation** box.
2. Click **Yes, Shrinkage** to improve the estimation of the covariances. (A JMP Alert will appear suggesting that you "Save As" because the data table has changed.)
3. Click **OK** and close the Explore Missing Value report window.

All the missing values are replaced by imputed values, and the data set is ready for further statistical analysis. If you check the data table, then the only remaining missing values are in the categorical columns of **Reason** and **Job**.

Finally, the next step would be to run a statistical model, such as a regression, with the missing data and to compare it to the regression with the imputed values.

Figure 3.13: Explore Missing Values Report with Only Continuous Variables

△ ▼ **Explore Missing Values**

△ **Commands**

Missing Value Report	Lists the number of missing values for each column.
Missing Value Clustering	Provides a hierarchical clustering analysis of the missing data to determine whether groups of columns have similar patterns of missingness.
Missing Value Snapshot	Finds patterns of missing values using a graphical map.
Multivariate Normal Imputation	Imputes missing values using least squares predictions from the nonmissing columns. Avoid this method when there are hundreds of columns. Use the shrinkage option to improve estimation of the covariance matrix.
Multivariate SVD Imputation	Imputes missing values quickly for large problems using an iterated low-rank SVD matrix completion method.
Multivariate RPCA Imputation	Imputes missing values using robust principal components, which replaces missing values using a low-rank matrix factorization (SVD) that is robust to outliers. This method is useful for wide problems.
Automated Data Imputation	Imputes missing values using a low-rank matrix approximation method. This method automatically selects the best dimension for the low-rank approximation based on the data.

▷ **Automated Data Imputation Controls**

△ **Missing Columns**

☐ Show only columns with missing

[Close]

Select columns and choose an action.

[Select Rows] [Color Cells]

[Exclude Rows] [Color Rows]

Column	Number Missing
Loan	0
Mortgage	518
Value	112
Reason_DebtCon	0
Reason_HomeImp	0
Job_Mgr	0
Job_Office	0
Job_Other	0
Job_ProfExe	0
Job_Sales	0
Job_Self	0
YOJ	515
Derogatories	708
Delinquencies	580
CLAGE	308
Inquiries	510
CLNO	222
DEBTINC	1267

This brings up the question whether cleaning the data will improve your (regression) model or not. The answer is that you are not sure. A clean data set could improve the model, and it could also make it worse. So why clean the data set?

A cleaned data set represents your population most accurately. Thus, statistics, inferences, and models accurately represent your population of interest. If the data set is not clean, you could possibly produce significant biases and inferences.

As discussed earlier in the chapter, if the MAR assumption is satisfied (that is, MCAR or MAR), then the missing data mechanism is said to be ignorable. This implies that there is no need to model the missing data mechanism as part of the analysis. However, if the MAR assumption is not satisfied (that is, if the missing data mechanism is assumed MNAR), the missing value issue must be addressed or corrected to produce correct estimates of the parameters of interest.

General First Steps on Receipt of a Data Set

Here is a list of recommended initial steps to clean a data set:

1. Understand all the columns/variables, their definitions, and coding. Who entered the data and how the data were entered might also be of interest. Identify any variables that are not being used or should not be used.
2. Perform univariate descriptive statistics on all the variables. Create some visualizations of the data.
3. Try to identify any typographical errors and correct them.
4. Try to identify outliers. If there is a typographical error, correct it if possible. Otherwise, note the degree of outliers.
5. Note the degree of missing values. If a significant percentage of values of a variable are missing, you might want to disregard that variable. There is no set rule. You're only concerned with what is significant. This might depend on the situation and data set. In general, if 40% or more of the data is missing, you might want to disregard that variable. And you might want to also explore why so much is missing.
6. Understand the basic distribution of the data for each variable.
7. Explore the pattern of missingness. If you believe that the MAR assumption is satisfied, the missing data mechanism is considered ignorable, and you do not have to impute the missing values. On the other hand, if you feel this MAR assumption is not satisfied, then you should impute the missing values.

Exercises

1. In the Titanic Passengers_new.jmp data set, identify if there are any outliers.

2. In the Promotions_new.jmp data set, identify if there are any outliers.

3. In the Sub_CC Churn.jmp data set, identify if there are any outliers.

4. In the Sub_Enrollment.jmp data set, identify if there are any outliers.

5. In the Titanic Passengers_new.jmp data set, do the following:

   a. Examine **Sex** and **Passenger Class**. Are there any typographical errors? If so, correct them.

   b. Examine **Lifeboat**. Are there any missing values? If so, how many?

   c. Examine **Age** and **Midpoint Age**. Are there any missing values? If so, how many? Impute them.

6. In the Promotions_new.jmp data set, do the following:

    a. Examine **Race** and **Position**. Are there any typographical errors? If so, correct them.

    b. Are there any missing values for all the variables? If so, impute them.

7. In the Sub_CC Churn.jmp data set, do the following:

    a. Examine **Marital Status, LTV Group,** and **Gender**. Are there any typographical errors? If so, correct them.

    b. Examine **Gender**. Are there any missing values? If so, how many?

    c. Examine **Age of Account (Months)** and **Age Group**. Are there any missing values? If so, how many? Impute them.

8. In the Sub_Enrollment.jmp data set, do the following:

    a. Examine **State Province**, **Nation Description**, **Citizenship Description** and **Ethnicity**. Are there any missing values? If so, how many?

    b. Examine **SAT Verbal, SAT Mathematics,** and **SAT Total Score**. Are there any missing values? If so, how many? Impute them.

Chapter 4: Data Discovery with Multivariate Data

Introduction

Most data sets in the real world are multivariate. That is, they contain more than two variables. Generally speaking, a data set can be viewed conceptually as shown in Figure 4.1, where the columns represent variables and the rows are objects. The rows, or *objects*, are the perspective from which the observations or measurements were taken (for example, by event, case, transaction, person, or company). The columns, or *variables*, are the characteristics by which the objects were measured. Multivariate data analysis is when more than two variables are analyzed simultaneously.

Figure 4.2 provides a framework of statistical and visual methods for analyzing multivariate data. The initial multivariate analytical steps should be the data discovery of relationships through tables and graphs. Some of this data discovery will include univariate descriptive statistics or distribution analysis and perhaps some bivariate analyses (for example, scatterplots and contingency tables, as discussed in Chapter 2). In this chapter, you will explore some of the multivariate tables and graphs.

Figure 4.1: A Conceptual View of a Data Set

			Variables	
	X_{11}	X_{12}	$\dots$	X_{1m}
	X_{21}	X_{22}	$\dots$	X_{2m}
	.		.	.
Objects	.		.	.
	.		.	.
	X_{n1}	X_{n2}	$\dots$	X_{nm}

Figure 4.2: A Framework for Multivariate Analysis

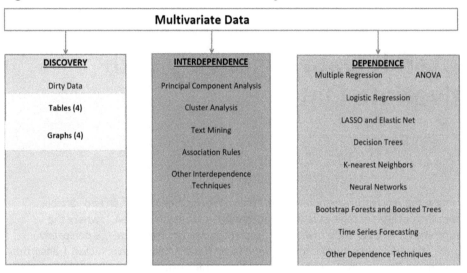

As shown in Figure 4.2, there are numerous multivariate statistical and data mining techniques available to analyze multivariate data. Several of the more popular multivariate and data mining techniques will be discussed in this text:

- principal components analysis
- cluster analysis
- multiple regression
- ANOVA
- logistic regression
- generalized regression
- decision trees
- time series forecasting
- *K*-nearest neighbors
- neural networks
- bootstrap forests
- boosted trees

Generally speaking, these techniques are categorized as *interdependence* and *dependence* techniques (Figure 4.2). The *interdependence* techniques examine relationships either between the variables (columns) or the observations (rows) without considering causality. With *dependence* techniques, one or more variables are identified as the dependent variables, and it is assumed that *X* variables cause *Y* values. The objective of these dependence techniques is to examine and measure the relationship between other (independent) variables and the dependent variable or variables. Two dependence techniques sometimes covered in an introductory statistics course, multiple regression and ANOVA, will be reviewed in Chapter 5.

One last word of caution and advice before you start your multivariate journey. (This is just a reiteration of the sixth fundamental concept discussed in Chapter 2.) All the many discovery tools and the numerous statistical techniques cannot guarantee useful insights until you try them. Successful results really depend on the data set. On the other hand, there are times when it is inappropriate to use a tool or technique. Throughout the following chapters, you will learn when and when not to use a tool or technique.

Use Tables to Explore Multivariate Data

Row and column tables, contingency tables, crosstabs, Excel PivotTables, and JMP Tabulate are basic OLAP tools that are used to produce tables to examine or summarize relationships between two or more variables. To illustrate, see the survey data from 20 students in the file Countif.xls and in the worksheet **rawdata** from Chapter 2, as shown in Table 2.2.

PivotTables

A PivotTable is one of the most powerful tools in Excel. It enables you to summarize and explore data. To generate a PivotTable in Excel, begin as follows:

1. Highlight cells **A1:G23**.
2. Click **Insert** on the top menu. A new set of icons appears.
3. All the way to the left, click **PivotTable**. When the dialog box appears, click **OK**. A new worksheet will appear similar to Figure 4.3.

Figure 4.3: PivotTable Worksheet

Continue with the following steps:

1. In the upper part of the PivotTable Field List box (on the right side of the worksheet, Figure 4.3), drag **Major** all the way to the left to Column A where it says Drop Row Fields Here and release the mouse button.
2. Similarly, drag **Gender** to where it says Drop Column Fields Here. Notice back in the upper part of the PivotTable Field List box (Figure 4.3), under **Choose fields to add to report**, that **Major** and **Gender** have check marks next to them. In the lower part of the box, under **Column labels**, see **Gender**. Under **Row labels**, see **Major**.
3. Drag **Salary** to the left where it says Drop Value Fields Here. **Salary** in the upper part of the PivotTable Field List box is now checked.
4. Below, under ∑ **Values,** is the **Sum of Salary**. Click the drop-down menu for the **Summary of Salary**.
5. Click the **Value Field Setting**, and a new dialog box similar to Figure 4.4 will appear.
6. In the dialog box, you can change the displayed results to various summary statistics. Click **Average** (notice that the Custom Name changes to **Average of Salary**). Click **OK**.

As the JMP diagram in the Fit Y by X dialog box directs you (see Figure 2.12 or 2.15), the rows and columns are categorical data in a contingency table. This is, in general, the same for these OLAP tools. The data in the PivotTable can be further sliced by dragging a categorical variable to the **Drop Report Filter Fields Here** area.

The resulting PivotTable should look similar to Figure 4.5, which shows the average salary by Gender and Major.

Figure 4.4: Value Field Setting Dialog Box

Figure 4.5: Resulting Excel PivotTable

	A	B	C	D
1	Drop Report Filter Fields Here			
2				
3	Average of Salary	Gender		
4	Major	Female	Male	Grand Total
5	A&S	41301	42273.6	41743.09091
6	Business	54484.66667	56968.375	56291
7	Grand Total	45695.55556	51316.53846	49017.04545

Tabulate in JMP

To generate a similar table in JMP, open Countif.jmp. Select **Analyze ▶ Tabulate**. The Tabulate dialog box appears (Figure 4.6).

Figure 4.6: The Tabulate Dialog Box

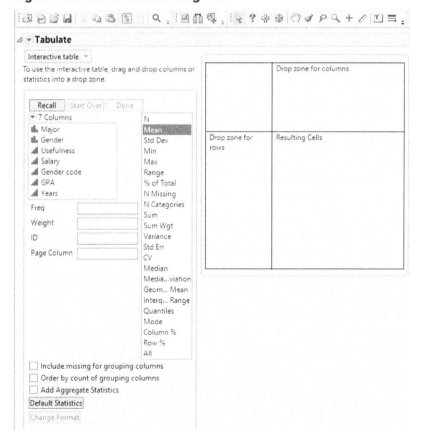

Then complete the following steps:

1. Drag **Salary** to the **Resulting Cells** area. The table now shows the sum of all the salaries (1078375).
2. In the Control Panel, drag **Mean** right on top of the word **Sum**. The average salary is 49017.0454.
3. Drag **Gender** to the top of the **Salary** box, just above the box that says **Mean**. It will now show Salary (Female Mean=45695.555556 and Male Mean=51316.538462).
4. Finally, drag **Major** to the white square to the left of the Mean for Females (45695.55).
5. Click the **Tabulate** red triangle and click **Show Chart**. The table and chart should now look like Figure 4.7.

If you want to copy and paste the JMP table and chart into Microsoft Word or Microsoft PowerPoint, then do as follows:

1. Click the Selection icon as shown in Figure 4.7.
2. Click on the table just outside its border. The table will be filled in the color blue. Right-click and select **Copy**.
3. Go to a Word or PowerPoint file and paste it in. The table and chart will appear like Figure 4.8.

To copy and paste JMP results from other JMP tools or techniques, you follow this same process.

Use Graphs to Explore Multivariate Data

Graphical presentation tools provide powerful insights into multivariate data. JMP provides a large selection of visualization tools beyond the simple *XY* scatterplots, bar charts, and pie charts. One such tool that is extremely useful in exploring multivariate data is the Graph Builder.

Graph Builder

Initially, look at and use the Graph Builder with the Countif.jmp data set.

Select **Graph ▶ Graph Builder**. The Graph Builder dialog box will appear, as shown in Figure 4.9. To the left of the dialog box, there is a window that has a list of your variables, and to the right is a graphical sandbox in which you can design your graph. As noted in Figure 4.9, there are several areas called *drop zones* where you can drop the variables. You can bring over to these drop zones either continuous or categorical (ordinal and nominal) data.

Figure 4.7: Selection Button to Copy the Output

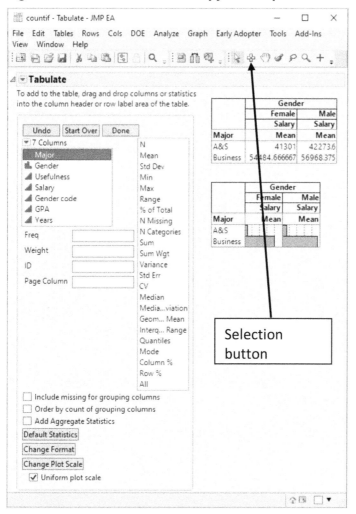

Figure 4.8: Resulting Copy of the Tabulate Table and Chart (into a Microsoft Word Document)

	Gender	
	Female	**Male**
	Salary	**Salary**
Major	**Mean**	**Mean**
A&S	41301	42273.6
Business	54484.666667	56968.375

Figure 4.9: Graph Builder Dialog Box

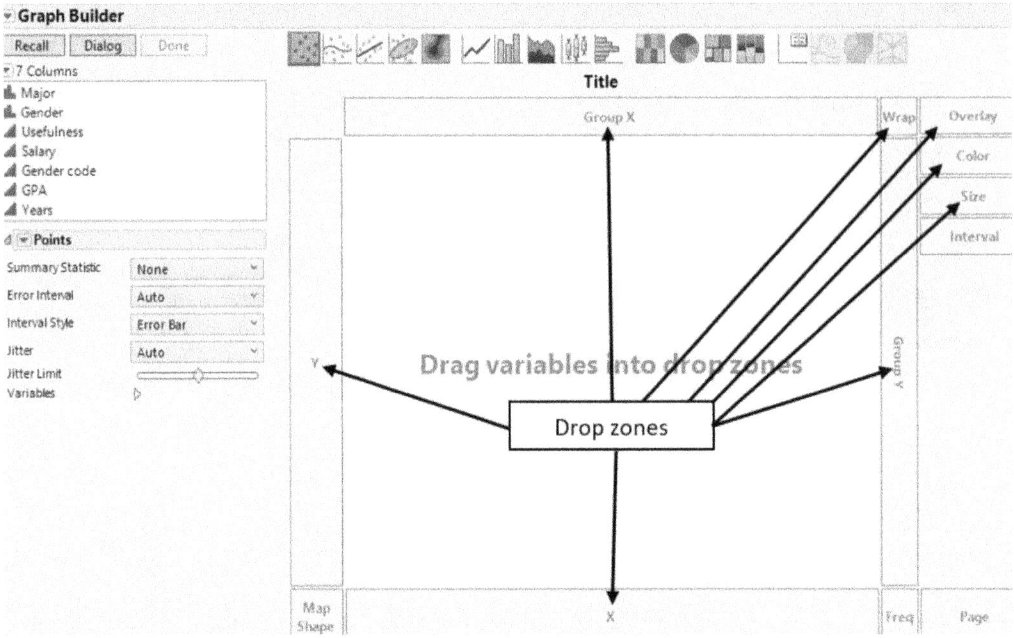

Complete the following steps:

1. Click **Salary** and drag it around to the different drop zones. The graph immediately reacts as you move over the drop zones.
2. Release **Salary** in the **Y** drop zone area.
3. Click **Years**, and again drag it around to the different drop zones and observe how the graph reacts.

Notice the following:

- When you move Years to Group X, you get several vertical graphs. This is further notice that years are grouped—or put into intervals (Figure 4.10).
- When you move Years to Group Y, you will get several horizontal graphs (Figure 4.11).
- When you move Years to Wrap and Overlay, Years is grouped into Year categories (Figures 4.12 and 4.13).

Figure 4.10: Graph of Salary and Year When Year Is in Drop Zone Group X

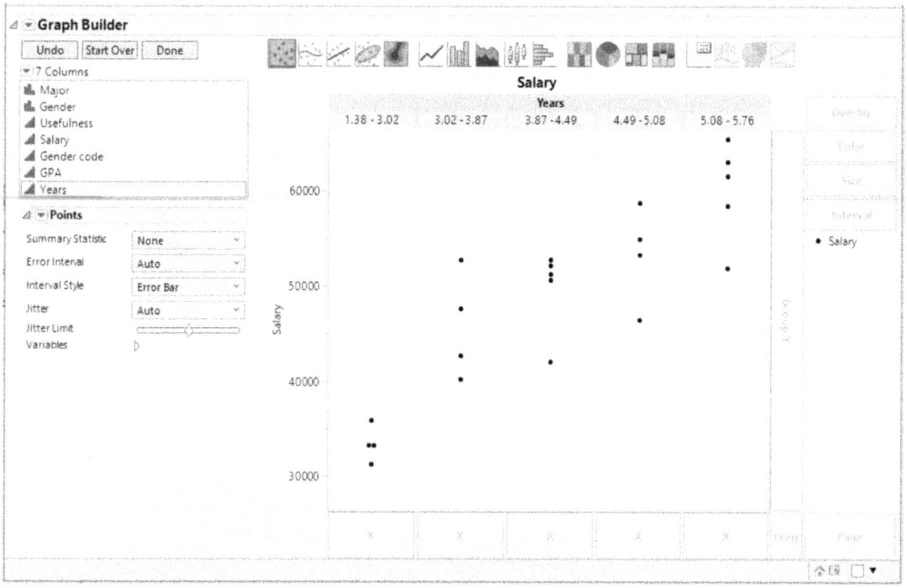

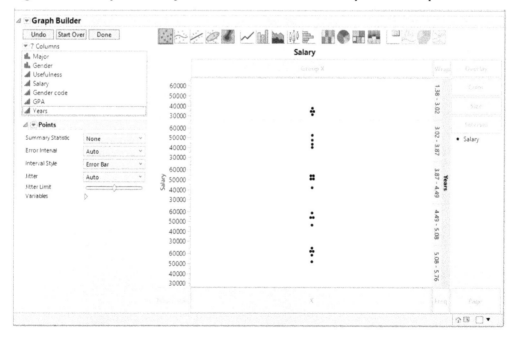

Figure 4.11: Graph of Salary and Year When Year Is in Drop Zone Group Y

Figure 4.12: Graph of Salary and Year When Year Is in Drop Zone Wrap

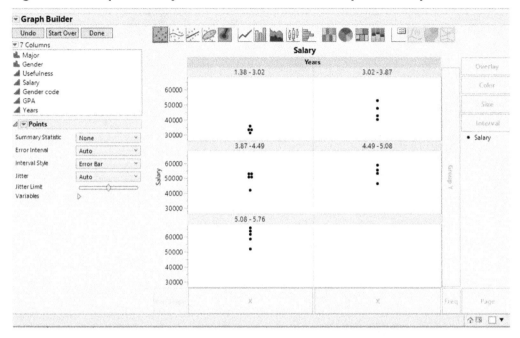

Figure 4.13: Graph of Salary and Year When Year Is in Drop Zone Overlap

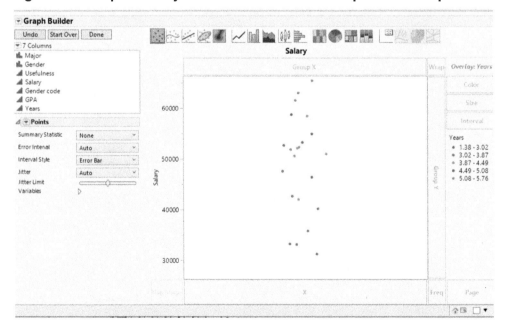

Next, complete the following steps to produce a trellis chart of Major, Gender by Usefulness:

1. First, let's clear the Graph Builder, click **Start Over**.
2. Click **Salary** and release **Salary** in the **Y** drop zone area.
3. Release **Years** in the **X** drop zone.
4. Click **Major** and drag it around to the drop zones.
5. Move **Major** over the **Y** and **X** drop zones, and observe how you can add another variable to those drop zones.
6. Release **Major** in the **Group X** drop zone.
7. Click **Gender** and drag it to the **Group Y** drop zone.

You now see four graphs as shown in Figure 4.14. You can quickly see that the Business students have higher salaries and are older (more years since they graduated). You can change the graphical display by click on one of the highlighted (suggested) graph element icons, as note in Figure 4.14.

Scatterplot

Another useful visualization tool for providing insights to multivariate data is the scatterplot matrix. Data that consists of k variables would require $k(k-1)$ two-dimensional XY scatterplots. Thus, every combination of two variables is in an XY scatterplot. The upper triangle of graphs is

Figure 4.14: Salary versus Year, by Major and Gender

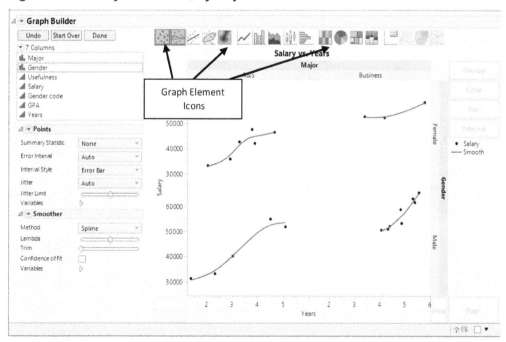

the same as the lower triangle of graphs, except that the coordinates are reversed. Thus, usually only one side of the triangle is shown. An advantage of the scatterplot matrix is that changes in one dimension can be observed by scanning across all the graphs in a particular row or column.

For example, produce a scatterplot matrix of the Countif.jmp data as follows:

1. Select **Graph ▶ Scatterplot Matrix**, and the scatterplot matrix dialog box will appear.
2. Hold down the **Ctrl** key and click every variable, one by one, except for **Gender Code**. All the variables are now highlighted except for **Gender Code**.
3. Click **Y, Columns**, and all the variables are listed.
4. Notice toward the lower left of the dialog box that there is **Matrix Format**. There is a drop-down menu with Lower Triangular selected. If you click the drop-down menu, you can see the different options available. Leave it as Lower Triangular. Click **OK**.

A scatterplot matrix similar to Figure 4.15 will appear.

For every scatterplot in the leftmost column of the scatterplot matrix (which is labeled *Major*), the X axis is **Major**. Move the mouse on top of any point and left-click. That observation is now highlighted in that scatterplot but also in the other scatterplots. So, you can observe how that observation performs in the other dimensions. The row number also appears.

Figure 4.15: Scatterplot Matrix of Countif.jmp

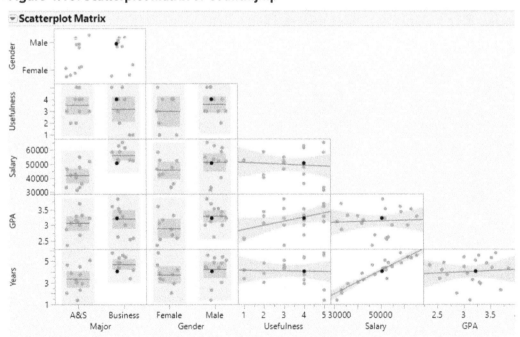

Similarly, you can hold down the left mouse button and encircle an area of points that will be highlighted. The corresponding selected points in the other scatterplots are also highlighted, as well as those observations in the data table.

Click the **Scatterplot Matrix** red triangle and **Fit Line**. In the scatterplots where one or both variables are continuous, a line is fitted with a confidence interval as shown in Figure 4.15. The smaller the width of the interval, the stronger the relationship. In the case of one variable being categorical, a line is fitted for each category within each scatterplot. That is, **Salary** and **Years** have a strong relationship.

Generally speaking, the scatterplots in a scatterplot matrix are more informative with continuous variables than with categorical variables. Nevertheless, insight into the effect of a categorical variable on the other variables can be visualized with the scatterplot matrix by using the Group option. Here is an example:

1. Select **Graph ▶ Scatterplot Matrix**.
2. Click **Recall**. All your variables are now listed under **Y, Columns**.
3. Select **Major ▶ Group**.
4. Click **OK**. The scatterplot matrix appears.
5. Click the **Scatterplot Matrix** red triangle and select **Density Ellipses ▶ Shaded Ellipses**.

As shown in Figure 4.16, when you examine the ellipses, it appears that Arts and Sciences (A&S) students have lower salaries than Business students (in the blue shaded ellipses), and, in the data set, there were more A&S students that have recently graduated than Business students.

Explore a Larger Data Set

Now explore HomePriceIndexCPI1.jmp, another data set that contains time as a variable. This file includes the quarterly home price index and consumer price index for each of the states in the United States and for the District of Columbia from May 1975 until September 2009. This table has been sorted by state and date.

Trellis Chart

Initially, you could examine all the variables in a scatterplot matrix. If you do, the scatterplots are not very helpful—there are too many dates and states. Instead, use the Graph Builder:

1. In JMP, open HomePriceIndexCPI1.jmp.
2. Select **Graph ▶ Graph Builder**.
3. Click **Date** and drag it to the **X** drop zone.
4. Click **Home Price Index**, and drag it to the **Y** drop zone. The graph is not too informative yet.
5. Now, click **State** and drag it to the **Wrap** drop zone.
6. Click the **Line Graph Element Icon**, as shown in Figure 4.17.

Figure 4.16: Scatterplot with Shaded Ellipses

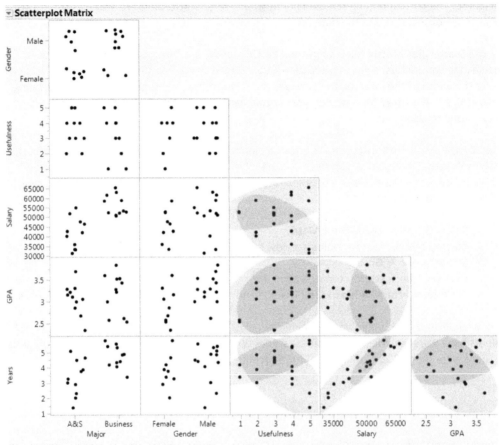

You now have 51 small charts, by **State**, of **Home Price Index** versus **Date**, as shown in Figure 4.17. This set of charts is called a *trellis chart*. A chart is created for each level of a categorical variable. (Similarly, the charts in Figure 4.14 are trellis charts.) Trellis charts can be extremely effective in discovering relationships with multivariate data. With this data, you can see the trend of each state's home price index. Some states increase significantly, for example, CA, DC, FL, HI, and WA (enclosed by a solid box), and some very slowly, such as GA, MN, MO, MS, and TX (enclosed by a dashed box).

You can add CPI to the charts by dragging **CPI** to the **Y** drop zone (just to the right of the **Y** axis label Home Price Index), as shown in Figure 4.18. But perhaps an easier way is to start over: Select **Home Price Index**, hold down the **Shift** key, click **CPI**, and then click **Y**.

Figure 4.17: Trellis Chart of the Home Price Indices, by State

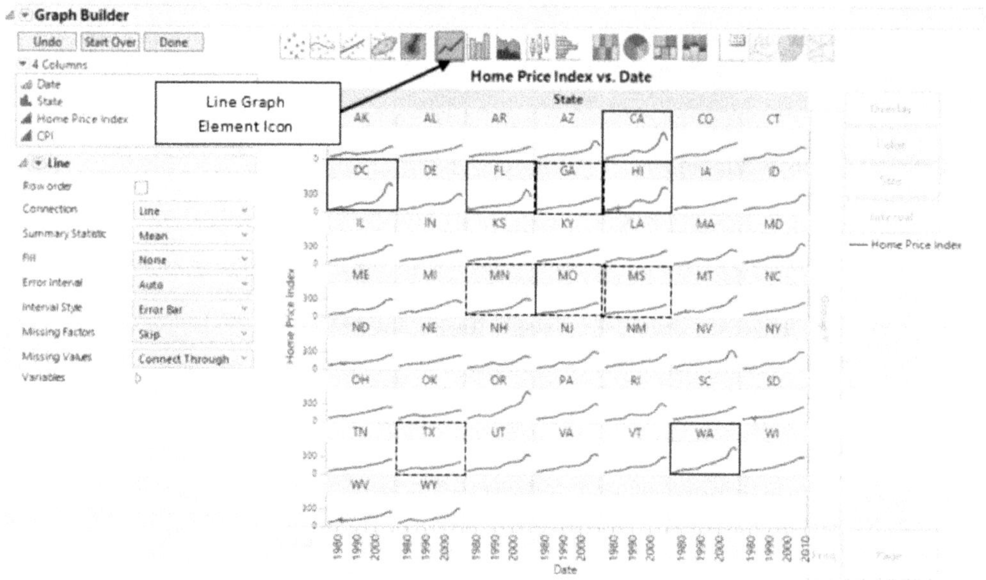

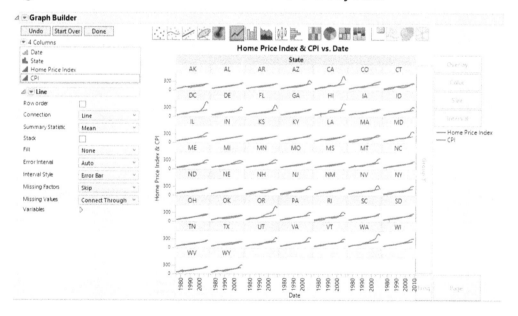

Figure 4.18: Trellis Chart of Home Price Index and CPI by State

Bubble Plot

Another informative visualization chart is the bubble plot, which can be very effective with data over time. To generate a bubble plot with the Home Price Index data, complete the following steps:

1. Select **Graph ▶ Bubble Plot**.
2. Drag **Home Price Index** to **Y**.
3. Drag **State** to **X**.
4. Drag **Date** to **Time**.
5. Drag **Home Price Index** to **Coloring**, as shown in Figure 4.19. Click **OK**.
6. Click the go arrow key icon (blue triangle, toward the bottom of the window), and observe how the home price indexes for the states increase over time until 2008, and then they decrease.

Figures 4.20 through 4.23 capture the bubble plot at four dates. You can increase the speed by moving the slider to the right. Further, you can record and save this as a GIF file so that you can send it in an email or include it as part of a presentation by clicking the red triangle at the bottom to record. When finished recording click the disk icon just to the right to save the recording as a GIF file.

Figure 4.19: Bubble Plot Dialog Box

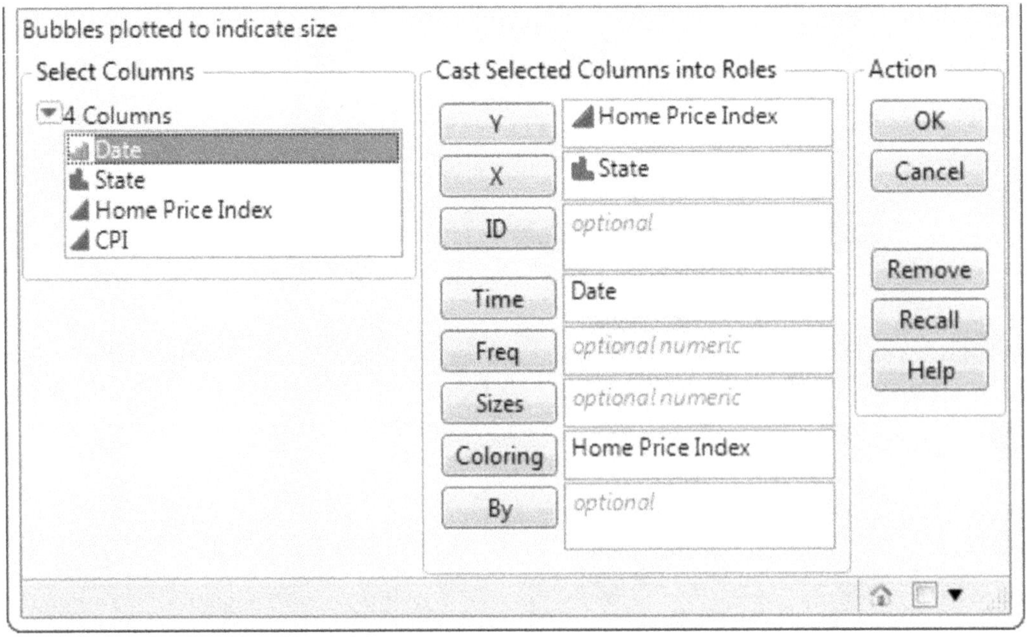

Figure 4.20: Bubble Plot of Home Price Index by State on 3/1975

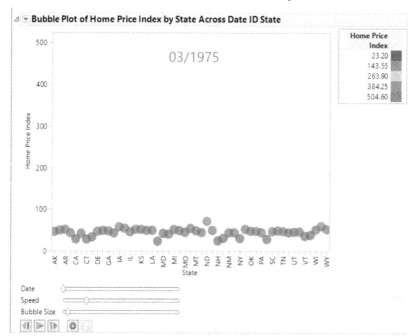

Figure 4.21: Bubble Plot of Home Price Index by State on 3/2005

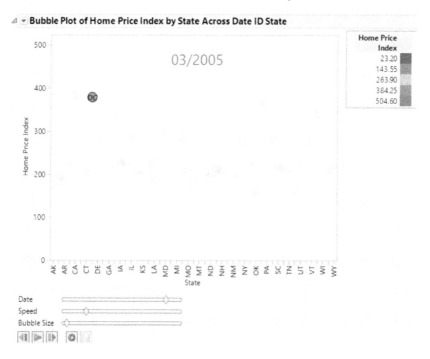

Figure 4.22: Bubble Plot of Home Price Index by State on 3/2008

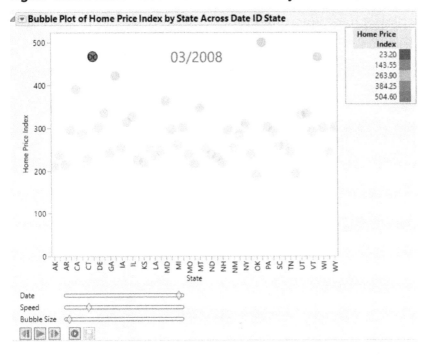

Figure 4.23: Bubble Plot of Home Price Index by State on 9/2009

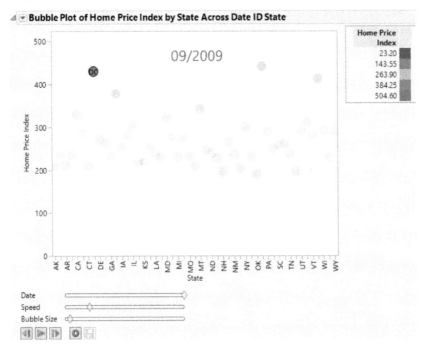

Explore a Real-World Data Set

Now you will examine another data set, profit by product.jmp. This file contains sales data, including **Revenue**, **Cost of Sales**, and two calculated columns—**Gross Profit** and **GP%** (percentage of gross profit). (Notice the plus sign to the right of the **Gross Profit** and **GP%** variables, respectively. Double-click the plus sign next to the variable. The Formula dialog box appears with the corresponding formulas.)

The data is organized by these items:

- time (quarter)
- distribution channel
- product line
- customer ID

Use Correlation Matrix and Scatterplot Matrix to Examine Relationships of Continuous Variables

If you were examining this data set "in the real world," the first step would be to generate and examine the results of some univariate and bivariate analyses with descriptive statistics, scatterplots, and tables. Next, since the data set is multivariate, analyses of the correlation matrix and scatterplot matrix of the continuous variables could provide insightful information:

1. Select **Analyze ▶ Multivariate Methods ▶ Multivariate**.
2. The Multivariate and Correlations dialog box appears. Select the four continuous variables (**Revenue, Cost of Sales, Gross Profit** and **GP%**) and click the **Y, Columns**.
3. Click **OK**.
4. The Multivariate output will appear. Click the **Scatterplot Matrix** red triangle. Click **Fit Line**.

A correlation matrix and scatterplot matrix appears similar to Figure 4.24. In this case, this set of continuous variables do not provide too much information except the Cost of Sales and Revenue have a strong positive relationship (correlation of 0.9371).

Use Graph Builder to Examine Results of Analyses

To provide further possible significant insights, use the JMP Graph Builder:

1. Select **Graph ▶ Graph Builder**.
2. Drag **Quarter** to the **X** drop zone.
3. Drag **Revenue** to the **Y** drop zone.

Figure 4.24: Correlation Matrix and Scatterplot Matrix

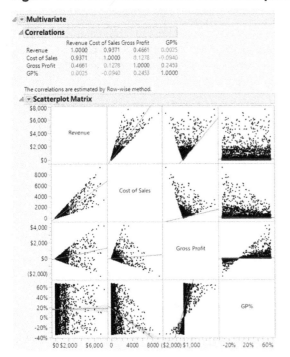

4. Instead of viewing the box plot, look at a line of the average revenue by quarter by right-clicking any open space in the graph and then selecting **Box Plot ▶ Change to ▶ Contour**. The density Revenue values are displayed by Quarter, similar to Figure 4.25. (Another approach to get the Contour graph is to click the **Contour Graph Element Icon** as shown in Figure 4.25.)

5. Now right-click inside any of the shaded revenue density areas. Then select **Contour ▶ Change to ▶ Line**. The line graph will resemble what is shown in Figure 4.26. (Another approach to get the Line graph is to click the **Line Graph Element Icon** as shown in Figure 4.25.)

6. To get a Bar Chart, select **Line ▶ Change to ▶ Bar** or click on the **Bar Chart Element Icon**.

Generate a Trellis Chart and Examine Results

Next complete the following steps:

1. First change back the graph to a line graph. Click on the **Line Graph Element Icon**
2. Add **Cost of Sales** and **Gross Profit** to the **Y** axis by dragging **Cost of Sales** to the **Y** drop zone. (Be careful to not remove **Revenue**—release the mouse button just to the right of the **Y** axis.)

Figure 4.25: Revenue by Quarter Using Contours

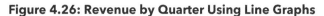

Figure 4.26: Revenue by Quarter Using Line Graphs

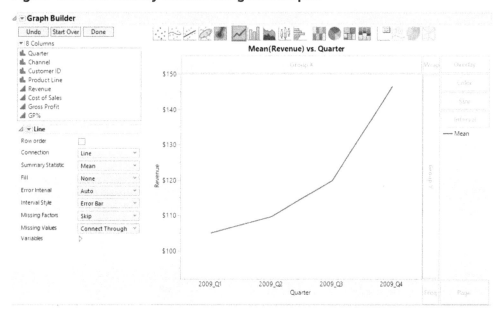

Figure 4.27: Trellis Chart of the Average Revenue, Cost of Sales, and Gross Product over Time (Quarter) by Product Line

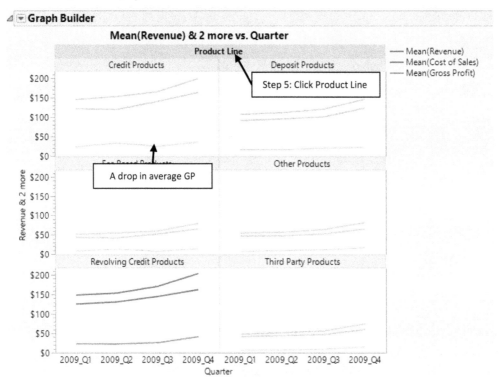

3. Similarly, drag **Gross Profit** just to the right of **Y axis**. (You could click on both variables and drag them over also.)
4. Drag **Product Line** to the **Wrap** drop zone.
5. Click **Done**.

These steps should produce a trellis chart similar to Figure 4.27.

Examining Figure 4.27, you can see that, in terms of average **Gross Profit**, the **Credit Products** product line (the upper left side graph) did not do too well in Quarter 3. You can focus or drill down on the **Revenue** and **Cost of Sales** of the **Credit Products** by using the Data Filter feature of JMP. The Data Filter, when used in concert with the Graph Builder, enhances your exploration capability.

1. On the main menu in the Data Table window, select **Rows ▶ Data Filter**.
2. Click **Product Line**, and click + to Add.
3. The Data Filter dialog box changes and shows the six Product Lines. Click **Credit Products**. Looking at the Graph Builder dialog box, except for the upper left side graph of Credit Products, the other graphs are grayed out.

Figure 4.28: Graph of the Average Revenue, Cost of Sales, and Gross Product, by Quarter for the Credit Products Product Line

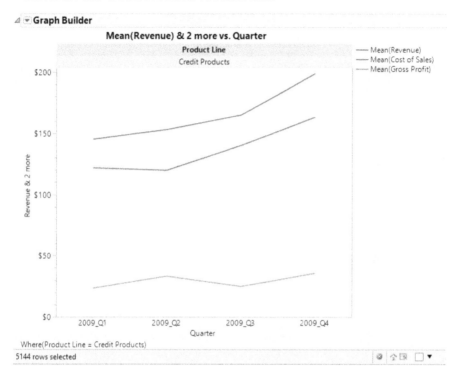

4. In the **Data Filter**, check the **Include** Option. Now there is one graph, similar to Figure 4.28. In the Rows Panel, note that 5,144 rows are selected and 19,402 rows are excluded. Only the Credit Products rows are included.
5. You can now focus on all your **Credit Products** customers. First, click the **Graph Builder** red triangle and click **Show Control Panel**. Next, you need to click **Product Line** (as shown in Figure 4.27) and drag and release it somewhere in the Columns panel.
6. Click **Customer ID** and drag it to the **Wrap** drop zone. The graph should look like Figure 4.29. It is interesting to see how the relationship over the quarters between **Revenue** and **Cost of Sales** varies from customer to customer.

However, if you have too many customers, this trellis chart might be much too busy. With the filter still in play, let's build another graph:

1. Click **Start Over** in the Graph Builder dialog box.
2. Drag **Revenue** to the **X** drop zone.
3. Drag **Customer ID** to the **Y** drop zone.
4. Click on the **Bar Chart Element Icon**.
5. Drag **GP%** to the **X** drop zone (toward the right, near the x-value of $500).
6. On the right side of the graph with GP%, right-click anywhere on the box plot and then select **Box Plot ▶ Change to ▶ Bar**. The graph should look similar to Figure 4.30.

Figure 4.29: Graph of the Average Revenue, Cost of Sales, and Gross Product, by Quarter for the Credit Products Product Line, by Customer ID

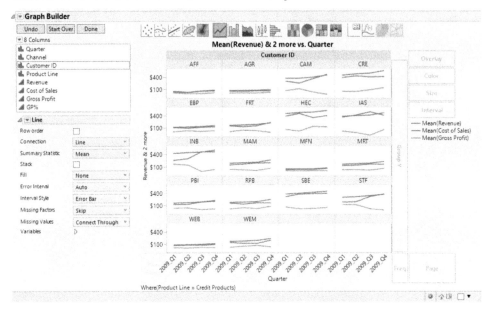

Figure 4.30: Bar Chart of the Average Revenue and %GP of Credit Products Customers

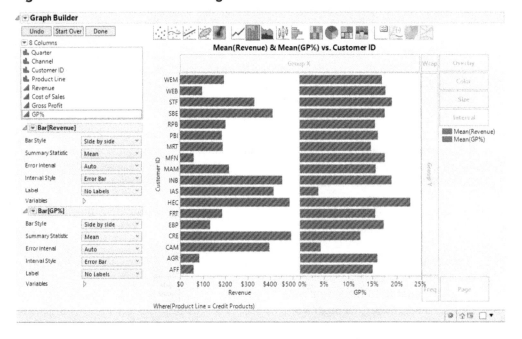

Use Dynamic Linking to Explore Comparisons in a Small Data Subset

You can quickly see for your Credit Products product line that the average sales (revenue) of customers IAS and CAM are relatively high, but their average percentage gross profit is rather low. You might want to further examine these customers separately. An effective feature of JMP is called dynamic linking. As you interact with the graph, you also interact with the data table. So, you can easily create a subset of the data with just these two customers:

1. Click on one of the bars for **IAS**. Then hold down the **Shift** key and click one of the bars for **CAM**. The bars for these two companies should be highlighted.
2. In the Data Table, 64 rows are selected. As before, right-click the 64 for **Selected** and click **Data View**. A new Data Table is created with 64 Credit Products observations from customers IAS and CAM only.
3. Select **File ▶ Save**. You can further analyze these two customers at a later time.

Now return to Graph Builder.

Return to Graph Builder to Sort and Visualize a Larger Data Set

If you have difficulty getting the Graph Builder dialog box back (Figure 4.30), navigate to the **JMP Home Window** and click **profit by product—Graph Builder**.

Those two customers were rather easy to identify. But what if you had a large number of customers? You can sort the customers by average percent gross profit by:

1. Again, drag **GP%** to the **Y** drop zone (release the mouse button just to the right of the Y axis).
2. With the cursor somewhere on the Y axis, right-click, and then click **Order By ▶ GP%, descending**. Now you can easily see the customers who are not doing well in terms of average percent gross profit as shown in Figure 4.31.

You can further explore the **Credit Products** product line and develop a better understanding of the data by adding another element to your filter. For example, you might postulate that there is a correlation between average size of sales and gross profit. You can visualize this relationship by following these next steps:

1. In the **Data Filter** dialog box, click the **AND** box.
2. In the new list of Columns, click **Revenue**.
3. Click **+** to Add. A scroll bar will appear as shown in Figure 4.32.
4. Double-click $0.5, change the value to **1350**, and press **Enter**. As a result, 169 rows are matched. The graph should look similar to Figure 4.33.

Figure 4.31: Bar Chart of the Average Revenue and %GP of Credit Products Customers in Ascending Order

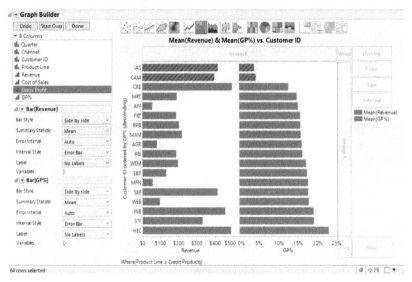

Figure 4.32: Two Data Filters with Scroll Bar

You can see that you are losing money with four customers. If you want to examine them further, you could subset these four customers to another JMP table.

With these examples, you have seen that by using several of the JMP visualization tools, and the additional layer of the data filter, you can quickly explore and develop a better understanding of a large amount of multivariate data.

Figure 4.33: Bar Chart Using Further Elements of the Data Filter

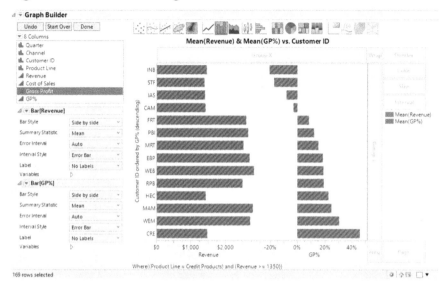

Exercises

1. Perform descriptive statistics and create some relevant graphs using the salesperfdata.jmp data set.

2. Perform descriptive statistics and create some relevant graphs using the churn.jmp data set.

3. Perform descriptive statistics and create some relevant graphs using the StateGDP2008.jmp data set.

4. Perform descriptive statistics and create some relevant graphs using the PublicUtilities.jmp data set.

5. Perform descriptive statistics and create some relevant graphs using the Kuiper.jmp data set.

Chapter 5: Regression and ANOVA

Introduction

Simple and multiple regression and ANOVA, as shown in the multivariate analysis framework in Figure 5.1, are the dependence techniques that are most likely covered in an introductory statistics course. In this chapter, you will review these techniques, illustrate the process of performing these analyses in JMP, and explain how to interpret the results.

Regression

One of the most popular applied statistical techniques and predictive analytics techniques is regression. Regression analysis typically has one or two main purposes. First, it might be used to understand the cause-and-effect relationship between one dependent variable and one or more independent variables: For example, it might answer the question, how does the amount of advertising affect sales? Or, secondly, regression might be applied for prediction—in particular, for the purpose of forecasting a dependent variable based on one or more independent variables. An example would be using trend and seasonal components to forecast sales. Regression analyses can handle linear or nonlinear relationships, although the linear models are mostly emphasized.

Figure 5.1: A Framework for Multivariate Analysis

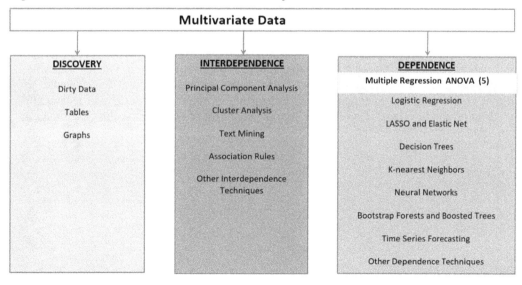

Perform a Simple Regression and Examine Results

Look at the data set salesperfdata.jmp. This data is from Cravens et al. (1972) and consists of the sales from 25 territories and seven corresponding variables:

- Salesperson's experience (Time)
- Market potential (MktPoten)
- Advertising expense (Adver)
- Market share (MktShare)
- Change in market share (Change)
- Number of accounts (Accts)
- Workload per account (WkLoad)

First, you will do only a simple linear regression, which is defined as one dependent variable Y and only one independent variable X. In particular, look at how advertising is related to sales:

1. Open the salesperfdata.jmp in JMP.
2. Select **Analyze ▶ Fit Y by X**.
3. In the Fit Y by X dialog box, click **Sales** and click **Y, Response**.
4. Click **Adver** and click **X, Factor**.
5. Click **OK**.
6. Click the **Bivariate Fit of Sales By Adver** red triangle and click **Fit Line**.

A scatterplot of sales versus advertising, similar to the top of Figure 5.2, will appear. There appears to be a positive relationship, which means that as advertising increases, sales increase.

The Fit Line causes a simple linear regression to be performed and the creation of the tables that contain the regression results. The output will look like the bottom half of Figure 5.2. The regression equation is: **Sales** = 2106.09 + 0.2911 * **Adver**. The y-intercept and **Adver** coefficient values are identified in Figure 5.2 under Parameter Estimates.

The *F* test and *t* test in simple linear regression are equivalent because they both test whether the independent variable (**Adver**) is significantly related to the dependent variable (**Sales**). As indicated in Figure 5.2, both *p*-values are equal to 0.0017 and are significant. (To assist you in identifying significant relationships, JMP puts an asterisk next to a *p*-value that is significant with $\alpha = 0.05$.) This model's goodness-of-fit is measured by the coefficient of determination (R^2 or RSquare) and the standard error (s_e or Root Mean Square Error), which in this case are equal to 35.5% and 1076.87, respectively.

Figure 5.2: Scatterplot with Corresponding Simple Linear Regression

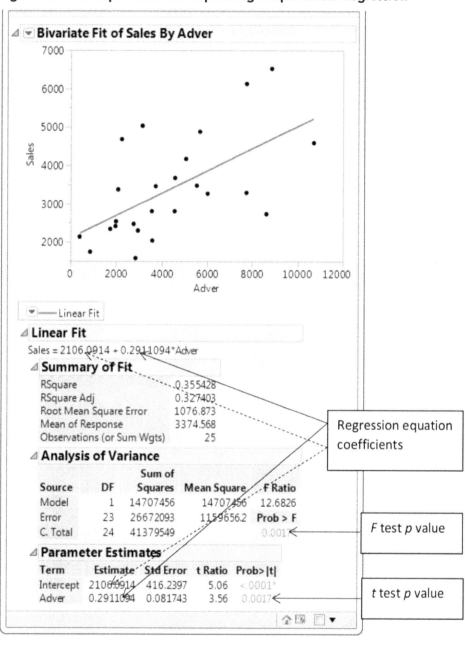

Understand and Perform Multiple Regression

You will next examine the multiple linear regression relationship between sales and the seven predictors (**Time**, **MktPoten**, **Adver**, **MktShare**, **Change**, **Accts**, and **WkLoad**), which is equivalent to those used by Cravens et al. (1972).

Examine the Correlations and Scatterplot Matrix

Before performing the multiple linear regression, you should first examine the correlations and scatterplot matrix:

1. Select **Analyze ▶ Multivariate Methods ▶ Multivariate**.
2. In the Multivariate and Correlations dialog box, in the Select Columns box, click **Sales**, hold down the **Shift** key, and click **WkLoad.**
3. Click **Y,Columns**, and all the variables will appear in the white box to the right of **Y, Columns**, as in Figure 5.3.
4. Click **OK**.
5. Click the **Scatterplot Matrix** red triangle. Click **Density Ellipses**.

Figure 5.3: The Multivariate and Correlations Dialog Box

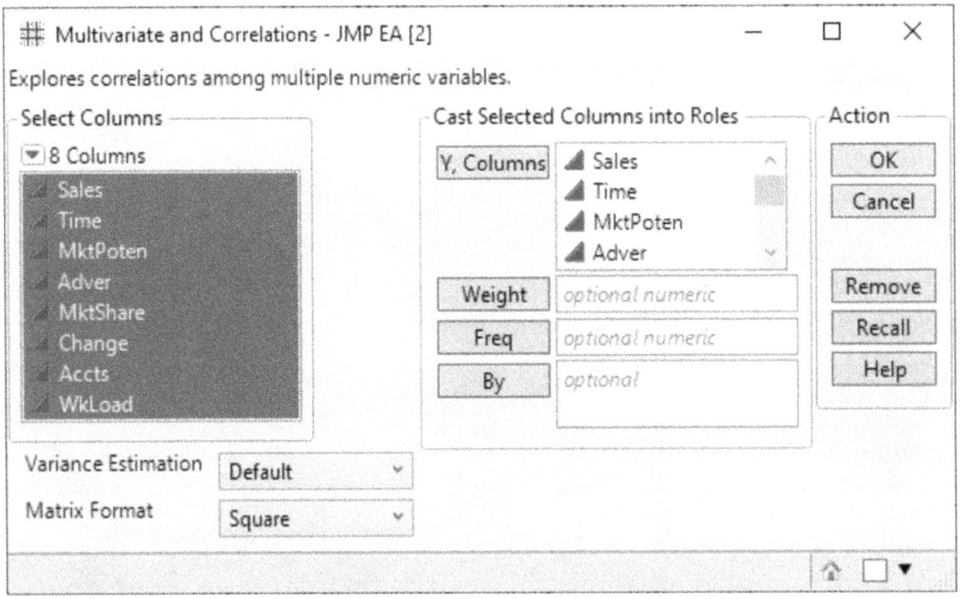

As shown in Figure 5.4, the correlation matrix and corresponding scatterplot matrix will be generated. Examine the first row of the Scatterplot Matrix. There appear to be several strong correlations, especially with the dependent variable **Sales**. All the variables, except for **Wkload**, have a strong positive relationship (or positive correlation) with **Sales**. The oval shape in each scatterplot is the corresponding bivariate normal density ellipse of the two variables. If the two variables are bivariate normally distributed, then about 95% of the points would be within the ellipse. If the ellipse is rather wide (round) and does not follow either of the diagonals, then the two variables do not have a strong correlation. For example, observe the ellipse in the scatterplot for **Sales** and **Wkload**, and notice that the correlation is –.1172. The more significant the correlation, the narrower the ellipse, and the more it follows along one of the diagonals (for example, **Sales** and **Accts**).

Figure 5.4: Correlations and Scatterplot Matrix for the salesperfdata.jmp Data

⊿ ▼ **Multivariate**

⊿ **Correlations**

	Sales	Time	MktPoten	Adver	MktShare	Change	Accts	WkLoad
Sales	1.0000	0.6229	0.5978	0.5962	0.4835	0.4892	0.7540	-0.1172
Time	0.6229	1.0000	0.4540	0.2492	0.1062	0.2515	0.7578	-0.1793
MktPoten	0.5978	0.4540	1.0000	0.1741	-0.2107	0.2683	0.4786	-0.2588
Adver	0.5962	0.2492	0.1741	1.0000	0.2645	0.3765	0.2000	-0.2722
MktShare	0.4835	0.1062	-0.2107	0.2645	1.0000	0.0855	0.4030	0.3493
Change	0.4892	0.2515	0.2683	0.3765	0.0855	1.0000	0.3274	-0.2877
Accts	0.7540	0.7578	0.4786	0.2000	0.4030	0.3274	1.0000	-0.1988
WkLoad	-0.1172	-0.1793	-0.2588	-0.2722	0.3493	-0.2877	-0.1988	1.0000

The correlations are estimated by Row-wise method.

⊿ ▼ **Scatterplot Matrix**

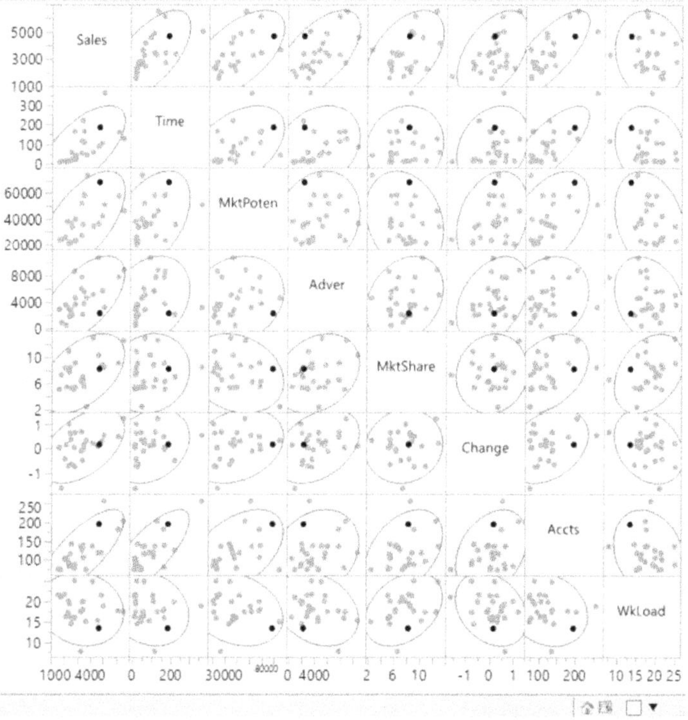

Perform a Multiple Regression

To perform the multiple regression, complete the following steps:

1. Select **Analyze ▶ Fit Model**.
2. In the Fit Model dialog box, as shown in Figure 5.5, click **Sales** and click **Y.**
3. Next, click **Time,** hold down the **Shift** key, and click **WkLoad**. Now all the independent variables from **Time** to **WkLoad** are highlighted.
4. Click **Add**, and now these independent variables are listed.
5. Notice the box to the right of Personality. It should say Standard Least Squares. Click the drop-down menu to the right and observe the different options, which include Stepwise Regression (which is discussed later in this chapter). Keep it at Standard Least Squares and click **Run**.
6. In the Fit Least Squares output, click the **Response Sales** red triangle and click **Regression reports ▶ Summary of Fit**.
7. Again, click the **Response Sales** red triangle and click **Regression reports ▶ Analysis of Variance.**
8. Also, farther down the output, click the display arrow to the left of **Parameter estimates.**

Figure 5.5: The Fit Model Dialog Box

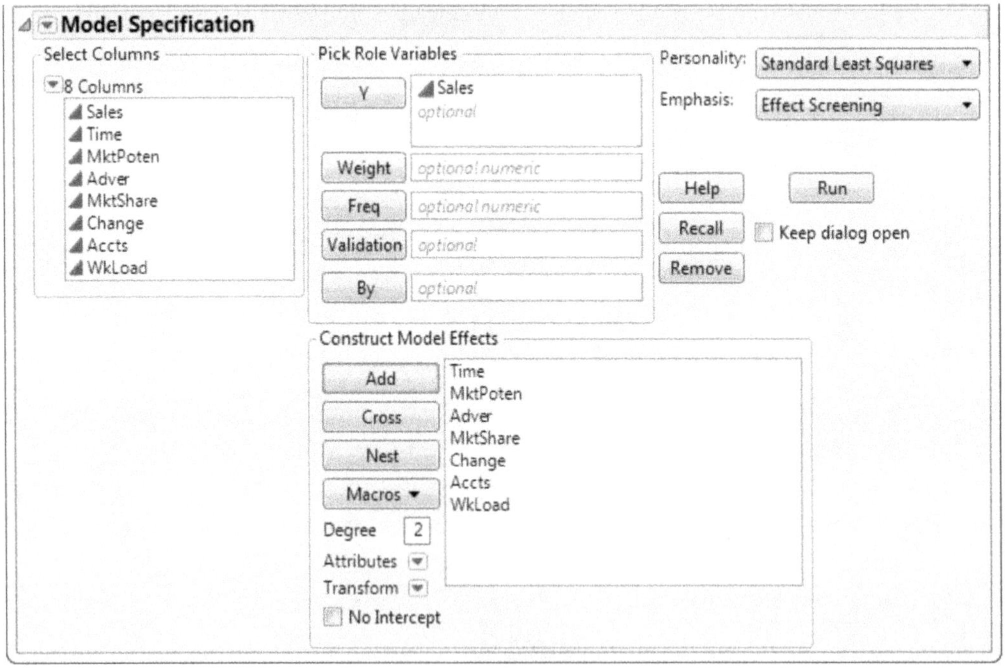

Examine the Effect Summary Report and Adjust the Model

The **Effect Summary** report, as shown in Figure 5.6, lists in ascending *p*-value order the LogWorth or False Discovery Rate (FDR) LogWorth values. These statistical values measure the effects of the independent variables in the model. A LogWorth value greater than 2 corresponds to a *p*-value of less than .01. The FDR LogWorth is a better statistic for assessing significance since it adjusts the *p*-values to account for the false discovery rate from multiple tests (similar to the multiple comparison test used in ANOVA).

Figure 5.6: Multiple Linear Regression Output (Top Half)

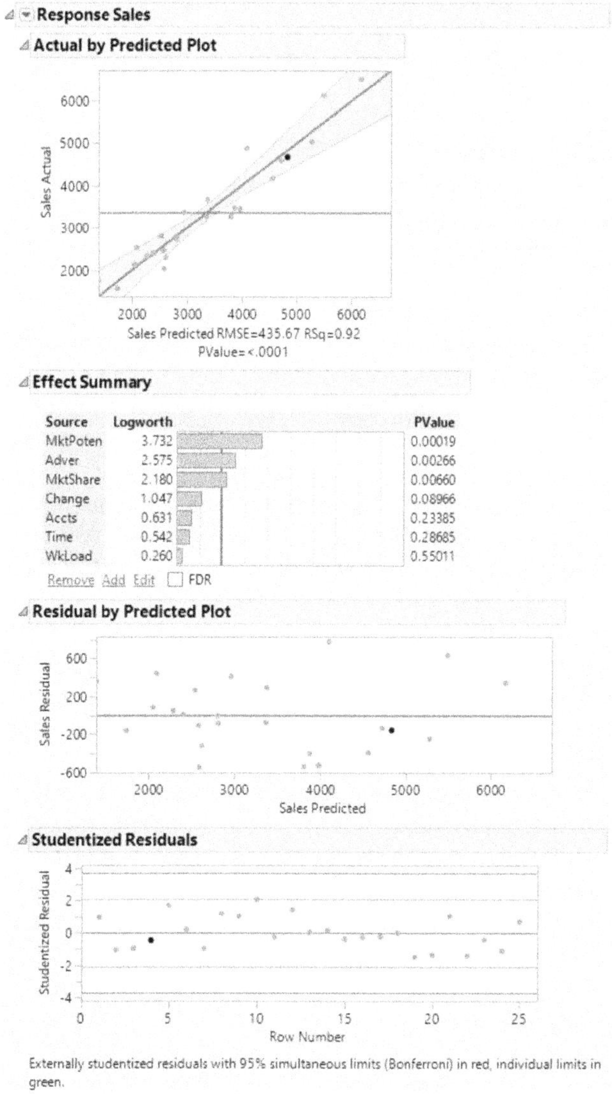

Complete the following steps:

1. Click the **FDR** box to view the FDR LogWorth values.
2. This report can be interactive by clicking **Remove**, **Add**, or **Edit**. For example, in the Effect Summary report, click **Change**, hold the **Shift** key down, and click **Workload**. The four variables of least significance are highlighted.
3. Click **Remove**. Observe that the regression output changed to reflect the removal of those variables. If you want these variables back in the regression model, click **Undo**.

As shown in Figure 5.7 listed under the Parameter estimates, the multiple linear regression equation is as follows:

Sales = −1485.88 + 1.97 * Time + 0.04 * MktPoten + 0.15 * Adver + 198.31*
MktShare + 295.87 * Change + 5.61 * Accts + 19.90 * WkLoad

Each independent variable regression coefficient represents an estimate of the change in the dependent variable to a unit increase in that independent variable while all the other independent variables are held constant. For example, the coefficient for **WkLoad** is 19.9. If **WkLoad** is increased by 1 and the other independent variables do not change, then **Sales** would correspondingly increase by 19.9.

The relative importance of each independent variable is measured by its standardized beta coefficient (which is a unitless value). The larger the absolute value of the standardized beta coefficient, the more important the variable.

To obtain the standardized beta values, move the cursor somewhere over the Parameter Estimates Table. Right-click to open a list of options. Select **Columns ▶ Std Beta**. Subsequently, the **Std Beta** column is added to the Parameter Estimates Table, as shown in Figure 5.8. With your sales performance data set, you can see that the variables **MktPoten**, **Adver**, and **MktShare** are the most important variables.

The Prediction Profiler displays a graph for each independent variable *X* against the dependent *Y* variable as shown in Figure 5.7. Each plot is basically a transformed *XY* plot of the X-residuals versus the Y-residuals. Added to each *X*-residual is the mean of the *X* and correspondingly added to each *Y*-residual is the *Y* mean. These transformed residuals are called *X leverage residuals* and *Y leverage residuals*. The black line represents the predicted values for individual *X* values, and the blue dotted line is the corresponding 95% confidence interval. If the confidence region between the upper and lower confidence interval crosses the horizontal line, then the effect of *X* is significant. The horizontal red dotted line shows the current predicted value of the *Y* variable as the vertical red dotted lines shows the current *X* value. You can observe changes in the current *X* or *Y* value by clicking in the graph and dragging the dotted line.

Figure 5.7: Multiple Linear Regression Output (Bottom Half)

◢ Summary of Fit

RSquare	0.922019	AICc	395.1501
RSquare Adj	0.88991	BIC	394.12
Root Mean Square Error	435.6742		
Mean of Response	3374.568		
Observations (or Sum Wgts)	25		

◢ Parameter Estimates

Term	Estimate	Std Error	t Ratio	Prob>|t|	VIF
Intercept	-1485.881	677.6727	-2.19	0.0425*	.
Time	1.9745433	1.79575	1.10	0.2868	3.071766
MktPoten	0.0372905	0.007851	4.75	0.0002*	1.9246054
Adver	0.1519609	0.043245	3.51	0.0027*	1.709946
MktShare	198.30849	64.11718	3.09	0.0066*	3.1450824
Change	295.86609	164.3865	1.80	0.0897	1.317864
Accts	5.6101882	4.544957	1.23	0.2339	5.4257278
WkLoad	19.899031	32.6361	0.61	0.5501	1.8139819

▷ Effect Tests

◢ ▾ Box-Cox Transformations

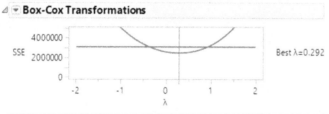

Best λ=0.292

◢ ▾ Prediction Profiler

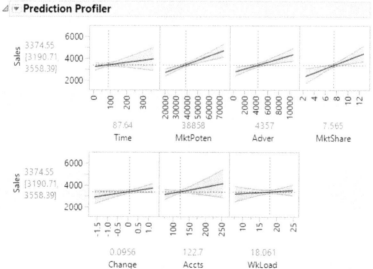

Figure 5.8: Parameter Estimates Table with Standardized Betas and Variance Inflation Factors

⊿ **Parameter Estimates**

Term	Estimate	Std Error	t Ratio	Prob>|t|	Std Beta	VIF
Intercept	-1485.881	677.6727	-2.19	0.0425*	0	.
Time	1.9745433	1.79575	1.10	0.2868	0.130522	3.071766
MktPoten	0.0372905	0.007851	4.75	0.0002*	0.446285	1.9246054
Adver	0.1519609	0.043245	3.51	0.0027*	0.311209	1.709946
MktShare	198.30849	64.11718	3.09	0.0066*	0.371494	3.1450824
Change	295.86609	164.3865	1.80	0.0897	0.139937	1.317864
Accts	5.6101882	4.544957	1.23	0.2339	0.194736	5.4257278
WkLoad	19.899031	32.6361	0.61	0.5501	0.055618	1.8139819

Evaluate the Statistical Significance of the Model

The process for evaluating the statistical significance of a regression model is as follows:

1. Determine whether it is good or bad:

   a. Conduct an *F* test.
   b. Conduct a *t* test for each independent variable.
   c. Examine the residual plot.
   d. Assess the degree of multicollinearity (variance inflation factor, VIF).

2. Determine the goodness of fit:

   a. Examine Adjusted R^2.
   b. Examine RMSE (or S_e).
   c. Examine AICc (or BIC).

Step 1a: Conduct an *F* Test

First, you should perform an *F* test. The *F* test in multiple regression is known as an *overall test*.

The hypotheses for the *F* test are as follows, where *k* is the number of independent variables:

$H_0 : \beta_1 = \beta_2 = ... = \beta_k = 0$

H_1 : not all equal to 0

If you fail to reject the *F* test, then the overall model is not statistically significant. The model shows no linear significant relationships. You need to start over, and you should not look at the numbers in the Parameter Estimates table. On the other hand, if you reject H_0, then you can conclude that one or more of the independent variables are linearly related to the dependent variable. So you want to reject H_0 of the *F* test.

In Figure 5.7, for your sales performance data set, you can see that the *p*-value for the *F* test is <0.0001. So you reject the *F* test and can conclude that one or more of the independent variables (that is, one or more of variables **Time**, **Mktpoten**, **Adver**, **Mktshare**, **Change**, **Accts**, and **Wkload**) is significantly related to Sales (linearly).

Step 1b: Evaluate the *T* Test for Each Independent Variable

The second step is to evaluate the *t* test for each independent variable. The hypotheses are as follows, where $k = 1, 2, 3, ... K$:

$H_0 : \beta_k = 0$

$H_1 : \beta_k \neq 0$

You are not testing whether independent variable k, x_k, is significantly related to the dependent variable. What you are testing is whether x_k is significantly related to the dependent variable above and beyond all the other independent variables that are currently in the model. That is, in the regression equation, you have the term $\beta_k x_k$. If β_k cannot be determined to be significantly different from 0, then x_k has no effect on Y. Again, in this situation, you want to reject H_0. You can see in Figures 5.6 and 5.7 that the independent variables **MktPoten**, **Adver**, and **MktShare** each reject H_0 and are significantly related to **Sales** above and beyond the other independent variables.

Step 1c: Examine the Residual Plot

One of the statistical assumptions of regression is that the residuals or errors (the difference between the actual value and the predicted value) should be random. That is, the errors do not follow any pattern. To visually examine the residuals, look at **Plot Residual by Predicted** in Figure 5.6 and in Figure 5.9. Examine the plot for any patterns—oscillating too often or increasing or decreasing in values or for outliers. The data appears to be random. There are statistical tests for randomness discussed in Chapter 17.

Figure 5.9: Residual Plot of Predicted versus Residual

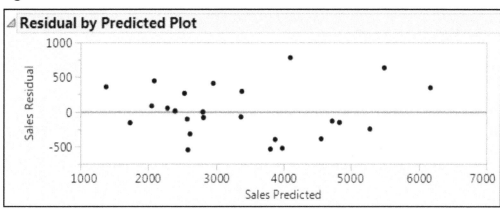

If the observations were taken in some time sequence, called a *time series* (not applicable to the sales performance data set), the Durbin-Watson test should be performed. (Click the red triangle next to the **Response Sales** heading; select **Row Diagnostics ▶ Durbin-Watson Test**.) The Durbin-Watson test examines the correlation between consecutive observations. In general, you want high *p*-values. High *p*-values of the Durbin-Watson test indicate that there is no problem with first order autocorrelation. In this case, the *p*-value is 0.2355.

Step 1d: Assess Multicollinearity

An important problem to address in the application of multiple regression is multicollinearity or collinearity of the independent variables (*X*s). Multicollinearity occurs when the two or more independent variables explain the same variability of *Y*. Multicollinearity does not violate any of the statistical assumptions of regression. However, significant multicollinearity is likely to make it difficult to interpret the meaning of the regression coefficients of the independent variables.

One method of measuring multicollinearity is the variance inflation factor (VIF). Each independent variable k has its own VIF_k. By definition, it must be greater than or equal to 1. The closer the VIF_k is to 1, the smaller the relationship between the kth independent variable and the remaining Xs. Although there are no definitive rules for identifying a large VIF_k, the basic guidelines (Marquardt 1980; Snee 1973) for identifying whether significant multicollinearity exists are as follows:

- $1 \leq VIF_k \leq 5$ means no significant multicollinearity.
- $5 < VIF_k \leq 10$ means that you should be concerned that some multicollinearity might exist.
- $VIF_k > 10$ means significant multicollinearity.

Note that exceptions to these guidelines are when you might have transformed the variables (such as nonlinear transformation). To display the VIF_k values for the independent variables (similar to what we illustrated to display the standardized beta values), move the cursor somewhere over the Parameter Estimates Table and right-click. Select **Columns ▶ VIF**. As shown before in Figure 5.8, a column of VIF values for each independent variable is added to the Parameter Estimate Table. The variable **Accts** has a VIF greater than 5, and we should be concerned about that variable.

If you want the VIF, summary fit table, Analysis of Variance table, and some other output to always appear when performing standard least squares:

1. Click the **Response Sales** red triangle, click **Platform Preferences ▶ Go To....**
2. A new Fit Least Squares window appears. Click **Show VIF; Set** and **Summary of Fit; Set** and **Analysis of Variance; Set** and **Parameter Estimates; AICc**.

Step 2: Determine the Goodness of Fit

There are two opposing points of views as to whether to include those nonsignificant independent variables (that is, those variables for which you failed to reject H_0 for the t test) or the high VIF_k variables. One perspective is to include those nonsignificant or high VIF_k variables because they explain some, although not much, of the variation in the dependent variable. And it does improve your understanding of these relationships. Taking this approach to the extremes, you can continue adding independent variables to the model so that you have almost the same number of independent variables as there are observations, which is somewhat unreasonable. However, this approach is sensible with a reasonable number of independent variables and when the major objective of the regression analysis is to understand the relationships of the independent variables to the dependent variable. Best Subsets regression lists performance measures for all possible models using a specified set of independent variables. To perform Best Subsets regression:

1. Click the **Response Sales** red triangle and select **Model Dialog**. The **Fit Model** dialog box as in Figure 5.5 will appear.
2. Click the **Recall** icon. The dialog box is repopulated and looks like Figure 5.5.
3. In the **Fit Model** dialog box, click the drop-down menu to the right of **Personality**. Change **Standard Least Squares** to **Stepwise**. Click **Run**.
4. The Fit Stepwise dialog box will appear, similar to the top portion of Figure 5.10. Click the **Stepwise Fit for Sales** red triangle; click **All Possible Models**.
5. The **All Possible Models** dialog box appears. Accept the default values and click **OK**.

A list of all possible models (up to the maximum number of terms in a model) with several performance measures are listed. One measure not listed is VIF_k values. Addressing the high VIF_k values (especially > 10) might be of concern, particularly if one of the objectives of performing the regression is the interpretation of the regression coefficients. Also, the p-values for the independent variables t tests do not appear, which could be imperative.

The other point of view follows the principle of *parsimony*, which states that the smaller the number of variables in the model, the better. This viewpoint is especially true when the regression model is used for prediction or forecasting (having such variables in the model might actually increase the RMSE). There are numerous approaches and several statistical variable selection techniques to achieve this goal of only significant independent variables in the model. Stepwise regression is one of the simplest approaches. Although it's not guaranteed to find the "best" model, it certainly will provide a model that is close to the "best." To perform stepwise regression:

6. You can continue on from the Stepwise Fit for Sales dialog box, similar to Figure 5.10 or you can start from the Data Table:

    a. Select **Analyze ▶ Fit Model**. Click the **Recall** icon. The dialog box is repopulated and looks like Figure 5.5.
    b. In the **Fit Model** dialog box, click the drop-down menu to the right of **Personality**. Change **Standard Least Squares** to **Stepwise**. Click **Run**.

7. With either approach, in the **Fit Stepwise for Sales** dialog box, in the drop-down box to the right of Stopping Rule, click the drop-down menu, and change the default from **Minimum BIC** to **P-Value Threshold**.
8. Two rows will appear, Prob to Enter and Prob to Leave. Click the drop arrow in the box next to Direction and change Forward to **Mixed**. (The **Mixed** option alternates the forward and backward steps.)
9. Click **Go**.

Figure 5.10 displays the stepwise regression results. The stepwise model did not include the variables **Accts** and **Wkload**. The Adjusted R² values improved slightly from 0.890 in the full model to 0.893. And the s_e, or root mean square error (RMSE), actually improved by decreasing from 435.67 to 430.23. And nicely, all the *p*-values for the *t* tests are now significant (less than .05).

10. You can click **Run Model** to get a more readable output similar to the standard least squares **(Fit Model)** output.

Figure 5.10: Stepwise Regression for the Sales Performance Data Set

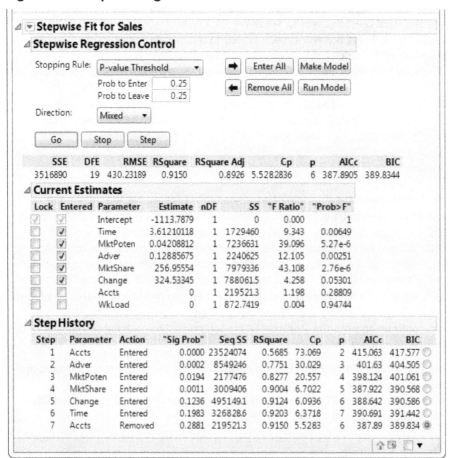

The goodness of fit of the regression model is measured by the Adjusted R^2 and the s_e or RMSE, as listed in Figure 5.7 and 5.10. The Adjusted R^2 measures the percentage of the variability in the dependent variable that is explained by the set of independent variables and is adjusted for the number of independent variables (*X*s) in the model. If the purpose of performing the regression is to understand the relationships of the independent variables with the dependent variable, the Adjusted R^2 value is a major assessment of the goodness of fit. What constitutes a good Adjusted R^2 value is subjective and depends on the situation. The higher the Adjusted R^2, the better the fit. On the other hand, if the regression model is for prediction or forecasting, the value of the RMSE or s_e (standard error) is of more concern. The residuals of the regression model are assumed to follow a normal distribution with a mean of 0 and a standard deviation equal to the RMSE. A smaller RMSE generally means a smaller forecasting error. Similar to Adjusted R^2, a good RMSE value is subjective and depends on the situation.

Many statistical techniques in JMP use a methodology called maximum likelihood to find the best fit. Rather than maximize the likelihood function, L(β), it is mathematically more convenient to work with the -2LogLikelihood (-2LL) function. The corrected Akaike's Information Criterion (AICc; the AICc corrects the AIC for small samples—similar to how the t distribution converges to the normal distribution) and Schwarz's Bayesian information criterion (BIC and sometimes referred to as SBC) are information-based criteria that assess model fit, including regression models, and both are based on -2LL function. In practice, the two criteria often produce identical results. For both criteria, the lower the value, the better. The two approaches have quite similar equations except that the BIC criterion imposes a greater penalty on the number of parameters than the AICc criterion, thus leading toward choosing more parsimonious models.

To apply these criteria, in the Stepwise dialog box, when you click the drop-down menu for Stopping Rule, there were several options listed, including **Minimum AICc** and **Minimum BIC.**

In evaluating a regression model, the user needs to evaluate the suite of performance measures, adjusted R^2, RMSE, AICc, and BIC as well as their domain knowledge to determine the best model.

Last of all, a significant statistical assumption of the least squares method of regression is that the dependent variable, y, follows a normal/symmetrical distribution. Regression is rather robust with this assumption. However, if the y-variable is significantly skewed and you observe residuals tailing off, steps should be taken, such as taking the log of the variable. Further discussion on identifying whether the data is bell-shaped or not and correcting it are covered in Chapter 17.

Further expanding the use of regression, in Chapter 8, you will learn two generalized regression approaches, LASSO and Elastic Net.

Understand and Perform Regression with Categorical Data

There are many situations in which a regression model that uses one or more categorical variables as independent variables might be of interest. For example, suppose that your dependent variable is sales. A few possible illustrations of using a categorical variable that could affect sales would be gender, region, store, or month. The goal of using these categorical variables would be to see whether the categorical variable significantly affects the dependent variable sales. That is, does the amount of sales differ significantly by gender, by region, by store, or by month? Or do sales vary significantly in combinations of several of these categorical variables?

Measuring ratios and distances are not appropriate with categorical data. That is, distance cannot be measured between male and female. So in order to use a categorical variable in a regression model, you must transform the categorical variables into continuous variables or integer (binary) variables. The resulting variables from this transformation are called *indicator* or *dummy variables.* How many indicator, or dummy, variables are required for a particular independent categorical variable X is equal to c – 1, where c is the number of categories (or levels) of the categorical X variable. For example, gender requires one dummy variable, and month requires 11 dummy variables. In JMP, indicator variables are coded 0 or 1. To create indicator variables, for example, click on a categorical variable in the Column area, such as **Process**:

1. Click **Cols** ▶ **Utilities** ▶ **Make Indicator Columns…**;
2. **The Make Indicator Columns** dialog box appears. Click the box next to **Append Column Name.**
3. Click **OK.**

Five new indicator variables columns appear with 0s and 1s in the Data Table.

However, in JMP, if a categorical variable is used in regression, the software does not use indicator variables. It uses dummy variables that are not limited to 0s or 1s. If a categorical variable has two categories (or levels) such as gender, then a single dummy variable is used with values of +1 and -1 (with +1 assigned to the alphabetically first category). If a categorical variable has more than two categories (or levels), the dummy variables are assigned values +1, 0, and –1.

Now look at a data set, in particular AgeProcessWords.jmp (Eysenck, 1974). Eysenck conducted a study to examine whether age and the amount remembered is related to how the information was initially processed. Fifty younger and fifty older people were randomly assigned to five learning process groups (Counting, Rhyming, Adjective, Imagery, and Intentional), where younger was defined as being younger than 54 years old. The first four learning process groups were instructed on ways to memorize the 27 items. For example, the rhyming group was instructed to read each word and think of a word that rhymed with it. These four groups were not told that they would later be asked to recall the words. On the other hand, the last group, the intentional group, was told that they would be asked to recall the words. The data set has three variables: **Age**, **Process**, and **Words**.

To run a simple regression using the categorical variable Age to see how it is related to the number of words memorized (the variable Words), complete the following steps:

1. Select **Analyze ▶ Fit Model**.
2. In the Fit Model dialog box, select **Words ▶ Y**.
3. Select **Age ▶ Add**.
4. Click **Run**.

Figure 5.11 shows the regression results. You can see from the *F* test and *t* test that **Age** is significantly related to **Words**. The regression equation is as follows: **Words** = 11.61 −1.55 * **Age[Older]**.

Figure 5.11: Regression of Age on Number of Words Memorized

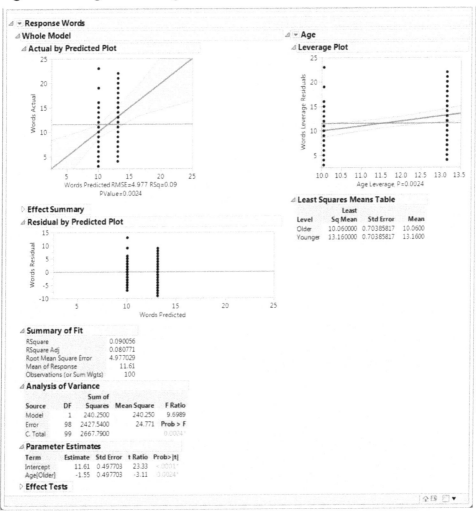

As we mentioned earlier, with a categorical variable with two levels, JMP assigns +1 to the alphabetical first level and −1 to the other level. So in this case, Age[Older] is assigned +1 and Age[Younger] is assigned −1. The regression equation for the Older age group is as follows:

Words = 11.61 − 1.55 * Age[Older] = 11.61 − 1.55(1) = 10.06

And the regression equation for the Younger age group is as follows:

Words = 11.61 − 1.55 * Age[Older] = 11.61 − 1.55(−1) = 13.16

Therefore, the Younger age group can remember more words. The y-intercept value of 11.61 is the overall mean number of Words memorized.

To verify the coding (and if you want to create a different coding in other situations), you can create a new variable called **Age1** by completing the following steps:

1. Select **Cols ▶ New Columns**. The **New Column** dialog box will appear.
2. In the text box for Column name, where Column 4 appears, enter **Age1**.
3. Select **Column Properties ▶ Formula**. The **Formula** dialog box will appear, as show in Figure 5.12.

Figure 5.12: Formula Dialog Box

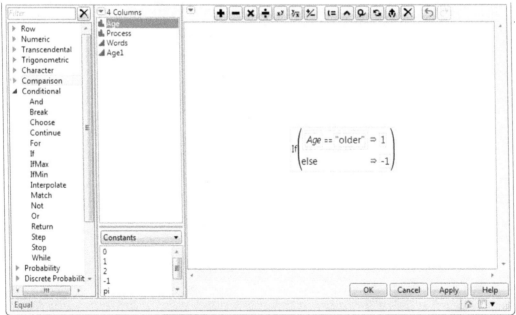

4. On the left side, there is a list of Functions. Click the arrow to the left of **Conditional ▶ If**. The If statement will appear in the formula area, similar to Figure 5.12. JMP has placed the cursor on expr (blue rectangle).
5. Click **Age** from the Columns area. Just above the Conditional Function that you clicked on the left side of the Formula dialog box, click **Comparison ▶ a==b**.
6. In the new blue rectangle, enter **"Older"** (include quotation marks), and then press the **Enter** key.
7. Click the **then clause**, type **1**, and then press the **Enter** key again.
8. Double-click on the lower **else clause**, type **–1**, and then press the **Enter** key. The dialog box should look like Figure 5.12.
9. Click **OK** and then click **OK** again.

A new column **Age1** with +1s and –1s will be in the data table. Now, run a regression with **Age1** as the independent variable. Figure 5.13 displays the results. Comparing the results in Figure 5.13 to the results in Figure 5.11, you can see that they are exactly the same.

A regression that examines the relationship between **Words** and the categorical variable **Process** would use four dummy variables. Complete the following steps:

1. Select **Analyze ▶ Fit Model**.
2. In the Fit Model dialog box, select **Words ▶ Y**.
3. Select **Process ▶ Add**.
4. Click **Run**.

The coding used for these four **Process** dummy variables is shown in Table 5.1. Figure 5.14 displays the regression results. The regression equation is as follows:

Words = 11.61 + 1.29 * **Adjective** – 4.86 * **Counting** + 3.89 * **Imagery** + 4.04 * **Intentional**

5. Given the dummy variable coding used by JMP, as shown in Table 5.1, the mean of the level displayed in the brackets is equal to the difference between its coefficient value and the mean across all levels (that is, the overall mean or the *y*-intercept which in this case is 11.61). So the *t* tests here are testing if the level shown is different from the mean across all levels. If you have used the dummy variable coding and substituted into the equation, the predicted number of Words that are memorized by process are as listed in Table 5.1. Intentional has the highest words memorized at 15.65, and Counting is the lowest at 6.75.

If you ran a regression with 4 of the 5 indicator variables (whichever indicator you do not include is considered the baseline), you would get similar statistical results—for example, the same R^2 and RMSE. The predicted number of Words to be memorized by process will also be the same. However, the regression coefficients are different. The y-intercept, b_0, coefficient with the dummy variables is the overall mean number of Words memorized, while the b_0 coefficient with indicator variables is equal to average number of Words memorized of the baseline indicator variable—the one not included in the model.

Figure 5.13: Regression of Age1 on Number of Words Memorized

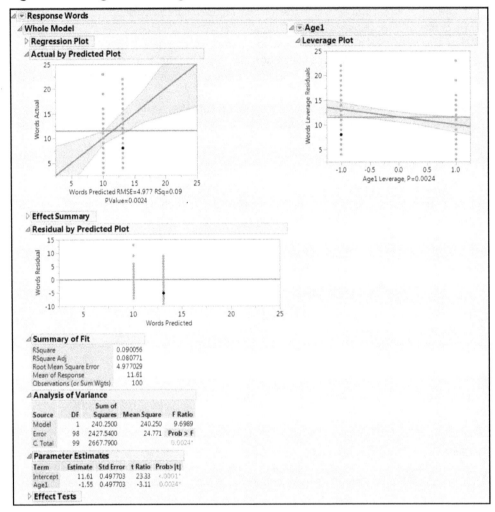

Table 5.1: Dummy Variable Coding for Process and the Predicted Number of Words Memorized

Row Process	Predicted Number of Words	Process Dummy Variable			
		[Adjective]	[Counting]	[Imagery]	[Intentional]
Adjective	12.90	1	0	0	0
Counting	6.75	0	1	0	0
Imagery	15.50	0	0	1	0
Intentional	15.65	0	0	0	1
Rhyming	7.25	−1	−1	−1	−1

Figure 5.14: Regression of Process on Number of Words Memorized

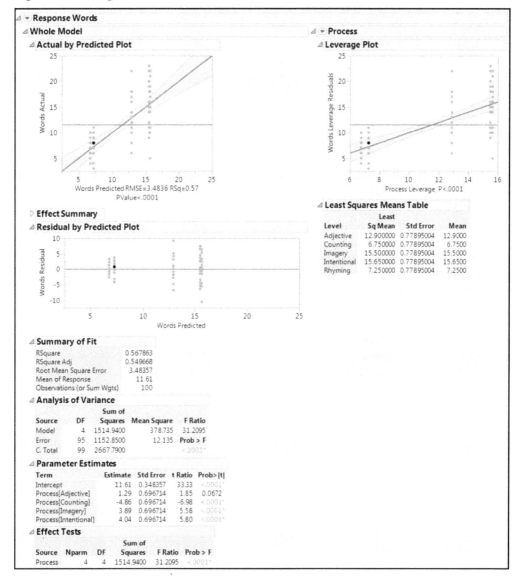

Analysis of Variance

Analysis of variance (more commonly called *ANOVA*), as shown in Figure 5.1, is a dependence multivariate technique. There are several variations of ANOVA, such as one-factor (or one-way) ANOVA, two-factor (or two-way) ANOVA, and so on, and also repeated measures ANOVA. (In JMP, repeated measures ANOVA is found under **Analysis ▶ Consumer Research ▶ Categorical**.) The factors are the independent variables, each of which must be a categorical variable. The dependent variable is one continuous variable. This book provides only a brief introduction to and review of ANOVA.

Assume that one independent categorical variable X has k levels. One of the main objectives of ANOVA is to compare the means of two or more populations:

$H_0 = \mu_1 = \mu_2 ... = \mu_k = 0$

H_1 = at least one mean is different from the other means

The average for each level is μ_k. If H_0 is true, you would expect all the sample means to be close to each other and relatively close to the grand mean. If H_1 is true, then at least one of the sample means would be significantly different. You measure the variability between means with the sum of squares between groups (SSBG). On the other hand, large variability within the sample weakens the capacity of the sample means to measure their corresponding population means. This within-sample variability is measured by the sum of squares within groups (or error) (SSE). As with regression, the decomposition of the total sum of squares (TSS) is as follows: TSS = sum of squares between groups + sum of squared error, or TSS = SSBG + SSE. (In JMP, TSS, SSBG, and SSE are identified as C.Total, Model SS, and Error SS, respectively.) To test this hypothesis, you do an F test (the same test that is done in regression).

If H_0 of the F test is rejected, which implies that one or more of the population means are significantly different, you then proceed to the second part of an ANOVA study and identify which factor level means are significantly different. If you have two populations (that is, two levels of the factor), you would not need ANOVA, and you could perform a two-sample hypothesis test. On the other hand, when you have more than two populations (or groups), you could take the two-sample hypothesis test approach and compare every pair of groups. This approach has problems that are caused by multiple comparisons and is not advisable, as will be explained.

If there are k levels in the X variable, the number of possible pairs of levels to compare is $k(k-1)/2$. For example, if you had three populations (call them A, B, and C), there would be 3 pairs to compare: A to B, A to C, and B to C. If you use a level of significance $\alpha = 0.05$, there is a 14.3% $(1-(.95)^3)$ chance that you will detect a difference in one of these pairs, even when there really is no difference in the populations; the probability of Type I error is 14.3%. If there are 4 groups, the likelihood of this error increases to 26.5%. This inflated error rate for the group of comparisons, not the individual comparisons, is not a good situation. However, ANOVA provides you with several multiple comparison tests that maintain the Type I error at α or smaller.

An additional plus of ANOVA is that if we are examining the relationship of two or more factors, ANOVA is good at uncovering any significant interactions or relationships among these factors. We will discuss interactions briefly when we examine two-factor (two-way) ANOVA. For now, let's look at one-factor (one-way) ANOVA.

Perform a One-Way ANOVA

One-way ANOVA has one dependent variable and one *X* factor. Let's return to the AgeProcessWords.jmp data set and first perform a one-factor ANOVA with **Words** and **Age**:

1. Select **Analyze ▶ Fit Y by X**.
2. In the Fit Y by X dialog box, select **Words ▶ Y, Response**.
3. Select **Age ▶ X, Factor**.
4. Click **OK**.
5. In the **Oneway Analysis of Words By Age** output, click the red triangle and select the **Means/Anova/Pooled t** option.

Figure 5.15 displays the one-way ANOVA results. The plot of the data at the top of Figure 5.15 is displayed by each factor level (in this case, the age group Older and Younger). The horizontal line across the entire plot represents the overall mean. Each factor level has its own mean diamond. The horizontal line in the center of the diamond is the mean for that level. The upper and lower vertices of the diamond represent the upper and lower 95% confidence limit on the mean, respectively. Also, the horizontal width of the diamond is relative to that level's (group's) sample size. That is, the wider the diamond, the larger the sample size for that level relative to the other levels.

In this case, because the level sample sizes are the same, the horizontal widths of all the diamonds are the same. As shown in Figure 5.15, the *t* test and the ANOVA *F* test (in this situation, since the factor **Age** has only two levels, a pooled *t* test is performed) show that there is a significant difference in the average **Words** memorized by **Age** level (p = 0.0024). In particular, examining the **Means for One-Way ANOVA** table in Figure 5.15, you can see that the Younger age group memorizes more words than the Older group (average of 13.16 to 10.06). Lastly, compare the values in the ANOVA table in Figure 5.15 to Figures 5.11 and 5.13. They have exactly the same values in the ANOVA tables as when you did the simple categorical regression using **AGE** or **AGE1**.

Evaluate the Model

The overall steps to evaluate an ANOVA model are as follows:

1. Conduct an *F* test.

   a. If you do not reject H0 (the p-value is not small), then stop because there is no difference in means.

   b. If you do reject H_0, then go to Step 2.

2. Consider unequal variances; look at the Levine test.

   a. If you reject H_0, then go to Step 3 because the variances are unequal.

   b. If you do not reject H_0, then go to Step 4.

Figure 5.15: One-Way ANOVA of Age and Words

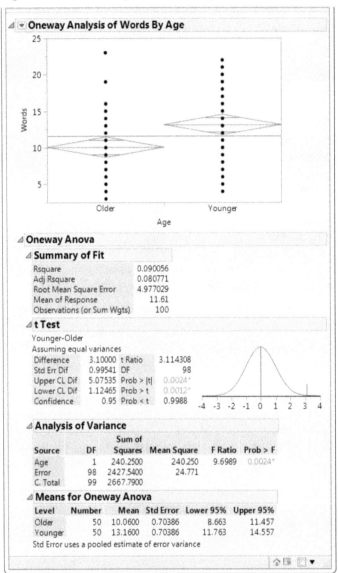

3. Conduct Welch's test, which tests differences in means, assuming unequal variances.

   a. If you reject H0 because the means are significantly different, then go to Step 4.
   b. If you do not reject H1, stop: Results are marginal, meaning that you cannot conclude that means are significantly different.

4. Perform multiple comparison test, Tukey's HSD.

Test Statistical Assumptions

ANOVA has three statistical assumptions to check and address. The first assumption is that the residuals should be independent. In most situations, ANOVA is rather robust in terms of this assumption. Furthermore, many times in practice this assumption is violated. So unless there is strong concern about the dependence of the residuals, this assumption does not have to be checked.

The second statistical assumption is that the variances for each level are equal. Violation of this assumption is of more concern because it could lead to erroneous *p*-values and hence incorrect statistical conclusions. You can test this assumption by clicking the red triangle and then clicking **Unequal Variances**. Added to the JMP ANOVA results is the report named **Tests that the Variances are Equal**.

Four tests are always provided. However, in this case, there are only two groups tested, and then an *F* test for unequal variance is also performed. This gives you five tests, as shown in Figure 5.16. If you fail to reject H_0 (that is, you have a large *p*-value), you have insufficient evidence to say that the variances are not equal. So you proceed as if they are equal, go to Step 4, and perform multiple comparison tests. On the other hand, if you reject H_0, the variances can be assumed to be unequal, and the ANOVA output cannot be trusted. In that case, you should go to Step 3. With your current problem in Figure 15.15 and 15.16, because for all the tests for unequal variances the *p*-values are small, you need to proceed to Step 3. In Step 3, you look at the Welch's Test, located at the bottom of Figure 5.16. The Welch's Test compares whether the means are equal, similar to ANOVA, however, assuming unequal variances. The *p*-value for the Welch ANOVA is .0025, which is also rather small. So you can assume that there is a significant difference in the population mean of Older and Younger.

Create a Normal Quantile Plot

The third statistical assumption is that the residuals should be normally distributed. The *F* test is very robust if the residuals are non-normal. That is, if slight departures from normality are detected, they will have no real effect on the *F* statistic. A normal quantile plot can confirm whether the residuals are normally distributed or not. To produce a normal quantile plot, complete the following steps:

1. In the **Oneway Analysis of Words By Age** output, click the red triangle and select **Save ▶ Save Residuals**. A new variable called **Words centered by Age** will appear in the Data Table.
2. Select **Analyze ▶ Distribution**. In the Distribution dialog box, in the Select Columns area, select **Words centered by Age ▶ Y, Response**.
3. Click **OK**.
4. The **Distributions** output will appear. Click the **Words centered by Age** red triangle and click **Normal Quantile Plot**.

Figure 5.16: Tests of Unequal Variances and Welch's Test for Age and Words

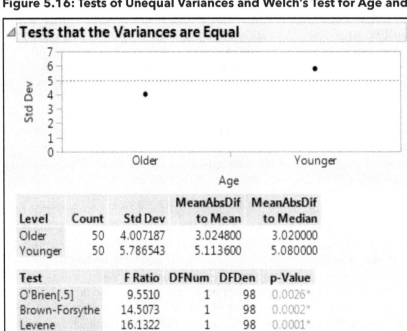

Level	Count	Std Dev	MeanAbsDif to Mean	MeanAbsDif to Median
Older	50	4.007187	3.024800	3.020000
Younger	50	5.786543	5.113600	5.080000

Test	F Ratio	DFNum	DFDen	p-Value
O'Brien[.5]	9.5510	1	98	0.0026*
Brown-Forsythe	14.5073	1	98	0.0002*
Levene	16.1322	1	98	0.0001*
Bartlett	6.4067	1	.	0.0114*
F Test 2-sided	2.0853	49	49	0.0114*

⊿ Welch's Test

Welch Anova testing Means Equal, allowing Std Devs Not Equal

F Ratio	DFNum	DFDen	Prob > F
9.6989	1	87.209	0.0025*

t Test
3.1143

The distribution output and normal quantile plot will look like Figure 5.17. If all the residuals fall on or near the straight line or within the confidence bounds, the residuals should be considered normally distributed. All the points in Figure 5.17 are within the bounds, so you can assume that the residuals are normally distributed.

Perform a One-Factor ANOVA

Now perform a one-factor ANOVA of **Process** and **Words**:

1. Select **Analyze ▶ Fit Y by X**. In the Fit Y by X dialog box, select **Words ▶ Y, Response**.
2. Select **Process ▶ X, Factor**.
3. Click **OK**.
4. Click the **Oneway Analysis of Words By Process** red triangle, and click **Means/Anova**.

Figure 5.17: Normal Quantile Plot of the Residuals

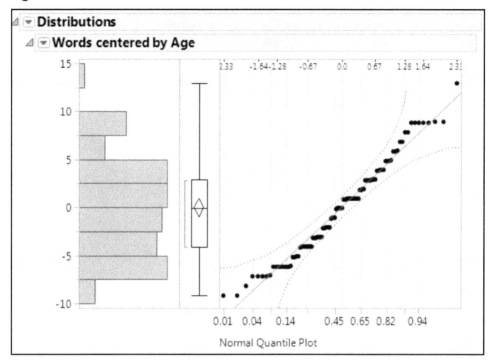

Figure 5.18 displays the one-way ANOVA results. The p-value for the F test is <.0001, so one or more of the Process means differ from each other. Also, notice that the ANOVA table in Figure 5.18 is the same as in the categorical regression output of **Words** and **Process** in Figure 5.14.

Examine the Results

5. Click the **Oneway Analysis of Words By Process** red triangle, and click **Unequal Variances**.

The results of the tests for unequal variances are displayed in Figure 5.19. In general, the Levene test is more widely used and more comprehensive, so you focus only on the Levene test. It appears that you should assume that the variances are unequal (for all the tests), so you should look at the Welch's Test in Figure 5.19. Because the p-value for the Welch's Test is small, you can reject the null hypothesis; the pairs of means are different from one another.

Figure 5.18: One-Way ANOVA of Process and Words

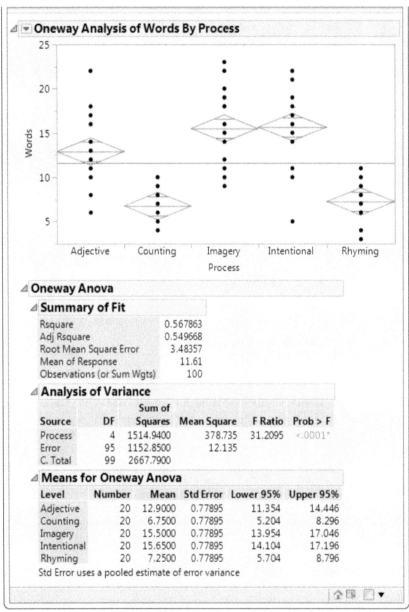

The second part of the ANOVA study focuses on identifying which factor level means differ from each other. With the AgeProcessWords.jmp data set, because you did not satisfy the statistical assumption that the variances for each level are equal, you needed to go to Step 3 to perform the Welch's test. You rejected the Welch's test, which suggests, assuming that the variances are different, that the means appear to be significantly different; therefore, you can perform

Figure 5.19: Tests of Unequal Variances and Welch's Test for Process and Words

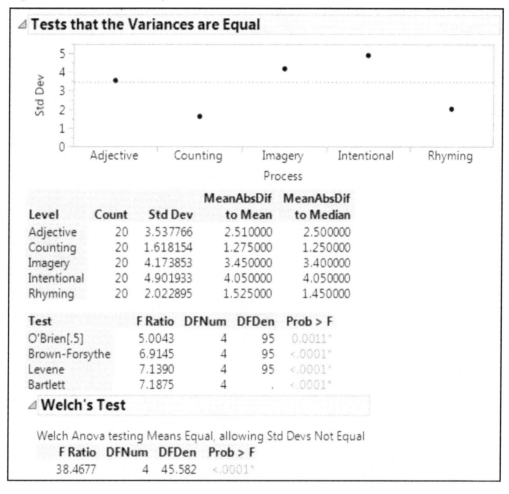

Tests that the Variances are Equal

Level	Count	Std Dev	MeanAbsDif to Mean	MeanAbsDif to Median
Adjective	20	3.537766	2.510000	2.500000
Counting	20	1.618154	1.275000	1.250000
Imagery	20	4.173853	3.450000	3.400000
Intentional	20	4.901933	4.050000	4.050000
Rhyming	20	2.022895	1.525000	1.450000

Test	F Ratio	DFNum	DFDen	Prob > F
O'Brien[.5]	5.0043	4	95	0.0011*
Brown-Forsythe	6.9145	4	95	<.0001*
Levene	7.1390	4	95	<.0001*
Bartlett	7.1875	4	.	<.0001*

Welch's Test

Welch Anova testing Means Equal, allowing Std Devs Not Equal

F Ratio	DFNum	DFDen	Prob > F
38.4677	4	45.582	<.0001*

the second part of an ANOVA and test for differences. If you had not rejected the Welch's test, then it would not be recommended that you perform these second-stage tests. In such a case, it is recommended that you perform some nonparametric tests that JMP provides but are not discussed in this text.

Test for Differences

To perform the second part of an ANOVA analysis, you will use a data set that does have equal variances, Analgesics.jmp. The Analgesics data table contains 33 observations and three variables: **Gender**, **Drug** (3 analgesics drugs: **A**, **B**, and **C**), and **Pain** (ranges from 2.13 and 16.64— the higher the value, the more painful).

Figures 5.20 and 5.21 display the two one-way ANOVAs. Males appear to have significantly higher **Pain**, and you do not have to go further since there are only two levels for gender. In terms of level of **Pain** by **Drug**, visually there does seem to be a significant difference in **Pain** and the *p*-value for the Levene test is .0587. So you fail to reject the null hypothesis of all equal variances and can

Figure 5.20: One-Way ANOVA of Gender and Pain

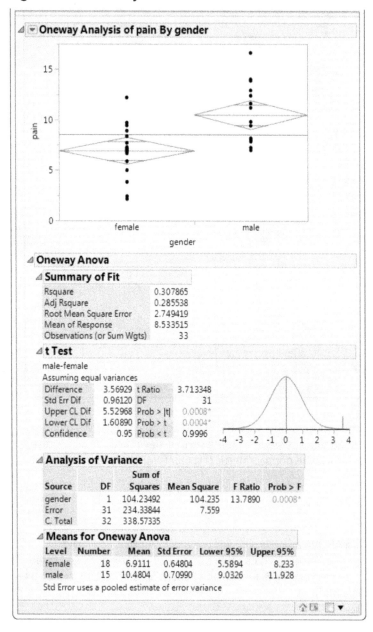

Figure 5.21: One-Way ANOVA of Drug and Pain

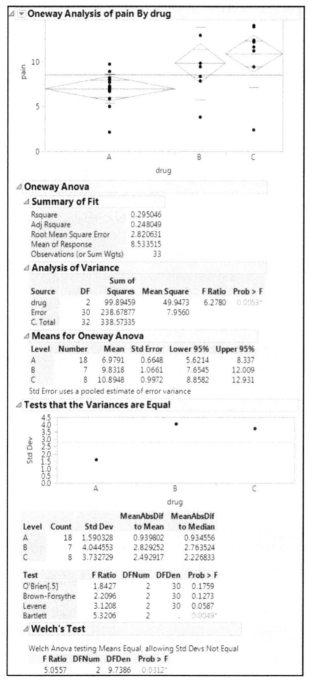

Oneway Analysis of pain By drug

Oneway Anova

Summary of Fit

Rsquare	0.295046
Adj Rsquare	0.248049
Root Mean Square Error	2.820631
Mean of Response	8.533515
Observations (or Sum Wgts)	33

Analysis of Variance

Source	DF	Sum of Squares	Mean Square	F Ratio	Prob > F
drug	2	99.89459	49.9473	6.2780	0.0053*
Error	30	238.67877	7.9560		
C. Total	32	338.57335			

Means for Oneway Anova

Level	Number	Mean	Std Error	Lower 95%	Upper 95%
A	18	6.9791	0.6648	5.6214	8.337
B	7	9.8318	1.0661	7.6545	12.009
C	8	10.8948	0.9972	8.8582	12.931

Std Error uses a pooled estimate of error variance

Tests that the Variances are Equal

Level	Count	Std Dev	MeanAbsDif to Mean	MeanAbsDif to Median
A	18	1.590328	0.939802	0.934556
B	7	4.044553	2.829252	2.763524
C	8	3.732729	2.492917	2.226833

Test	F Ratio	DFNum	DFDen	Prob > F
O'Brien[.5]	1.8427	2	30	0.1759
Brown-Forsythe	2.2096	2	30	0.1273
Levene	3.1208	2	30	0.0587
Bartlett	5.3206	2	.	0.0049*

Welch's Test

Welch Anova testing Means Equal, allowing Std Devs Not Equal

F Ratio	DFNum	DFDen	Prob > F
5.0557	2	9.7386	0.0312*

comfortably move on to the second part of an ANOVA study. On the other hand, in Figure 5.21 the diamonds under **Oneway analysis of pain by Drug** appear different. Looking vertically, Drug A distribution is tighter, and the distributions of drugs B and C are somewhat similar. Each distribution has some significantly low values, especially drug C, suggesting possible differences in variances. On the other hand, looking horizontally, Drug A is wide and Drug B and C are somewhat similarly narrower. The horizontal width is related to sample size. The number of individuals with Drug B and C are about the same (7 and 8), while the sample size for Drug A is over twice the size (18).

JMP provides several multiple comparison tests, which can be found by clicking the red triangle, clicking **Compare Means**, and then selecting the test.

Student's *t* Test

The first test, the **Each Pair, Student's *t* test**, computes individual pairwise comparisons. As discussed earlier, the likelihood of a Type I error increases with the number of pairwise comparisons. Unless the number of pairwise comparisons is small, this test is not recommended.

Tukey Honest Significant Difference Test

The second means comparison test is the **All Pairs, Tukey HSD** test. If the main objective is to check for any possible pairwise difference in the mean values, and there are several factor levels, the Tukey HSD (honest significant difference), also called *Tukey-Kramer HSD test,* is the most desired test. Figure 5.22 displays the results of the Tukey-Kramer HSD test. To identify mean differences, either examine:

- the HSD Threshold Matrix. Positive values indicate a significant difference in the pair of means. In this example, **Drug A** is significantly different from **Drug C**.
- the Connecting Letters Report. Groups that do not share the same letter are significantly different from one another. The mean pain for **Drug A** is significantly different from the mean pain of **Drug C**.

Hsu's Multiple Comparison with Best

The third means comparison test is **With Best, Hsu MCB**. The Hsu's MCB (multiple comparison with best) is used to determine whether each factor level mean can be rejected as the "best" of all the other means, where "best" means either a maximum or minimum value. Figure 5.23 displays the results of Hsu's MCB test. The *p*-value report and the maximum and minimum LSD (Least Squares Differences) matrices can be used to identify significant differences. The *p*-value report identifies whether a factor level mean is significantly different from the maximum and from the minimum of all the other means. **Drug A** is significantly different from the maximum, and **Drugs B** and **C** are significantly different from the minimum. The maximum LSD matrix compares the means of the groups against the unknown maximum and, correspondingly, compares the means of the groups against the same for the minimum LSD matrix. Follow the directions on the output below each matrix, looking at positive values for the maximum and negative values for the minimum.

Figure 5.22: The Tukey-Kramer HSD Test

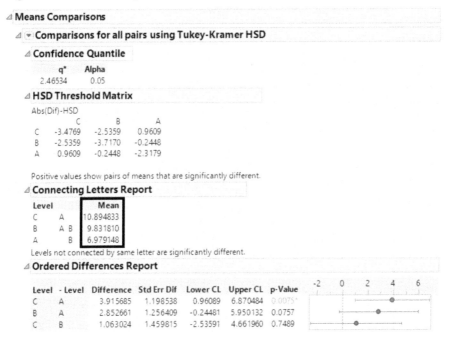

Examining the matrices in Figure 5.23, you can see that the Drug groups AC and AB are significantly less than the maximum and significantly greater than the minimum.

Differences with the Hsu's MCB test are less conservative than those found with the Tukey-Kramer test. Also, Hsu's MCB test should be used if there is a need to make specific inferences about the maximum or minimum values.

Dunnett's Test

The last means comparison test provided, **With Control, Dunnett's**, is applicable when you do not wish to make all pairwise comparisons, but rather only compare one of the levels (the "control") with each other level. Thus, fewer pairwise comparisons are made. This is beyond the focus of this book, so this test is discussed no further here.

The JMP Fit Model Platform

In addition, you can perform one-way ANOVA by using the JMP Fit Model platform. Most of the output is identical to the Fit Y by X results, but with a few differences.

To perform a one-way ANOVA on **Pain** with **Drug**:

Figure 5.23: Hsu's MCB Test

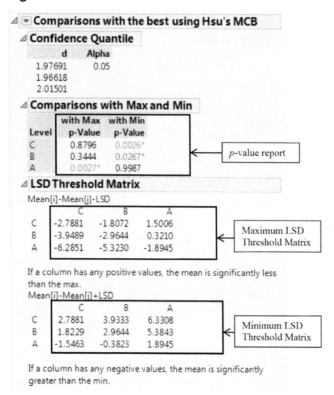

1. Select **Analyze ▶ Fit Model**.
2. In the Fit Model dialog box, click **Pain ▶ Y**.
3. Select **Drug ▶ Add**.
4. Click **Run**.
5. On the right side of the output, click the red triangle next to **Drug,** and select **LSMeans Plot** and then **LSMeans Tukey HSD**.

The output will look similar to Figure 5.24. The LSMeans plot shows a plot of the factor means. The LSMeans Tukey HSD is similar to the All Pairs, Tukey HSD output from the Fit Y by X option. In Figure 5.24 and Figure 5.22, notice the same Connecting Letters Report. The Fit Model output does not have the LSD matrices but does provide you with a crosstab report. The Fit Model platform does not directly provide an equal variance test. But you can visually evaluate the Residual by Predicted Plot on the left side of Figure 5.24.

Perform a Two-Way ANOVA

Two-way ANOVA is an extension of the one-way ANOVA in which there is one continuous dependent variable, but now you have two categorical independent variables.

Figure 5.24: One-Way ANOVA Output Using Fit Model

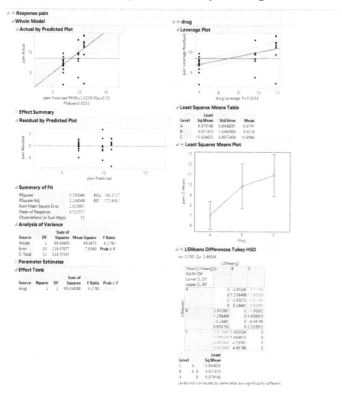

There are three basic two-way ANOVA designs: without replication, with equal replication, and with unequal replication. The two two-way designs with replication not only enable you to address the influence of each factor's contribution to explaining the variation in the dependent variable, but also enable you to address the interaction effects due to all the factor level combinations. Only the two-way ANOVA with equal replication is discussed here.

Using the **Analgesics.jmp**, perform a two-way ANOVA of **Pain** with **Gender** and **Drug** as independent variables:

1. Select **Analyze ▶ Fit Model**.
2. In the Fit Model dialog box, select **Pain ▶ Y**.
3. Click **Gender**, hold down the shift key, and click **Drug**.
4. Click **Add**.
5. Again, click **Gender**, hold down the shift key, and click **Drug**.
6. This time, click **Cross**. (Another approach is to highlight **Gender** and **Drug**, click **Macros**, and click **Full Factorial**.)
7. Click **Run**.

Examine the Results

Figures 5.25 to 5.28 display the two-way ANOVA results. The *p*-value for the *F* test in the ANOVA table is 0.0006 in Figure 5.26, so there are significant differences in the means. To find where the differences are, examine the *F* tests in the **Effect Tests** table, toward the bottom of Figure 5.26. You can see that there are significant differences in the **Gender, Drug** (which you found out already when you did the one-way ANOVAs). But observe a moderately significant difference in the interaction means, *p*-value = 0.0916. To understand these differences, go back to the top of the output and click the red triangles for each factor. Then complete the following steps:

1. For **Gender**, click the red triangle, select **LSMeans Plot;** click the red triangle, select **LSMeans Student's t** (since you have only two levels).
2. For **Drug**, click the red triangle, select **LSMeans Plot;** click the red triangle, select **LSMeans Tukey HSD.**
3. For **Gender*Drug**, click the red triangle, select **LSMeans Plot,** in the dialog box, click **Create an Interaction Plot,** click **gender;** click **OK,** click the **Least Square Means Plot** red triangle, click off **Show Confidence Limits;** click the red triangle, select **LSMeans Tukey HSD.**

The results for **Gender and Drug** displayed in Figures 5.25 and Figure 5.26 are equivalent to what you observed earlier in the chapter when one-way ANOVA was discussed. Figure 5.27 also has the LSMeans Plot and the Connecting Letter Report for the interaction effect **Gender*Drug**. If there were no significant interaction, the lines in the LSMeans Plot would not cross and would be mostly parallel.

There does appear to be some interaction. The Connecting Letter Report identifies further the significant interactions. Overall, and clearly in the LS Means Plot, it appears that **Females** have lower **Pain** than **Males**. However, for **Drug A, Females** have higher than expected **Pain**.

Evaluate the Model for Equal Variances

To check for equal variances in two-way ANOVA, you need to create a new column that is the interaction **Gender*Drug**, and then run a one-way ANOVA on that variable. To create a new column when both variables are in character format, complete the following steps:

1. Select **Cols ▶ New Columns**. The new column dialog box will appear.
2. In the text box for Column name where Column 4 appears, type **Gender*Drug**.
3. Click the drop-down menu for Column Properties and click **Formula**. The Formula dialog box will appear.
4. Click the arrow next to **Character** and click **Concat**. The Concat statement will appear in the formula area with two rectangles. JMP has placed the cursor on the left rectangle (blue rectangle).

Figure 5.25: Two-Way ANOVA Output (Top Half)

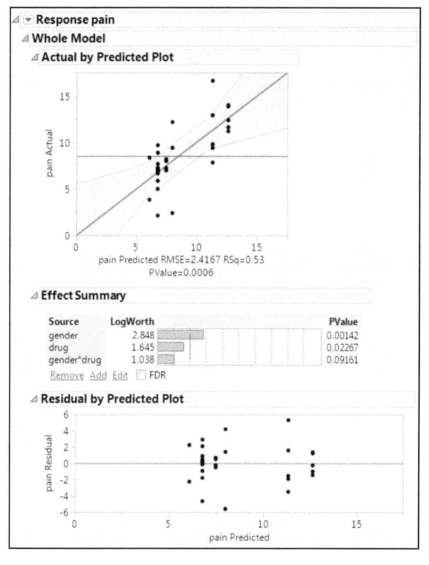

5. Click **Gender** from the Columns; click the right **Concat** rectangle, and click **Drug** from the Columns. The dialog box should look like Figure 5.29.

6. Click **OK** and then Click **OK** again.

The results of running a one-way ANOVA of **Gender*Drug** and **Pain** are shown in Figure 5.30. The *F* test rejects the null hypothesis. So, as you have seen before, there is significant interaction.

Figure 5.26: Two-Way ANOVA Output (Bottom Half)

△ Summary of Fit

RSquare	0.534258
RSquare Adj	0.448009
Root Mean Square Error	2.41667
Mean of Response	8.533515
Observations (or Sum Wgts)	33

△ Analysis of Variance

Source	DF	Sum of Squares	Mean Square	F Ratio
Model	5	180.88537	36.1771	6.1944
Error	27	157.68799	5.8403	Prob > F
C. Total	32	338.57335		0.0006*

△ Parameter Estimates

Term	Estimate	Std Error	t Ratio	Prob>|t|
Intercept	8.7207484	0.494984	17.62	<.0001*
gender[female]	-1.759652	0.494984	-3.55	0.0014*
drug[A]	-1.585892	0.616267	-2.57	0.0159*
drug[B]	-0.009982	0.765306	-0.01	0.9897
gender[female]*drug[A]	1.409308	0.616267	2.29	0.0303*
gender[female]*drug[B]	-0.856115	0.765306	-1.12	0.2731

△ Effect Tests

Source	Nparm	DF	Sum of Squares	F Ratio	Prob > F
gender	1	1	73.808295	12.6378	0.0014*
drug	2	2	51.059196	4.3713	0.0227*
gender*drug	2	2	30.542763	2.6148	0.0916

Examining the Levene test for equal variances, you have a *p*-value of .0084, rejecting the null hypothesis of all variances being equal. However, the results show a warning that the sample size is relatively small. So, in this situation, you will disregard these results. Examining the Welch's Test, we reject H_o, so we can perform multiple comparisons. In Figure 5.31 are the Tukey-Kramer HSD multiple comparison results, showing some significant differences.

Figure 5.27: Two-Way ANOVA Output for Gender*Drug

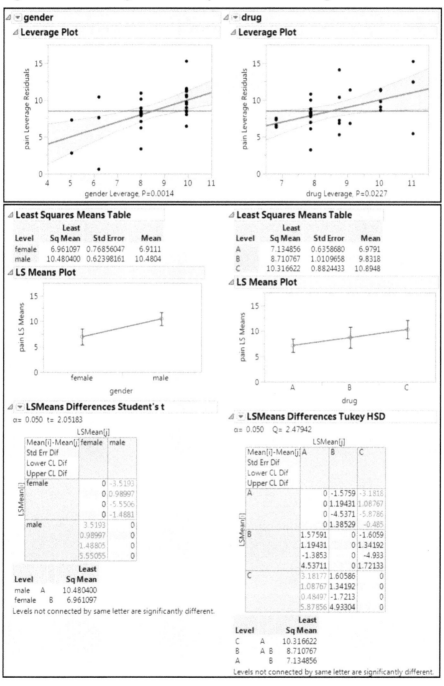

Figure 5.28: Two-Way ANOVA Output for Gender*Drug

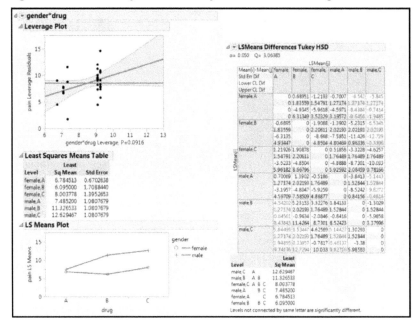

Figure 5.29: Formula Dialog Box

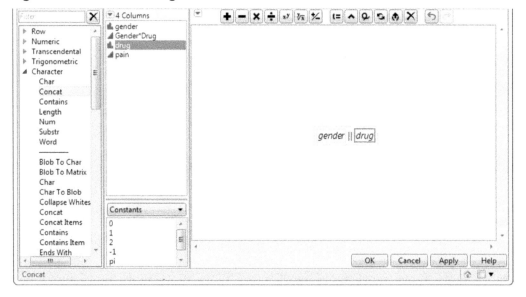

Figure 5.30: One-Way ANOVA with Pain and Interaction Gender*Drug

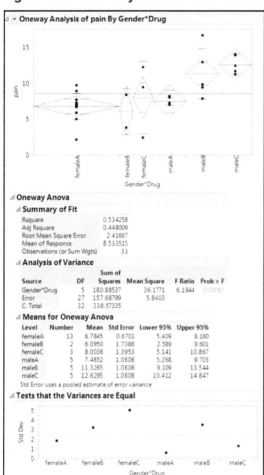

Oneway Analysis of pain By Gender*Drug

Oneway Anova

Summary of Fit

Rsquare	0.534258
Adj Rsquare	0.448009
Root Mean Square Error	2.41667
Mean of Response	8.533515
Observations (or Sum Wgts)	33

Analysis of Variance

Source	DF	Sum of Squares	Mean Square	F Ratio	Prob > F
Gender*Drug	5	180.88537	36.1771	6.1944	0.0006*
Error	27	157.68799	5.8403		
C. Total	32	338.57335			

Means for Oneway Anova

Level	Number	Mean	Std Error	Lower 95%	Upper 95%
femaleA	13	6.7845	0.6703	5.409	8.160
femaleB	2	6.0950	1.7088	2.589	9.601
femaleC	3	8.0038	1.3953	5.141	10.867
maleA	5	7.4852	1.0808	5.268	9.703
maleB	5	11.3265	1.0808	9.109	13.544
maleC	5	12.6295	1.0808	10.412	14.847

Std Error uses a pooled estimate of error variance

Tests that the Variances are Equal

Level	Count	Std Dev	MeanAbsDif to Mean	MeanAbsDif to Median
femaleA	13	1.824411	1.149239	1.106205
femaleB	2	3.191880	2.257000	2.257000
femaleC	3	5.044267	3.732741	3.262889
maleA	5	0.565866	0.484907	0.436533
maleB	5	3.495135	2.765173	2.461600
maleC	5	1.277130	1.054293	1.008133

Test	F Ratio	DFNum	DFDen	Prob > F
O'Brien[.5]	2.8604	4	26	0.0434*
Brown-Forsythe	1.5777	5	27	0.2000
Levene	3.9209	5	27	0.0084*
Bartlett	2.9507	5	.	0.0115*

Warning: Small sample sizes. Use Caution.

Welch's Test

Welch Anova testing Means Equal, allowing Std Devs Not Equal

F Ratio	DFNum	DFDen	Prob > F
11.0754	5	5.8537	0.0059*

Figure 5.31: Multiple Comparison of Gender*Drug

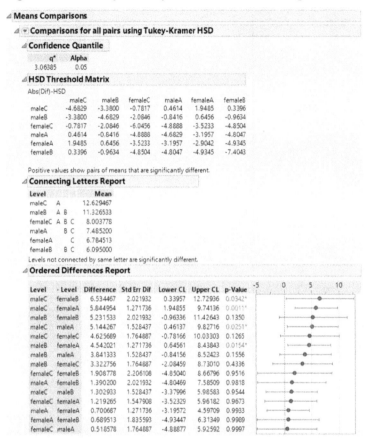

⊿ **Means Comparisons**

⊿ ▾ **Comparisons for all pairs using Tukey-Kramer HSD**

⊿ **Confidence Quantile**

q*	Alpha
3.06385	0.05

⊿ **HSD Threshold Matrix**

Abs(Dif)-HSD

	maleC	maleB	femaleC	maleA	femaleA	femaleB
maleC	-4.6829	-3.3800	-0.7817	0.4614	1.9485	0.3396
maleB	-3.3800	-4.6829	-2.0846	-0.8416	0.6456	-0.9634
femaleC	-0.7817	-2.0846	-6.0456	-4.8888	-3.5233	-4.8504
maleA	0.4614	-0.8416	-4.8888	-4.6829	-3.1957	-4.8047
femaleA	1.9485	0.6456	-3.5233	-3.1957	-2.9042	-4.9345
femaleB	0.3396	-0.9634	-4.8504	-4.8047	-4.9345	-7.4043

Positive values show pairs of means that are significantly different.

⊿ **Connecting Letters Report**

Level		Mean
maleC	A	12.629467
maleB	A B	11.326533
femaleC	A B C	8.003778
maleA	B C	7.485200
femaleA	C	6.784513
femaleB	B C	6.095000

Levels not connected by same letter are significantly different.

⊿ **Ordered Differences Report**

Level	- Level	Difference	Std Err Dif	Lower CL	Upper CL	p-Value
maleC	femaleB	6.534467	2.021932	0.33957	12.72936	0.0342*
maleC	femaleA	5.844954	1.271736	1.94855	9.74136	0.0011*
maleB	femaleB	5.231533	2.021932	-0.96336	11.42643	0.1350
maleC	maleA	5.144267	1.528437	0.46137	9.82716	0.0251*
maleC	femaleC	4.625689	1.764887	-0.78166	10.03303	0.1265
maleB	femaleA	4.542021	1.271736	0.64561	8.43843	0.0154*
maleB	maleA	3.841333	1.528437	-0.84156	8.52423	0.1556
maleB	femaleC	3.322756	1.764887	-2.08459	8.73010	0.4336
femaleC	femaleB	1.908778	2.206108	-4.85040	8.66796	0.9516
maleA	femaleB	1.390200	2.021932	-4.80469	7.58509	0.9818
maleC	maleB	1.302933	1.528437	-3.37996	5.98583	0.9544
femaleC	femaleA	1.219265	1.547908	-3.52329	5.96182	0.9673
maleA	femaleA	0.700687	1.271736	-3.19572	4.59709	0.9933
femaleA	femaleB	0.689513	1.835593	-4.93447	6.31349	0.9989
femaleC	maleA	0.518578	1.764887	-4.88877	5.92592	0.9997

Exercises

1. Using the Countif.xls file, develop a regression model to predict Salary by using all the remaining variables. Use α = 0.05. Evaluate this model—perform all the tests. Run a stepwise model and evaluate it.

2. Using the hmeq.jmp file, develop the best model you can to predict loan amount. Evaluate each model and use α = 0.05.

3. Using the Promotion_new.jmp file, develop each model, evaluate it, and use α = 0.05:

   a. Develop a model to predict Combine score, using the variable Position.
   b. Create an indicator variable for the variable Position, and use the new indicator variable Captain in a regression model to predict Combine.

   c. Create a new variable called Position_2 that assigns 1 to Captain or –1 otherwise (leave blank as *missing*). Now run a regression model using this new variable, Position_2, to predict Combine.

   d. What are the differences and similarities among parts a, b, and c?

   e. Develop a model using Race and Position to predict Combine.

4. Using the Countif.xls file, address the following:

   a. Is there significant interaction between Major and Gender and the average salary?

   b. Create a new variable, GPA_greater_3, which is equal to High if GPA ≥ 3; otherwise, it is equal to Low. See how this new variable, GPA_greater_3, has different salary means.

   c. Continuing with part b, test to see whether there is significant interaction between GPA_greater_3 and Major and in average Salary.

5. Using the Promotion_new.jmp file, test to see whether there is significant interaction with Race and Position and the average Combine score.

6. Using the Titanic_Passengers_new.jmp file, test to see whether there is significant interaction between whether a passenger survived and passenger class and the passengers' average age.

7. Using the MassHousing.jmp file, let the variable crim be the dependent variable:

   a. Run descriptive statistics on all the variables and comment on the results.

   b. Run a multiple regression with crim as the dependent variable and all the other variables. Evaluate the model.

   c. Run stepwise regression and evaluate the model.

   d. Try to improve the model. Evaluate your new model.

   e. Compare your models from parts b, c, and d. Which one would you consider the best? Explain why.

8. Using the MassHousing.jmp file, test to see whether there are significant differences between

   a. crim and the variable chas;

   b. crim and the variable mvalue.

9. Use the datasets_finance.xlsx file, answer the following:

Do various financial indicators differ significantly according to type of company? Use ANOVA in JMP with the financial database to answer this question.

The financial database contains observations on eight variables for 100 companies. The variables are Type of Industry, Total Revenues ($ millions), Total Assets ($ millions), Return on Equity (%), Earnings per Share ($), Average Yield (%), Dividends per Share ($), and Average Price per Earnings (P/E) ratio. The data were gathered from *Moody's Handbook of Common Stocks*. The companies represent seven different types of industries. The variable "Type" displays a company's industry type as follows:

1 = apparel

2 = chemical

3 = electric power

4 = grocery

5 = health care products

6 = insurance

7 = petroleum

10. Use the datasets_hospital_only.xls file and answer the following:

Do Admissions and/or Births vary by the seven different geographic regions. Control is a variable with four levels of classification denoting the type of control the hospital is under (such as federal government or for-profit). Use this variable as the independent variable and test to determine whether there is a significant difference in the Admissions of a hospital by Control. Perform the same test using Births as the dependent variable.
Overall, you need to run these ANOVAs:

- Admissions/Region
- Admissions/Control
- Admissions/Region*Control
- Births/Region
- Births/Control
- Births/Region*Control

Chapter 6: Logistic Regression

Introduction

Linear regression is designed for a continuous dependent variable such as interest rate, budget, and so on. Very often the dependent variable is not continuous, but discrete. There are many important situations in which the dependent variable is binary–that is, it can take on only two possible values. For example, will the loan applicant default? Will the cellphone customer switch to another carrier? Will a consumer buy a particular product? All these situations have a binary dependent variable, and as will be seen in this chapter, linear regression cannot be used for a binary dependent variable. Consequently, statisticians have developed a specialized form of regression call *logistic regression* to handle these situations. This chapter shows you how to use logistic regression to run a regression when the dependent variable is binary.

Dependence Technique

Logistic regression, as shown in the multivariate analysis framework in Figure 6.1, is one of the dependence techniques in which the dependent variable is discrete and, more specifically, binary. That is, it takes on only two possible values. The following are some examples:

- Will a credit card applicant pay off a bill or not?
- Will a mortgage applicant default?
- Will someone who receives a direct mail solicitation respond to the solicitation?

In each of these cases, the answer is either "yes" or "no." Such a categorical variable cannot directly be used as a dependent variable in a regression. But a simple transformation solves the problem: Let the dependent variable Y take on the value 1 for "yes" and 0 for "no."

Because Y takes on only the values 0 and 1, you know $E[Y_i] = 1 * P[Y_i = 1] + 0 * P[Y_i = 0] = P[Y_i = 1]$. But from the theory of regression, you also know that $E[Y_i] = a + b * X_i$. (Simple regression is used here, but the same holds true for multiple regression.) Combining these two results, you have $P[Y_i = 1] = a + b * X_i$. You can see that, in the case of a binary dependent variable, the regression might be interpreted as a probability. You then seek to use this regression to estimate the probability that Y takes on the value 1. If the estimated probability is high enough (for example, above .5), then you predict 1. Conversely, if the estimated probability of a 1 is low enough (for example, below .5), then you predict 0.

Figure 6.1: A Framework for Multivariate Analysis

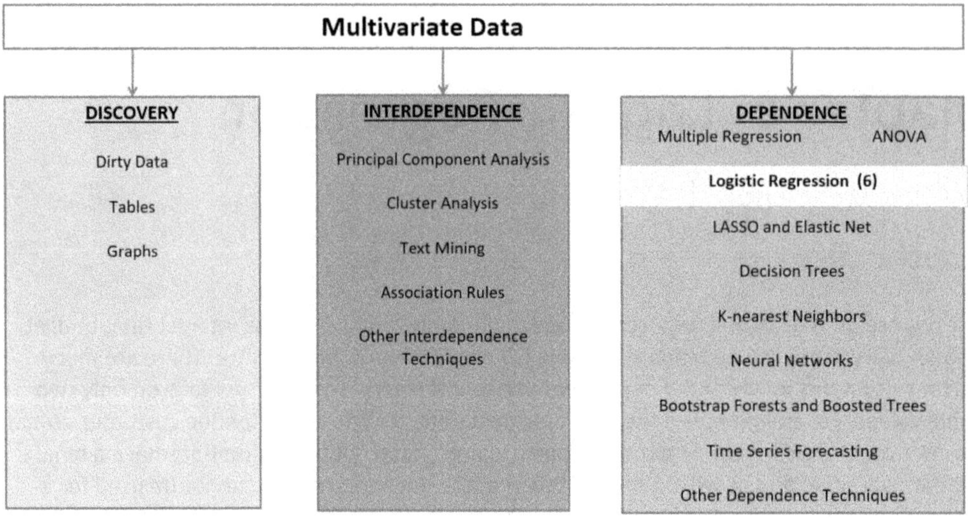

Multivariate Data		
DISCOVERY	**INTERDEPENDENCE**	**DEPENDENCE**
Dirty Data	Principal Component Analysis	Multiple Regression ANOVA
Tables	Cluster Analysis	Logistic Regression (6)
Graphs	Text Mining	LASSO and Elastic Net
	Association Rules	Decision Trees
	Other Interdependence Techniques	K-nearest Neighbors
		Neural Networks
		Bootstrap Forests and Boosted Trees
		Time Series Forecasting
		Other Dependence Techniques

The Linear Probability Model

When linear regression is applied to a binary dependent variable, it is commonly called the *linear probability model* (LPM). Traditional linear regression is designed for a continuous dependent variable and is not well-suited to handling a binary dependent variable. Three primary difficulties arise in the LPM. First, the predictions from a linear regression do not necessarily fall between zero and one. What are you to make of a predicted probability greater than one? How do you interpret a negative probability? A model that is capable of producing such nonsensical results does not inspire confidence.

Second, for any given predicted value of y (denoted $\hat{y}$), the residual (resid = $y - \hat{y}$) can take only two values. For example, if $\hat{y} = 0.37$, then the only possible values for the residual are resid = -0.37 or resid = 0.63 (= 1 -0.37), because it has to be the case that $\hat{y}$ + resid equals zero or 1. Clearly, the residuals will not be normal. Plotting a graph of $\hat{y}$ versus resid will not produce a nice scatter of points, but two parallel lines. You should verify this assertion by running such a regression and making the requisite scatterplot. A further implication of the fact that the residual can take on only two values for any $\hat{y}$ is that the residuals are heteroscedastic. This violates the linear regression assumption of homoscedasticity (constant variance). The estimates of the standard errors of the regression coefficients will not be stable, and inference will be unreliable.

Third, the linearity assumption is likely to be invalid, especially at the extremes of the independent variable. Suppose that you are modeling the probability that a consumer will pay back a $10,000 loan as a function of his or her income. The dependent variable is binary: 1 = the consumer pays back the loan, and 0 = the consumer does not pay back the loan. The independent variable is income, measured in dollars. A consumer whose income is $50,000 might have a probability of 0.5 of paying back the loan. If the consumer's income is increased by $5,000, then the probability of paying back the loan might increase to 0.55, so that every $1,000 increase in income increases the probability of paying back the loan by 1%. A person with an income of $150,000 (who can pay the loan back very easily) might have a probability of 0.99 of paying back the loan. What happens to this probability when the consumer's income is increased by $5,000? Probability cannot increase by 5%, because then it would exceed 100%. Yet, according to the linearity assumption of linear regression, it must do so.

The Logistic Function

A better way to model $P[Y_i =]$ would be to use a function that is not linear, one that increases slowly when $P[Y_i = 1]$ is close to zero or one and that increases more rapidly in between. It would have an "S" shape. One such function is the logistic function whose cumulative distribution function is shown in Figure 6.2:

$$G(z) = \frac{1}{1+e^{-z}} = \frac{e^z}{1+e^z}$$

Figure 6.2: The Logistic Function

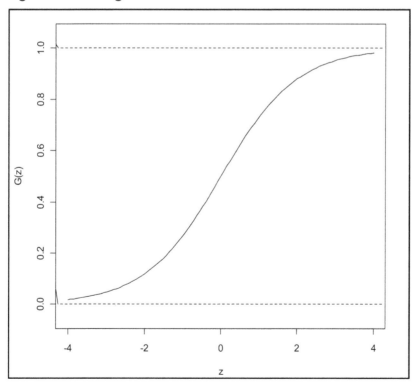

Another useful representation of the logistic function is the following:

$$1 - G(z) = \frac{e^{-z}}{1 + e^{-z}}$$

Recognize that the Y axis, G(z), is a probability, and let G(z) = π, the probability of the event's occurring. You can form the odds ratio (the probability of the event occurring divided by the probability of the event not occurring) and do some simplifying:

$$\frac{\pi}{1 - \pi} = \frac{G(z)}{1 - G(z)} = \frac{\dfrac{1}{1 + e^{-z}}}{\dfrac{e^{-z}}{1 + e^{-z}}} = \frac{1}{e^{-z}} = e^{z}$$

Consider taking the natural logarithm of both sides. The left side will become log[π/(1 − π)]. The log of the odds ratio is called the *logit*. The right side will become z (since log (e^z) = z), so that you have the following relation, which is called the *logit transformation*:

$$\log\left[\frac{\pi}{1 - \pi}\right] = z$$

If you model the logit as a linear function of X (that is, let z = β₀ = β₁X), then you have the following:

$$\log\left[\frac{\pi}{1 - \pi}\right] = \beta_0 + \beta_1 X$$

You could estimate this model by linear regression and obtain estimates b_0 of β_0 and b_1 of β_1 if only you knew the log of the odds ratio for each observation. Since you do not know the log of the odds ratio for each observation, you will use a form of nonlinear regression called *logistic regression* to estimate the following model:

$$E[Y_i] = \pi_i = G\left(\beta_0 + \beta_1 X_i\right) = \frac{1}{1 + e^{-\beta_0 - \beta_1 X_i}}$$

In so doing, you obtain the desired estimates b_0 of β_0 and b_1 of β_1. The estimated probability for an observation X_i will be as follows:

$$P[Y_i = 1] = \hat{\pi}_i = \frac{1}{1 + e^{-b_0 - b_1 X_i}}$$

And the corresponding estimated logit will be the following:

$$\log\left[\frac{\hat{\pi}}{1-\hat{\pi}}\right] = b_0 + b_1 X$$

This leads to a natural interpretation of the estimated coefficient in a logistic regression: b_1 is the estimated change in the logit (log odds) for a one-unit change in X.

A Straightforward Example Using JMP

To make these ideas concrete, suppose you open a small data set toylogistic.jmp that contains students' midterm exam scores (**MidtermScore**) and whether the student passed the class (**PassClass** = 1 if pass, **PassClass** = 0 if fail). A passing grade for the midterm is 70.

Create a Dummy Variable

The first thing to do is create a dummy variable to indicate whether the student passed the midterm: **PassMidterm** = 1 if **MidtermScore** ≥ 70; and **PassMidterm** = 0 otherwise.

1. Select **Cols** ▶ **New Columns** to open the New Column dialog box.
2. In the Column Name text box, for your new dummy variable, type **PassMidterm**.
3. Click the drop-down menu for modeling type and change it to **Nominal**.
4. Click the drop-down menu for Column Properties and select **Formula**. The Formula dialog box appears.
5. Under Functions, click **Conditional** ▶ **If**.
6. Under Table Columns, double click **MidtermScore** so that it appears in the top box to the right of the **If**.
7. Under Functions, click **Comparison** ▶ "a>=b". In the formula box to the right of >=, enter 70. Press the **Enter** key.
8. Click in the box to the right of the arrow, the then clause, enter the number **1**. Similarly, enter **0** for the else clause. The Formula dialog box should look like Figure 6.3. Click **OK**, and then click **OK** again.

Use a Contingency Table to Determine the Odds Ratio

First, you will use a traditional contingency table analysis to determine the odds ratio. Make sure that both **PassClass** and **PassMidterm** are classified as nominal variables:

1. Right-click in the data grid of the column **PassClass** and select **Column Info**.
2. Click the black triangle next to Modeling Type and select **Nominal** ▶ **OK**. Do the same for **PassMidterm**. (Another approach to changing type of variable is to position your pointer over the blue triangle or blue/green bar chart symbol to the left of the variable

Figure 6.3: Formula Dialog Box

listed in the Columns section on the Data Table; right-click and change to whatever type of variable you desire.)

3. Select **Analyze ▶ Tabulate** to open the Tabulate dialog box. It shows the general layout for a table.
4. Drag **PassClass** to the Drop zone for columns. Now that data have been added, the words **Drop zone for rows** will no longer be visible. But the **Drop zone for rows** will still be in the lower left panel of the table. See Figure 6.4.
5. Drag **PassMidterm** to the panel immediately to the left of the 8 in the table, as shown in Figure 6.4. Click **Done**. A contingency table identical to Figure 6.5 will appear.

The probability of passing the class when you did not pass the midterm is as follows:

$$P(\text{PassClass} = 1) \mid P(\text{PassMidterm} = 0) = 2/7$$

The probability of not passing the class when you did not pass the midterm is as follows (similar to row percentages):

$$P(\text{PassClass} = 0) \mid P(\text{PassMidterm} = 0) = 5/7$$

The odds of passing the class when you have failed the midterm are as follows:

$$\frac{P(\text{PassClass} = 1) \mid P(\text{PassMidterm} = 0)}{P(\text{PassClass} = 0) \mid P((\text{PassMidterm} = 0)} = \frac{2/7}{5/7} = \frac{2}{5}$$

Figure 6.4: Control Panel for Tabulate

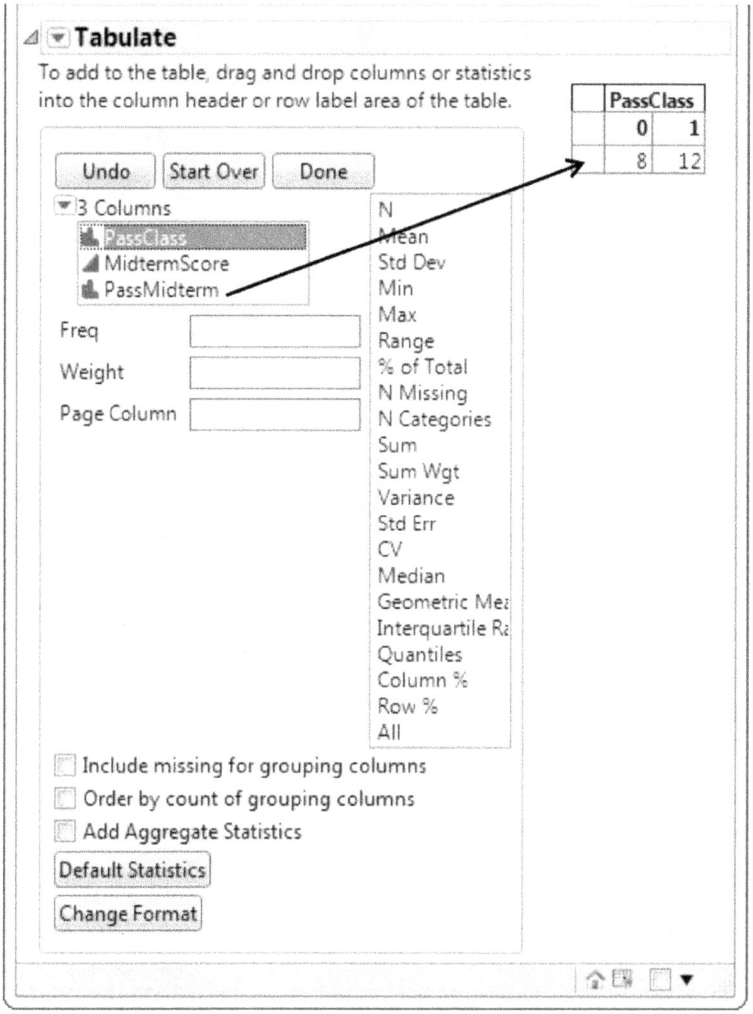

Similarly, you calculate the odds of passing the class when you have passed the midterm as follows:

$$\frac{P(\text{PassClass}=1)\,|\,P(\text{PassMidterm}=1)}{P(\text{PassClass}=0)\,|\,P(\text{PassMidterm}=1)} = \frac{10/13}{3/13} = \frac{10}{3}$$

Of the students that did pass the midterm, the odds are the number of students that pass the class divided by the number of students that did not pass the class.

Figure 6.5: Contingency Table from toylogistic.jmp

	PassClass	
PassMidterm	0	1
0	5	2
1	3	10

Calculate the Odds Ratio

So far, you have considered only odds. Now calculate an odds ratio. It is important to note that this can be done in two equivalent ways.

Method 1: Compute the Probabilities

Suppose you want to know the odds ratio of passing the class by comparing those who pass the midterm (**PassMidterm** = 1 in the numerator) to those who fail the midterm (**PassMidterm** = 0 in the denominator). The usual calculation leads to the following:

$$\frac{\text{Odds of passing the class; given passed the Midterm}}{\text{Odds of passing the class; given failed the Midterm}} = \frac{10/3}{2/5} = \frac{50}{6} = 8.33$$

This equation has the following interpretation: if you pass the midterm, the odds of passing the class are 8.33 times the odds of failing the course. This odds ratio can be converted into a probability. You know that P(Y=1)/P(Y=0)=8.33. And by definition, P(Y=1)+P(Y=0)=1. So solving two equations in two unknowns yields P(Y=0) = (1/(1+8.33)) = (1/9.33)= 0.1072 and P(Y=1) = 0.8928. As a quick check, observe that 0.8928/0.1072=8.33. Note that the log-odds are ln(8.33) = 2.120. Of course, the user doesn't have to perform all these calculations by hand; JMP will do them automatically. When a logistic regression has been run, simply clicking the red triangle and selecting **Odds Ratios** will do the trick.

Method 2: Run a Logistic Regression

Equivalently, you could compare those who fail the midterm (**PassMidterm**=0 in the numerator) to those who pass the midterm (**PassMidterm** = 1 in the denominator) and calculate as follows:

$$\frac{\text{Odds of passing the class; given failed the Midterm}}{\text{Odds of passing the class; given passed the Midterm}} = \frac{2/5}{10/3} = \frac{6}{50} = \frac{1}{8.33} = 0.12$$

This calculation tells us that the odds of failing the class are 0.12 times the odds of passing the class for a student who passes the midterm. Since $P(Y = 0) = 1 - \pi$ (the probability of failing the midterm) is in the numerator of this odds ratio (OR), you must interpret it in terms of the event failing the midterm. It is easier to interpret the odds ratio when it is less than 1 by using the following transformation: (OR − 1) * 100%. Compared to a person who passes the midterm, a person who fails the midterm is 12% as likely to pass the class. Or equivalently, a person who fails the midterm is 88% less likely, (OR − 1) * 100% = (0.12 − 1) * 100% = −88%, to pass the class than someone who passed the midterm. Note that the log-odds are $ln(0.12) = -2.12$.

The relationships between probabilities, odds (ratios), and log-odds (ratios) are straightforward. An event with a small probability has small odds, and also has small log-odds. An event with a large probability has large odds and also large log-odds. Probabilities are always between zero and unity. Odds are bounded below by zero but can be arbitrarily large. Log-odds can be positive or negative and are not bounded, as shown in Figure 6.6. In particular, if the odds ratio is 1 (so the probability of either event is 0.50), then the log-odds equal zero. Suppose $\pi = 0.55$, so the odds ratio is 0.55/0.45 = 1.222. Then you say that the event in the numerator is (1.222 − 1) = 22.2% more likely to occur than the event in the denominator.

Different software applications adopt different conventions for handling the expression of odds ratios in logistic regression. By default, JMP uses the "log odds of 1/0" convention, which puts the 1 in the numerator and the 0 in the denominator. This is a consequence of the sort order of the columns, which will be addressed shortly.

To see the practical importance of this, rather than compute a table and perform the above calculations, you can simply run a logistic regression. It is important to make sure that **PassClass** is nominal and that **PassMidterm** is continuous. If **PassMidterm** is nominal, JMP will fit a different but mathematically equivalent model that will give different (but mathematically equivalent) results. The scope of the reason for this is beyond this book, but in JMP, interested readers can consult **Help ▶ Books ▶ Modeling and Multivariate Methods** and see Appendix A.

If you have been following along with this book, both variables ought to be classified as *nominal*, so **PassMidterm** needs to be changed to *continuous*:

Figure 6.6: Ranges of Probabilities, Odds, and Log-odds

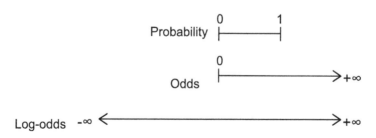

1. Right-click in the column **PassMidterm** in the Data Table and select **Column Info**.
2. Click the black triangle next to **Modeling Type** and select **Continuous**.
3. Click **OK**.

Now that the dependent and independent variables are correctly classified as Nominal and Continuous, respectively, run the logistic regression:

1. From the top menu, select **Analyze ▶ Fit Model**.
2. Select **PassClass ▶ Y**.
3. Select **PassMidterm ▶ Add**. The Fit Model dialog box should now look like Figure 6.7.
4. Notice the **Target Level** value is initially equal to 1. The **Target Level** specifies the level whose probability you want to model. So, in this case, click the drop arrow and change the **Target Level** to **0**.
5. Click **Run**.

Figure 6.8 displays the logistic regression results.

Examine the Parameter Estimates

Examine the parameter estimates in Figure 6.8. The intercept is 0.91629073, and the slope is −2.1202635. The slope gives the expected change in the logit for a one-unit change in the independent variable (the expected change on the log of the odds ratio). However, if you simply exponentiate the slope (compute), $e^{-2.1202635} = 0.12$, then you get the 0/1 odds ratio.

Figure 6.7: Fit Model Dialog Box

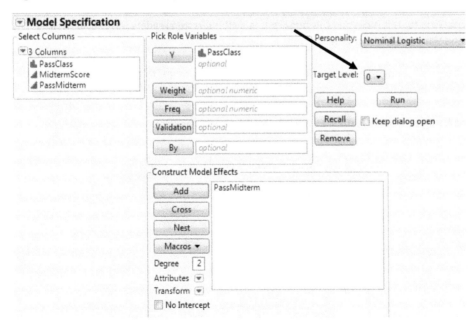

Figure 6.8: Logistic Regression Results for toylogistic.jmp

⊿ ▼ **Nominal Logistic Fit for PassClass**
▷ **Effect Summary**
⊿ **Logistic Plot**

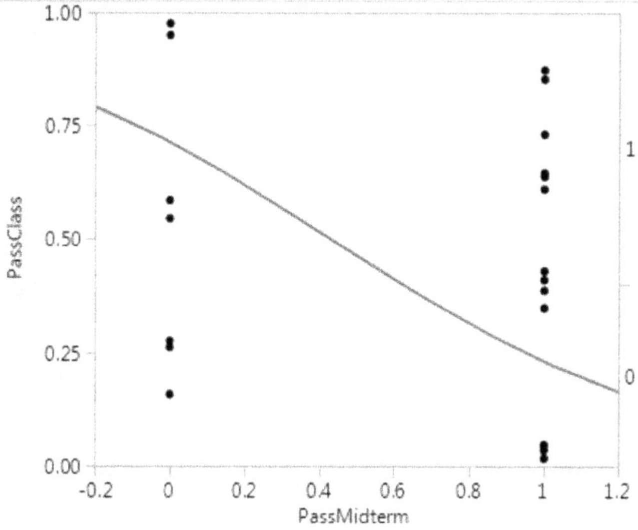

Converged in Gradient, 4 iterations

▷ **Iterations**

⊿ **Whole Model Test**

Model	-LogLikelihood	DF	ChiSquare	Prob>ChiSq
Difference	2.249692	1	4.499385	0.0339*
Full	11.210541			
Reduced	13.460233			

RSquare (U)	0.1671
AICc	27.127
BIC	28.4125
Observations (or Sum Wgts)	20

▷ **Fit Details**

⊿ **Parameter Estimates**

Term	Estimate	Std Error	ChiSquare	Prob>ChiSq
Intercept	0.91629073	0.83666	1.20	0.2734
PassMidterm	-2.1202635	1.0645813	3.97	0.0464*

For log odds of 0/1

▷ **Covariance of Estimates**

⊿ **Effect Likelihood Ratio Tests**

Source	Nparm	DF	L-R ChiSquare	Prob>ChiSq
PassMidterm	1	1	4.49938474	0.0339*

There is no need for you to exponentiate the coefficient manually. JMP will do this for you:

Click the red triangle and click **Odds Ratios**. The Odds Ratios tables are added to the JMP output as shown in Figure 6.9.

Unit Odds Ratios refers to the expected change in the odds ratio for a one-unit change in the independent variable. **Range Odds Ratios** refers to the expected change in the odds ratio when the independent variable changes from its minimum to its maximum. Since the present independent variable is a binary 0/1 variable, these two definitions are the same. You get not only the odds ratio, but also a confidence interval. Notice the right-skewed confidence interval; this is typical of confidence intervals for odds ratios.

Change the Default Convention

To change from the default convention (log odds of 1/0), which puts the 1 in the numerator and the 0 in the denominator, do as follows:

1. In the Data Table, select the **PassClass** column.
2. Right-click to select **Column Properties ▶ Value Order**.
3. In the new dialog box, click on the value **1,** and click ⬆ as in Figure 6.10.
4. Click **OK**.

Then, when you rerun the logistic regression, although the parameter estimates will be the same values but multiplied by -1, the odds ratios will change to reflect the fact that the 0 is now in the numerator and the 1 is in the denominator.

Figure 6.9: Odds Ratios Tables Using the Nominal Independent Variable PassMidterm

◢ **Odds Ratios**

For PassClass odds of 0 versus 1
Tests and confidence intervals on odds ratios are likelihood ratio based.

◢ **Unit Odds Ratios**

Per unit change in regressor

Term	Odds Ratio	Lower 95%	Upper 95%	Reciprocal
PassMidterm	0.12	0.011664	0.855944	8.3333333

◢ **Range Odds Ratios**

Per change in regressor over entire range

Term	Odds Ratio	Lower 95%	Upper 95%	Reciprocal
PassMidterm	0.12	0.011664	0.855944	8.3333333

Figure 6.10: Changing the Value Order

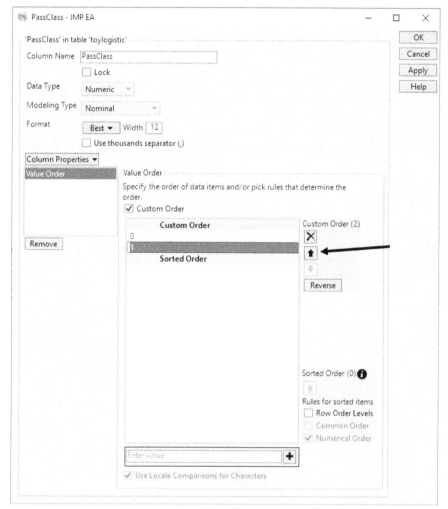

Examine with Continuous Independent Variable

The independent variable is not limited to being only a nominal (or ordinal) dependent variable; it can be continuous. In particular, examine the results, using the actual score on the midterm, with **MidtermScore** as an independent variable:

1. Select **Analyze ▶ Fit Model**.
2. Select **PassClass ▶ Y**.
3. Select **MidtermScore ▶ Add**.
4. Click **Run**.

Figure 6.11: Parameter Estimates

Parameter Estimates				
Term	Estimate	Std Error	ChiSquare	Prob>ChiSq
Intercept	25.6018754	11.184069	5.24	0.0221*
MidtermScore	-0.3637609	0.1581661	5.29	0.0215*
For log odds of 0/1				

This time the intercept is 25.6018754, and the slope is –0.3637609. You expect the log-odds to decrease by 0.3637609 for every additional point scored on the midterm, as shown in Figure 6.11.

To view the effect on the odds ratio itself, click the **Nominal Logistic Fit for PassClass** red triangle as before and click **Odds Ratios**. Figure 6.12 displays the Odds Ratios tables.

For a one-unit increase in the midterm score, the new odds ratio will be 69.51% of the old odds ratio. Or, equivalently, you expect to see a 30.5% reduction in the odds ratio (0.695057 – 1) * (100%=–30.5%). For example, suppose a hypothetical student has a midterm score of 75%. The student's log odds of failing the class would be as follows:

25.6018754 – 0.3637609 * 75 = –1.680192

The student's odds of failing the class would be exp(–1.680192) = 0.1863382. That is, the student is much more likely to pass than fail. Converting odds to probabilities (0.1863328/(1 + 0.1863328) = 0.157066212786159), you see that the student's probability of failing the class is 0.15707, and the probability of passing the class is 0.84293. Now, if the student's score increased by one point to 76, then the log odds of failing the class would be 25.6018754 – 0.3637609 * 76 = –2.043953. Thus, the student's odds of failing the class become exp(–2.043953) = 0.1295157. So,

Figure 6.12: Odds Ratios Tables Using the Continuous Independent Variable MidtermScore

Odds Ratios

For PassClass odds of 0 versus 1
Tests and confidence intervals on odds ratios are likelihood ratio based.

Unit Odds Ratios

Per unit change in regressor

Term	Odds Ratio	Lower 95%	Upper 95%	Reciprocal
MidtermScore	0.695057	0.451212	0.879069	1.4387302

Range Odds Ratios

Per change in regressor over entire range

Term	Odds Ratio	Lower 95%	Upper 95%	Reciprocal
MidtermScore	0.000335	2.491e-8	0.058681	2989.1384

the probability of passing the class would rise to 0.885334, and the probability of failing the class would fall to 0.114666. With respect to the Unit Odds Ratio, which equals 0.695057, you see that a one-unit increase in the test score changes the odds ratio from 0.1863382 to 0.1295157. In accordance with the estimated coefficient for the logistic regression, the new odds ratio is 69.5% of the old odds ratio because 0.1295157/0.1863382 = 0.695057.

Compute Probabilities for Each Observation

Finally, you can use the logistic regression to compute probabilities for each observation. As noted, the logistic regression will produce an estimated logit for each observation. These estimated logits can be used, in the obvious way, to compute probabilities for each observation. Consider a student whose midterm score is 70. The student's estimated logit is 25.6018754 − 0.3637609(70) = 0.1386124. Since exp(0.1386129) = 1.148679 = $\pi/(1 - \pi)$, you can solve for π (the probability of failing) = 0.534597.

You can obtain the estimated logits and probabilities by clicking the **Nominal Logistic Fit for PassClass** red triangle and selecting **Save Probability Formula**. Four columns will be added to the worksheet: **Lin[0]**, **Prob[0]**, **Prob[1]**, and **Most Likely PassClass**. For each observation, these four columns give the estimated logit, the probability of failing the class, and the probability of passing the class, respectively. Observe that the sixth student has a midterm score of 70. Look up this student's estimated probability of failing (**Prob[0]**); it is very close to what you just calculated above. See Figure 6.13. The difference is that the computer carries 16 digits through its calculations, but you carried only six.

The fourth column (**Most Likely PassClass**) classifies the observation as either 1 or 0, depending on whether the probability is greater than or less than 50%. You can observe how well your model classifies all the observations (using this cut-off point of 50%) by producing a confusion matrix. Click the **Nominal Logistic Fit for PassClass** red triangle and click **Confusion matrix**.

Figure 6.14 displays the confusion matrix for the example. The rows of the confusion matrix are the actual classification (that is, whether **PassClass** is 0 or 1). The columns are the predicted classification from the model (that is, the predicted 0/1 values from that last fourth column using your logistic model and a cutpoint of .50). Correct classifications are along the main diagonal from upper left to lower right. You see that the model has classified 6 students as not passing the class, and actually they did not pass the class. The model also classifies 10 students as passing the class when they actually did. The values on the other diagonal, both equal to 2, are misclassifications. The results of the confusion matrix will be examined in more detail when in the discussion on model comparison in Chapter 14.

Figure 6.13: Verifying Calculation of Probability of Failing

	PassClass	MidtermScore	PassMidterm	Lin[0]	Prob[0]	Prob[1]	Most Likely PassClass
1	0	62	0	3.048697664	0.9547262676	0.0452737324	0
2	0	63	0	2.6849367335	0.936131922	0.063868078	0
3	0	64	0	2.3211758029	0.9106156911	0.0893843089	0
4	0	65	0	1.9574148724	0.8762529099	0.1237470901	0
5	0	66	0	1.5936539419	0.8311295662	0.1688704338	0
6	0	70	1	0.1386102197	0.5345971803	0.4654028197	0
7	0	72	1	-0.588911641	0.3568846133	0.6431153867	1
8	0	74	1	-1.316433502	0.2114122777	0.7885877223	1
9	1	68	0	0.8661320808	0.7039402276	0.2960597724	0
10	1	69	0	0.5023711503	0.6230163983	0.3769836017	0
11	1	71	1	-0.225150711	0.4439489049	0.5560510951	1
12	1	73	1	-0.952672572	0.2783476639	0.7216523361	1
13	1	75	1	-1.680194433	0.1570697245	0.8429302755	1
14	1	78	1	-2.771477225	0.0588850958	0.9411149042	1
15	1	79	1	-3.135238155	0.0416768925	0.9583231075	1
16	1	80	1	-3.498999086	0.0293407232	0.9706592768	1
17	1	81	1	-3.862760016	0.0205775978	0.9794224022	1
18	1	82	1	-4.226520947	0.0143929258	0.9856070742	1
19	1	83	1	-4.590281877	0.0100480097	0.9899519903	1
20	1	84	1	-4.954042808	0.0070054079	0.9929945921	1

Check the Model's Assumptions

Of course, before you can use the model, you have to check the model's assumptions. The first step is to verify the linearity of the logit. This can be done by plotting the estimated logit against **PassClass**:

1. Select **Graph ▶ Scatterplot Matrix**.
2. Select **Lin[0] ▶ Y, columns**.
3. Select **MidtermScore ▶ X**.
4. Click **OK**. As shown in Figure 6.15, the linearity assumption appears to be perfectly satisfied.

Continuing to evaluate the model, with our second logistic model with **MidtermScore** as an independent variable, we can further evaluate the logistic output. The analog to the ANOVA *F* test for linear regression is found under the **Whole Model Test** (Figure 6.16), in which the Full and Reduced models are compared. The null hypothesis for this test is that all the slope parameters are equal to zero. Since **Prob>ChiSq** is 0.0004, this null hypothesis is soundly rejected. For a discussion of other statistics found here, such as BIC and Entropy R^2, see the JMP Help.

The next important part of model checking is the **Lack of Fit test**. Figure 6.17 compares the model actually fitted to the saturated model. The saturated model is a model generated by

Figure 6.14: Confusion Matrix

Confusion Matrix

Training

Actual	Predicted Count	
PassClass	0	1
0	6	2
1	2	10

Actual	Predicted Rate	
PassClass	0	1
0	0.750	0.250
1	0.167	0.833

Figure 6.15: Scatterplot of Lin[0] and MidtermScore

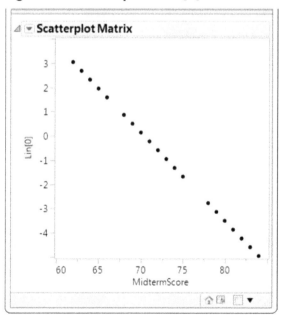

Figure 6.16: Whole Model Test for the Toylogistic Data Set

Whole Model Test				
Model	-LogLikelihood	DF	ChiSquare	Prob>ChiSq
Difference	6.264486	1	12.52897	0.0004*
Full	7.195748			
Reduced	13.460233			
RSquare (U)	0.4654			
AICc	19.0974			
BIC	20.383			
Observations (or Sum Wgts)	20			

JMP that contains as many parameters as there are observations. So, it fits the data very well. The null hypothesis for this test is that there is no difference between the estimated model and the saturated model. If this hypothesis is rejected, then more variables (such as cross-product or squared terms) need to be added to the model. In the present case, as can be seen, **Prob>ChiSq** = 0.7032. You can therefore conclude that you do not need to add more terms to the model.

A Realistic Logistic Regression Statistical Study

Turn now to a more realistic data set with several independent variables. This discussion will also briefly present some of the issues that should be addressed and some of the thought processes during a statistical study.

Cellphone companies are very interested in determining which customers might switch to another company. This switching is called *churning*. Predicting which customers might be about to churn enables the company to make special offers to these customers, possibly stemming their defection. Churn.jmp contains data on 3,333 cellphone customers, including the variable **Churn** (0 means that the customer stayed with the company and 1 means that the customer left the company).

Figure 6.17: Lack of Fit Test for Current Model

Lack Of Fit			
Source	DF	-LogLikelihood	ChiSquare
Lack Of Fit	18	7.1957477	14.3915
Saturated	19	0.0000000	Prob>ChiSq
Fitted	1	7.1957477	0.7032

Understand the Model-Building Approach

Before you can begin constructing a model for customer churn, you need to understand model building for logistic regression. Statistics and econometrics texts devote entire chapters to this concept. In several pages, only a sketch of the broad outline can be given.

The first thing to do is make sure that the data are loaded correctly. Observe that **Churn** is classified as Continuous; be sure to change it to Nominal. One way is to make that change is to right-click in the **Churn** column in the Data Table, select **Column Info**, and under Modeling Type, click **Nominal**. Another way is to look at the list of variables on the left side of the Data Table, find **Churn**, click the blue triangle (which denotes a continuous variable), and change it to **Nominal** (the blue triangle then becomes a red histogram).

Make sure that all binary variables are classified as Nominal. This includes **Intl_Plan**, **VMail_ Plan**, **E_VMAIL_PLAN**, and **D_VMAIL_PLAN**. Should **Area_Code** be classified as Continuous or Nominal? (Nominal is the correct answer!) **CustServ_Call**, the number of calls to customer service, could be treated as either continuous or nominal/ordinal; you treat it as continuous.

Suppose that you are building a linear regression model and you find that the number of variables is not so large that this cannot be done manually. One place to begin is by examining histograms and scatterplots of the continuous variables and crosstabs of the categorical variables as discussed in Chapters 2 and 4. Another very useful device as discussed in Chapter 4 is the scatterplot/correlation matrix, which can, at a glance, suggest potentially *useful* independent variables that are correlated with the dependent variable. The scatterplot/correlation matrix approach cannot be used with logistic regression, which is nonlinear, but a similar method similar can be applied.

You are now faced with a situation similar to that discussed in Chapter 4. Your goal is to build a model that follows the principle of parsimony—that is, a model that explains as much as possible of the variation in Y and uses as few significant independent variables as possible. However, now with multiple logistic regression, you are in a nonlinear situation. You have four approaches that you could take. These approaches and some of their advantages and disadvantages are as follows:

- **Inclusion of all the variables**. In this approach, you just enter all the independent variables into the model. An obvious advantage of this approach is that it is fast and easy. However, depending on the data set, most likely several independent variables will be insignificantly related to the dependent variable. This includes variables that are not significant can cause severe problems, which weakens the interpretation of the coefficients and lessens the prediction accuracy of the model. This approach definitely does not follow the principle of parsimony, and it can cause numerical problems for the nonlinear solver that can lead to a failure to obtain an answer.
- **Bivariate method**. In this approach, you search for independent variables that might have predictive value for the dependent variable by running a series of bivariate logistic

regressions. That is, you run a logistic regression for each of the independent variables, searching for "significant" relationships. A major advantage of this approach is that it is the one most agreed upon by statisticians (Hosmer and Lemeshow, 2001). On the other hand, this approach is not automated, is very tedious, and is limited by the analyst's ability to run the regressions. That is, it is not practical with very large data sets. Further, it misses interaction terms, which, as you shall see, can be very important.

- **Stepwise approach.** In this approach, you would use the Fit Model platform, change the Personality to **Stepwise** and Direction to **Mixed**. The Mixed option is like Forward Stepwise, but variables can be dropped after they have been added. An advantage of this approach is that it is automated; so, it is fast and easy. The disadvantage of the stepwise approach is that it can lead to possible interpretation errors and prediction errors, depending on the data set. However, using the Mixed option, as opposed to the Forward or Backward Direction option, tends to lessen the magnitude and likelihood of these problems.

- **Decision trees.** A *decision tree* is a data mining technique that can be used for variable selection and will be discussed in Chapter 10. The advantage of using the decision tree technique is that it is automated, fast, and easy to run. Further, it is a popular variable reduction approach taken by many data mining analysts (Pollack, 2008). However, somewhat like the stepwise approach, the decision tree approach can lead to some statistical issues. In this case, significant variables identified by a decision tree are very sample-dependent. These issues will be discussed further in Chapter 10.

No one approach is a clear winner. Nevertheless, it is recommended that you use the "Include all the variables" approach. If the data set is too large or you do not have the time, you should run both the stepwise and decision trees models and compare the results. The data set **Churn.jmp** is not too large, so you will apply the bivariate approach.

It is traditional to choose $\alpha = 0.05$. But in this preliminary stage, you adopt a more lax standard, $\alpha = 0.25$. The reason for this is that you want to include, if possible, a group of variables that are not individually significant but together are significant. Having identified an appropriate set of candidate variables, run a logistic regression that includes all of them. Compare the coefficient estimates from the multiple logistic regression with the estimates from the bivariate logistic regressions. Look for coefficients that have changed in sign or have dramatically changed in magnitude, as well as changes in significance. Such changes indicate the inadequacy of the simple bivariate models, and confirm the necessity of adding more variables to the model.

Three important ways to improve a model are as follows:

- If the logit appears to be nonlinear when plotted against some continuous variable, one resolution is to convert the continuous variable to a few dummy variables (for example, three) that cut the variable at its 25th, 50th, and 75th percentiles.
- If a histogram shows that a continuous variable has an excess of observations at zero (which can lead to nonlinearity in the logit), add a dummy variable that equals one if the continuous variable is zero and equals zero otherwise.

- Finally, a seemingly numeric variable that is actually discrete can be broken up into a handful of dummy variables (for example, ZIP codes).

Before you can begin modeling, you must first explore the data. With your churn data set, creating and examining the histograms of the continuous variables reveals nothing much of interest, except **VMail_Message**, which has an excess of zeros. (See the second point in the previous paragraph.) Figure 6.18 shows plots for **Intl_Calls** and **VMail_Message**. To produce such plots, follow these steps:

1. Select **Analyze ▶ Distribution**,
2. Click **Intl_Calls** and then **Y, Columns.**
3. Select **VMail_Message ▶ Y, Columns** and then click **OK**.
4. To add the Normal Quantile Plot, click the **Intl_Calls** red triangle and select **Normal Quantile Plot**.
5. Similarly, for **VMail_Message**, click the **VMail_Message** red triangle and select **Normal Quantile Plot**.

Here it is obvious that **Intl_Calls** is skewed right. Note that a logarithmic transformation of this variable might be needed in order to reduce the skewness, but you need not pursue the idea here.

A correlation matrix of the continuous variables (select **Graph ▶ Scatterplot Matrix** and put the desired variables in **Y, Columns**) turns up a curious pattern. **Day_Charge** and **Day_Mins**, **Eve_Charge** and **Eve_Mins**, **Night_Charge** and **Night_Mins**, and **Intl_Charge** and **Intl_Mins** all are perfectly correlated. The charge is obviously a linear function of the number of minutes. Therefore, you can drop the Charge variables from your analysis. (You could also drop the "Mins" variables instead; it doesn't matter which one you drop.) If your data set had a very large number of variables, the scatterplot matrix would be too big to comprehend. In such a situation, you would choose groups of variables for which to make scatterplot matrices, and examine those. (Another, yet similar, approach is to use **Analyze ▶ Multivariate Methods ▶ Multivariate**.)

Figure 6.18: Distribution of Intl_Calls and VMail_Message

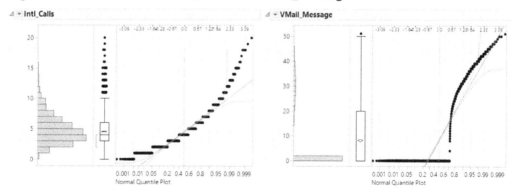

A scatterplot matrix for the four binary variables turns up an interesting association. **E_VMAIL_ PLAN** and **D_VMAIL_PLAN** are perfectly correlated. Both have common 1s, and where the former has -1, the latter has zero. It would be a mistake to include both of these variables in the same regression (try it and see what happens). Delete **E_VMAIL_PLAN** from the data set, and also delete **VMail_Plan** because it agrees perfectly with **E_VMAIL_PLAN**: When the former has a "no," the latter has a "−1," and similarly for "yes" and "+1."

Phone is more or less unique to each observation. (You ignore the possibility that two phone numbers are the same but have different area codes.) Therefore, it should not be included in the analysis. So, you will drop **Phone** from the analysis.

A scatterplot matrix between the remaining continuous and binary variables produces a curious pattern. **D_VMAIL_PLAN** and **VMailMessage** have a correlation of 0.96. They have zeros in common, and where the former has 1s, the latter has numbers. (See again point two in the above paragraph. You won't have to create a dummy variable to solve the problem because **D_VMAIL_PLAN** will do the job nicely.)

To summarize, you have dropped 7 of the original 23 variables from the data set (**Phone**, **Day_ Charge**, **Eve_Charge**, **Night_Charge**, **Intl_Charge**, **E_VMAIL_PLAN**, and **VMail_Plan**). So there are now 16 variables left, one of which is the dependent variable, Churn. You have 15 possible independent variables to consider.

Run Bivariate Analyses

Next comes the time-consuming task of running several bivariate (two variables, one dependent and one independent) analyses, some of which will be logistic regressions (when the independent variable is continuous) and some of which will be contingency tables (when the independent variable is categorical). In total, you have 15 bivariate analyses to run. What about Area Code? JMP reads it as a continuous variable, but it's really nominal. So be sure to change it from continuous to nominal. Similarly, make sure that **D_VMAIL_PLAN** is set as a nominal variable, not continuous.

Do *not* try to keep track of the results in your head, or by referring to the 15 bivariate analyses that would fill your computer screen. Make a list of all 15 variables that need to be tested, and write down the test result (for example, the relevant *p*-value) and your conclusion (for example, "include" or "exclude"). This not only prevents simple errors; it is a useful record of your work should you have to come back to it later. There are few things more pointless than conducting an analysis that concludes with a 13-variable logistic regression, only to have some reason to rerun the analysis and now wind up with a 12-variable logistic regression. Unless you have documented your work, you will have no idea why the discrepancy exists or which is the correct regression.

Below you will see how to conduct both types of bivariate analyses, one for a nominal independent variable and one for a continuous independent variable. The other 14 are left to the reader.

Make a contingency table of **Churn** versus **State**:

1. Select **Analyze ▶ Fit Y by X**.
2. Click **Churn** (which is nominal) and then click **Y, Response**.
3. Click **State** and then click **X, Factor**.
4. Click **OK**.

At the bottom of the table of results are the Likelihood Ratio and Pearson tests, both of which test the null hypothesis that **State** does not affect **Churn**, and both of which reject the null. The conclusion is that the variable **State** matters. On the other hand, perform a logistic regression of **Churn** on **VMail_Message**:

1. Select **Analyze ▶ Fit Y by X**.
2. Click **Churn**.
3. Click **Y, Response**.
4. Click **VMail_Message** and click **X, Factor**.
5. Click **OK**.

Under **Whole Model Test**, the Prob>ChiSq, which means that the *p*-value is less than 0.0001, so you conclude that **VMail_message** affects **Churn**. Remember that for all these tests, you are setting α (probability of Type I error) = 0.25.

In the end, you have 10 candidate variables for possible inclusion in your multiple logistic regression model:

- **State**
- **Intl_Plan**
- **D_VMAIL_PLAN**
- **VMail_Message**
- **Day_Mins**
- **Eve_Mins**
- **Night_Mins**
- **Intl_Mins**
- **Intl_Calls**
- **CustServ_Call**

Remember that the first three of these variables should be set to *nominal*, and the rest to *continuous*. (Of course, leave the dependent variable Churn as nominal!)

Run the Initial Regression and Examine the Results

Run your initial multiple logistic regression with **Churn** as the dependent variable and the above 10 variables as independent variables:

1. Select **Analyze ▶ Fit Model ▶ Churn ▶ Y**.
2. Select the above 10 variables. (To select variables that are not consecutive, click on each variable while holding down the **Ctrl** key.) Click **Add**.
3. Change the **Target Level** to **0**.
4. Check the box next to Keep dialog open.
5. Click **Run**.

The effect summary report, as shown in Figure 6.19, is similar to the effect summary report discussed in Chapter 5 in Figure 5.6, for multiple regression. Likewise, here the report identifies the significant effects of the independent variables in the model.

The **Whole Model Test** lets you know that your included variables have an effect on the Churn and a *p*-value less than .0001, as shown in Figure 6.19.

The lack of fit test tells you that you have done a good job explaining **Churn**. From the **Lack of Fit**, you see that −LogLikelihood for the Full model is 1037.4471. Linear regression minimizes the sum of squared residuals. So, when you compare two linear regressions, the preferred one has the smaller sum of squared residuals. In the same way, the nonlinear optimization of the logistic regression minimizes the −LogLikelihood (which is equivalent to maximizing the LogLikelihood). The model with the smaller −LogLikelihood is preferred to a model with a larger −LogLikelihood.

Examining the *p*-values of the independent variables in the **Parameter Estimates**, you find that a variable for which Prob>ChiSq is less than 0.05 is said to be significant. Otherwise, it is said to be insignificant, similar to what is practiced in linear regression. The regression output gives two sets of tests, one for the **Parameter Estimates** and another for **Effect Likelihood Ratio Tests**. The following focuses on the latter. To see why, consider the **State** variable, which is really not one variable but many dummy variables. You are not so much interested in whether any particular state is significant or not (which is what the **Parameter Estimates** tell you) but whether, overall, the collection of state dummy variables is significant. This is what the **Effect Likelihood Ratio Tests** tells you: The effect of all the state dummy variables is significant with a Prob>ChiSq of 0.0010. True, many of the **State** dummies are insignificant, but overall **State** is significant. You will keep this variable as it is. It might prove worthwhile to reduce the number of state dummy variables into a handful of significant states and small clusters of "other" states that are not significant, but you will not pursue this line of inquiry here.

You can see that all the variables in the model are significant. You might be able to derive some new variables that help improve the model. Below are two examples of deriving new variables: (1) converting a continuous variable into discrete variables and (2) producing interaction variables.

Convert a Continuous Variable to Discrete Variables

Try to break up a continuous variable into a handful of discrete variables. An obvious candidate is **CustServ_Call**. Look at its distribution in Figure 6.20:

Figure 6.19: Whole Model Test and Lack of Fit for the Churn Data Set

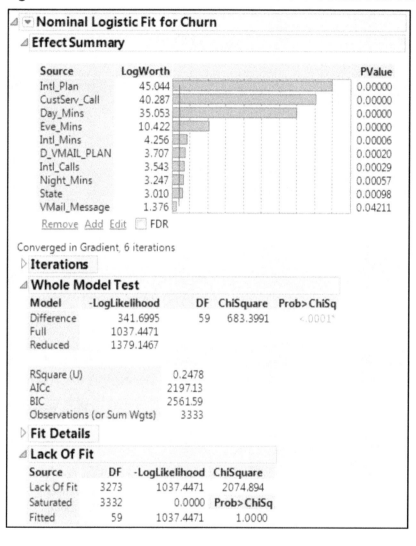

1. Select **Analyze ▶ Distribution**.
2. Select **CustServ_Call ▶ Y, Columns** and click **OK**.
3. Click the **CustServ_Call** red triangle and uncheck **Outlier Box Plot**.
4. Again, click the **CustServ_Call** red triangle and select **Histogram Options ▶ Show Counts**.

Create a new nominal variable called **CustServ** so that all the counts for 5 and greater are collapsed into a single cell:

Figure 6.20: Histogram of CustServ_Call

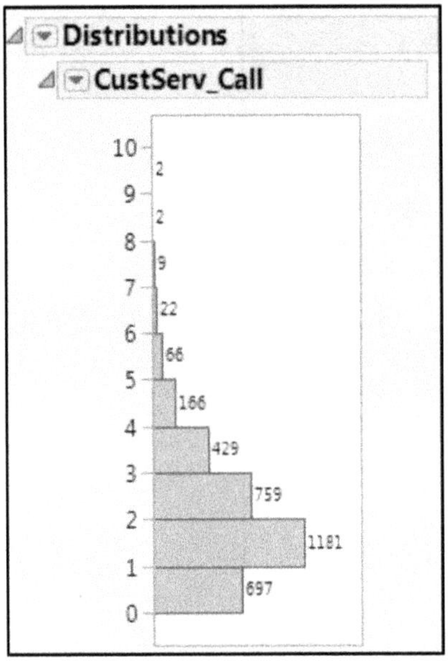

1. Select **Cols ▶ New Columns**.
2. For column name, enter **CustServ**. Change Modeling Type to **Nominal**. Then click the drop-down menu for **Column Properties**, and click **Formula**.
3. In the Formula dialog box, select **Conditional ▶ If**. Then, in the top left, click **CustServ_Call**, type **<=4, and click Enter.**
4. In the top then clause, click **CustServ_Call**. For the else clause, type **5** and click **Enter**. See Figure 6.21.
5. Click **OK,** and click **OK**.

Now drop the **CustServ_Call** variable from the Logistic Regression and add the new **CustServ** nominal variable, which is equivalent to adding some dummy variables. Your new value of – LogLikelihood is 970.6171, which constitutes a very substantial improvement in the model.

Producing Interaction Variables

Another possible important way to improve a model is to introduce interactions terms–that is, the product of two or more variables. Best practice would be to consult with subject-matter experts and seek their advice. Some thought is necessary to determine meaningful interactions, but it can pay off in substantially improved models.

Thinking about what might make a cell phone customer want to switch to another carrier, you have all heard a friend complain about being charged an outrageous amount for making an international call. Based on this observation, you might conjecture those customers who make

Figure 6.21: Creating the CustServ Variable

international calls and who are not on the international calling plan might be more irritated and more likely to churn. A quick bivariate analysis shows that there are more than a few such persons in the data set:

1. Select **Analyze ▶ Tabulate** and drag **Intl_Plan** to **Drop zone for columns**.
2. Drag **Intl_Calls** to **Drop zone for rows**.
3. Right-click **Int_Calls** in the table and choose **Use as Grouping column**.

Observe that almost all customers make international calls, but most of them are not on the international plan (which gives cheaper rates for international calls). For example, for the customers who made no international calls, all 18 of them were not on the international calling plan. For the customers who made 8 international calls, 106 were not on the international calling plan, and only 10 of them were. There is quite the potential for irritated customers here! This is confirmed by examining the output from the previous logistic regression. The **Parameter Estimate** for **Intl_Plan[no]** is positive and significant. This means that when a customer does not have an international plan, the probability is that the churn increases.

Customers who make international calls and don't get the cheap rates are perhaps more likely to churn than customers who make international calls and get cheap rates. Hence, the interaction term **Int_Plan * Intl_Mins** might be important. To create this interaction term, you have to create a new dummy variable for **Intl_Plan**, because the present variable is not numeric and cannot be multiplied by **Intl_Mins**:

1. Click on the **Intl_Plan** column in the Data Table to select it.
2. Right-click and select **Recode**.

3. Under **New Value**, where it has **No**, enter **0**, and right below that where it has **Yes**, enter **1**.
4. The new column name is **Intl_Plan2**. However, it is still nominal. Click **OK**.
5. Right-click on this new column. Click **Column Info.** Change the **Data Type** to **Numeric** and the **Modeling Type** to **Continuous**. Click **OK**. (This variable has to be continuous so that you can use it in the interaction term, which is created by multiplication. Nominal variables cannot be multiplied.)

To create the interaction term, complete the following steps:

1. Select **Cols ▶ New Columns** and call the new variable **IntlPlanMins**.
2. Under Column Properties, click **Formula**.
3. Click **Intl_Plan2**, click the times sign (**x**) in the middle of the dialog box, click **Intl_Mins**, and click **OK**.
4. Click **OK** again.

Now add the variable **IntlPlanMins** as the 11th independent variable in multiple logistic regression that includes **CustServ** and run it. The variable **IntlPlanMins** is significant, and the −LogLikelihood has dropped to 947.1450, as shown in Figure 6.22. This is a substantial drop for adding one variable. Undoubtedly, other useful interaction terms could be added to this model.

Validate and Confusion Matrix

Now that you have built an acceptable model, it is time to validate the model. You have already checked the Lack of Fit, but now you have to check linearity of the logit. From the **Nominal Logistic Fit for Churn** red triangle, click **Save Probability Formula**, which adds four variables to the data set: **Lin[0]** (which is the logit), **Prob[0]**, **Prob[1]**, and the predicted value of Churn, **Most Likely Churn**.

Now you have to plot the logit against each of the continuous independent variables. The categorical independent variables do not offer much opportunity to reveal nonlinearity (plot some, and see this for yourself). All the relationships of the continuous variables can be quickly viewed by generating a scatterplot matrix and then clicking the red triangle and **Fit Line**. Nearly all the red fitted lines are horizontal or near horizontal. For all of the logit versus independent variable plots, there is no evidence of nonlinearity.

Figure 6.22: Logistic Regression Results with Interaction Term Added

Whole Model Test				
Model	-LogLikelihood	DF	ChiSquare	Prob>ChiSq
Difference	431.9626	64	863.9252	<.0001*
Full	947.1841			
Reduced	1379.1467			

Figure 6.23: Confusion Matrix

⊿ **Confusion Matrix**

Training

Actual Churn	Predicted Count 0	1
0	2749	101
1	327	156

Actual Churn	Predicted Rate 0	1
0	0.965	0.035
1	0.677	0.323

You can also see how well your model is predicting by examining the Confusion Matrix, which is shown in Figure 6.23.

The actual number of churners in the data set is 327 + 156 = 483. The model predicted a total of 257 (= 101 + 156) churners. The number of bad predictions made by the model is 327 + 101 = 428, which indicates that 327 that were predicted not to churn actually did churn, and 101 that were predicted to churn did not churn. Further, observe in the Prob[1] column of the Data Table that you have the probability that any customer will churn. Right-click this column and select **Sort**. This will **sort** all the variables in the data set according to the probability of churning. Scroll to the top of the data set.

Look at the **Churn** column. It has mostly ones and some zeros here at the top where the probabilities are all above 0.85. Scroll all the way to the bottom and see that the probabilities now are all below 0.01, and the values of **Churn** are all zero. You really have modeled the probability of churning.

Now that you have built a model for predicting churn, how might you use it? You could take the next month's data (when you do not yet know who has churned) and predict who is likely to churn. Then these customers can be offered special deals to keep them with the company, so that they do not churn.

Exercises

1. Consider the logistic regression for the toy data set, where π is the probability of passing the class:

$$\log\left[\frac{\hat{\pi}}{1-\hat{\pi}}\right] = 25.60188 - 0.363761 \text{ MidtermScore}$$

Consider two students, one who scores 67% on the midterm and one who scores 73% on the midterm. What are the odds that each fails the class? What is the probability that each fails the class?

2. Consider the first logistic regression for the Churn data set, the one with 10 independent variables. Consider two customers, one with an international plan and one without. What are the odds that each churns? What is the probability that each churns?

3. You have already found that the interaction term **IntlPlanMins** significantly improves the model. Find another interaction term that does so.

4. Without deriving new variables such as **CustServ** or creating interaction terms such as **IntlPlanMins**, use a stepwise method to select variables for the Churn data set. Compare your results to the bivariate method used in the chapter; pay particular attention to the fit of the model and the confusion matrix.

5. Use the Freshmen1.jmp data set and build a logistic regression model to predict whether a student returns. Perhaps the continuous variables **Miles from Home** and **Part Time Work Hours** do not seem to have an effect. See whether turning them into discrete variables makes a difference. (*In essence*, turn **Miles from Home** into some dummy variables, such as 0–20 miles, 21–100 miles, or more than 100 miles.)

6. Use the purchase.xls file and build a logistic regression model to predict whether a person purchases or not. The data set has 431 observations and contains the variables, purchase (0—no, 1—yes), gender, income (low, medium, high) and another income variable income2 (lowmed and high). Create three new variables:
   gender: female = 2, male = 1
   income: Low = 1, Medium = 2, High = 3
   income2: lowmed = 1, High = 2
   Build the logistic regression model using these variables and age. Evaluate this new model.

7. Use the logit.xls data set and build a logistic regression model to predict whether a student is admitted to graduate school or not. The data set has 400 observations and contains the following variables: the binary variable admitted to graduate school (where 0—don't admit, 1—admit), GRE (Graduate Record Exam scores), undergraduate GPA (grade point average), and prestige of the undergraduate program (1—yes, 0—no). The question is: do GRE, undergraduate GPA, and the prestige of the undergraduate program affect admission into graduate school? Run the appropriate analysis to evaluate this question.

Chapter 7: Principal Components Analysis

Introduction

Principal component analysis (PCA) is an exploratory multivariate technique with two overall objectives. One objective is "dimension reduction"—to turn a collection of, for example, 100 variables into a collection of 10 variables that retain almost all the information that was contained in the original 100 variables. The other objective is to discover the structure in the relationships between the variables. As shown in Figure 7.1, PCA is a technique that does not require a dependent variable.

PCA assesses the structure of the interrelationships (correlations) among the variables by defining a set of common underlying dimensions called *components* or *factors*. PCA achieves this goal by eliminating unnecessary correlations between variables. To the extent that two variables are correlated, there are really three sources of variation:

Figure 7.1: A Framework for Multivariate Analysis

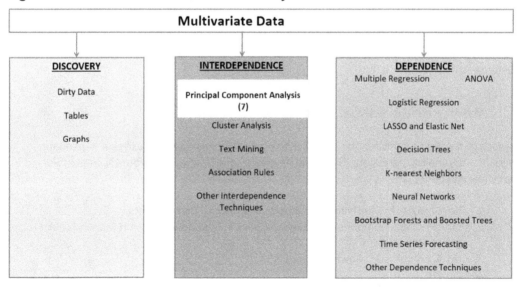

- variation unique to the first variable
- variation unique to the second variable
- variations common to the two variables

The method of PCA transforms the two variables into uncorrelated variables (with no common variation) that still preserve two sources of unique variation so that the total variation in the two variables remains the same.

Basic Steps in JMP

The following steps are the basics for performing a PCA with the use of JMP. To see how PCA works in JMP, examine a small data table toyprincomp.jmp, which contains the three variables, *x*, *y*, and *z*.

Produce the Correlations and Scatterplot Matrix

Before performing the PCA, first examine the correlations and scatterplot matrix. To produce them, complete the following steps:

1. Select **Analyze ▶ Multivariate Methods ▶ Multivariate**.
2. For the Select Columns option in the Multivariate and Correlations dialog box, click **x**, hold down the shift key, and click **y** to select all three variables.
3. Click **Y, Columns**, and all the variables will appear in the white box to the right of **Y, Columns**.
4. Click **OK**.
5. Click the **Scatterplot Matrix** red triangle, then click **Density Ellipses**.

As shown in Figure 7.2, the correlation matrix and corresponding scatterplot matrix will be generated. There appear to be strong correlations among all the variables. The correlation between *y* and *z* is almost 0.8; the correlation between *y* and *x* is over 0.70; and the correlation between *x* and *z* is almost .60.

Create the Principal Components

Treat *x* and *z* as a pair of variables on which to apply PCA. Reserve *y* for use as a dependent variable for running regressions. Since you have two variables, *x* and *z*, you will create two principal components:

1. Click **Analyze ▶ Multivariate Methods ▶ Principal Components**.
2. In the Principal Components dialog box, click **x**, hold down the shift key, and click **z** to select both variables.
3. Click **Y, Columns** as shown in Figure 7.3.
4. Click **OK**.

Figure 7.2: Correlations and Scatterplot Matrix for the toyprincomp.jmp Data Set

△ ▼ **Multivariate**

△ **Correlations**

	x	z	y
x	1.0000	0.5752	0.7143
z	0.5752	1.0000	0.7912
y	0.7143	0.7912	1.0000

The correlations are estimated by Row-wise method.

△ ▼ **Scatterplot Matrix**

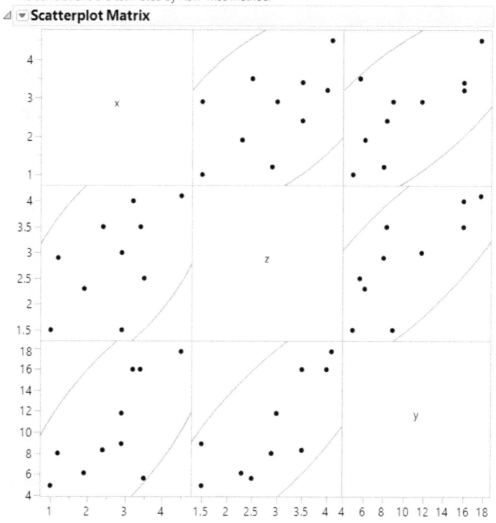

Figure 7.3: Principal Components Dialog Box

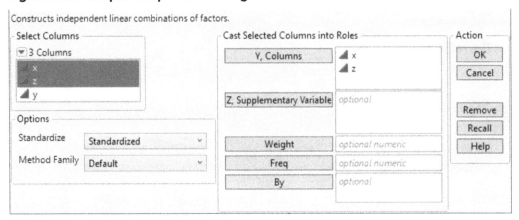

Three principal component summary plots, as shown in Figure 7.4, will appear. These plots show how the principal components explain the variations in the data. The leftmost graph is a listing and bar chart of the eigenvalue and percentage of variation accounted for by each principal component. (In this case, with only two principal components, the graph is not too informative.)

The first eigenvalue, 1.5752, is much larger than the second eigenvalue, 0.4248. This suggests that the first principal component, Prin1, is much more important (in terms of explaining the variation in the pair of variables) than the second principal component, Prin2. Also, the bar for the percentage of variation accounted for by Prin1 is about 80%. (As you can see in the other two plots, Prin1 accounted for 78.8%, and Prin2 accounted for 21.2%.)

The second graph is a scatter plot of the two principal components; this is called a *score plot*. Notice that the scatter is approximately flat, indicating a lack of correlation between the principal components. A correlation between the principal components would be indicated by a scatter with a positive or negative slope.

The third graph is called a *loadings plot*, and it shows the contribution made to each principal component (the principal components are the axes of the graph) by the original variables (which are the directed points on the graph). In this case, reading from the plot, you see that x and z each contribute about 0.90 to Prin1; x contributes about a positive 0.50 to Prin2; and z contributes about a negative 0.50 to Prin2. This graph is not particularly useful when there are only two variables. When there are many variables, it is possible to see which variables group together in the principal component space. Examples of this will be presented in a later section.

Linear combinations of x and z have been formed into Prin1 and Prin2. To show that Prin1 and Prin2 represent the same overall correlation as x and z, you use the dependent variable

Figure 7.4: Principal Components Summary Plots

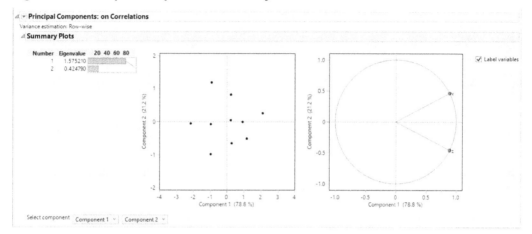

y and run two regressions. First regress *y* on *x* and *z*. Then regress *y* on Prin1 and Prin2. (The variables Prin1 and Prin2 can be created by clicking the red triangle, clicking **Save Columns ▶ Save Principal Components**, and then entering **2** as the number of components to save. Click **OK**.) Both regressions have the exact same R^2 and Root Mean Square Error (or s_e as shown in Table 7.1).

Table 7.1: Regression Results of *y* on Prin1 and Excluding Prin2

	R^2	Root Mean Square Error (s_e)
y|*x, z*	0.726336	2.811032
y| Prin1, Prin2	0.726336	2.811032
y| Prin1	0.719376	2.662706

Run a Regression of *y* on Prin1 and Excluding Prin2

To see the true value of the principal components method, now run a regression of *y* on Prin1, excluding Prin2. You get almost the same R^2 (which is slightly lower as shown in Table 7.1), which implies that the predicted *y* values from both models are essentially the same. You also see a drop in the Root Mean Square Error, which implies a tighter prediction interval. If your interest is not in interpreting coefficients but simply in predicting by use of principal components, you get practically the same prediction with a tighter prediction interval. The attraction of PCA is obvious.

Understand Eigenvalue Analysis

The method of principal components, or PCA, works by transforming a set of *k* correlated variables into a set of *k* uncorrelated variables that are called, not coincidentally, *principal components* or simply *components*. The first principal component (Prin1) is a linear combination of the original variables:

$$Prin1 = w_{11}x_1 + w_{12}x_2 + w_{13}x_3 + ... + w_{1k}x_k$$

Prin1 accounts for the most variation in the data set. The second principal component is uncorrelated with the first principal component, and accounts for the second-most variation in the data set. Similarly, Prin3 is uncorrelated with Prin1 and Prin2 and accounts for the third-most variation in the data set. The general form for the *i*th principal component is as follows. Where w_{i1} is the weight of the first variable in the *i*th principal component:[1]

$$Prin(i) = w_{i1}x_1 + w_{i2}x_2 + w_{i3}x_3 + ... + w_{ik}x_k$$

The weights w_{ij} are computed by a mathematical method called *eigenvalue analysis* that is applied to the correlation matrix of the original data set. This is equivalent to standardizing each variable by subtracting its mean and dividing by its standard deviation. This standardization is important, lest results depend on the units of measurement. For example, if one of the variables is dollars, measuring that variable in cents or thousands of dollars will produce completely different sets of principal components. The eigenvalue analysis of the correlation matrix of k variables produces *k* eigenvalues, and for each eigenvalue there is an eigenvector of *k* elements. For example, the *k* elements of the first eigenvector are $w_{11}, w_{12}, w_{13} ..., w_{1k}$

Conduct the Eigenvalue Analysis and the Bartlett Test

To see how these weights work, continue with the toyprincomp.jmp data set:

1. Click the **Principal Components: on Correlations** red triangle and click **Eigenvectors**. Added to the principal component report will be the eigenvectors as shown in Figure 7.5. Accordingly, the equations for Prin1 and Prin2 are Prin1 = 0.70711 *x* + 0.70711 *z* and Prin2 = 0.70711 *x* – 0.70711 *z*.
2. Again, click the **Principal Components: on Correlations** red triangle and click **Eigenvalues**.
3. Click the **Principal Components: on Correlations** red triangle and click **Bartlett Test**. (The Bartlett Test assesses whether the variances of the eigenvalues are equal or not. If you fail to reject, PCA is inappropriate.) The eigenvalues are displayed as shown in Figure 7.5.

---

[1] A related multivariate technique is *factor analysis*. Although superficially similar, the techniques are quite different and have different purposes. First, the PCA approach accounts for all the variance, common and unique; factor analysis analyzes only common variance. Further, with PCA, each principal component is viewed as a weighted combination of input variables. On the other hand, with factor analysis, each input variable is viewed as a weighted combination of some underlying theoretical construct. In sum, the principal components method is just a transformation of the data to a new set of variables and is useful for prediction; factor analysis is a model for the data that seeks to explain the data.

Figure 7.5: Eigenvectors and Eigenvalues for the toyprincomp.jmp Data Set

◢ **Eigenvectors**

	Prin1	Prin2
x	0.70711	0.70711
z	0.70711	-0.70711

◢ **Eigenvalues**

Number	Eigenvalue	Percent	20 40 60 80	Cum Percent	ChiSquare	DF	Prob>ChiSq
1	1.575210	78.760		78.760	3.415	0.425	0.0206*
2	0.424790	21.240		100.000	0.000	.	.

Observe that Prin1 accounts for 78.76% of the variation in the data because its eigenvalue (1.5752) is 0.7876 of the sum of all the eigenvalues (1.5752 + 0.4248 = 2). The fact that the sum of the eigenvalues equals 2 is not a mere coincidence. Remember that the variables are standardized, so each variable has a variance equal to 1. Therefore, the sum of the standardized variances equals the number of variables, in this case, 2.

Verify Lack of Correlation

Finally, you can verify that the principal components, Prin1 and Prin2, are uncorrelated by computing the correlation matrix for the principal components. You can generate the correlation matrix:

1. Click **Analyze ▶ Multivariate Methods ▶ Multivariate**.
2. Select **Prin1** and **Prin2**.
3. Click **OK**. The correlation matrix clearly shows that the correlation between Prin1 and Prin2 equals zero.

Dimension Reduction

One of the main objectives of PCA is to reduce the information contained in all the original variables into a smaller set of components with a minimum loss of information. So, the question is how do you determine how many components should be considered. To answer this question, look at another data set, princomp.jmp, which has 12 independent variables, $x1$ through $x12$; a single dependent variable, y; and 100 observations.

Produce the Correlations and Scatterplot Matrix

As you did earlier in this chapter with the toyprincomp.jmp data set, first generate the correlation matrix and scatterplot matrix:

1. Select **Analyze ▶ Multivariate Methods ▶ Multivariate**.
2. For the Select Columns option in the Multivariate and Correlations dialog box, click **x1**, hold down the shift key, and click **x12** to select all twelve *x* variables.
3. Click **Y, Columns**, and all the variables will appear in the white box to the right of **Y, Columns**.
4. Click **OK**.

It is rather hard to make sense of this correlation matrix and the associated scatterplots, so try another way to see this information:

1. Click the **Multivariate** red triangle and select **Pairwise Correlations**.
2. Scroll to the bottom of the screen to see a table listing of the pairwise correlations. Right-click in the table and select **Sort by Column**.
3. Select **Signif Prob** and check the box for **Ascending**.
4. Click **OK**.

You should observe that most of the correlations are rather low with four correlations in the 60% range and several variables simply uncorrelated. The correlations for about half the correlations are significant, indicated by an asterisk in the **Signif Prob** column, while about half the correlations are insignificant.

Conduct the Principal Component Analysis

Next, perform the PCA on the variables *x*1 through *x*12:

1. Select **Analyze ▶ Multivariate Methods ▶ Principal Components**.
2. In the Principal Components dialog box, click **x1,** hold down the shift key, and click **x12**.
3. Then click **Y, Columns**.
4. Click **OK**.
5. On the **Principal Components: on Correlations** output, click the red triangle and click **Eigenvalues**.
6. Click the **Principal Components: on Correlations** red triangle and click **Bartlett Test**.
7. Click the **Principal Components: on Correlations** red triangle and click **Scree Plot**. Figure 7.6 displays the Scree Plot and eigenvalues.

Examining the Scree Plot, it appears that there might be an "elbow" at 2 or 3 or 4 principal components. When you examine the histogram of eigenvalues, it appears that the first three principal components account for about 60% of the variation in the data, and the first four principal components might account for about 68% of the variation.

Determine the Number of Principal Components to Select

How many principal components should you select? There are three primary methods for choosing this number, and any one of them can be satisfactory. (No one is necessarily better

Figure 7.6: Scree Plot and Eigenvalues for *x1* to *x12* from the princomp.jmp Data Set

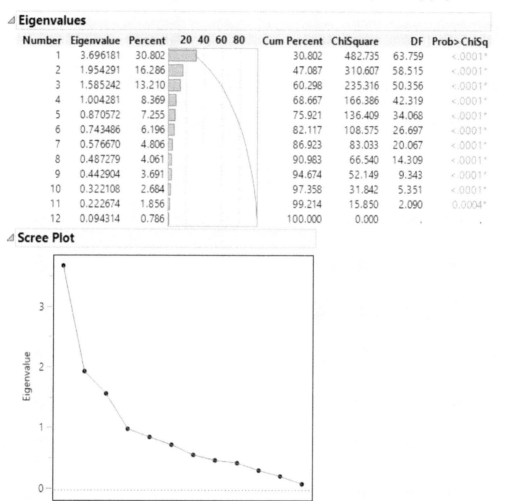

⊿ **Eigenvalues**

Number	Eigenvalue	Percent	20 40 60 80	Cum Percent	ChiSquare	DF	Prob>ChiSq
1	3.696181	30.802		30.802	482.735	63.759	<.0001*
2	1.954291	16.286		47.087	310.607	58.515	<.0001*
3	1.585242	13.210		60.298	235.316	50.356	<.0001*
4	1.004281	8.369		68.667	166.386	42.319	<.0001*
5	0.870572	7.255		75.921	136.409	34.068	<.0001*
6	0.743486	6.196		82.117	108.575	26.697	<.0001*
7	0.576670	4.806		86.923	83.033	20.067	<.0001*
8	0.487279	4.061		90.983	66.540	14.309	<.0001*
9	0.442904	3.691		94.674	52.149	9.343	<.0001*
10	0.322108	2.684		97.358	31.842	5.351	<.0001*
11	0.222674	1.856		99.214	15.850	2.090	0.0004*
12	0.094314	0.786		100.000	0.000	.	.

⊿ **Scree Plot**

than any of the others in all situations, so selecting the number of principal components is an art form.)

Method 1

Look for an "elbow" in the scree plot of eigenvalues. In the above scree plot, there is a clear elbow at 3, which suggests keeping the first three principal components.

Method 2

How many eigenvalues are greater than one? Each principal component accounts for a proportion of variation related to its corresponding eigenvalue, and the sum of the eigenvalues equals the variance in the data set. Any principal component with an eigenvalue greater than one is contributing more than its share to the variance. Those principal components associated with eigenvalues that are less than one are not accounting for their share of the variation in the data. This suggests that you should retain principal components associated with eigenvalues greater than one. It is important not to be too strict with this rule. For example, if the fourth eigenvalue equals 1.01 and the fifth eigenvalue equals 0.99, it would be silly to use the first four principal components because the fifth principal component makes practically the same contribution as the fourth principal component. This method is especially useful if there is no clear elbow in the scree plot. In the princomp.jmp example, you would choose 4 components.

Method 3

Account for a specified proportion of the variation. This can be used in two ways. First, the researcher can desire to account for at least 70% or 80% of the variation, for example, and retain enough principal components to achieve this goal. Second, the researcher can keep any principal component that accounts for more than, for example, 5% or 10% of the total variation. For the princomp.jmp example, we choose to explain at least 70% of the variation. We would then choose five principal components because four principal components only account for 68.667% of the variation.

Compare Methods for Determining the Number of Components

Now see what difference each of these methods makes with this data set. First, if you run a regression of y on all 12 x variables ($x1$ to $x12$), the R^2 is .834434. The R^2 when you regress y on three, four, and five principal components is listed in Table 7.2. The difference in R^2 between three and four principal components is more than 4% (and the maximum R^2 is 100%), but the difference in R^2 between four and five is a negligible .001637. This suggests that four might be a good number of principal components to retain. The predictions that you get from keeping four or five principal components will be practically the same.

Table 7.2: Regression Results

	R^2
$y \mid x1, x2, \ldots, x12$	0.834434
$y \mid$ Princomp1 through Princomp3	0.723898
$y \mid$ Princomp1 through Princomp4	0.766565
$y \mid$ Princomp1 through Princomp5	0.768202

Discovery of Structure in the Data

In addition to dimension reduction, PCA can also be used to gain insight into the structure of the data set in two ways. First, the factor loadings can be used to plot the variables in the principal components space (this is the "Loading Plot"). And it is sometimes possible to see which variables are "close" to each other in the principal components space. Second, the principal component scores can be plotted for each observation (this is the "Score Plot"), and aberrant observations or small, unusual clusters might be noted. In this section, we consider both of these uses of PCA. You will first use a data set of track and field records in which the results are very clean and easy to interpret. You will then use a real-world economic data set where the results are messier and more typical of the results obtained in practice.

A Straightforward Example

The olymp88sas.jmp data set contains decathlon results for 34 contestants in the 1988 Summer Olympics in Seoul. In the decathlon, each contestant competes in 10 events, and an athlete's performance in each event makes a contribution to the final score. The contestant with the highest score wins.

Produce the Correlations and Scatterplot Matrix

First, as you have done before, generate the correlation matrix and scatterplot matrix:

1. Select **Analyze ▶ Multivariate Methods ▶ Multivariate**.
2. Select all the variables, click **Y, Columns**, and click **OK**.
3. In the **Multivariate** red triangle, click **Pairwise Correlations**.
4. Right-click in the table of pairwise correlations, and select **Sort by Column**.
5. Select **Signif Pro**.
6. Check the **Ascending Box**.
7. Click **OK**.

You should observe that most of the correlations are rather significant with only a couple of correlations less than (absolute value, that is) 0.15.

Conduct the Principal Component Analysis

Next, perform the PCA on this data set, but be sure to exclude "score." Why? Because "score" is a combination of all the other variables! After running the PCA:

1. Click the **Principal Components: on Correlations** red triangle and click **Eigenvalues.**
2. Click the **Principal Components: on Correlations** red triangle and click **Bartlett Test.**
3. Click the **Principal Components: on Correlations** red triangle and click and **Scree Plot.**
   Figure 7.7 displays the PCA summary plots, eigenvalues, and Scree Plot for the data set.

Figure 7.7: PCA Summary Plots, Eigenvalues, and Scree Plot for the olymp88sas.jmp Data Set

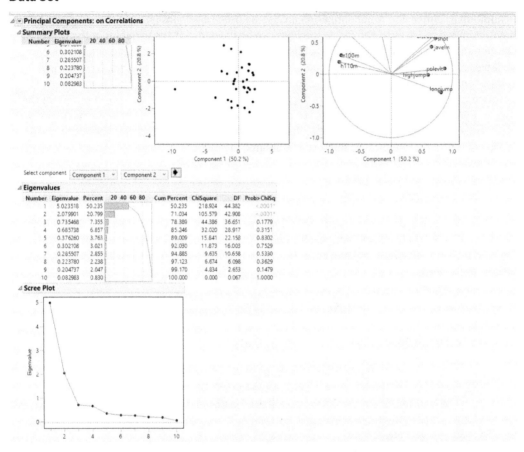

The bar chart of the eigenvalues indicates that two principal components dominate the data set, contributing 70% of the variability. The Score Plot shows that almost all the observations cluster near the origin of the space, which is defined by the first two principal components. But there is a noticeable outlier on the far left. Clicking on this observation reveals that it is observation 34, the contestant with the worst score. Examine the score column further. First, realize that the observations were sorted from highest to lowest score. Next, notice that the difference between any two successive contestants' scores is usually less than 50, and occasionally one hundred or two hundred points. Contestant 34, however, finished 1568 points behind contestant 33; contestant 34 certainly is an outlier.

Back to the PCA output and Figure 7.7, you can see in the Loading Plot how neatly the variables cluster into three groups. In the upper left quadrant are the races, in the upper right quadrant are the throwing events, and along the right side of the X axis are the jumping events. With economic data, structures are rarely so well-defined and easily recognizable, as you shall see next.

An Example with Less Well-Defined Data

The Stategdp2008.jmp data set contains state gross domestic product (GDP) for each state and the District of Columbia for the year 2008 in billions of dollars. Each state's total GDP is broken down into twenty categories of state GDP, with total GDP given for each state in the second column and the total for the United States and each category given in the top row.

First, generate the correlation matrix and scatterplot matrix. The correlation matrix of the data set shows that the variables are highly correlated, with many correlations exceeding 0.9. This makes sense, because the data are measured in dollars and states with large economies.

For example, California, Texas, and New York tend to have large values for each of the categories, and small states tend to have small values for each of the categories.

Conduct a Principal Component Analysis and Correct Mistakes

The fact that the data set is highly correlated suggests that the data set might have very few or even only one principal component. You can see this by running a PCA on the data set. Select all the numeric variables except total. Why? Try it both ways and see what happens.

The eigenvalue plot shows that the first eigenvalue accounts for practically all of the variation; this confirms the earlier suspicion. Notice how the score plot shows almost all of the observations clustered at the origin, with a single observation on the X axis near the value of 30. Click on that observation. What mistake has been made?

You included the "US" observation in the analysis, which should not have been done. To exclude this row from the analysis, on the JMP data table, in the list of row numbers in the first column (with the observation numbers), right-click the first observation **1**, and click **Exclude/Unexclude**. A red circle with a line through it should appear next to the row number.

Rerun the Principal Component Analysis

Now rerun the PCA, and the output will look like Figure 7.8. From the bar chart of the eigenvalues, you can see that the first eigenvalue dominates, but that a second eigenvalue might also be relevant. In the score plot, click on each of the three right-most data points to see that they represent NY, TX, and CA. This plot just shows you what you already know: that these are the three largest state economies. In the factor loadings plot, all the variables except mining are clustered together.

Refine Results by Expressing Data in Proportional Form

To obtain a more informative plot, it might be more useful to express the data in proportional form to show what proportion each category constitutes of the state's total GDP. For example, the proportion of Alaska's (AK) state GDP by agriculture is 2.368/170.14 = 0.0139. Now perform

Figure 7.8: PCA Summary Plots for the StateGDP2008.jmp Data Set

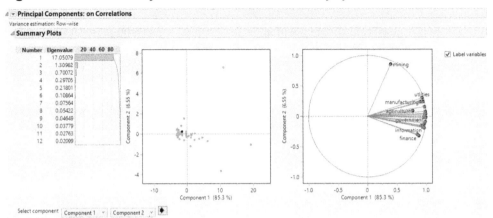

the analysis again, using the StateGDP2008percent.jmp data set that has the relative proportions. Examine the correlation matrix of the data set. Another way of producing the correlation matrix is to run the PCA. Then click the **Principal Components: on Correlations** red triangle and click **Correlations**.

Besides the main diagonal, which has to be all ones, there are no large correlations. You can expect to find a few important principal components, not just one. Indeed, as can be seen in Figure 7.9, the bar chart of the eigenvalues shows that the first two principal components account for barely 40% of the variation. In the lower left quadrant of the score plot, you find two observations that belong to Alaska and Wyoming, which are very negative on both the first and second principal components. Referring to the data table, you see that only two states have a proportion for mining that exceeds 20%; those two are Alaska and Wyoming. If you identify the other four observations that fall farthest from the origin in this quadrant, you find them to be LA, WV, NM, and OK, the states that derive a large proportion of GDP from mining activities. In the lower right corner, is a single observation DC that gets 32% of its GDP from government.

When there are only two or three important principal components, analyzing the loading plots involves looking at only one or perhaps three plots. (In the former case, the first and second principal components; in the latter case, plots of first versus second, second versus third, and first versus third are necessary.) For more than two important principal components, examining all the possible principal component plots becomes problematic. Nonetheless, for expository purposes, look at the loadings plot. You see in the lower left quadrant that both "transport" and "mining" are negatively correlated with both the first and second principal components. In the lower right quadrant, "other" is negatively correlated with the second principal component but positively correlated with the first principal component, as are "services" and "government."

This chapter has included two examples to illustrate the use of PCA for exploring the structure of a data set. But it is important to keep in mind that the primary use of PCA in multivariate analysis and data mining is data reduction—that is, reducing several variables to a few. This concept is explored further in the exercises.

Figure 7.9: PCA Summary Plots for the StateGDP2008percent.jmp Data Set

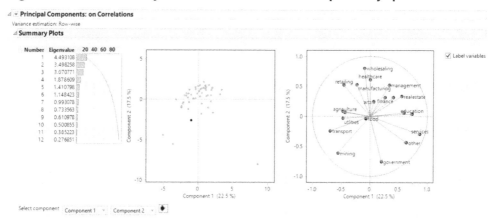

Exercises

1. Use the PublicUtilities.jmp data set. Run a regression to predict **return** using all the other variables. Run a PCA and use only a few principal components to predict **return** (remember not to include **return** in the variables on which the PCA is conducted).

2. Use the MassHousing.jmp data set. Run a regression to predict market value (**mvalue**) using all the other variables. Run a PCA and use only a few principal components to predict **mvalue.** (Remember not to include **mvalue** in the variables on which the PCA is conducted.)

3. Use the olymp88excel.xls data set. Run a PCA and use only a few principal components to predict **score.** (Remember not to include **score** in the variables on which the PCA is conducted.)

4. Use the stockreturns.xls data set. The weekly (100 weeks) rates of return for five stocks (Allied Chemical, DuPont, Union Carbide, Exxon, and Texaco) are listed in the file. Since 1926, the stock market has an average rate of return of 11.3%. Investors have earned more or less depending on the type of investments and risks taken. It is very important to note that this return is before costs have been factored. Run a principal component analysis (PCA) to find (and define) the dimensions that best summarize these stock returns.

Chapter 8: Least Absolute Shrinkage and Selection Operator and Elastic Net

Introduction

In Chapter 5, you learned about stepwise regression, which is a method to select a few from many possible regressors for inclusion in a regression equation. In this chapter, you will learn two more such methods: *least absolute shrinkage and selection operator* (LASSO) and *elastic net*, which each take a different approach to reducing the number of regressors.

As shown in the multivariate analysis framework in Figure 8.1, these new generalized regression techniques are dependence techniques. To motivate the development of these two new methods, you will consider a method called *ridge regression*.

Figure 8.1: A Framework for Multivariate Analysis

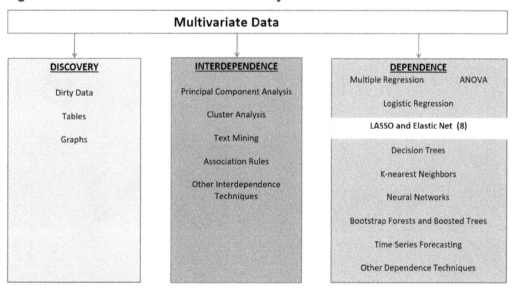

The Importance of the Bias-Variance Tradeoff

Suppose that your focus is on good predictions, not the interpretation of the coefficients and their effects on the dependent variable. Suppose as well that you are going to make predictions using linear regression. Suppose that the true value that you want to predict is 10.0, and you have two estimators available; their distributions are given in Figure 8.2.

One estimator is unbiased: it is symmetric and centered on 10. The other estimator is biased: its expected value does not equal 10, but instead equals 10.5. The former distribution obviously has much more variance than the latter. A moment's reflection tells you that if all you care about is a prediction, you might well want to use the biased estimator rather than the unbiased estimator.

The unbiased estimator has a much higher probability of returning a prediction that is far from 10—for example, between 0 and 5 or between 15 and 20. The biased estimator will practically never return such extreme predictions. In choosing to use the biased estimator, you are trading off a lot of variance for a little bit of bias and obtaining a much higher probability of getting an estimate that is close to the truth. This *bias-variance tradeoff* appears frequently in advanced statistical methods and is rarely discussed in introductory texts. It is an especially important concept for predictive analytics.

Figure 8.2: Two Estimation Distributions

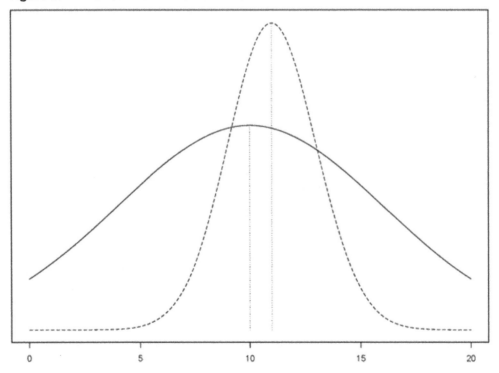

Ridge Regression

To motivate the rest of this chapter, a brief treatment of ridge regression and its limitations follow.

Technique and Limitations

The usual linear regression that you saw in Chapter 5 is based on minimizing the residual sum of squares (RSS):

$$\text{RSS} = \sum_{i=1}^{n} (y_i - (\beta_0 + \beta_1 x_1 + \beta_2 x_2 + ... + \beta_k x_k))^2$$

In Chapter 5, we called the RSS the sum of square errors (SSE).

The ridge regression minimizes a different criterion:

$$\sum_{i=1}^{n} (y_i - (\beta_0 + \beta_1 x_1 + \beta_2 x_2 + ... + \beta_k x_k))^2 + \lambda \sum_{j=1}^{k} \beta_j^2$$

Here, $\lambda > 0$. The second term on the right imposes a penalty on large values of β. So the minimization process introduces a bias by making the squared slope coefficients smaller than they otherwise would be. (Note that the penalty is not applied to the intercept term, β_0.) As is obvious, the closer λ gets to zero, the closer the ridge regression coefficients get to the least squares coefficients. And when $\lambda = 0$, the ridge solution equals the least squares coefficients. Increasing λ has the effect of moving both positive and negative coefficients toward zero—that is, shrinking the slope coefficients toward zero.

Hence, ridge regression is one of a general class of estimators called *shrinkage estimators,* and λ is called a *shrinkage penalty*. This bias introduced by shrinkage makes the variance smaller than it otherwise would be, thus effecting the bias-variance tradeoff (you hope!). It is not *always* true that ridge regression will have a smaller prediction error than linear regression, but it is usually true.

Use of JMP

Critical to getting good results from ridge regression is a good choice of the value for the shrinkage penalty, λ. JMP chooses λ by choosing a large upper bound and a small lower bound, and then searching for the best value of λ. For example, it might choose to search between 1 and 10 in increments of 1, yielding the results in Table 8.1.

Table 8.1: Hypothetical Values of Ridge Criterion for Various Values of λ

Type	Values									
λ	1.0	2.0	3.0	4.0	5.0	6.0	7.0	8.0	9.0	10.0
Ridge criterion	32.1	36.2	37.5	33.4	31.3	30.2	31.5	34.7	35.8	39.2

Inspection of Table 8.1 suggests that the value of λ that minimizes the ridge criterion falls somewhere between 5 and 7. So a new search would be executed between 5 and 7 in increments of 0.01. The search continues until adding more decimals to λ really doesn't change the value of the ridge criterion.

There is an important difference between linear regression and ridge regression. For linear regression, the scale of the variables doesn't matter. If a variable is multiplied by 10, its slope coefficient will be divided by 10. The same is not true of ridge regression. Therefore, it is best to standardize the independent variables. The dependent variable does not need to be standardized. The purpose of the standardization is to put all the penalized variables on an even footing by removing the effects of the units of measurement, and no penalty is applied to the dependent variable. JMP automatically centers and scales the predictor variables.

Use the Mass Housing data set, MassHousing.jmp, for this example. The treatment of ridge regression here will be rather perfunctory because it is introduced only to motivate other methods. In particular, only a few the many options for this method are discussed.

1. Open MassHousing.jmp.
2. Click **Analyze ▶ Fit Model** and select **mvalue** as the **Y** variable.
3. Select all other variables and select **Construct Model Effects ▶ Add**.
4. In the top right of the box, for **Personality**, select **Generalized Regression**.
5. Click **Run**.
6. In the Generalized Regression dialog box that appears, as shown in Figure 8.3, select **Estimation Method ▶ Ridge**. Two validation methods are offered: **Holdback** (discussed in Chapter 14) and **KFold** (discussed in Chapter 12). Don't worry about these for present purposes. Leave the validation method as the default **Holdback** with **Holdback Proportion = 0.3**.
7. Click **Go**.

Because this method relies on the use of the random number generator, and because new random numbers are used every time this method is invoked, you will get slightly different answers every time you run it.

Near the top of the Generalized Regression output, similar to Figure 8.4, you should see that the Number of rows equals 354 for Training and 152 for Validation. At the bottom of the output are the regression coefficients, together with **Scale**, which is the value of λ calculated by the program. To give a sense of the variation that can be expected because of the random number generator, you run this model five times and obtain values of **Scale** (with estimates of the **crim** coefficient in parentheses) equal to 5.03 (–0.125), 4.34 (–0.132), 4.33 (–0.094), 4.94 (–0.10), and 4.72 (–0.134).

Figure 8.3: The Generalized Regression Dialog Box

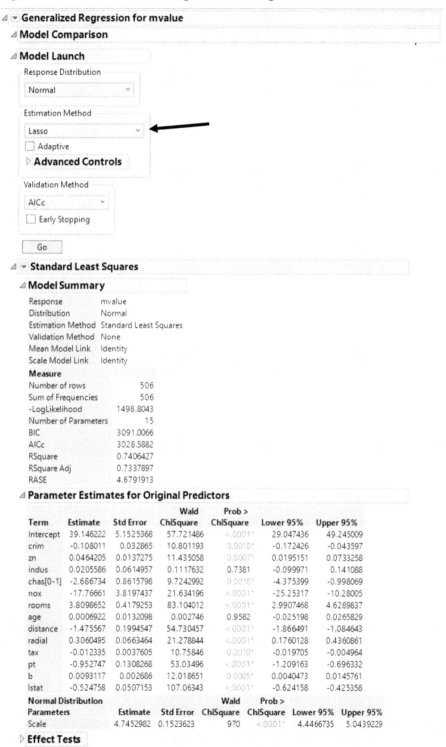

Term	Estimate	Std Error	Wald ChiSquare	Prob > ChiSquare	Lower 95%	Upper 95%
Intercept	39.146222	5.1525368	57.721486	<.0001*	29.047436	49.245009
crim	-0.108011	0.032865	10.801193	0.0010*	-0.172426	-0.043597
zn	0.0464205	0.0137275	11.435058	0.0007*	0.0195151	0.0733258
indus	0.0205586	0.0614957	0.1117632	0.7381	-0.099971	0.141088
chas[0-1]	-2.686734	0.8615798	9.7242992	0.0018*	-4.375399	-0.998069
nox	-17.76661	3.8197437	21.634196	<.0001*	-25.25317	-10.28005
rooms	3.8098652	0.4179253	83.104012	<.0001*	2.9907468	4.6289837
age	0.0006922	0.0132098	0.002746	0.9582	-0.025198	0.0265829
distance	-1.475567	0.1994547	54.730457	<.0001*	-1.866491	-1.084643
radial	0.3060495	0.0663464	21.278844	<.0001*	0.1760128	0.4360861
tax	-0.012335	0.0037605	10.75846	0.0010*	-0.019705	-0.004964
pt	-0.952747	0.1308268	53.03496	<.0001*	-1.209163	-0.696332
b	0.0093117	0.002686	12.018651	0.0005*	0.0040473	0.0145761
lstat	-0.524758	0.0507153	107.06343	<.0001*	-0.624158	-0.425358

Figure 8.4: Generalized Regression Output for the Mass Housing Data Set

◢ ▾ Generalized Regression for mvalue
◢ ▾ Standard Least Squares
▷ Effect Tests
◢ ▾ Normal Ridge with Holdback Validation

◢ Model Summary

Response	mvalue
Distribution	Normal
Estimation Method	Ridge
Validation Method	Holdback
Mean Model Link	Identity
Scale Model Link	Identity

◢ Estimation Details

Number of Grid Points	150
Minimum Penalty Fraction	0
Grid Scale	Square Root

Measure	Training	Validation
Number of rows	354	152
Sum of Frequencies	354	152
-LogLikelihood	1040.7721	463.20952
Number of Parameters	15	15
BIC	2169.5836	1001.7773
AICc	2112.9643	959.94846
RSquare	0.7389499	0.7280921
RASE	4.5772371	5.0449251
Lambda Penalty	0.0060757	

◢ Solution Path

◢ Parameter Estimates for Original Predictors

Term	Estimate	Std Error	Wald ChiSquare	Prob > ChiSquare	Lower 95%	Upper 95%
Intercept	37.218917	8.8520747	17.678171	<.0001*	19.869169	54.568664
crim	-0.109432	0.0288662	14.37163	0.0002*	-0.166008	-0.052855
zn	0.0352273	0.0181927	3.749452	0.0528	-0.00043	0.0708843
indus	0.0125805	0.0625961	0.0403924	0.8407	-0.110106	0.1352666
chas[0-1]	-1.28462	1.3968732	0.845737	0.3578	-4.022441	1.4532013
nox	-16.42346	3.8392533	18.299354	<.0001*	-23.94826	-8.898661
rooms	4.0642536	0.9400465	18.692307	<.0001*	2.2217963	5.9067109
age	-0.011663	0.0176834	0.4349965	0.5095	-0.046322	0.0229959
distance	-1.412792	0.2469337	32.733764	<.0001*	-1.896773	-0.928811
radial	0.3121534	0.0808447	14.908481	0.0001*	0.1537007	0.470606
tax	-0.014459	0.0039244	13.574093	0.0002*	-0.022151	-0.006767
pt	-1.008147	0.14037	51.582171	<.0001*	-1.283268	-0.733027
b	0.0083761	0.0027791	9.0841206	0.0026*	0.0029292	0.0138229
lstat	-0.438641	0.1073391	16.699456	<.0001*	-0.649022	-0.22826

Normal Distribution Parameters	Estimate	Std Error	Wald ChiSquare	Prob > ChiSquare	Lower 95%	Upper 95%
Scale	4.5772371	0.3519921	169.09901	<.0001*	3.8873454	5.2671289

▷ Effect Tests

Least Absolute Shrinkage and Selection Operator

The problem with ridge regression from the perspective of predictive analytics is that it does not do variable selection for you—all the variables are still included. The ability to shrink some of the regression coefficients (those of the less important variables) all the way to zero would be nice.

To achieve this desirable goal, JMP offers two methods, the first of which goes by the rather tedious name of *least absolute shrinkage and selection operator*, commonly known by its acronym, *LASSO*. This method minimizes the LASSO criterion as follows:

$$\sum_{i=1}^{n}(y_i - (\beta_0 + \beta_1 x_1 + \beta_2 x_2 + ... + \beta_k x_k))^2 + \lambda \sum_{j=1}^{k}|\beta_j|$$

The big difference between ridge regression and the LASSO can be seen in the second term on the right. Ridge regression minimizes the sum of the squared coefficients, but the LASSO minimizes the sum of the absolute values of the coefficients. Just as was the case with ridge regression, increasing λ makes the coefficients smaller. And when $\lambda = 0$, the LASSO solution equals the least squares solution. As with ridge regression, the predictor variables should be standardized and, again, JMP will do this automatically.

Perform the Technique

To run the LASSO on the Mass Housing data set MassHousing.jmp, do as follows:

1. Expand the **Model Launch** arrow. Click the **Estimation Method ▶ LASSO.** Note the **Adaptive** box. The Adaptive LASSO method attempts to give a smaller penalty to variables that contribute more to the prediction. Keep the **Adaptive** box unchecked. Several validation methods are listed. Click **AICc** so that the random number generator will not come into play. Other validation methods such as **KFold** or **Holdback** use a random number generator and slightly different results would be produced each time.
2. Click **Go**. Your results should include that λ, given as Scale in the list of regression coefficients, equals 4.6807981.

Examine the Results

The two graphs in Figure 8.5 present two solution paths. Focus on the left one. Click the black triangle at the top of the red line and drag it to the far right. The value of Scale will now equal 4.6791913. By convention, the X axis does not show λ but instead shows **Magnitude of Scaled Parameter Estimates**. However, there is a one-to-one relationship between them. When **Magnitude of Scaled Parameter Estimates** (MoSPE) is larger, λ is smaller, and the converse is also true.

The Y axis shows the coefficient value. Click on the top-most curved line in the graph. It should become bold, and the variable **rooms** should be highlighted in the coefficient table. What this curved line tells us is that **rooms** is a very powerful variable in this model, and even as λ increases the coefficient, **rooms** stays the same for a long time. Click on the black triangle and drag it to the left, until the red line gets to the point where MoSPE is about 150.

Figure 8.5: LASSO Regression for the Mass Housing Data Set

◢ ▾ **Normal Lasso with AICc Validation**

◢ **Model Summary**

Response	mvalue
Distribution	Normal
Estimation Method	Lasso
Validation Method	AICc
Mean Model Link	Identity
Scale Model Link	Identity

Measure

Number of rows	506
Sum of Frequencies	506
-LogLikelihood	1498.978
Number of Parameters	13
BIC	3078.901
AICc	3024.6959
ERIC	3100.3088
RSquare	0.7404645
RASE	4.6807981
Lambda Penalty	0.3364947

◢ **Estimation Details**

Number of Grid Points	150
Minimum Penalty Fraction	0
Grid Scale	Square Root

◢ **Solution Path**

Reset Solution

◢ **Parameter Estimates for Original Predictors**

Term	Estimate	Std Error	Wald ChiSquare	Prob > ChiSquare	Lower 95%	Upper 95%
Intercept	38.041515	7.659778	24.665121	<.0001*	23.028626	53.054404
crim	-0.10321	0.0289562	12.704613	0.0004*	-0.159963	-0.046457
zn	0.0435362	0.0132664	10.769474	0.0010*	0.0175345	0.0695379
indus	0	0	0	1.0000	0	0
chas[0-1]	-2.699679	1.2814816	4.4381251	0.0351*	-5.211337	-0.188021
nox	-16.8115	3.2377737	26.960017	<.0001*	-23.15742	-10.46558
rooms	3.8351821	0.776629	24.386238	<.0001*	2.3130173	5.3573469
age	0	0	0	1.0000	0	0
distance	-1.441673	0.2143247	45.246948	<.0001*	-1.861742	-1.021605
radial	0.275387	0.0585128	22.150579	<.0001*	0.160704	0.3900699
tax	-0.010769	0.0027807	14.998685	0.0001*	-0.016219	-0.005319
pt	-0.937915	0.110679	71.81192	<.0001*	-1.154842	-0.720988
b	0.0091511	0.0026393	12.022233	0.0005*	0.0039783	0.014324
lstat	-0.522515	0.0839894	38.703365	<.0001*	-0.687131	-0.357899

Normal Distribution

Parameters	Estimate	Std Error	Wald ChiSquare	Prob > ChiSquare	Lower 95%	Upper 95%
Scale	4.6807981	0.2812283	277.02674	<.0001*	4.1296007	5.2319955

▷ **Effect Tests**

Look at the regression output. Only four coefficients are nonzero (**Intercept, rooms, pt,** and **lstat**), and Scale is about 5.6. What this tells us is that when λ is increased from 4.6791913 to 5.6, the coefficients on ten variables are driven to zero. If MoSPE is increased to about 250, then only four or five coefficients are zeroed out. (Just above 250 four variables are zeroed; just below 250 five variables are zeroed.) Scale is about 5 at this point. Which variable is even more powerful than **rooms**? Click on the most negative of the curved lines to find out that it is **lstat**.

In order from strongest to weakest, the LASSO says that the four most important variables are **lstat, rooms, pt,** and **b**. Click on the curves that hit the zero line closest to the Y axis to see this.

This graph is used to inform a qualitative judgment as to which variables should be included in a regression model, in much the same way that stepwise regression informs variable selection. An advantage of the LASSO is that the variables often hit the zero axis in groups, enabling the modeler to drop several variables at a time. For example, first drop the variables whose curves hit the zero line closest to the right side.

Elastic Net

The next method for variable selection is the *elastic net,* which minimizes a function that is a combination of both ridge regression (see the middle term below, which has λ_1 in it) and the LASSO (see the last term below, which has λ_2 in it). The elastic net criterion is as follows:

$$\sum_{i=1}^{n}(y_i - (\beta_0 + \beta_1 x_1 + \beta_2 x_2 + ... + \beta_k x_k))^2 + \lambda_1 \sum_{j=1}^{k} |\beta_j| + \lambda_2 \sum_{j=1}^{k} \beta_j^2$$

where $\lambda1 = \alpha$; $\lambda2 = (1-\alpha)/2$ and $\alpha \in (0,1)$.

Perform the Technique

The elastic net is implemented almost the same way as the LASSO. To run the elastic net on the Mass Housing data set MassHousing.jmp, complete the following steps:

1. Expand the **Model Launch** arrow. Click the **Estimation Method** ▶ **Elastic Net**. Leave the Validation Method at the default **AICc** and click **Go**.

The list of parameter estimates again includes a value for **Scale**. This time it is 4.680967 as shown in Figure 8.6.

Compare with LASSO

In Figure 8.5, notice how different the solution path for the LASSO is from the solution path for the elastic net in Figure 8.6. The elastic net can be used in much the same way as the LASSO. Click the black triangle and drag the red line to the point where MoSPE = 250. See that only two variables have been zeroed out, whereas the LASSO had four or five variables zeroed out at this point. Drag the red line farther to the left, to the point where MoSPE = 100. See that the elastic net approach has one more nonzero variable, **tax**. This shows that the two methods can behave very differently.

With the Mass Housing data set, the LASSO gives you a nice group of predictors, whereas the elastic net does not. The elastic net keeps almost all the variables in until MoSPE drops below 50. The LASSO sometimes does not perform well when the variables are highly correlated. In the presence of highly correlated variables, the elastic net can perform better in the sense of producing more accurate predictions.

Figure 8.6: Elastic Net Regression for the Mass Housing Data Set

▲ ▼ **Normal Elastic Net with AICc Validation**

▲ Model Summary			▲ Estimation Details	
Response	mvalue		Elastic Net Alpha	0.99
Distribution	Normal		Number of Grid Points	150
Estimation Method	Elastic Net		Minimum Penalty Fraction	0
Validation Method	AICc		Grid Scale	Square Root
Mean Model Link	Identity			
Scale Model Link	Identity			

Measure	
Number of rows	506
Sum of Frequencies	506
-LogLikelihood	1498.9963
Number of Parameters	13
BIC	3078.9375
AICc	3024.7324
RSquare	0.7404458
RASE	4.680967
Lambda Penalty	0.2497177

▲ **Solution Path**

▲ **Parameter Estimates for Original Predictors**

Term	Estimate	Std Error	Wald ChiSquare	Prob > ChiSquare	Lower 95%	Upper 95%
Intercept	37.898686	7.6559022	24.505048	<.0001*	22.893394	52.903979
crim	-0.103387	0.028932	12.769386	0.0004*	-0.160092	-0.046681
zn	0.0435094	0.013264	10.760153	0.0010*	0.0175125	0.0695063
indus	0	0	0	1.0000	0	0
chas[0-1]	-2.713466	1.2825719	4.4759494	0.0344*	-5.22726	-0.199671
nox	-16.7568	3.2337368	26.851749	<.0001*	-23.0948	-10.41879
rooms	3.8412597	0.7772529	24.424328	<.0001*	2.317872	5.3646474
age	0	0	0	1.0000	0	0
distance	-1.435686	0.2138742	45.061127	<.0001*	-1.854872	-1.0165
radial	0.2737325	0.0584027	21.967851	<.0001*	0.1592654	0.3881996
tax	-0.010697	0.0027784	14.823362	0.0001*	-0.016143	-0.005252
pt	-0.936902	0.110584	71.77996	<.0001*	-1.153643	-0.720161
b	0.0091851	0.0026385	12.118469	0.0005*	0.0040137	0.0143564
lstat	-0.520856	0.0839363	38.506875	<.0001*	-0.68537	-0.356345

Normal Distribution Parameters	Estimate	Std Error	Wald ChiSquare	Prob > ChiSquare	Lower 95%	Upper 95%
Scale	4.680967	0.2812563	276.99154	<.0001*	4.1297147	5.2322193

▷ **Effect Tests**

As can be seen from the formulas for the various methods, a penalty is applied to the coefficients, and this penalty is the same for all the coefficients. That is, the penalty is applied to each coefficient with the same weight. There exists a more sophisticated approach that uses weighted penalties, and this is called *adaptive estimation*. To invoke this method, all that is necessary is to leave the box for **Adaptive** checked.

In this chapter, you have learned two new methods for variable selection, each of which has many options. Thus, you have the ability to produce many different groups of predictor variables. Which one should you use? You should use the group that produces the best predictions! But to see how to determine which group of predictors produces the best predictions, you will have to wait until Chapter 14.

Exercises

1. For the Mass Housing data set, MassHousing.jmp, explore the effects of using adaptive estimation, as well as various form of validation. Already you have used both the LASSO and the elastic net without adaptive estimation and with **AICc** validation. Now try it with **Adaptive Estimation** and **AICc** validation. Then try it without **Adaptive Estimation** and with **KFold** validation, and so on.

2. Do exercise 1 above, except use the Churn data set from Chapter 6 on Logistic Regression. Be sure to change the **Distribution** from **Normal** to **Binomial**.

3. Using the Sales Performance data set, Salesperfdata.xls, run a regression and stepwise regression. Then use LASSO and elastic net approaches. Compare the models. Which is best?

4. Using the Financial data set, Financial.jmp, run a regression and stepwise regression. Then use LASSO and elastic net approaches. Compare the models. Which is best?

5. Using the Freshman data set, Freshman1.jmp, run a regression and stepwise regression. Then use LASSO and elastic net approaches. Compare the models. Which is best?

Chapter 9: Cluster Analysis

Introduction

Cluster analysis is an exploratory multivariate technique designed to uncover natural groupings of the rows in a data set. If data are two-dimensional, it can be very easy to find groups that exist in the data; a scatterplot will suffice. When data have three, four, or more dimensions, how to find groups is not immediately obvious. As shown in Figure 9.1, cluster analysis is a technique where no dependence in any of the variables is required. The object of cluster analysis is to divide the data set into groups where the observations within each group are relatively homogeneous, yet the groups are unlike each other.

Example Applications

A standard clustering application in the credit card industry is to segment its customers into groups based on the number of purchases made, whether balances are paid off every month, where the purchases are made, and the like. In the cell-phone industry, clustering is used to identify customers who are likely to switch carriers. Grocery stores with loyalty-card programs

Figure 9.1: A Framework for Multivariate Analysis

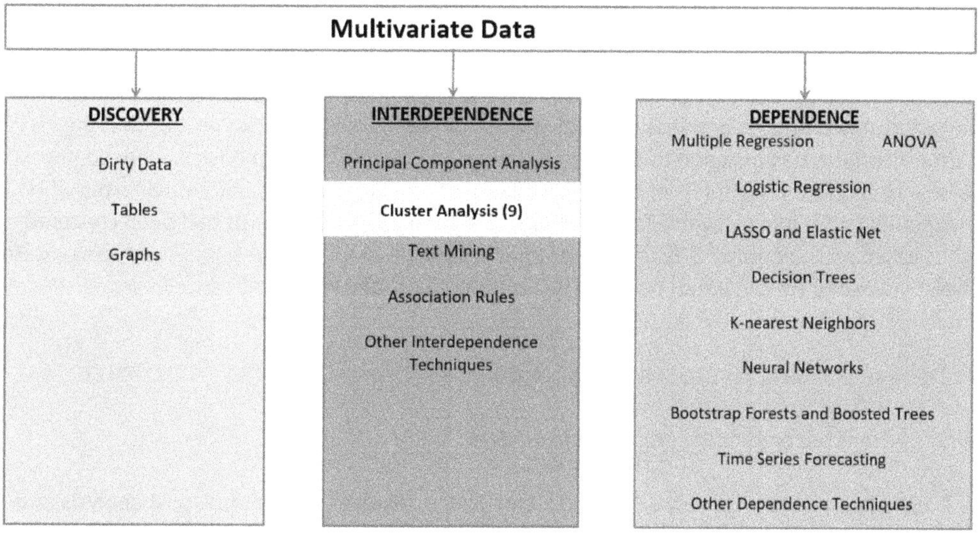

cluster their customers based on the number, frequency, and types of purchases. After customers are segmented, advertising can be targeted. For example, there is no point in sending coupons for baby food to all the store's customers, but sending the coupons to customers who have recently purchased diapers might be profitable. Indeed, coupons for premium baby food can be sent to customers who have recently purchased filet mignon, and coupons for discount baby food can be sent to customers who have recently purchased hamburger.

An Example from the Credit Card Industry

A cluster analysis of 1,000 credit card customers from a commercial bank in Shanghai identified three clusters (market segments). The analysis described them as follows (Ying and Yuanuan, 2010):

1. First Class: married, 30 to 45 years old, above average salaries with long credit histories and good credit records.
2. Second Class: single, younger than 30 years old, fashionable, no savings and good credit records, with a tendency to carry credit card balances over to the next month.
3. Third Class: single or married, 30-45, average to below-average incomes with good credit records.

Each cluster was then analyzed in terms of contribution to the company's profitability and associated risk of default. Then an appropriate marketing strategy was designed for each group.

The book *Scoring Points* by Humby, Hunt, and Phillips (2007) tells the story of how the company Tesco used clustering and other data mining techniques to rise to prominence in the British grocery industry. After much analysis, Tesco determined that its customers could be grouped into 14 clusters. For example, one cluster always purchased the cheapest commodity in any category; Tesco named them "shoppers on a budget." Another cluster contained customers with high incomes but little free time, and they purchased high-end, ready-to-eat food.

Thirteen of the groups had interpretable clusters, but the buying patterns of the 14th group, which purchased large amounts of microwavable food, didn't make sense initially. After much investigation, it was determined that this 14th group actually consisted of two groups that the clustering algorithm had assigned to a single cluster: young people in group houses who did not know how to cook (so bought lots of microwavable food) and families with traditional tastes who just happened to like microwavable food. The two otherwise disparate groups had been clustered together based on their propensity to purchase microwavable food. But the single-purchase pattern had been motivated by the unmet needs of two different sets of customers.

The Need to Understand Statistics and the Business Problem

Two morals from the credit card example are evident:

1. Clustering is not a purely data-driven exercise. It requires careful statistical analysis and interpretation by an industry business expert to produce good clusters.

2. Many iterations might be needed to achieve the goal of producing good clusters, and some of these iterations might require field testing.

In this chapter, you will learn two important clustering algorithms: hierarchical clustering and *k*-means clustering. Just as clustering is not purely data driven; it is also not purely a statistical exercise. A good use of the method requires knowledge not only of statistics, but also the characteristics of the business problem and the industry.

Hierarchical Clustering

This method builds a tree by successively merging similar points or groups of points.

Understand the Dendrogram

The specific form of hierarchical clustering used in JMP is called an *agglomerative algorithm*. At the start of the algorithm, each observation is considered as its own cluster. The distance between each cluster and all other clusters is computed, and the nearest clusters are merged. If there are *n* observations, this process is repeated *n* − 1 times until there is only one large cluster. Visually, this process is represented by a tree-like figure called a *dendrogram*.

Inspecting the dendrogram enables the user to make a judicious choice about the number of clusters to use. Sometimes an analyst wants to perform *k*-means clustering—which requires that the number of clusters be specified. But the analyst might have no idea of how many clusters are in the data. Perhaps the analyst wants to name the clusters based on a *k*-means clustering. In such a situation, one remedy is to perform hierarchical clustering first in order to determine the number of clusters. Then *k*-means clustering is performed.

Understand the Methods for Calculating Distance between Clusters

Except at the very first step when each observation is its own cluster, clusters are not individual observations (subjects or customers), but collections of observations (subjects or customers). There are many ways to calculate the distance between two clusters. Figure 9.2 shows four methods of measuring the distance between two clusters. Another method, which is not amenable to graphical depiction, is Ward's method, which is based on minimizing the information loss that occurs when two clusters are joined.

The various methods of measuring distance tend to produce different types of clusters. Average linkage is biased toward producing clusters with the same variance. Single linkage imposes no constraint on the shape of clusters, and makes it easy to combine two clumps of observations that other methods might leave separate. Hence, single linkage has a tendency toward what is called "chaining" and can produce long and irregularly shaped clusters. Complete linkage is biased toward producing clusters with similar diameters. The centroid method is more robust to

Figure 9.2: Ways to Measure Distance between Two Clusters

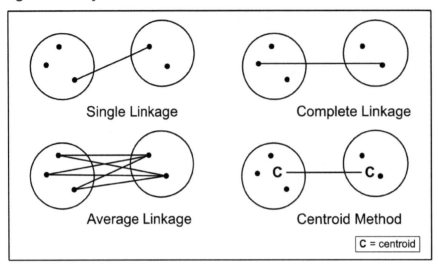

outliers than other methods, but Ward's method is biased toward producing clusters with the same number of observations.

Figure 9.3 shows how single linkage can lead to combining clusters that produce long strings, but complete linkage can keep them separate. The horizontal lines indicate the distance computed by each method. By the single linkage method, the left and right groups are very close together and, hence, are combined into a single cluster. In contrast, by the complete linkage method, the two groups are far apart and are kept as separate clusters.

Perform Hierarchical Clustering with Complete Linkage

To get a feeling for how hierarchical clustering works, consider the toy data set in Table 9.1 and in the file Toy-cluster.jmp.

Figure 9.3: The Different Effects of Single and Complete Linkage

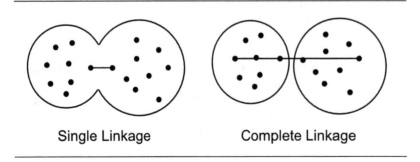

To perform hierarchical clustering with complete linkage on the Toy-cluster.jmp data table, complete the following steps:

1. Open Toy-cluster.jmp in JMP.
2. Select **Analyze** ▶ **Clustering** ▶ **Hierarchical Cluster**.
3. From the Clustering dialog box, select both **X** and **Y**. Click **Y, Columns**.
4. Select **Label** and click **Label**.
5. Because the units of measurement can affect the results, make sure that **Standardize By Columns** is selected.
6. Under Options, select **Ward** (Figure 9.4).
7. Click **OK**.

The clustering output includes a dendrogram similar to Figure 9.5.

Examine the Results

Now complete the following steps:

1. Click the **Hierarchical Clustering** red triangle and click **Color Clusters** and **Mark Clusters**.
2. Click the drop-down menu to the left of **Clustering History.**
3. Notice the two diamonds, one at the top and one at the bottom of the dendrogram. Click one of them, and the number 2 should appear. The 2 is the current number of clusters, and you can see how the observations are broken out.
4. Click one of the diamonds again and drag it all the way to the left where you have each observation, alone, in its individual cluster.
5. Now arrange the JMP windows so that you can see both the data table and the dendrogram. Slowly drag the diamond to the right and watch how the clusters change, as well as the corresponding colors and symbols.

Table 9.1: Toy Data Set for Illustrating Hierarchical Clustering

X	Y	Label
1	1	A
1	0	B
2	2	C
3	2	D
4	3	E
5	4	F
6	5	G
6	6	H
2	5	I
3	4	J

Figure 9.4: The Clustering Dialog Box

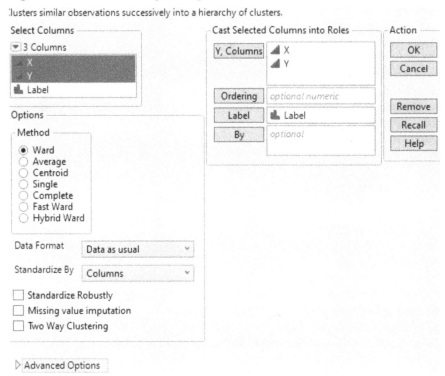

Looking at the scatterplot in Figure 9.6, you see that the clusters are numbered in the order in which they were created. Click the arrow to the left of **Clustering History**. When you move the diamond from left to right, the dendrogram and the clustering history can be read as follows:

1. H and G are paired to form a cluster.
2. A and B are paired to form a cluster.
3. C and D are paired to form a cluster.
4. E and F are paired to form a cluster.
5. I and J are paired to form a cluster.
6. The AB and CD clusters are joined.
7. The EF and IJ clusters are combined.
8. HG is added to the EFIJ cluster.
9. The ABCD and EFIJGH clusters are combined.

The clustering process is more difficult to imagine in higher dimensions, but the idea is the same.

Consider a Scree Plot to Discern the Best Number of Clusters

The fundamental question when you are applying any clustering technique—and hierarchical clustering is no exception—is "What is the best number of clusters?" There is no target variable

Figure 9.5: Dendrogram of the Toy Data Set

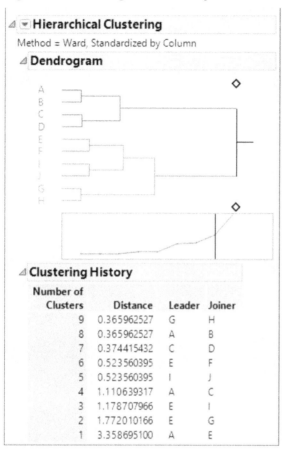

and no a priori knowledge to tell you which customer belongs to which group. So there is no gold standard by which you can determine whether any particular classification of observations into groups is successful.

Sometimes it is enough simply to recognize that a particular classification has produced groups that are interesting or useful in some sense or another. If there are no such compelling anecdotal justifications, one common method is to use the scree plot beneath the dendrogram to gain some insight into what the number of clusters might be. The ordinate (Y axis) is the distance that was bridged in order to join the clusters. A natural break in this distance produces a change in the slope of the line (often described as an "elbow") that suggests an appropriate number of clusters. At the middle of the box in Figure 9.5 is a small scree plot, a series of dots connected by lines. Each dot represents the level of clustering at each step, where the number of clusters decreases from left to right. Dragging the diamond in the dendrogram moves the vertical line in the scree plot so that the optimal number of clusters can be easily identified. The elbow appears to be around 2 or 3 clusters, so 2 or 3 clusters might be appropriate for these data.

Figure 9.6: Scatterplot of the Toy Data Set

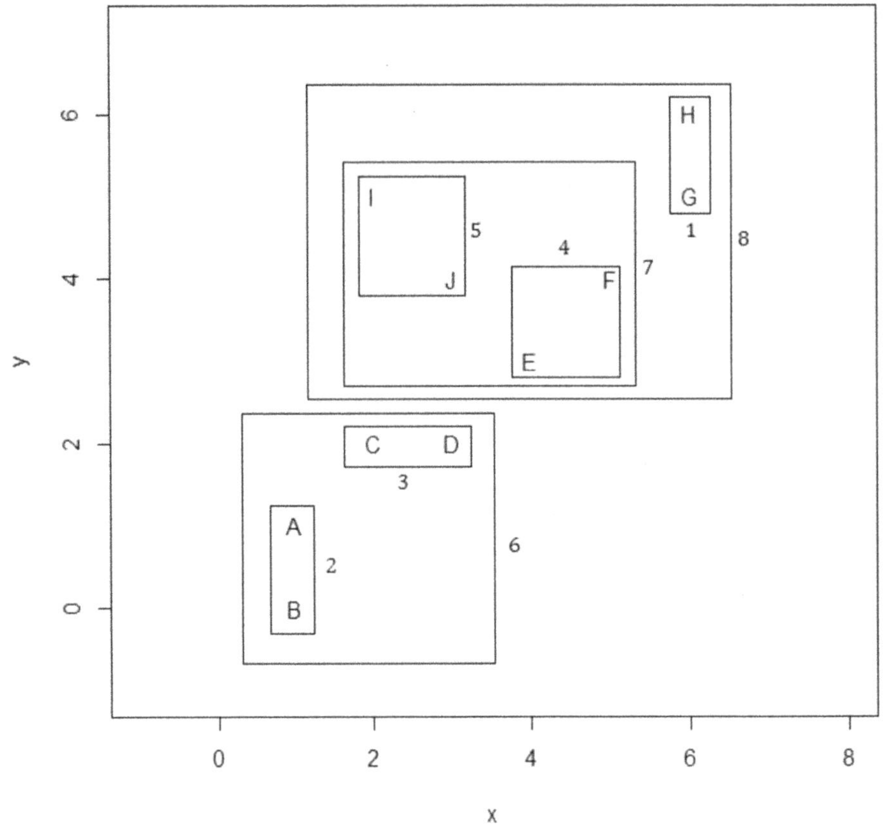

Apply the Principles to a Small but Rich Data Set

Now apply these principles to a data set, Thompson's "1975 Public Utility Data Set" (Johnson and Wichern, 2002). The data set is small enough that all the observations can be comprehended, and rich enough that it provides useful results. It is a favorite for exhibiting clustering methods.

Table 9.2 shows the Public Utility Data found in PublicUtilities.jmp, which has eight numeric variables that will be used for clustering: coverage, the fixed-charge coverage ratio; return, the rate of return on capital; cost, cost per kilowatt hour; load, the annual load factor; peak, the peak kilowatt hour growth; sales, in kilowatt hours per year; nuclear, the percent of power generation by nuclear plants; and fuel, the total fuel costs. "Company" is a label for each observation; it indicates the company name.

To perform hierarchical clustering on the Public Utility Data Set:

1. Open PublicUtilities.jmp in JMP.

2. Select **Analyze ▶ Clustering ▶ Hierarchical Cluster**.
3. From the Clustering dialog box, select **Coverage**, **Return**, **Cost**, **Load**, **Peak**, **Sales**, **Nuclear**, and **Fuel.** Click **Y, Columns**.
4. Select **Company**. Click **Label**.
5. Make sure that **Standardize By Columns** is selected and under Options, Ward is selected.
6. Click **OK**.
7. Click the **Hierarchical Clustering** red triangle and click **Color Clusters** and **Mark Clusters**.

The results are shown in Figure 9.7. The vertical line in the box goes through the third (from the right) x, which indicates that three clusters might be a good choice. The first cluster is Arizona Public through Consolidated Edison (14 firms). The second cluster is Idaho, Puget Sound, and Nevada (three firms), and the third cluster is Hawaiian through San Diego (five firms).

Move the vertical line and look at the different clusters. It appears that clusters of size 3, 4, 5, or 6 would be "best." For now, assume that the Ward's method with five clusters suffices. Move the vertical line so that it produces five clusters. Now produce a report or profile of this "5-cluster solution." (In practice, you might well produce similar reports for the 3-, 4-, and 6-cluster solutions for review by a subject-matter expert who could assist you in determining the appropriate number of clusters.)

To create a column in the worksheet that indicates each firm's cluster, click the red triangle and click **Save Clusters**. To help you interpret the clusters, you will produce a table of means for each cluster:

1. In the Data Table, select **Tables ▶ Summary**.
2. Select **Coverage, Return, Cost, Load, Peak, Sales, Nuclear,** and **Fuel**.
3. Click the **Statistics** box, and select **Mean**.
4. Select the variable **Cluster**, and click **Group**.
5. Click **OK**.
6. Because the output contains far too many decimal places, select all the columns. Then select **Cols ▶ Column Info**. Under **Format**, select **Fixed Dec**, and then change **Dec** from 0 to 2 for each variable.
7. Click **OK**.

The result is shown in Figure 9.8. Or click the **Hierarchical Clustering** red triangle and click **Cluster Summary** and you will get a similar table.

To understand a data set via clustering, it can be useful to try to identify the clusters by looking at summary statistics. In the present case, you can readily identify all the clusters: Cluster 1 is highest return; Cluster 2 is highest nuclear; Cluster 3 is the singleton; Cluster 4 is highest cost; and Cluster 5 is highest load. Here you have been able to characterize each cluster by appealing to a single variable. But often it will be necessary to use two or more variables to characterize a cluster.

You should also recognize that you have clustered based on standardized variables and identified them by using the original variables. Sometimes it might be necessary to refer to the summary statistics of the standardized variables to be able to identify the clusters.

Table 9.2: Thompson's 1975 Public Utility Data Set

Coverage	Return	Cost	Load	Peak	Sales ($)	Nuclear	Fuel	Company
1.06	9.20	151	54.4	1.6	9,077	0.0	0.630	Arizona Public
0.89	10.30	202	57.9	2.2	5,088	25.3	1.555	Boston Edison
1.43	15.40	113	53.0	3.4	9,212	0.0	1.058	Central Louisiana
1.02	11.20	168	56.0	0.3	6,423	34.3	0.700	Commonwealth Edison
1.49	8.80	192	51.2	1.0	3,300	15.6	2.044	Consolidated Edison
1.32	13.50	111	60.0	−2.2	11,127	22.5	1.241	Florida Power & Light
1.22	12.20	175	67.6	2.2	7,642	0.0	1.652	Hawaiian Electric
1.10	9.20	245	57.0	3.3	13,082	0.0	0.309	Idaho Power
1.34	13.00	168	60.4	7.2	8,406	0.0	0.862	Kentucky Utilities
1.12	12.40	197	53.0	2.7	6,455	39.2	0.623	Madison Gas
0.75	7.50	173	51.5	6.5	17,441	0.0	0.768	Nevada Power
1.13	10.90	178	62.0	3.7	6,154	0.0	1.897	New England Electric
1.15	12.70	199	53.7	6.4	7,179	50.2	0.527	Northern States Power
1.09	12.00	96	49.8	1.4	9,673	0.0	0.588	Oklahoma Gas
0.96	7.60	164	62.2	−0.1	6,468	0.9	1.400	Pacific Gas
1.16	9.90	252	56.0	9.2	15,991	0.0	0.620	Puget Sound Power
0.76	6.40	136	61.9	9.0	5,714	8.3	1.920	San Diego Gas
1.05	12.60	150	56.7	2.7	10,140	0.0	1.108	The Southern Co.
1.16	11.70	104	54.0	2.1	13,507	0.0	0.636	Texas Utilities
1.20	11.80	148	59.9	3.5	7,287	41.1	0.702	Wisconsin Electric
1.04	8.60	204	61.0	3.5	6,650	0.0	2.116	United Illuminating
1.07	9.30	174	54.3	5.9	10,093	26.6	1.306	Virginia Electric

Figure 9.7: Hierarchical Clustering of the Public Utility Data Set

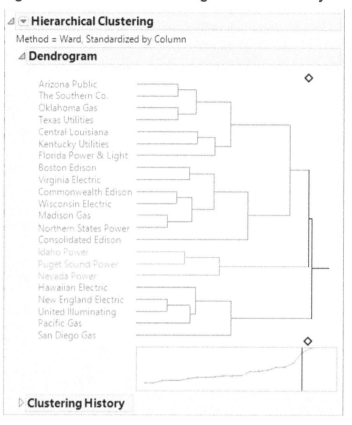

Consider Adding Clusters in a Regression Analysis

Using a well-chosen cluster variable in regression can prove to be very useful. Consider running a regression on the Public Utilities data by using Sales as a dependent variable and Coverage, Return, Cost, Load, Peak, Nuclear, and Fuel as independent variables. The model had an R^2 of 59.3%. Not too high, and the adjusted R^2 is only 38.9%.

Figure 9.8: Cluster Means for Five Clusters

Cluster	N Rows	Mean(Coverage)	Mean(Return)	Mean(Cost)	Mean(Load)	Mean(Peak)	Mean(Sales)	Mean(Nuclear)	Mean(Fuel)
1	7.00	1.21	12.49	127.57	55.47	1.71	10163.14	3.21	0.87
2	6.00	1.08	11.28	181.33	55.80	3.50	7087.50	36.12	0.90
3	1.00	1.49	8.80	192.00	51.20	1.00	3300.00	15.60	2.04
4	3.00	1.00	8.87	223.33	54.83	6.33	15504.67	0.00	0.57
5	5.00	1.02	9.14	171.40	62.94	3.66	6525.60	1.84	1.80

What if you add the nominal variable Clusters to the regression model? The model improves significantly with an R^2 of 88.3%, and the adjusted R^2 is only 75.5%. But now you have 12 parameters to estimate (8 numeric variables and 4 dummy variables) and only 22 observations. This high R^2 is perhaps a case of overfitting. Overfitting occurs when the analyst includes too many parameters and therefore fits the random noise rather than the underlying structure. This concept is discussed in more detail in Chapter 14. Nevertheless, if you run the multiple regression with only the Cluster variable (thus, 4 dummy variables), then the R^2 is 83.6%, and the adjusted R^2 is 79.8%. You have dropped the eight numeric variables from the regression, and the R^2 dropped only from 88.3% to 83.6%. This result strongly suggests that the clusters contain much of the information that is in the eight numeric variables.

k-Means Clustering

Form clusters based on an initial guess of how many clusters there are, and then refine the guess.

Understand the Benefits and Drawbacks of the Method

Although hierarchical clustering allows examination of several clustering solutions in one dendrogram, it has two significant drawbacks when applied to large data sets. First, it is computationally intensive and can have long run times. Second, the dendrogram can become large and unintelligible when the number of observations is even moderately large.

One of the oldest and most popular methods for finding groups in multivariate data is the *k*-means clustering algorithm, which has five steps:

1. Choose *k*, the number of clusters.
2. Guess at the multivariate means of the *k* clusters. If there are ten variables, each cluster will be associated with ten means, one for each variable. Very often this collection of means is called a centroid. JMP will perform this guessing with the assistance of a random number generator, which is a mathematical formula that produces random numbers on demand. It is much easier for the computer to create these guesses than for the user to create them by hand.
3. For each observation, calculate the distance from that observation to each of the *k* centroids, and assign that observation to the closest cluster (the closest centroid).
4. After all the observations have been assigned to one and only one cluster, calculate the new centroid for each cluster using the observations that have been assigned to that cluster. The cluster centroids "drift" toward areas of high density, where there are many observations.
5. If the new centroids are very different from the old centroids, the centroids have drifted. So return to Step 3. If the new centroids and the old centroids are the same so that additional iterations will not change the centroids, then the algorithm terminates.

The effect of the *k*-means algorithm is to minimize the differences within each group, and to maximize the differences between groups, as shown in Figure 9.9.

Figure 9.9: The Function of *k*-Means Clustering

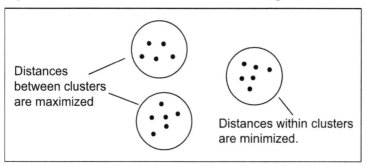

A primary advantage of the *k*-means clustering algorithm is that it has low complexity. That is, its execution time is proportional to the number of observations, so it can be applied to large data sets. By contrast, when you use an algorithm with high complexity, doubling the size of the data set can increase the execution time by a factor of four or more. Hence, algorithms with high complexity are not desirable for use with large data sets.

A primary disadvantage of the algorithm is that its result, the final determination of which observations belong to which cluster, can depend on the initial guess (as in Step 1 above). As a consequence, if group stability is an important consideration for the problem at hand, it is sometimes advisable to run the algorithm more than once to make sure that the groups do not change appreciably from one run to another. All academics advise multiple runs with different starting centroids, but practitioners rarely do this, though they should. However, they have to be aware of two things: (1) comparing solutions from different starting points can be tedious, and the analyst often ends up observing, "this observation was put in cluster 1 on the old output, and now it is put in cluster 5 on the new output—I think"; and (2) doing this will add to the project time.

If the data were completely dependent, there would be a single cluster. If the data were completely independent, there would be as many clusters as there are observations. Almost always the true number of clusters is somewhere between these extremes, and the analyst's job is to find that number. If there is, in truth, only one cluster, but *k* is chosen to be five, the algorithm will impose five clusters on a data set that consists of only a single cluster, and the results will be unstable. Every time the algorithm is run, a completely different set of clusters will be found. Similarly, if there are really 20 clusters and *k* is chosen for the number of clusters, the results will again be unstable.

Choose *k* and Determine the Clusters

After the algorithm has successfully terminated, each observation is assigned to a cluster, each cluster has a centroid, and each observation has a distance from the centroid. The distance of each observation from the centroid of its cluster is calculated. Square them, and sum them all to obtain the sum of squared errors (SSE) for that cluster solution. When this quantity is computed for various numbers of clusters, it is traditional to plot the SSE and to choose the number of clusters that minimizes the sum of squared errors. For example, in Figure 9.10, the value of *k* that minimizes the sum of squared errors is four.

There is no automated procedure for producing a graph such as that in Figure 9.10. Every time the clustering algorithm is run, you have to write down the sum of squared errors, perhaps entering both the sum of squared errors and the number of clusters in appropriately labeled columns in a JMP Data Table. Complete the following steps:

1. Select **Graph ▶ Overlay Plot**.
2. Select the sum of squared errors as **Y** and the number of clusters as **X**.
3. Click **OK** to produce a plot of points.
4. To draw a line through the points, in the overlay plot window, click the red arrow and select **Connect Thru Missing**.

As shown in Figure 9.11, it is not always the case that the SSE will take on a U-shape for increasing number of clusters. Sometimes the SSE decreases continuously as the number of clusters increases. In such a situation, choosing the number of clusters that minimizes the SSE would produce an inordinately large number of clusters. In this situation, the graph of SSE versus the number of clusters is called a *scree plot*.

Often there is a natural break where the distance jumps up suddenly. These breaks suggest natural cutting points to determine the number of clusters. The "best" number of clusters is typically chosen at or near this "elbow" of the curve. The elbow suggests which clusters should be profiled and reviewed with the subject-matter expert. Based on Figure 9.11, the number of clusters would probably be 3, but 2 or 4 would also be possibilities. Choosing the "best" number of clusters is as much an art form as it is a science. Sometimes a particular number of clusters produces a particularly interesting or useful result. In such a case, SSE can probably be ignored.

Figure 9.10: U-Shaped Sum of Squared Errors Plot for Choosing the Number of Clusters

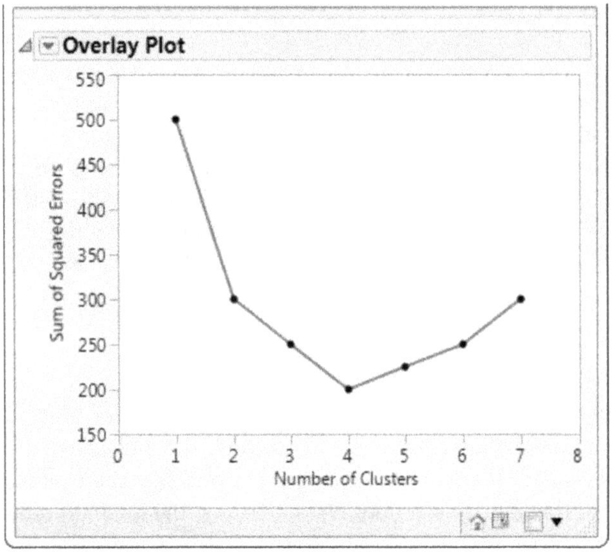

Figure 9.11: A Scree Plot for Choosing the Number of Clusters

The difference between two and three or three and four clusters (indeed between any pair of partitions of the data set) is not always statistically obvious. The fact is that it can be difficult to decide on the number of clusters. Yet this is a very important decision because the proper number of clusters can be of great business importance. In Figure 9.12 it is difficult to say

Figure 9.12: Determining How Many Clusters Are in the Data Set

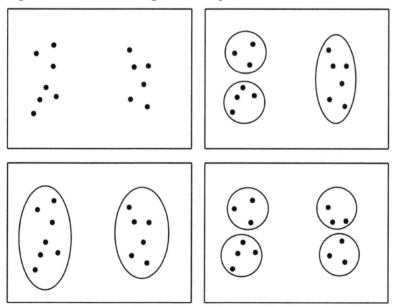

whether the data set has two, three, or four clusters. A pragmatic approach is necessary in this situation: choose the number of clusters that produces useful clusters.

Perform *k*-Means Clustering

Once *k* has been chosen and clusters have been determined, the centroid (multivariate) means of the clusters can be used to give descriptions (and descriptive names) to each cluster or segment. For example, a credit card company might observe that in one cluster, the customers charge large balances and pay them off every month. This cluster might be called "transactors." Another cluster of customers might occasionally make a large purchase and then pay the balance down over time; they might be "convenience users." A third cluster would be customers who always have a large balance and roll it over every month, incurring high interest fees; they could be called "revolvers" since they use the credit card as a form of revolving debt. Of course, there would be other clusters, and perhaps not all of them would have identifiable characteristics that lead to names. The idea, however, should be clear.

To perform *k*-means clustering on the PublicUtilities data set:

1. Open PublicUtilities.jmp in JMP and select **Analyze ▶ Clustering ▶ K Means Cluster.**
2. From the Clustering dialog box, select **Coverage, Return, Cost, Load, Peak, Sales, Nuclear,** and **Fuel** (click **Coverage**, hold down the **Shift** key, and click **Fuel**), and click **Y, Columns**.
3. The *k*-means algorithm is sensitive to the units in which the variables are measured. If you have three variables (length, weight, and value), you will get one set of clusters if the units of measurement are inches, pounds, and dollars, and (probably) a radically different set of clusters if the units of measurement are feet, ounces, and cents. To avoid this problem, make sure the box for **Columns Scaled Individually** is checked.
4. Click **OK**.

A new pop-up box similar to Figure 9.13 appears. The Method menu indicates *k*-Means Clustering, and the number of clusters is 3. But you will change the number of clusters shortly.

Normal Mixtures, Robust Normal Mixtures, and Self Organizing Map are other clustering methods about which you can read in the online user guide and with which you might wish to experiment. To access this document, from the JMP Home Window, select **Help ▶ Books ▶ Multivariate Methods,** and consult the appropriate chapters.

Change the Number of Clusters

Suppose you wanted more than three clusters. Then you would change the number of clusters to 5. If interested, consult the online Help files to learn about "Single Step," "Use within-cluster std deviations," and "Shift distances using sampling rates." But do not check these boxes until you have read about these methods. The JMP input box should look like Figure 9.13. Click **Go** to perform *k*-means clustering. The output is shown in Figure 9.14.

Figure 9.13: *k*-**Means Dialog Box**

Iterative Clustering

Columns Scaled Individually

Control Panel

Method | K Means Cluster ˅

Number of Clusters | Range of Clusters (Optional)

5 | .

Go

☐ Single Step

☐ Use within-cluster std deviations

☐ Shift distances using sampling rates

Under **Cluster Summary** in Figure 9.14, you can see that clusters 2 and 5 have a single observation; perhaps five clusters with the *k*-means is too coarse of a breakdown. So rerun the *k*-means analysis with three clusters:

Figure 9.14: Output of Means Clustering with Five Clusters

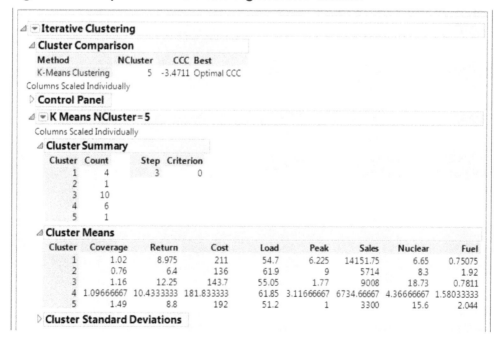

Iterative Clustering

Cluster Comparison

Method	NCluster	CCC	Best
K-Means Clustering	5	-3.4711	Optimal CCC

Columns Scaled Individually

▷ **Control Panel**

K Means NCluster=5

Columns Scaled Individually

Cluster Summary

Cluster	Count	Step	Criterion
1	4	3	0
2	1		
3	10		
4	6		
5	1		

Cluster Means

Cluster	Coverage	Return	Cost	Load	Peak	Sales	Nuclear	Fuel
1	1.02	8.975	211	54.7	6.225	14151.75	6.65	0.75075
2	0.76	6.4	136	61.9	9	5714	8.3	1.92
3	1.16	12.25	143.7	55.05	1.77	9008	18.73	0.7811
4	1.09666667	10.4333333	181.833333	61.85	3.11666667	6734.66667	4.36666667	1.58033333
5	1.49	8.8	192	51.2	1	3300	15.6	2.044

▷ **Cluster Standard Deviations**

1. In the **Iterative Clustering** output, click the drop-down menu next to **Control Panel**.
2. Change **Number of Clusters** to **3**.
3. Click **Go**. Right below the 5-Cluster output will be the 3-Cluster output as shown in Figure 9.15.

Create a Profile of the Clusters with Parallel Coordinate Plots (Optional)

1. Click on the **K Means NCluster=3** red triangle and click **Parallel Coord Plots**.
2. Position your pointer over one of the X-axis labels plots, right-click, and click **Axis Setting...**

Figure 9.15: Output of *k*-Means Clustering with Three Clusters

3. Under the **Tick/Bin Increment** box and in the **Increment** input box, change the 2 to 1. Click **OK**.

This command sequence creates plots of the variable means within each cluster, as shown in Figure 9.16.

Parallel coordinate plots can be helpful in the interpretation of the clusters. This is a fast way to create a "profile" of the clusters and can be of great use to a subject-matter expert. In Figure 9.1, you can see that Cluster 1 is the "high nuclear" group. This can be confirmed by referring to the results in Figure 9.15. For an excellent and brief introduction to parallel coordinate plots, see Few (2006).

Under **Cluster Summary**, the program identifies three clusters with five, six, and eleven companies in each. Examining the numbers under **Cluster Means**, you can identify Cluster 1 as the "high nuclear" cluster and Cluster 3 as the "high sales" cluster. Nothing really stands out about Cluster 2, but perhaps it might not be exaggerating to refer to it as the "high load" or "high fuel" cluster. Because you are going to try other values of *k* before leaving this screen, you should calculate the SSE for this partition of the data set.

1. Click the **K Means NCluster = 3** red triangle and click **Save Clusters**. Two new columns will appear on the right of the Data Table. **Cluster** indicates the cluster to which each company

Figure 9.16: Parallel Coordinate Plots for *k* = 3 Clusters

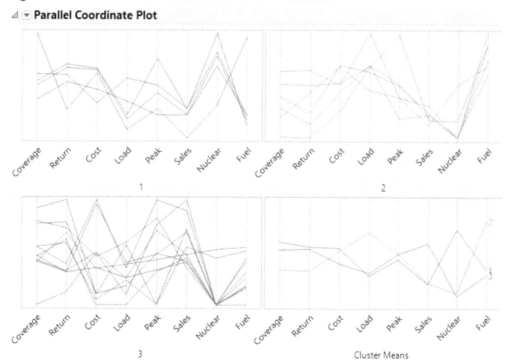

Figure 9.17: Formula Editor for Creating Distance Squared

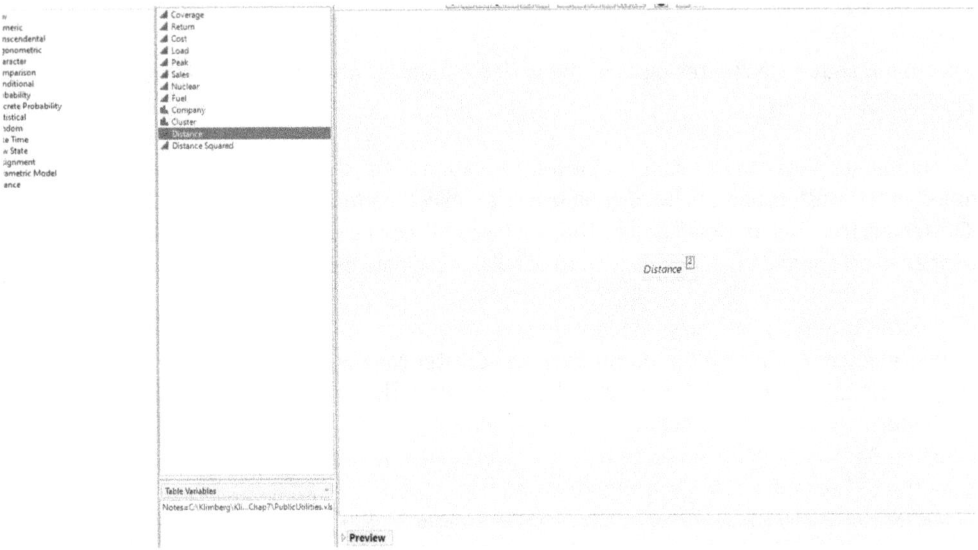

has been assigned. **Distance** gives the distance of each observation from the centroid of its cluster. You need to square all these distances and sum them to calculate the SSE.

2. From the top menu select **Cols ▶ New Columns**. For **Column Name**, enter **Distance Squared**. Go to the bottom of the dialog box, click **Column Properties** and select **Formula**.

3. The Formula Editor appears, as shown in Figure 9.17, and from the list of Columns select the variable **Distance** and double-click.

4. Across the top of the Formula editor dialog box are several operator buttons. Click the operator button x^y. The operator defaults to squaring the variable (that is, the number **2**). See Figure 9.17.

5. Click **OK**. The original **New Column** dialog box is still present, so click **OK** in it. The variable Distance Squared has been created, and you now need its sum.

6. On the Data Table menu, select **Analyze ▶ Distribution**. Click **Distance Squared** and then click **Y, Columns**. Click **OK.**

7. In the **Distribution** window, click the **Summary Statistics** red triangle (which is beneath Quantiles, which, in turn, is beneath the histogram/boxplot). Click **Customize Summary Statistics** and check the box for **Sum**. Click **OK**. Sum is now displayed along with the other summary statistics and is seen to be 814.5612. (Alternatively, on the top menu, select **Tables ▶ Summary**. The Summary dialog box appears. From the list of Select Columns, click **Distance Squared**. Click the drop-down menu next to Statistics and click **Sum**. Click **OK**.)

Perform Iterative Clustering

With the same number of clusters, the members of clusters will most likely differ from the Hierarchical Clustering and the *k*-means clustering. As a result, this procedure of producing the SSE using the *k*-means clustering should be performed for *k* = 4, 5, and 6.

This iterative process can be facilitated by clicking the right arrow next to the **Control Panel** in the **Iterative Clustering** output and entering 4 in the **Number of Clusters field** and 6 in the **Range of clusters (Optional)** field. When both of these boxes have numbers, the former is really the lower limit of the number of clusters desired, and the latter is really the upper limit of the number of clusters desired. Note that if you were planning to run iterative clustering using k-means clustering when you initially have the **Control Panel** dialog box, you could send the range of clusters there.

Scroll to the top of the **Iterative Clustering** output under **Cluster Comparison.** The CCC for the different cluster sizes are as follows:

- *k* = 3 is -2.2661
- *k* = 4 is -3.0663
- *k* = 5 is -3.4711
- *k* = 6 is -1.7213.

The cubic clustering criterion (CCC) can be used to estimate the number of clusters using k-means clustering. The CCC values should be plotted against the number of clusters. It is recommended to vary the number of clusters from 1 to about 1/10 the number of observations. If the average number of observations per cluster is less than 10, the CCC values might not be well-behaved (SAS 1983). A guideline of good range of CCC values are:

Table 9.3: Five Clusters and Their Members for the Public Utility Data

Cluster Designation	Number of Members	Member Names
1	4	Idaho Power, Nevada Power, Puget Sound Electric, Virginia Electric
2	1	San Diego Gas
3	8	Arizona Public, Central Louisiana, Commonwealth Edison, Madison Gas, Northern States Power, Oklahoma Gas, The Southern Co., Texas Utilities
4	8	Boston Edison, Florida Power & Light, Hawaiian Electric, Kentucky Utilities, New England Electric, Pacific Gas, Wisconsin Electric, United Illuminating
5	1	Consolidated Edison

Figure 9.18: Cluster Means for Five Clusters Using *k*-Means

Cluster	Coverage	Return	Cost	Load	Peak	Sales	Nuclear	Fuel
1	1.02	8.975	211	54.7	6.225	14151.75	6.65	0.75075
2	0.76	6.4	136	61.9	9	5714	8.3	1.92
3	1.16	12.25	143.7	55.05	1.77	9008	18.73	0.7811
4	1.09666667	10.4333333	181.833333	61.85	3.11666667	6734.66667	4.36666667	1.58033333
5	1.49	8.8	192	51.2	1	3300	15.6	2.044

⊿ **Cluster Means**

- "Peaks in the plot of the cubic clustering criterion with values greater than 2 or 3 indicate good clusters."
- "Peaks with values between 0 and 2 indicate possible clusters."
- "Large negative values of the CCC can indicate outliers" (SAS 1983).

In this case, JMP suggests the number of clusters should be 6 based on the CCC values.

While the SSE for the different cluster sizes are as follows:

- k = 3 is 814.56.
- k = 4 is 656.10.
- k = 5 is 402.86.
- k = 6 is 213.46.

You see that a plot of k by SSE declines at the same rate, dropping about 200 units for each one unit increase in k. To choose a proper value of k, you would hope to see an "elbow" in the plot. This problem is explored in the exercises at the end of the chapter. For now, let us pretend that k = 5 is the correct number of clusters.

Returning to the k-means with five clusters, as mentioned, you see two singletons, which can be considered outliers that belong in no cluster. The clusters are given in Table 9.3.

Since clusters 2 and 5 are singletons that might be considered outliers, you need try to interpret only Clusters 1, 3, and 4. The cluster means are given in Figure 9.18. Cluster 1 could be highest cost, and cluster 3 could be highest nuclear. Cluster 4 does not immediately stand out for any one variable, but might accurately be described as high (but not highest) load and high fuel.

As might be deduced from this simple example and examining it using hierarchical clustering and k-means clustering, if the data set is large with numerous variables, the prospect of searching for k is daunting. But that is the analyst's task: to find a good number for k.

Score New Observations

After you have performed a cluster analysis, one of your possible next tasks is to score new observations. In this case, *scoring* means assigning the new observation to existing clusters without rerunning the clustering algorithm.

Suppose another public utility named "Western Montana" is brought to your attention. It has the following data:

- Coverage = 1
- Return = 5
- Cost = 150
- Load = 65
- Peak = 5
- Sales = 6000
- Nuclear = 0
- Fuel = 1

You would like to know to which cluster it belongs. To score this new observation, complete the following steps:

1. Rerun *k*-means clustering with five clusters.
2. This time, instead of saving the clusters, save the cluster formula. From the **K Means NCluster=5** red triangle, select **Save Cluster Formula**.
3. Go to the Data Table, which has 22 rows, right-click in the 23rd row, and select **Add Rows**. For **How many rows to add**, enter **1**.
4. Click **OK**.

Enter the data for Western Montana in the appropriate cells in the Data Table. When you enter the last datum in **fuel** and then click in the next cell to enter the company name, a value will appear in the 23rd cell of the **Cluster Formula** column: 2. According to the formula created by the *k*-means clustering algorithm, the company Western Montana should be placed in the second cluster. You have scored this new observation.

k-Means Clustering versus Hierarchical Clustering

The final solution to the *k*-means algorithm can depend critically on the initial guess for the *k*-means. For this reason, it is recommended that *k*-means be run several times, and these several answers should be compared. Hopefully, a consistent pattern will emerge from the several solutions, and one of them can be chosen as representative of the many solutions. In contrast, for hierarchical clustering, the solution for *k* clusters depends on the solution for *k* + 1 clusters, and this solution will not change when the algorithm is run again on the same data set.

Usually, it is a good idea to run both algorithms and compare their outputs. Standard bases to choose between the methods are interpretability and usefulness. Does one method produce clusters that are more interesting or easier to interpret? Does the problem at hand lend itself to finding small groups with unusual patterns? Often one method will be preferable on these bases, and the choice is easy.

Exercises

1. Use hierarchical clustering on the Public Utilities data set. Be sure to use the company name as a label. Use all six methods (for example, Average, Centroid, Ward, Single, Complete, and Fast Ward), and run each with the data standardized. How many clusters does each algorithm produce?

2. Repeat exercise 1, this time with the data not standardized. How does this affect the results?

3. Use hierarchical clustering on the Freshmen1.jmp data set. How many clusters are there? Use this number to perform a *k*-means clustering. (Be sure to try several choices of *k* near the one that is indicated by hierarchical clustering.) Note that *k*-means will not permit ordinal data. Based on the means of the clusters for the final choice of *k*, try to name each of the clusters.

4. *Use k*-means clustering on the churn data set. Try to name the clusters.

5. Use usagesas.jmp data set. The data were whether or not an individual has used different statistical packages starting with the base package, and professional statistics to advanced statistics with the following variables: ts—time series (forecasting); present—presentation; permap—perception maps; chaid—a data mining techniques; map—maps; and neurnet—another data mining technique (neural nets). Jobarea is a code for what type of job the person has. Perform some clustering to see whether these individuals form any interesting groups.

6. Use the HousingPrices.jmp data set. A real estate company that manages properties around a ski resort in the United States wishes to improve its method for pricing homes. Sample data is obtained on a number of measures, including size of the home and property, location, age of the house, and a strength-of-market indicator.

   The data set contains information about 45 residential properties near a popular North American ski resort sold during a recent 12-month period. The data is a representative sample of the full set of properties sold during that time period. The variables in the data set are:

   Price: Selling price of the property (in $000)
   Beds: # of bedrooms in the house
   Baths: # of bathrooms in the house
   Square Feet: Size of the house in square feet
   Miles to Resort: Miles from the property to the downtown resort area
   Miles to Base: Miles from the property to the base of the ski resort's facing mountain

Acres: Lot size in number of acres
Cars: # of cars that will fit into the garage
Years Old: Age of the house at the time it was listed in years
DoM: # of days the house wan on the market before it was sold

The dependent variable is price. Do a cluster analysis. Evaluate the clusters and determine your best cluster size. Run a regression with all the variables plus dummy variables for cluster evaluate the model. If necessary, try to improve the model.

Chapter 10: Decision Trees

Introduction

The decision tree is one of the most widely used techniques for describing and organizing multivariate data. As shown in Figure 10.1, a decision tree is one of the dependence techniques in which the dependent variable can be either discrete (the usual case) or continuous.

Benefits and Drawbacks

A decision tree is usually considered to be a data mining technique as well as a dependence technique. One of its strengths is its ability to categorize data in ways that other methods cannot. For example, it can uncover nonlinear relationships that might be missed by techniques such as linear regression.

A decision tree is easy to understand and easy to explain, which is always important when an analyst has to communicate results to a nontechnical audience. Decision trees do not always

Figure 10.1: A Framework for Multivariate Analysis

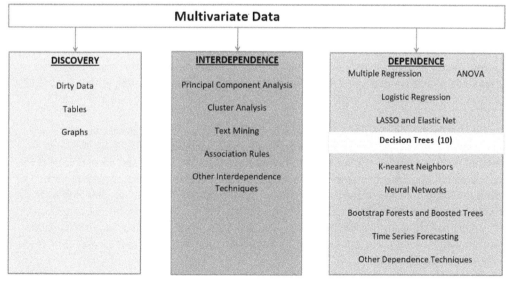

produce the best results, but they offer a reasonable compromise between models that perform well and models that can be simply explained. Decision trees are useful not only for modeling, but also for exploring a data set, especially when you have little idea of how to model the data.

The primary drawback of trees is that they are a high-variance procedure: growing trees on two similar data sets probably will not produce two similar trees. As an example of a low-variance procedure, consider that if you run the same regression model on two different (but similar) samples, you will likely get similar results: both regressions will have about the same coefficients. By contrast, if you run the same tree on two different (but similar) samples, you will likely get quite different trees.

The reason for the variance is that, in a tree, an error in any one node does not stay in that node. Instead, the error is propagated down the tree. Specifically, if two variables (for example, Variable A and Variable B) are close contenders for the first split in a decision tree, a small change in the data might affect which of those variables is chosen for the top split. Splitting on Variable A might well produce a markedly different tree than splitting on Variable B. There are methods such as *boosting* and *bagging* to combat this issue by growing multiple trees on the same data set and averaging them. But these methods are beyond the scope of this text. The interested reader should consult the text by Berk (2008).

Definitions and an Example

A *decision tree* is a hierarchical collection of rules that specify how a data set is to be broken up into smaller groups based on a target variable (a dependent *y* variable). If the target variable is categorical, then the decision tree is called a *classification tree*. If the target variable is continuous, then the decision tree is called a *regression tree*. In either case, the tree starts with a single root node. Here a decision is made to split the node based on some non-target variable, creating two (or more) new nodes or leaves. Each of these nodes can be similarly split into new nodes, if possible.

Suppose you have historical data on whether bank customers defaulted on small, unsecured personal loans, and you are interested in developing rules to help you decide whether a credit applicant is a good risk or a bad risk. You might build a decision tree as shown in Figure 10.2.

Your target variable, risk, is categorical (good or bad), so this is a *classification* tree. We first break income into two groups: high and low (for example, income above $75,000 and income below $75,000). Savings is also broken into two groups, high and low. Based on the historical data, persons with high incomes who can easily pay off the loan out of current income have low default rates and are categorized as good risks without regard to their savings. Persons with low incomes cannot pay off the loan out of current income. But they can pay it off out of savings if they have sufficient savings, which explains the rest of the tree. In each "good risk" leaf, the historical data indicate more persons paid back the loan than not. In each "bad risk" leaf, more persons defaulted than not.

Figure 10.2: Classifying Bank Customers as "Good" or "Bad" Risks for a Loan

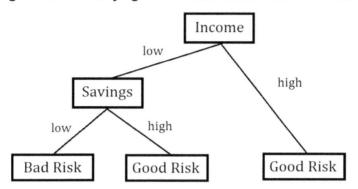

Theoretical Questions

Several questions come to mind. Why only binary splits? Why not split into three or more groups? As Hastie et al. (2009) explain, the reason is that multiway splits use up the data too quickly. Besides, multiway splits can always be accomplished by some number of binary splits. You might ask, "What are the cut-off levels for low and high income?" These might be determined by the analyst who enters the Income variable as categorical, or it might be determined by the computer program if the Income variable is entered as a continuous variable. You might also ask, "Why is *income* grouped first and then *savings?* Why not *savings* first and then *income?*" The tree-building algorithm determined that splitting first on Income produced "better groups" than splitting first on Savings. Most of the high-income customers did not default, whereas most of the low-income customers defaulted. However, further separating on the basis of savings revealed that most of the low-income customers with high savings did not default.

A common question is, "Can you just put a data set into a tree and expect good results?" The answer is a decided "no!" Thought must be given to which variables should be included. Theory and business knowledge must guide variable selection. For example, beware of including a variable that is highly correlated with the target variable. To see the reason for this warning, suppose the target variable (*y*) is whether a prospective customer purchases insurance. If the variable "premium paid" is included in the tree, it will soak up all the variance in the target variable, since only customers who actually do purchase insurance pay premiums.

There is also the question of whether an *x* variable should be transformed, and, if so, how. For example, should Income be entered as continuous, or should it be binned into a discrete variable? If it is to be binned, what should be the cutoffs for the bins? Still more questions remain. If you had many variables, which variables would be used to build the tree? When should you stop splitting nodes?

Classification Trees

The questions raised in the previous subsection are best answered by means of a simple example. A big problem on college campuses is "freshman retention." For a variety of reasons, many freshmen do not return for their sophomore year. If the causes for departures could be identified, then perhaps remedial programs could be instituted that might enable these students to complete their college education. Open the Freshmen1.jmp data set, which contains 100 observations on several variables that are thought to affect whether a freshman returns for the sophomore year. These variables are described in Table 10.1.

Begin Tree and Observe Results

Note that in the JMP data table, all the variables are correctly labeled as continuous or categorical, and whether they are *x* or *y* variables. Usually, the user has to make these assignments. JMP knows that **Return** is the target variable (see the small "y" in the blue circle to the right of **Return** in the columns window), which has 23 zeros and 77 ones. To begin building a decision tree, select **Analyze ▶ Predictive Modeling ▶ Partition**. Click **OK**. Figure 10.3 will appear.

Table 10.1: The Variables in the Freshmen1.jmp Data Set

Variable	Coding and Theoretical Reason for Including an x Variable
Return	=1 if the student returns for sophomore year; =0 otherwise.
Grade point average (GPA)	Students with a low freshman GPA fail out and do not return.
College	The specific college in which the students enroll might affect the decision to return; the engineering college is very demanding and might have a high failure rate.
Accommodations	Whether students live in a dorm or on campus might affect the decision to return. There is not enough dorm space, and some students might hate living off campus.
Part-time work hours	Students who have to work a lot might not enjoy college as much as other students.
Attendance at office hours	Students who never attend office hours might be academically weak, need more help, and are inclined to fail out; or they might be very strong and never need to attend office hours.
High school GPA	Students who were stronger academically in high school might be more inclined to return for sophomore year.
Miles from home	Students who live farther from home might be homesick and want to transfer to a school closer to home.

Figure 10.3: Partition Initial Output with Discrete Dependent Variable

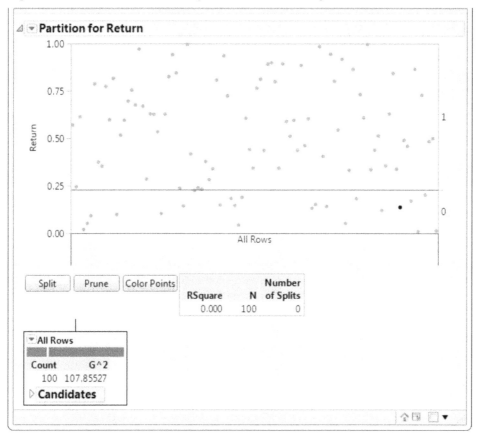

The data are represented in the graph at the top of the window (Figure 10.3). Above the horizontal line are 77 data points, and below it (or touching it) are 23 points, which correspond to the number of ones and zeros in the target variable. Points that represent observations are placed in the proper area above or below the line separating 1 (return) and 0 (not return). As the tree is built, this graph will be subdivided into smaller rectangles, but it can then be difficult to interpret. It is much easier to interpret the tree, so you will largely focus on the tree and not on the graph of the data.

Next, notice the box immediately under the graph, which shows information about how well the tree represents the data. Since the tree has yet to be constructed, the familiar RSquare statistic is zero. The number of observations in the data set, *N*, is 100. No splits have been made.

Next, observe the box in the lower left corner, which is the root node of the tree. You can see that there are 100 observations in the data set. The bar indicates how many zeros (red) and ones (blue) are in this node. The "G^2" statistic is displayed; this is the likelihood ratio goodness-of-fit test statistic, and it (like the LogWorth statistic, which is not shown yet) can be used to make splits. What drives the creation of a tree is a criterion function—something to be maximized or minimized. In the case of a classification tree, the criterion function by which nodes are split is the LogWorth statistic, which is to be maximized. The Chi-square test of Independence can be applied to the case of multi-way splits and multi-outcome targets. The *p*-value of the test will indicate the likelihood of a significant relationship between the observed value and the target proportions for each branch. These *p*-values tend to be very close to zero with large data sets, so the quality of a split is reported by LogWorth = (−1)*ln(chi-squared *p*-value).

Use JMP to Choose the Split That Maximizes the LogWorth Statistic

JMP automatically checks all the predictor, or independent, variables and all the possible splits for them and chooses the variable and split that maximize the LogWorth statistic:

1. Click the **Partition for Return** red triangle at the top of the partition window.
2. Under **Display Options**, select **Show Split Prob**. For each level in the data set (zeros and ones), **Rate** and **Prob** numbers appear. The **Rate** shows the proportion of each level in the node, and the **Prob** shows the proportion that the model predicts for each level, as shown in Figure 10.4.
3. Under **Display Options**, select **Show Split Count**. The number of observations, **Count**, is displayed for each level, as shown in Figure 10.4.
4. Click the gray arrow to expand the **Candidates** box. These are "candidate" variables for the next split.

Split the Root Node According to Rank of Variables

As shown in Figure 10.4, see that GPA has the highest G^2 as well as the highest LogWorth. That LogWorth and G^2 are both maximized for the same variable as indicated by the asterisk between them. (In the case that G^2 and LogWorth are not maximized by the same variable, the "greater than" (>) and "less than" (<) symbols are used to indicate the respective maxima.) In some sense, the LogWorth and G^2 statistics can be used to rank the variables in terms of their importance for explaining the target variable, a concept to which we shall return.

Clearly, the root node should be split on the GPA variable. Click **Split** to see several changes in the window as shown in Figure 10.5.

In Figure 10.5, the graph has new rectangles in it. These rectangles represent the effect this split has on the data. RSquare has increased from zero to 0.334. The number of splits is 1, and in the root node, suddenly the LogWorth statistic has appeared.

More importantly, the first split divides the data into two nodes, depending on whether GPA is above or below 1.0159. The node that contains students whose GPA is less than 1.0159 has

Figure 10.4: Initial Rate, Probabilities, and LogWorths

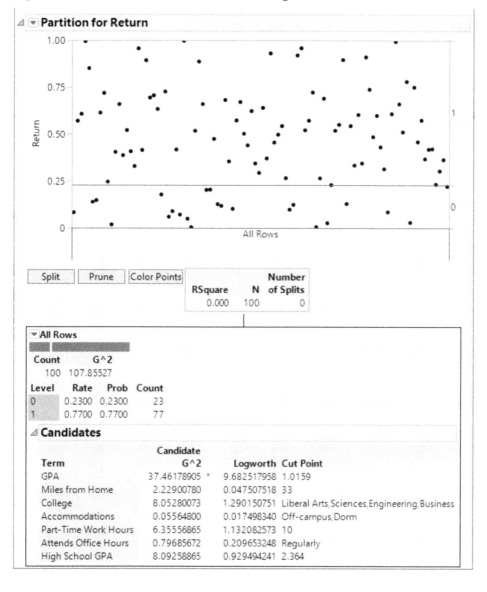

11 students, all of whom are zeros: they did not return for their sophomore year. This node cannot be split anymore because it is pure ($G^2 = 0$). Splitting the data to create nodes, or subsets, of increasing purity is the goal of tree building. This node provides us with an estimate of the probability that a freshman with a GPA of less than 1.0159 will return for sophomore year: zero— though perhaps the sample size might be a bit small.

Figure 10.5: Decision Tree after First Split

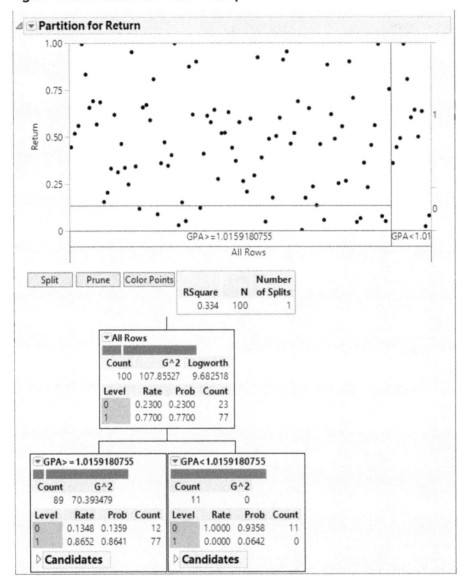

Split Second Node According to the College Variable

Perhaps further examination of these students might shed some light on the reasons for their deficient GPAs, and remedial help (extra tutoring, better advising, and specialized study halls) could prevent such students from failing out in the future. In considering the event that a freshman with a GPA above 1.0159 returns for sophomore year, we see that our best estimate of this probability is .86 or so. (The simple ratio of returning students to total students in this node is 0.8652, while the model's estimate of the probability is 0.8641.)

At the top of the decision tree output, click the **Partition for Return** red triangle and click **Show Fit Details**. Notice at the bottom of the decision tree output that there is the misclassification rate, 0.12, and the confusion matrix, as shown in Figure 10.6.

The other node, for freshmen with a GPA above 1.0159, contains 89 students. From the blue portion of the bar, you see that most of them are 1s (who returned for their sophomore year). Expanding the **Candidates** box in the GPA above 1.0159 node, you see that the largest LogWorth is College, as shown in Figure 10.7.

The next split will be on the College variable. Click **Split** and expand the **Candidates** boxes in both of the newly created nodes. As can be seen in Figure 10.8, the R^2 has increased substantially to 0.553.

The parent node has been split into two child nodes, one with 62 students and one with 27 students. The bar for the former indicates one or two zeros (the Count shows it is 1 student)—that the node is

Figure 10.6: Fit Model Details

⊿ **Fit Details**

Measure	Training	Definition
Entropy RSquare	0.3338	1-Loglike(model)/Loglike(0)
Generalized RSquare	0.4581	$(1-(L(0)/L(model))^{(2/n)})/(1-L(0)^{(2/n)})$
Mean -Log p	0.3593	$\sum -Log(p[j])/n$
RASE	0.3229	$\sqrt{\sum(y[j]-p[j])^2/n}$
Mean Abs Dev	0.2154	$\sum |y[j]-p[j]|/n$
Misclassification Rate	0.1200	$\sum (p[j] \neq pMax)/n$
N	100	n

⊿ **Confusion Matrix**

Training

	Predicted Count	
Actual	0	1
Return		
0	11	12
1	0	77

	Predicted Rate	
Actual	0	1
Return		
0	0.478	0.522
1	0.000	1.000

Figure 10.7: Candidate Variables for Splitting an Impure Node

```
GPA>=1.0159180755
▀▀       ▀▀▀▀▀
Count       G^2
   89  70.393479
Level    Rate    Prob  Count
0      0.1348  0.1359    12
1      0.8652  0.8641    77
```

⊿ Candidates

Term	Candidate G^2		LogWorth	Cut Point
GPA	18.61968454		3.771459948	3.6242
Miles from Home	5.09984838		0.422254132	33
College	23.65677128	*	4.593602824	Business,Liberal Arts,Sciences,Engineering
Accommodations	4.79426880		1.164259923	Other
Part-Time Work Hours	3.55608173		0.519047040	30
Attends Office Hours	1.99835034		0.501935536	Sometimes
High School GPA	6.45939980		0.641257835	2.364

not pure can be seen by observing that G^2 = 10.238. (If the node were pure, then G^2 would be zero.) The bar for the latter indicates a substantial number of zeros, though still less than half.

What you can see from these splits is that almost all the students who do not return for sophomore year and have not failed out are all in the School of Social Sciences. The schools of

Figure 10.8: Splitting a Node (*n* = 89)

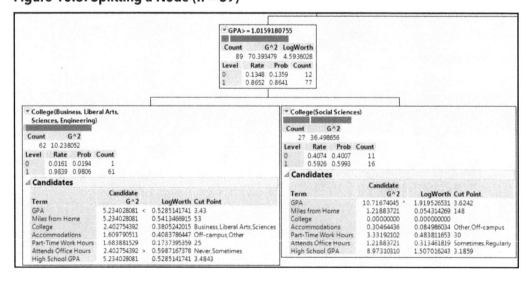

Business, Liberal Arts, Sciences, and Engineering do not have a problem retaining students who have not failed out; only one of 62 did not return. What is it about the School of Social Sciences that it leads all the other schools in freshmen not returning?

Examine Results and Predict the Variable for a Third Split

Before clicking **Split** again, try to figure out what will happen next. Check the candidate variables for both nodes. For the node with 62 observations, the largest LogWorth is 0.5987 for the variable **Attends Office Hours**. For the node with 27 observations, the largest LogWorth is 1.919 for the variable **GPA**. You can expect that the node with 27 observations will split next, and it will split on the **GPA** variable.

Look again at the node with 62 observations. You can tell by the Rate for zero that there is only one non-returning student in this group. As if there were any doubt, look at the counts next to the probabilities. There is really no point in developing further branches from this node, because there is no point in trying to model a 1-out-of-62 occurrence. Click **Split** to see a tree that contains the nodes shown in Figure 10.9.

Examine Results and Predict the Variable for a Fourth Split

You now have a leaf of non-returning students whose GPA exceeds 3.624. We can conjecture that these students, having achieved a high GPA in their freshman year, are transferring out to

Figure 10.9: Splitting a Node (*n* = 27)

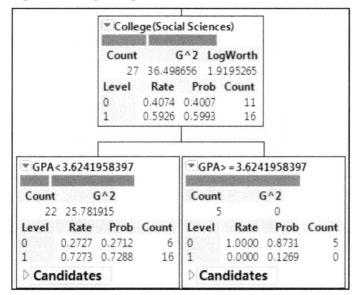

better schools. Perhaps they find the current school too easy and seek more demanding courses; perhaps the creation of "honors" courses might retain these students.

Check the candidate variables for the newly created node for students whose GPA is less than 3.624. The highest LogWorth is 2.4039 for the variable **GPA**. When you click **Split** again, what will happen? Will the node with 62 observations split, or will the split be on the node for students with a GPA lower than 3.624? Which has the higher LogWorth for a candidate variable?

It's the node for students with a GPA lower than 3.624, so that's where the next split will occur. The node with 62 observations will not split until all nodes in the branch for GPA < 3.624 have a LogWorth less than 0.5987. Notice that the misclassification rate has decreased to 0.07. Click **Split**.

Examine Results and Continue Splitting to Gain Actionable Insights

The node for GPA < 3.624 has been split into a leaf for GPA > 2.01. These students all return. And a node for GPA < 2.01 is split about 50-50. Check the candidate variables for this node; the highest LogWorth is 0.279 for the variable **Part Time Work Hours**. Since 0.279 is less than 0.5987, the next split will be on the node with 62 observations. But since you're only pursuing a couple of zeros in this branch, there is not much to be gained by analyzing this newest split.

Continue clicking **Split** until the GPA < 2.01 node is split into two nodes with five observations each. (This is really far too few observations to make a reliable inference. But for now pretend anyway—30 is a much better minimum number of observations for a node, as recommended by Tuffery, 2011.)

Figure 10.10: Splitting a Node (n = 22)

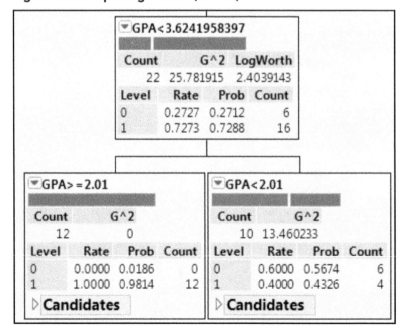

The clear difference is that students who work more than 30 hours a week tend to not return with higher probability than students who work fewer than 30 hours a week. More financial aid to these students might decrease their need to work so much, resulting in a higher grade point and a return for their sophomore year. A simple classification tree analysis of this data set has produced a tree with 7 splits and an RSquare of 0.796, and has revealed some actionable insights into improving the retention of freshmen. Note that the algorithm, on its own, found the critical GPA cutoffs of 1.0159 (student has a "D" average) and 2.01 (student has a "C" average).

Prune to Simplify Overgrown Trees

Suppose that you had not examined each leaf as it was created. Suppose that you built the tree quickly, looking only at R^2 or AICc to guide your efforts, and ended up with a tree with several splits, some of which you suspect will not be useful. What would you do? You would look for leaves that are predominantly nonreturners. This is easily achieved by examining the bars in each node and looking for bars that are predominantly red or looking at the **Count** for each level.

Look at the node with 62 observations; this node has but a single nonreturning student in it. All the branches and nodes that extend from this node are superfluous; you can "prune" them from the tree. By pruning the tree, you will end up with a smaller, simpler set of rules that still predicts almost as well as the larger, unpruned tree. Click the red triangle for this node, and click **Prune Below**.

Observe that the RSquare has dropped to 0.764, and the number of splits has dropped to 5. You can see how much simpler the tree has become, without losing any substantive nodes or much of its ability to predict *y*.

After you grow a tree, it is very often useful to go back and prune nonessential branches. In pruning, you must balance two dangers. A tree that is too large can overfit the data, while a tree that is too small might overlook important structures in the data. There do exist automated methods for growing and pruning trees, but they are beyond the scope of this book. A nontechnical discussion can be found in Linoff and Berry (2011).

Restore the tree to its full size by undoing the pruning. Click the red triangle in the node that was pruned, and click **Split Here**. Next click the just-created **Attends Office Hours (Regularly)** node and click **Split Here**. The RSquare is again 0.796, and the number of splits is again 7.

Examine Receiver Operator Characteristic and Lift Curves

Conclude this analysis by using two more important concepts. First, observe that the seventh and final split increased the R^2 only from 0.782 to 0.796. Remove the nodes created by the last split. In keeping with the arborist's terminology, click **Prune** to undo the last split so that the number of splits is 6 and the RSquare is 0.782. Very often you will grow a tree larger than you need, and then you will need to prune it back to the desired size.

After having grown the proper-size classification tree, it is often useful to consider summaries of the tree's predictive power. The first of these summaries of the ability of a tree to predict the value of Y is to compute probabilities for each observation, as was done for Logistic Regression. Click the **Partition for Return** red triangle and select **Save Columns ▶ Save Prediction Formula**. In the data table will appear Prob(Return==0), Prob(Return==1) and Most Likely Return. As you look down the rows, there will be much duplication in the probabilities for observations because all the observations in a particular node are assigned the same probabilities.

Next are two important graphical summaries, the Receiver Operating Characteristic (ROC) curve and the Lift curve. To see these two curves, click the **Partition for Return** red triangle and click **ROC Curve**, and repeat by clicking **Lift Curve**. See that these curves are now displayed in

Figure 10.11: Receiver Operator Characteristic and Lift Curves

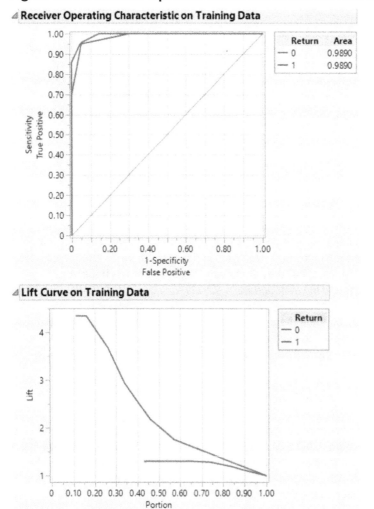

the output, as shown in Figure 10.11. Although they are very useful, for now simply note their existence; they will be explained in great detail in Chapter 14.

Regression Trees

The type of tree created depends on the target variable. In the last section, you created a classification tree because the *y* variable was binary. To use the regression tree approach on the same data set you have been using, you need a continuous target variable.

Suppose we want to explore the components of GPA:

1. In the Data Table, click the blue **x** next to **GPA** and change its role to Y.
2. Click the blue **y** next to **Return** and change its role to **No Role**.
3. As before, select **Analyze ▶ Predictive Modeling ▶ Partition**.

See that the root node contains all 100 observations with a mean of 2.216 as shown in Figure 10.12. (If you like, you can verify this by selecting **Analyze ▶ Distributions**.)

In Figure 10.12, observe the new statistic in the results box, RASE, which stands for root average square error. RASE is similar to RMSE (root mean square error), which can be interpreted as the standard deviation of the target variable in that node, except that RMSE adjusts for degrees of freedom while RASE does not.

In the present case, GPA is the continuous target variable. Click **Candidates** to see that the first split will be made on **Attends Office Hours**. Click **Split**.

Understand How Regression Trees Work

The two new nodes contain 71 and 29 observations. The former has a mean GPA of 2.00689, and the latter has a mean GPA of 2.728. This is quite a difference in GPA! The regression tree algorithm simply runs a regression of the target variable on a constant for the data in each node, effectively calculating the mean of the target variable in each node.

It is important to understand that this is how regression trees work, so it is worthwhile to spend some time exploring this idea. Before continuing, pause to explore the value 2.2160642 that you see in Figure 10.12. Create a new variable called *Regularly* that equals 1 if **Attends Office Hours** is **Regularly,** and equals zero otherwise:

4. In the Data Table, click in the column **Attends Office Hours**.
5. Select **Cols ▶ Recode**.
6. For **Never**, change the New Value to **0**; for **Regularly**, change the New Value to **1**; and for **Sometimes**, change the New Value to **0**.
7. Click **Recode** to create a new variable called **Attends Office Hours 2**.

Figure 10.12: Partition Initial Output with Continuous Discrete Dependent Variable

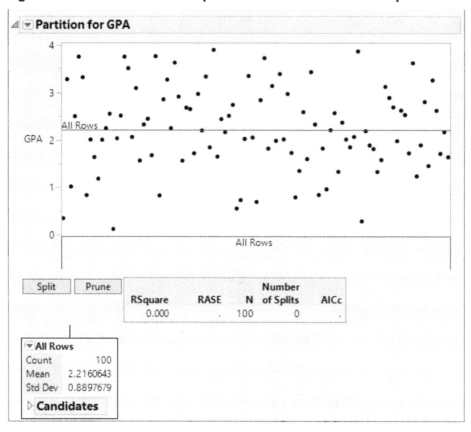

Observe that **Attends Office Hours** is clearly a nominal variable because it is character data. **Attends Office Hours 2** consists of numbers, but should be a nominal variable. Make sure that it is nominal.

To calculate the mean GPA for the **Attends Office Hours** regularly (Regularly = 1) and **Attends Office Hours** rarely or never (Regularly = 0), proceed as follows:

1. Select **Analyze ▶ Distribution**.
2. Under **Y, Columns, Remove** all the variables except **GPA**.
3. Click **Attends Office Hours 2,** and then click **By**.
4. Click **OK**.

In the Distributions window, you should see that mean GPA is 2.00689 when **Attends Office Hours 2** = 0 and that GPA is 2.728 when **Attends Office Hours 2** = 1. Regression trees really do calculate the mean of the target variable for each node.

Be sure to delete the variable **Attends Office Hours 2** from the Data Table so that it is not used in subsequent analyses. In the Data Table, right-click **Attends Office Hours 2,** and select **Delete Columns**.

Resume with the tree building. Click the red triangle in the first node (with 100 observations) and select **Prune Below**. You are going to split several times, and each time you split you are going to record some information from the RSquare Report Table as shown in Figure 10.13: the RSquare, the RASE, and the AICc. You can write this down on paper or use JMP. For now, use JMP.

Right-click in the RSquare Report Table and select **Make into Data Table**. A new data table appears that shows the following:

- RSquare
- RASE
- *N*
- Number of Split
- AICc

Every time you click **Split**, you produce a data table. After splitting 14 times, there will be 14 such tables. Copy and paste the information into a single table, as shown in Figure 10.14.

Continue splitting until the number of splits is 14 and the R^2 is 0.543. For each split, write down the R^2, the RASE, and the AICc. To use the AICc as a model selection criterion, you would interpret the AICc as a function of the number of splits, with the goal of minimizing the AICc. It sometimes occurs that the AICc simply continues to decrease, perhaps ever so slightly, as the number of splits increases. In such a case, the AICc is not a useful indicator for determining the number of splits. In other cases, the AICc decreases as the number of splits increases, reaches a minimum, and then begins to increase. In such a case, it might be useful to stop splitting when the AICc reaches a minimum.

The RASE and AICc are plotted in Figure 10.15. In the present case, the number of splits that minimizes the AICc is 9, with an AICc of 217.01. It is true that AICc is 219.6 on Split 14 and 220.27 on Split 13. So the plot of AICc versus splits is not a perfect bowl shape. But it is still true that AICc has a local minimum at 9 splits. All these comments are not to suggest that you cannot continue splitting past 9 splits if you continue to uncover useful information.

Figure 10.13: RSquare Report Table before Splitting

RSquare	RASE	N	Number of Splits	AICc
0.000	0.8853079	100	0	263.547

Figure 10.14: Table Containing Statistics from Several Splits

	RSquare	RASE	N	Number of Splits	AICc
1	0.000	0.8853078558	100	0	263.54745101
2	0.137	0.8225877196	100	1	250.97767622
3	0.274	0.7543296384	100	2	235.82359521
4	0.302	0.7395153027	100	3	234.07394375
5	0.356	0.7106789006	100	4	228.3840189
6	0.408	0.6813680288	100	5	222.274559
7	0.429	0.6689173837	100	6	220.95118047
8	0.447	0.6583586062	100	7	220.18660627
9	0.474	0.6419799974	100	8	217.61999024
10	0.490	0.631986405	100	9	217.01022741
11	0.498	0.6274553426	100	10	218.157358
12	0.507	0.6215311382	100	11	218.90641127
13	0.520	0.6135277152	100	12	219.02291504
14	0.527	0.6088610506	100	13	220.26895289
15	0.543	0.5983722853	100	14	219.63348991

Untitled 6 — Make Into Data Table

Columns (5/0): RSquare, RASE, N, Number of Splits, AICc

Rows: All rows 15; Selected 0; Excluded 0; Hidden 0; Labeled 0

Figure 10.15: Plot of AIC and RMSE by Number of Splits

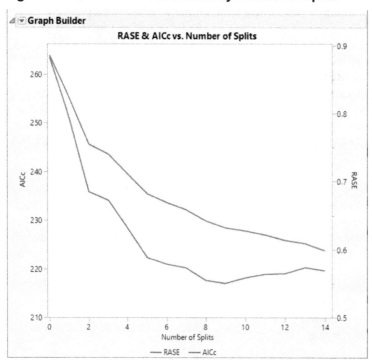

Restart a Regression Driven by Practical Questions

Start over again by pruning everything below the first node. Now create a tree with 9 splits, the number of splits suggested in Figure 10.14. A very practical question is this: What can you say that might be useful to a college administrator about the effect on GPA of the variables in the data set? The largest driver of GPA appears to be whether a student attends office hours regularly. This split (and all other splits) effectively divides the node into two groups: high GPA (for this node, students with an average GPA of 2.728) and low GPA (for this node, students with an average GPA of 2.00689). Furthermore, there appears to be no difference between students who attend Never and those who attend Sometimes. You can say this because there is no split between Never and Sometimes students.

For the group of high GPA students (attends office hours regularly with GPA above 2.728), those who live off-campus have substantially lower GPAs than other students. This suggests that the off-campus lifestyle is conducive to many more non-studying activities than living on campus. Among the high GPA students who live in dorms, those who attend school close to home have higher GPAs (3.40 versus 2.74), though the sample size is too small to merit much trust in this node. Certainly, if this result were obtained with a larger sample, then it might be interesting to investigate the reasons for such a relationship. Perhaps the ability to go home for a non-holiday weekend is conducive to the mental health necessary to sustain a successful studying regimen.

On the low-GPA side of the tree (attends office hours never or sometimes with a GPA of 2.00), you again see that students who attend school closer to home have higher GPAs (2.83 versus 1.82—nearly a "B" versus less than a "C"). For those lower-GPA students who live far from home, it really matters whether the student is enrolled in Social Sciences or Liberal Arts on the one hand, or Sciences, Business, or Engineering on the other hand. This might be symptomatic of grade inflation in the former two schools, or it might be a real difference in the quality of the students that enroll in each school. Or it might be some combination of the two. We see also that among low-GPA students in Sciences, Business, and Engineering, more hours of part-time work result in a lower GPA.

Many of these explanations are interesting, but you wouldn't want to believe any of them—yet. You should run experiments or perform further analyses to document that any effect is real and not merely a chance correlation.

As an illustration of this important principle, consider the credit card company Capital One, which grew from a small division of a regional bank to a behemoth that dominates its industry. Capital One conducts thousands of experiments every year in its attempts to improve the ways that it acquires customers and keeps them. A Capital One analyst might examine some historical data with a tree and find some nodes indicating that blue envelopes with a fixed interest rate offer receive more responses than white envelopes with a variable interest rate offer. Before rolling out such a campaign on a large scale, Capital One would first run a limited experiment to make sure the effect was real and not just a quirk of the small number of customers in that node of the tree. This could be accomplished by sending out 5,000 offers of each type and comparing the responses within a six-week period.

Use Column Contributions and Leaf Reports for Large Data Sets

With a large data set, a tree can grow very large—too large to be viewed on a computer screen. Even if printed out, one might have too many leaves for you to comprehend them all. Continue with the Freshmen1.jmp Data Table, and once again consider the example in which the target variable **Return** is nominal.

1. In the data table, click the blue *y* next to GPA and make it an *x* variable.
2. There is no blue letter next to **Return**, so highlight the **Return** column.
3. Click **Cols** from the top menu and select **Preselect Role ▶ Y**.
4. Build a tree with 7 splits as before; the RSquare is 0.796.
5. Under the **Partition for Return** red triangle, select **Column Contributions**.

The chart that appears (Figure 10.16) tells you which variables are more important in explaining the target variable.

If you ever happen to have a large data set and you're not sure where to start looking, build a tree on the data set and look at the **Column Contributions**. (To do so, click the red arrow for the Partition window, and then select **Column Contributions**.) In the **Column Contributions** box, right-click anywhere in the SS column or G^2 column (whichever one appears), and select **Sort by Column**.

Another useful tool for interpreting large data sets is the Leaf Report. To see it, under the **Partition for Return** red triangle, select **Leaf Report**, which is shown in Figure 10.17. The Leaf Report gives the probability and counts of the bottom-level leaves. The top set of horizontal bar charts make it very easy to see which leaves have high and low concentrations of the target variable. The bottom set of horizontal bar charts show the counts for the various leaves. The splitting rules for each leaf also are shown. With a little practice, you ought to be able to read a Leaf Report almost as easily as you can read a tree.

Figure 10.16: Column Contributions

Term	Number of Splits	G^2		Portion
GPA	3	60.5002114		0.6715
College	1	23.6567713		0.2626
Attends Office Hours	1	2.40275439		0.0267
Accommodations	1	1.80697534		0.0201
Part-Time Work Hours	1	1.72609243		0.0192
Miles from Home	0	0		0.0000
High School GPA	0	0		0.0000

Figure 10.17: Leaf Report

Leaf Report

Response Prob

Leaf Label	0	1
GPA>=1.0159180755&College(Business, Liberal Arts, Sciences, Engineering)&Attends Office Hours(Never, Sometimes)	0.0046	0.9954
GPA>=1.0159180755&College(Business, Liberal Arts, Sciences, Engineering)&Attends Office Hours(Regularly)&Accommodations(Off-campus, Other)	0.0155	0.9845
GPA>=1.0159180755&College(Business, Liberal Arts, Sciences, Engineering)&Attends Office Hours(Regularly)&Accommodations(Dorm)	0.1318	0.8682
GPA>=1.0159180755&College(Social Sciences)&GPA<3.6241958397&GPA>=2.01	0.0186	0.9814
GPA>=1.0159180755&College(Social Sciences)&GPA<3.6241958397&GPA<2.01&Part-Time Work Hours<30	0.3791	0.6209
GPA>=1.0159180755&College(Social Sciences)&GPA<3.6241958397&GPA<2.01&Part-Time Work Hours>=30	0.7124	0.2876
GPA>=1.0159180755&College(Social Sciences)&GPA>=3.6241958397	0.8731	0.1269
GPA<1.0159180755	0.9358	0.0642

Response Counts

Leaf Label	0	1
GPA>=1.0159180755&College(Business, Liberal Arts, Sciences, Engineering)&Attends Office Hours(Never, Sometimes)	0	43
GPA>=1.0159180755&College(Business, Liberal Arts, Sciences, Engineering)&Attends Office Hours(Regularly)&Accommodations(Off-campus, Other)	0	11
GPA>=1.0159180755&College(Business, Liberal Arts, Sciences, Engineering)&Attends Office Hours(Regularly)&Accommodations(Dorm)	1	7
GPA>=1.0159180755&College(Social Sciences)&GPA<3.6241958397&GPA>=2.01	0	12
GPA>=1.0159180755&College(Social Sciences)&GPA<3.6241958397&GPA<2.01&Part-Time Work Hours<30	2	3
GPA>=1.0159180755&College(Social Sciences)&GPA<3.6241958397&GPA<2.01&Part-Time Work Hours>=30	4	1
GPA>=1.0159180755&College(Social Sciences)&GPA>=3.6241958397	5	0
GPA<1.0159180755	11	0

Exercises

1. Build a classification tree on the churn data set. Remember that you are trying to predict churn, so focus on nodes that have many churners. What useful insights can you make about customers who churn?

2. After building a tree on the churn data set, use the **Column Contributions** to determine which variables might be important. Could these variables be used to improve the Logistic Regression developed in Chapter 5?

3. Build a Regression Tree on the Masshousing.jmp data set to predict market value.

4. A non-profit health care group, similar to AARP, conducted a survey of 360 members. The survey asked various questions about their diet and state of health. The data from the survey is in the Excel file blood_pressure.xlsx. On the next two pages, the coding of some of the variables is provided. They would like a report discussing the results of the survey and also provide some life-style suggests to their members.

TYPE OF MILK

1-WHOLE
2-2%
3-SKIM
4-POWDER
5-NO MILK

SALT IN FOOD

1-A LOT
2-MODERATE
3-VERY LITTLE
4-NONE
5-??? UNKNOWN

SALT CONSUMPTION

1-VERY LOW
2-LOW
3-MODERATE
4-HIGH
5-VERY HIGH
6-??? UNKNOWN

BUTTER FOOD

1-FREQUENTLY
2-SOMETIMES
3-NEVER

SPORTS ACTIVITY

1-DAILY
2-WEEKLY
3-OCCASIONALLY
4-RARELY
5-NEVER
6-??? UNKNOWN

SMOKING

1-REGULAR
2-OCCASIONAL
3-FORMER
4-NEVER
5-??? UNKNOWN

DRINK PATTERN

1-REGULAR
2-OCCASIONAL
3-FORMER
4-NEVER

DRINKS EVERY DAY

1-YES
2-NO
3-??? UNKNOWN

AGE

1-32-50
2-51-62
3-63-72

GENDER

1-MALE
2-FEMALE

HYPERTENSION

1-LOW
2-NORMAL
3-HIGH

5. Use the salesperfdata.jmp data set. Run a stepwise regression with sales as the dependent variable. Build a regression tree to predict sales. Which model is better?

Chapter 11: *k*-Nearest Neighbors

Introduction

The *k*-nearest neighbors algorithm is a simple and powerful method that can be used either for classification or for regression and is one of the dependence techniques as shown in Figure 11.1.

Example–Age and Income as Correlates of Purchase

As a first example, consider the data in Figure 11.2, which gives Age, Income, and Purchase decision for some product. Two individuals made the purchase, indicated by a plus sign (+). Two individuals did not purchase, indicated by a minus sign (−). A prospective customer is indicated by a question mark (?) because you do not know whether this customer will make a purchase. Your task is to predict whether the prospective customer is a likely purchaser. If this customer is a likely purchaser, then perhaps you will target him or her for special marketing materials. If he or she is not a likely purchaser, you will forgo sending him or her such materials.

Figure 11.1: A Framework for Multivariate Analysis

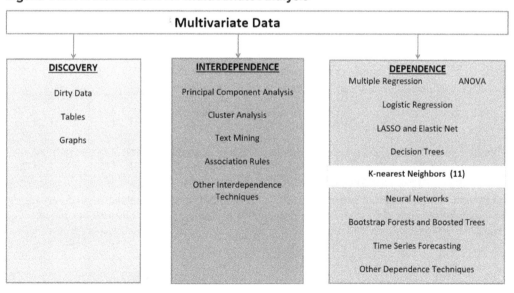

Figure 11.2: Whether Purchased or Not, by Age and Income

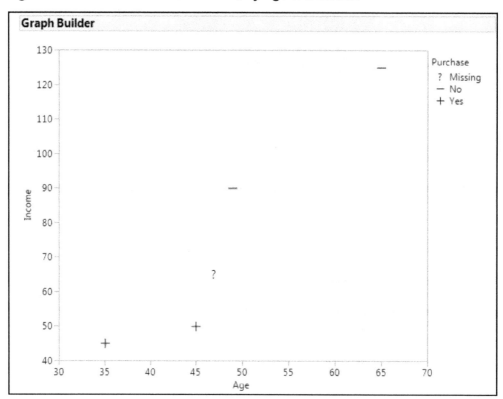

If you classify this new customer by his or her nearest neighbor, you will consider him or her to be a purchaser, because the nearest neighbor in this case is the observation at the point (45, 50), Customer C, which is a plus sign. If you use this customer's two nearest neighbors, you had better do some calculations because eyeballing the second nearest neighbor will be difficult. The distance is calculated by the usual Euclidean metric, in this case as follows:

$$\text{Distance} = \sqrt{(\text{Age} - 47)^2 + (\text{Income} - 65)^2}$$

Table 11.1 gives the data, together with the distance that each observation is from the point (47, 65).

The second nearest neighbor is the point (35, 45), Customer A, which is also a plus. If you use the two nearest neighbors to classify the prospective customer, you will label him or her as a "plus."

Table 11.1: Customer Data and Distance from Customer E

Customer	Age	Income	Purchase	Distance from Customer E
A	35	45	Yes	23.3
B	49	90	No	25.1
C	45	50	Yes	15.1
D	65	125	No	62.6
E	47	65	?	00.0

The Way That JMP Resolves Ties

Suppose that the second nearest neighbor had been a minus instead of a plus. Then you would have had a tie—one plus and one minus. Ties represent a situation in which there is no good solution, only a variety of less-bad solutions. If the data set is large, then there are not likely to be many ties, and the few ties that exist will not much affect the overall analysis. So, you will concern yourself no further with ties except to note that JMP resolves ties by selecting one of the tied levels at random.

The Need to Standardize Units of Measurement

Second, the Euclidean distance is affected by the units of measurement. When the variables are measured in different units, it might be necessary to standardize (subtract the mean and divide by the standard deviation):

1. Select **Analyze ▶ Distribution**.
2. In the red triangle for the variable in question, select **Save** and then **Standardized**).

This method only works for numerical independent variables and perhaps for binary independent variables that are represented as zeros and ones. It does not work for categorical data. Suppose "political affiliation" was a relevant independent variable? It is not immediately obvious how to calculate the distance between "liberal" and "conservative."

Moving on to the three nearest neighbors, there are two plusses and one minus. Majority vote means that you again classify the prospective customer as a "Yes." The idea underlying the algorithm should be clear now: find the k-nearest neighbors, and use those k observations to make an inference. For purposes of classification, you want to choose the value of k that gives the best confusion matrix.

Observe that the data for income is given in thousands of dollars, and the age is given in years. What would happen if income was measured in dollars and age was measured in months instead? You would get Table 11.2:

Table 11.2: Customer Raw Data and Distance from Customer E

Customer	Age (Months)	Income ($)	Purchase	Distance from Customer E
A	420	45,000	Yes	56,237
B	588	90,000	No	26,490
C	540	50,000	Yes	17,371
D	780	125,000	No	99,074
E	564	65,000	?	0

As before, Customer C is still the nearest neighbor to Customer E. However, the second nearest neighbor has changed, and is now Customer B. This dependence on the units of measurement suggests that standardizing the units of measurement might be in order. If you standardize the data in Table 11.1 (subtracting the mean and dividing by the standard deviation) for both income and age, you get Table 11.3.

Table 11.3: Customer Standardized Data

Customer	Standardized Age	Standardized Income	Purchase	Distance from Customer E
A	−1.082	−0.866	Yes	1.315
B	0.040	0.333	No	0.671
C	−0.281	−0.733	Yes	0.566
D	1.322	1.266	No	2.000
E	0.120	−0.333	?	0.000

Now you find that the first nearest neighbor to Customer E is Customer C, and the second nearest neighbor is Customer B.

k-Nearest Neighbors Analysis

The k-nearest neighbors method is very straightforward to apply, interpret, and use. You first motivate the method using a toy data set, and then move on to analyze a real data set.

Perform the Analysis

Open the toylogistic.jmp file that was used in Chapter 6. It has two variables: **PassClass**, a binary variable indicating whether the student passed the class (1 = yes, 0 = no), and **MidTermScore**, a continuous variable. Be sure to turn **PassClass** into a nominal variable (click the blue triangle and select nominal). Complete the following steps:

1. Select **Analyze** ▶ **Predictive Modeling** ▶ **Partition**.
2. In the Options area of the Partition dialog box, on the Method menu, change **Decision Tree** to **K Nearest Neighbors**.
3. Still in the Options area, the default value of **Number of Neighbors K** is 10, but you have only 20 observations, so change it to **5**.
4. Select **PassClass,** and click **Y, response**.
5. Select **MidTermScore,** and click **X, Factor**.
6. Click **OK**.

or

1. Select **Analyze** ▶ **Predictive Modeling** ▶ **K Nearest Neighbors**.
2. Chang **K** to **5**.
3. Select **PassClass,** and click **Y, response**.
4. Select **MidTermScore,** and click **X, Factor**.
5. Click **OK**.

The output window is given below in Figure 11.3. Because the random number generator determines the training and validation data sets, your numbers might be different.

As can be seen, JMP provides a summary for each possible value of k, giving the number of observations, the misclassification rate, and the number of misclassifications. The lowest number of misclassifications in this example is 5, which occurs for $k = 4$. JMP presents the confusion matrix for this best value of k.

It might sometimes be necessary to save the predicted values for each observation. Perhaps you might wish to do further analysis on the predictions from this model. To do so, on the **PassClass** red triangle select **Save Predicteds**, and the Data Table will be augmented with five Predicted PassClass columns because you chose $k = 5$.

Make Predictions for New Data

Making predictions for new data is easy:

1. On the **PassClass** red triangle, select **Save Prediction Formula** and enter the number of neighbors of the best model. Since your best model was for $k = 4$, enter **4**. Click **OK**. The **Predicted Formula** column now appears in the Data Table.
2. Suppose a student scores 76 on the midterm and you want to predict the student's eventual success in the class. In Row 21, under **MidtermScore**, enter the value **76**, leaving **PassClass** empty.
3. Click in any other cell, and the prediction will appear in the 21st row of the **Predicted Formula** column. In this case, the model predicts that a student who scores 76 on the midterm will pass the class.
4. Change the 76 to a 74 and click in another cell. See that the prediction has now changed from a 1 to a zero. The prediction automatically updates when the input data are changed.

Figure 11.3: *k*-Nearest Neighbor Output for toylogistic.jmp File

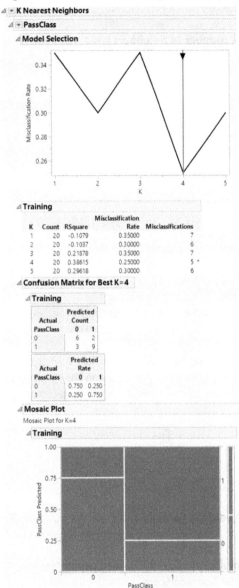

You might be tempted to think that if some point B is the nearest neighbor of another point A, then A is also the nearest neighbor to B. However, the nearest neighbor relationship is not symmetrical, as Figure 11.4 makes clear. The nearest neighbor to A is B, but the nearest neighbor to B is C.

Figure 11.4: Example of the Nonsymmetrical Nature of the *k*-Nearest Neighbor Algorithm

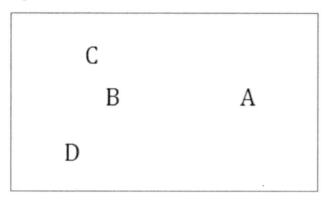

k-Nearest Neighbor for Multiclass Problems

Nearest neighbors can address multiclass problems very easily. To see this approach, use the glass data set.

Understand the Variables

For forensic purposes, it might be of interest to identify the source of a shard of broken glass. Given appropriate chemical measurements on the piece of glass, this becomes a classification problem. By way of technical background, there are two manufacturing processes for producing window glass: float and nonfloat. In the data set, there are six different types of glass whose variable names are given in Table 11.4.

Table 11.4: Types of Glass

Type of Glass	Category Name
Float glass from a building window	WinF
Nonfloat glass from a building window	WinNF
Glass from a vehicle window	Veh
Glass from a container	Con
Glass from tableware	Tabl
Glass from a vehicle headlight	Head

Table 11.5: Ten Attributes of Glass

Measured Attribute	Variable Name
Refractive index	RI
Sodium	Na
Magnesium	Mg
Aluminum	Al
Silicon	Si
Potassium	K
Calcium	Ca
Barium	Ba
Iron	Fe

Ten measurements are taken on each of 214 pieces of glass. The variable names and definitions are given in Table 11.5.

Perform the Analysis and Examine Results

Follow these steps to analyze the data:

1. Open the file **glass.jmp.**
2. Select **Analyze ▶ Predictive Modeling ▶ Partition**.
3. Select **type** as **Y, Response** and all the other variables as **X, Factor**.
4. On the Method menu that shows **Decision Tree,** choose instead **K Nearest Neighbors**.
5. Keep the **Number of Neighbors K** to 10.
6. Click **OK**.

The results are given in Figure 11.5.

The number of classification errors is minimized when $k = 3$. The resulting confusion matrix shows that most of the errors are in the lower right corner, where the algorithm has difficulty distinguishing between **WinF** and **WinNF**. Of course, the correct classifications are all on the main diagonal from upper left to lower right.

Looking at the Data Table and running the **Distribution** option on variables **K** and **Si**, you see that the variable **K** takes on small values between zero and 1, and the variable **Si** takes on values between 70 and 80. Might this be a partial cause for so many misclassifications? Perhaps scaling is in order. This idea will be explored in the exercises at the end of the chapter.

Figure 11.5: *k*-Nearest Neighbor for the glass.jmp File

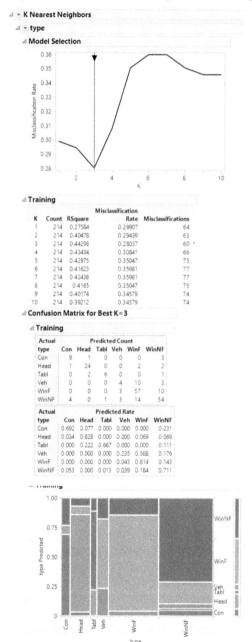

⊿ ▾ K Nearest Neighbors

⊿ ▾ type

⊿ Model Selection

⊿ Training

K	Count	RSquare	Misclassification Rate	Misclassifications
1	214	0.27584	0.29907	64
2	214	0.40478	0.29439	63
3	214	0.44298	0.28037	60 *
4	214	0.43434	0.30841	66
5	214	0.42975	0.35047	75
6	214	0.41623	0.35981	77
7	214	0.42438	0.35981	77
8	214	0.4165	0.35047	75
9	214	0.40174	0.34579	74
10	214	0.39212	0.34579	74

⊿ Confusion Matrix for Best K = 3

⊿ Training

Actual type	Predicted Count					
	Con	Head	Tabl	Veh	WinF	WinNF
Con	9	1	0	0	0	3
Head	1	24	0	0	2	2
Tabl	0	2	6	0	0	1
Veh	0	0	0	4	10	3
WinF	0	0	0	3	57	10
WinNF	4	0	1	3	14	54

Actual type	Predicted Rate					
	Con	Head	Tabl	Veh	WinF	WinNF
Con	0.692	0.077	0.000	0.000	0.000	0.231
Head	0.034	0.828	0.000	0.000	0.069	0.069
Tabl	0.000	0.222	0.667	0.000	0.000	0.111
Veh	0.000	0.000	0.000	0.235	0.588	0.176
WinF	0.000	0.000	0.000	0.043	0.814	0.143
WinNF	0.053	0.000	0.013	0.039	0.184	0.711

The *k*-Nearest Neighbor Regression Models

The *k*-nearest neighbor techniques can be used not only for classification, but also for regression when the target variable is continuous. In this case, rather than take a majority vote of the neighbors to determine classification, the average value of the neighbors is computed, and this becomes the predicted value of the target variable. It can improve on linear regression in some cases.

Perform a Linear Regression as a Basis for Comparison

To see this, return to the Mass Housing data set, MassHousing.jmp, which was analyzed in the exercises for Chapter 7. The goal is to predict the median house price. To establish a basis for comparison, first run a linear regression with **mvalue** as the dependent variable and all other variables as independent variables. You should find that the RSquare is 0.740643, and the Root Mean Square Error is 4.745298.

Apply the *k*-Nearest Neighbors Technique

Now apply the *k*-nearest neighbors technique:

1. Click **Analyze ▶ Modeling ▶ Partition**.
2. Change the method from **Decision Trees** to **K Nearest Neighbors**.
3. Select **mvalue** as **Y, Response** and all the other variables as **X, Factor.**
4. Click **OK**.

The results are given in Figure 11.6.

Compare the Two Methods

Observe that the RASE traces out a bowl shape as a function of *k*, and both RASE and SSE are minimized when *k* = 4. Note that the RASE produced by *k*-nearest neighbors is much less than the RMSE produced by linear regression. (RASE is similar to RMSE, but RMSE adjusts for degrees of freedom.) So, you could expect that if you had to make predictions, *k*-nearest neighbors would produce better predictions than linear regression.

To see more clearly what such a reduction in RMSE means, it is useful to compare the residuals from the two methods. Plot the residuals from *k*-nearest neighbors. You will have to create the residuals manually, subtracting predicted values from actual values. To do so, complete the following steps:

1. On the **mvalue** red triangle, select **Save Predicteds.** Doing so will save one column of predicted values for each K (in the present case, ten columns). You will focus on the fourth column of predicted values, **Predicted mvalue 4**. (You could use **Save Prediction Formula** with *k* = 4 to show only this column.)

Figure 11.6: *k***-Nearest Neighbor Results for the MassHousing.jmp File**

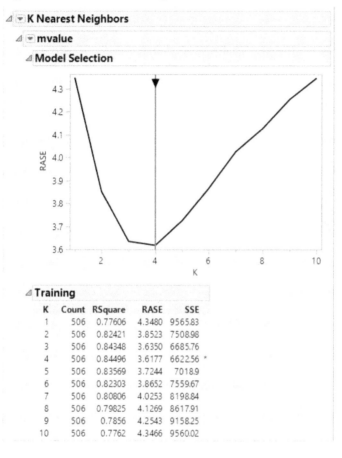

2. Create a new variable by right-clicking at the top of a blank column and selecting **Column Info...** Call the new column **residuals**.
3. Select **Column Properties** and **Formula**. From the list of column variables, select **mvalue**, and then click the **minus sign** at the middle of the box. Then click in the fourth column of predicted values called **Predicted mvalue 4**. Click **OK**.
4. Click **OK**.
5. Select **Graph ▶ Legacy ▶ Overlay Plot**. Select **residuals** and click **Y**.
6. Click **OK**.

The results appear in Figure 11.7.

To get the residuals from the linear regression, complete the following steps:

1. In the regression window, click the **Response mvalue** red triangle and select **Row Diagnostics ▶ Plot Residuals by Row**.

Figure 11.7: Overlap Plot for the MassHousing.jmp File

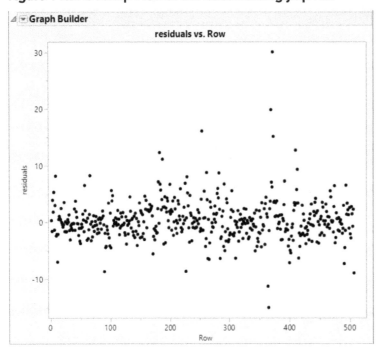

2. You might have to scroll down to see this plot, and it might be too tiny to see clearly. To enlarge the plot, right-click the plot, select **Size/Scale ▶ Frame Size**, and enter **400** for horizontal and **200** for vertical.

The results appear in Figure 11.8.

Comparing these two figures shows how much more variable the residuals are compared to linear regression. To see this, focus on the range between 100 and 300. In Figure 11.7, the residuals are largely between –5 and +5, whereas in Figure 11.7 they are between –5 and +10 or even +15. Further, we can compare the distributions and their standard deviation. First, in the regression window:

1. Click the **Response mvalue** red triangle and select **Save Columns ▶ Residuals.** A new column called **Residual mvalue** is created.

Then generate and examine the distribution output for the variables **Residual mvalue** and **residuals** as shown in Figure 11.9. The regression standard deviation is 4.68, and the k-nearest neighbors standard deviation is 3.60.

As mentioned, you should expect *k*-nearest neighbors to yield better predictions in this case.

Figure 11.8: Residual Plot for Multiple Linear Regression

◢ **Residual by Row Plot**

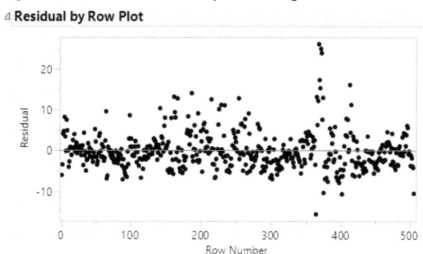

Figure 11.9: Distribution of *k*-Nearest Neighbors Residuals and the Regression Residual mvalue

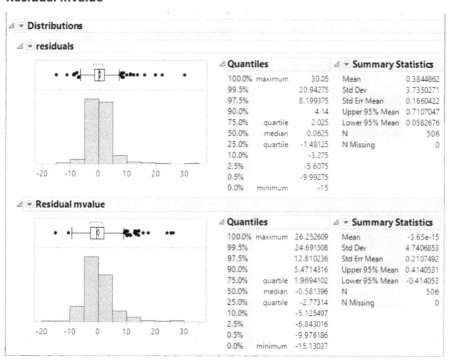

Make Predictions for New Data

To see how easy it is to make predictions, complete the following steps:

1. In the *k*-nearest neighbors output, click the **mvalue** red triangle and select **Save Prediction Formula**. Click **OK**.
2. On the data table, in the row directly beneath the last observation, enter the following values: crim = 0.5, zn = 0, indus = 10, chas = 0, nox = 0.5, rooms = 5, age = 50, distance = 3.5, radial = 5, tax = 500, pt = 15, b = 375, and lstat = 15. Of course, no value should be entered for the dependent variable, which will remain a black dot in the last cell.
3. Now, click in any other cell in the data table to see that the **K Nearest Neighbors** predicts a value of 19.375 for this new observation.

Limitations and Drawbacks of the Technique

It is intuitively obvious that when observations are close together, *k*-nearest neighbors will work better than when observations are far apart. In low-dimension problems (those with few variables), *k*-nearest neighbors can work quite well. In higher dimensions (those with a large number of variables), the nearest neighbor algorithm runs into trouble. In many dimensions, the nearest observation can be far away, resulting in bias and poor performance.

The probability of observations being close together is related to the number of variables in the data set. To motivate this claim, consider two points in one dimension, on the unit line (a line that is one unit long). The farthest away that they can be is one unit: place one point at 0 and the other point at 1. In two dimensions, place one point at (0, 0) and the other at (1, 1): the distance between them is $\sqrt{2} = 1.414$. In three dimensions, place one point at (0,0,0) and the other at (1,1,1): the distance between them is $\sqrt{3} = 1.732$. As is obvious, the more dimensions in the data, the farther apart the observations can be. This phenomenon is sometimes referred to as "the curse of dimensionality."

Although *k*-nearest neighbors requires no assumptions of normality, linearity, and the like, it does have one major drawback: computational demands. Suppose that you want to make predictions for ten new observations. The entire data set must be used to make each of the ten predictions, and the entire data set must be analyzed ten times. Contrast this situation with regression, where the entire data set would be analyzed once, a formula would be computed, and then the formula would be used ten times. So *k*-nearest neighbors would not be useful for real-time predictions with large data sets, whereas other methods would be better suited to such a situation.

Exercises

1. Is there any point in extending *k* beyond 10 in the case of the glass data? Set the maximum value of *k* at 20 and then at 30.

2. Are the results for the glass data affected by the scaling? Standardize all the variables and apply *k*-nearest neighbors.

3. Run a linear regression problem of your choice and compare it to *k*-nearest neighbors.

Chapter 12: Neural Networks

Introduction

The neural networks technique is one of the dependence techniques as shown in the multivariate analysis framework in Figure 12.1. Neural networks were originally developed to understand biological neural networks and were specifically studied by artificial intelligence researchers to allow computers to develop the ability to learn. In the past 30 years, neural networks have been successfully applied to a wide variety of problems, including predicting the solvency of mortgage applicants, detecting credit card fraud, validating signatures, forecasting stock prices, speech recognition programs, predicting bankruptcies, mammogram screening, determining the probability that a river will flood, and countless others.

Drawbacks and Benefits

Neural networks are a black box as far as statistical methods are concerned. The data go in, the prediction comes out, and nobody really knows what goes on inside the network. No hypotheses are tested, there are no *p*-values to determine whether variables are significant, and there is

Figure 12.1: A Framework for Multivariate Analysis

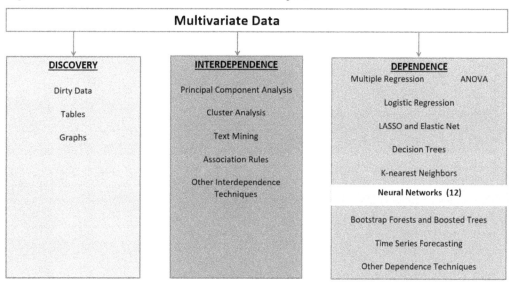

no way to determine precisely how the model makes its predictions. Neural networks can be quite useful to a statistician, but they are probably not useful when you need to present a model with results to a management team. The management team is not likely to put much faith in the statistician's presentation: "We don't know what it does or how it does it, but here is what it did." At least trees are intuitive and easily explained, and logistic regression can be couched in terms of relevant variables and hypothesis tests, so these methods are better when you need to present results to a management team.

Neural networks do have their strong points. They are capable of modeling extremely nonlinear phenomena, require no distributional assumptions, and they can be used for either classification (binary dependent variable) or prediction (continuous dependent variable). Selecting variables for inclusion in a neural network is always difficult because there is no test for whether a variable makes a contribution to a model. Naturally, consultation with a subject-matter expert can be useful. Another way is to apply a tree to the data, check the "variable importance" measures from the tree, and use the most important variables from the tree as the variables to be included in the neural network.

A Simplified Representation

Neural networks are based on a model of how neurons in the brain communicate with each other. In a very simplified representation, a single neuron takes inputs (electrical signals of varying strengths) from an input layer of other neurons, weights them appropriately, and combines them to produce outputs (again, electrical signals of varying strengths) as an output layer, as shown in Figure 12.2. This figure shows two outputs in the output layer, but most applications of neural networks have only a single output.

Figure 12.2: A Neuron Accepting Weighted Inputs

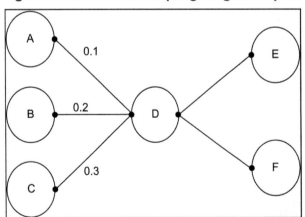

Figure 12.3: A Neuron with a Bias Term

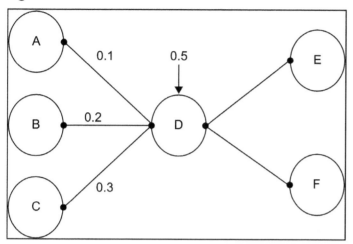

To make things easy, see Figure 12.3. Suppose that the strength of each signal emanating from neurons A, B, and C equals one. Now D might accept input from A with a weight of 0.1, from B with a weight of 0.2, and from C with a weight of 0.3. Then the output from D would be 0.1(1) + 0.2(1) + 0.3(1) = 0.6. Similarly, neurons E and F will accept the input of 0.6 with different weights. The linear activation function (by which D takes the inputs and combines them to produce an output) looks like a regression with no intercept. If you add what is called a "bias term" of 0.05 to the neuron D as shown in Figure 12.3, then the linear activation function by which D takes the inputs and produces an output is: output = 0.05 + 0.1(1) + 0.2(1) + 0.3(1) = 0.65.

More generally, if Y is the output and the inputs are X1, X2, and X3, then the activation function could be written Y = 0.05 + 0.1 * X1 + 0.2 * X2 + 0.3 * X3. Similarly, neurons E and F would have their own activation functions.

The activation functions used in neural networks are rarely linear as in the above examples. They are usually nonlinear transformations of the linear combination of the inputs. One such nonlinear transformation is the hyperbolic tangent, *tanh*, which would turn the value 0.65 into 0.572 as shown in Figure 12.4. Observe that in the central region of the input, near zero, the relationship between the input and the output is nearly linear; 0.65 is not that far from 0.572. However, farther away from zero, the relationship becomes decidedly nonlinear. Another common activation function is the Gaussian radial basis function.

Figure 12.4: Hyperbolic Tangent Activation Function

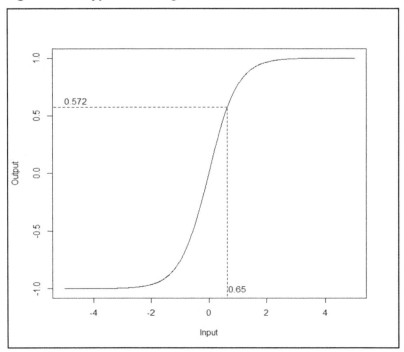

A More Realistic Representation

In practice, neural networks are slightly more complicated than those shown in Figures 12.2 and 12.3 and usually look like Figure 12.5. Rather than move directly from input to output, to obtain modeling flexibility, the inputs (what are called the Xs in a regression problem) are transformed into features (essentially, nodes labeled as Z in Figure 12.5). These are new variables that are combinations of the input variables. Then these variables are used as the inputs that produce the output.

To achieve this goal of flexibility, between the input and output layers is a hidden layer that models the features (in essence, creates new variables). As usual, let X represent inputs, Y represent outputs, and let Z represent features. A typical representation of such a neural network is given in Figure 12.5. Let there be *k* input variables, *p* features (which means *p* nodes in the hidden layer), and a single output. Each node of the input layer connects to each node of the hidden layer. Each of these connections has a weight, and each hidden node has a bias term. Each of the hidden nodes has its own activation function that must be chosen by the user.

Similarly, each node of the hidden layer connects to the node in the output layer, and the output node has a bias term. The activation function that produces the output is not chosen by the user. If

Figure 12.5: A Standard Neural Network Architecture

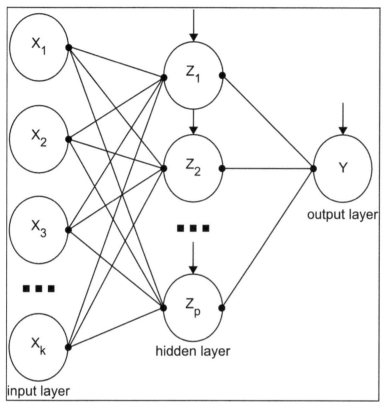

the output is continuous, it will be a linear combination of the features, and if the output is binary, it will be based on a logistic function as discussed in Chapter 6.

A neural network with k inputs, p hidden nodes, and 1 output has $p(k + 2) + 1$ weights to be estimated. So if $k = 20$ inputs and $p = 10$ hidden nodes, then there are 221 weights to be estimated. How many observations are needed for each weight? It depends on the problem and is, in general, an open question with no definitive answer. But suppose it's 100. Then you need 22,100 observations for such an architecture.

The weights for the connections between the nodes are initially set to random values close to zero and are modified (trained) on an iterative basis. By default, the criterion for choosing the weights is to minimize the sum of squared errors; this is also called the least squares criterion. The algorithm chooses random numbers close to zero as weights for the nodes, and creates an initial prediction for the output. This initial prediction is compared to the actual output, and the prediction error is calculated. Based on the error, the weights are adjusted, and a new prediction is made that has a smaller sum of squared errors than the previous prediction. The process stops when the sum of squared errors is sufficiently small.

The phrase "sufficiently small" merits elaboration. If left to its own devices, the neural network will make the error smaller and smaller on subsequent iterations, changing the weights on each iteration, until the error cannot be made any smaller. In so doing, the neural network will overfit the model (see Chapter 14 for an extended discussion of this concept) by fitting the model to the random error in the data. Essentially, an overfit model will not generalize well to other data sets. To combat this problem, JMP offers two validation methods: holdback and cross validation.

Understand Validation Methods

In traditional statistics, and especially in the social sciences and business statistics, you need only run a regression and report an R^2. (This is a bit of an oversimplification, but not much of one.) Little or no thought is given to the idea of checking how well the model actually works. In data mining, it is of critical importance that the model "works"; it is almost unheard of to deploy a model without checking whether the model actually works. The primary method for doing such checking is called *validation*.

Holdback Validation

The holdback validation method works in the following way. The data set is randomly divided into two parts, the training sample and the validation (holdback) sample. Both parts have the same underlying model, but each has its own unique random noise. The weights are estimated on the training sample. Then, these weights are used on the holdback sample to calculate the error. It is common to use two thirds of the data for the training and one third for the validation. Initially, as the algorithm iterates, the error on both parts will decline as the neural network learns the model that is common to both parts of the data set. After a sufficient number of iterations (that is, recalculations of the weights) the neural network will have learned the model, and it will then begin to fit the random noise in the training sample. Since the holdback sample has different random noise, its calculated error will begin to increase.

One way to view this relationship between the error (which you want to minimize) and the number of iterations is displayed in Figure 12.6. After n iterations, the neural network has determined the weights that minimize the error on the holdback sample. Any further iterations will only fit the noise in the training data and not the underlying model (and obviously will not fit the noise in the validation sample). Therefore, the weights based on n iterations that minimize the error on the holdout sample should be used. The curves in Figure 12.6 and the divergence between them as the number of iterations increases is a general method of investigating overfitting.

Figure 12.6: Typical Error Based on the Training Sample and the Holdback Sample

Error

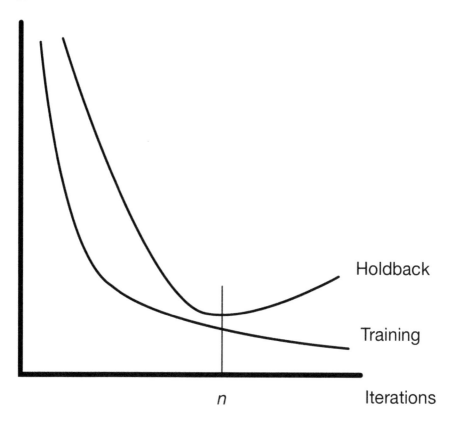

k-fold Cross Validation

A second way to validate, called *k-fold cross validation*, works in a different way to determine the number of iterations at which to stop, but the basic idea is the same. Divide the data set into k groups, or folds, that contain approximately the same number of observations. Consider $k - 1$ folds to be the training data set, and the kth fold to be the validation data set. Compute the relevant measure of accuracy on the validation fold. Repeat this k times, each time leaving out a different fold, thus obtaining k measures of accuracy. Average the k measures of accuracy to obtain an overall estimate of the accuracy. As with holdback validation, to avoid overfitting, compare the training error to the validation error. Cross validation is most often used when there are not enough data to divide the data into training and validation samples.

If randomly splitting the data set into two parts is not desirable for some reason, there is a third way to divide the data into training and validation samples. The user can manually split the data into two parts by instructing JMP to include specific rows for the training sample and to exclude others that will constitute the holdback sample. There are two ways to do this.

First, the user can select some observations in the Data Table, right-click, and set them to **Exclude**. Then, when executing a neural net, under Validation Method, the user can choose Excluded Rows Holdback. Second, the user creates a new variable that indicates by zeros and ones whether a particular observation should be for training (zero) or validation (1). In the Neural dialog box when variables are cast as *Y* or *X*, the user will also set a variable as **Validation**. It will automatically be used for the validation method.

Understand the Hidden Layer Structure

Figure 12.5 shows a neural network architecture with one hidden layer that has *p* nodes. The nodes do not all have to have the same activation function. They can have any combination of the three types of activation functions, tanh, linear, or Gaussian. For example, six nodes in the hidden layer could have all tanh, or could have two each of the three types of the activation functions. Nor is the network limited to one hidden layer: JMP allows up to two hidden layers.

A Few Guidelines for Determining Number of Nodes

Concerning the architecture of a neural network, the two fundamental questions are as follows: How many nodes for the input layer, and how many nodes for the output layer? For the former, the number of variables is the answer. This number cannot be large for two reasons. First, a large number of variables greatly increases the possibility of local optima and correspondingly decreases the probability of finding the global optimum. Second, as the number of variables increases, the amount of time it takes to solve the problem increases even more. A tree or a logistic regression can easily accommodate hundreds of variables. A neural network might not be able to tolerate tens of variables, depending on the sample size and also depending on how long you can wait for JMP to return a solution. The number of nodes in the output layer depends on the problem. To predict a single continuous variable or a binary variable, use one output node. For a categorical variable with five levels, use five output nodes, one for each level.

Suppose that there is only a single hidden layer. The guiding principle for determining the number of nodes is that there should be enough nodes to model the target variable, but not so many as to overfit. There are many rules of thumb to follow. Some of those rules are for setting the number of nodes:

- to be between the number of inputs and the number of outputs
- to equal the number of inputs plus the number of outputs times two-thirds
- to be no more than twice the number of inputs
- to be approximately ln(T) where T is the sample size
- to be between 5% and 10% of the number of variables

This list is a set of rules of thumb; notice that the first and second are contradictory. No citations are given here for these rules of thumb because they are all, in some sense, misleading. The fact is that there is no widely accepted procedure for determining the number of nodes in a hidden layer, and there is no formula that will give a single number to answer this question. (Of course, good advice is to find an article that describes successful modeling of the type in question, and use that article as a starting point.)

Practical Strategies for Determining Number of Nodes

The necessary number of hidden nodes is a function of, among other things, the sample size, the complexity of the function to be modeled (and this function is usually unknown!), and the amount of noise in the system (which you cannot know unless you know the function!). With too few hidden nodes, the network cannot learn the underlying model and therefore cannot make good predictions on new data. But with too many nodes, the network memorizes the random noise (overfits) and cannot make good predictions on new data. Yoon et al. (1994) indicate that performance improves with each additional hidden node up to a point, after which performance deteriorates.

Therefore, a useful strategy is to begin with some minimum number of hidden nodes and increase the number of hidden nodes, keeping an eye on prediction error via the holdback sample or cross validation, adding nodes so long as the prediction error continues to decline, and stopping when the prediction error begins to increase. If the training error is low and the validation error (either holdback or *k*-fold cross validation) is high, then the model has been overfit, and the number of hidden nodes should be decreased. If both the training and validation errors are high, then more hidden nodes should be added. If the algorithm will not converge, then increase the number of hidden nodes. The bottom line is that extensive experimentation is necessary to determine the appropriate number of hidden nodes. It is possible to find successful neural network models built with as few as three nodes (predicting river flow) and as many as hundreds of hidden nodes (speech and handwriting recognition). The vast majority of analytics applications of neural networks seen by the authors have fewer than thirty hidden nodes.

The number of hidden layers is usually one. The reason to use a second layer is because it greatly reduces the number of hidden nodes that are necessary for successful modeling (Stathakis, 2009). There is little need to resort to using the second hidden layer until the number of nodes in the first hidden layer has become untenable—that is, the computer fails to find a solution or takes too long to find a solution. However, using two hidden layers makes it easier to get trapped at a local optimum, which makes it harder to find the global optimum.

The Method of Boosting

Boosting is an option that can be used to enhance the predictive ability of the neural network. Boosting is one of the great statistical discoveries of the 20th century. A simplified discussion follows. Consider the case of a binary classification problem (for example, zero or one). Suppose you have a classification algorithm that is a little better than flipping a coin—for example, it is correct 55% of the time. This is called a *weak classifier*. Boosting can turn a weak classifier into a strong classifier.

The method of boosting is to run the algorithm once where all the observations have equal weight. In the next step, give more weight to the incorrectly classified observations and less weight to the correctly classified observations, and run the algorithm again. Repeat this re-weighting process until the algorithm has been run T times, where T is the "Number of Models" that the user specifies. Each observation then has been classified T times. If an observation has been classified more times as a zero than a one, then zero is its final classification. If it has been classified more times as a one, then that is its final classification. The final classification model, which uses all T of the weighted classification models, is usually more accurate than the initial classification, and sometimes much more accurate. It is not unusual to see the error rate (the proportion of observations that are misclassified) drop from 20% on the initial run of the algorithm to below 5% for the final classification.

Boosting methods have also been developed for predicting continuous target variables. Gradient boosting is the specific form of boosting used for neural networks in JMP, and a further description can be found in the JMP help files. In the example in the manual, a 1-layer/2-node model is run when $T = 6$, and the "final model" has 1 layer and $2 \times 6 = 12$ nodes (individual models are retained and combined at the end). This corresponds to the general method described above in the sense that the T re-weighted models are combined to form the final model.

The method of gradient boosting requires a learning rate, which is a number greater than zero and less than or equal to one. The learning rate describes how quickly the algorithm learns: the higher the learning rate, the faster the method converges, but a higher learning rate also increases the probability of overfitting. When the Number of Models (T) is high, the learning rate should be low, and vice versa.

Understand Options for Improving the Fit of a Model

One approach to improving the fit of the model is to transform all the continuous variables to near normality. This can be especially useful when the data contain outliers or are heavily skewed, and it is recommended in most cases. JMP offers two standard transformation methods, the Johnson Su and Johnson Sb methods. JMP automatically selects the preferred method.

In addition to the default least squares criterion, which minimizes the sum of squared errors, another criterion can be used to choose the weights for the model. The robust fit method minimizes the absolute value of the errors rather than the squared errors. This can be useful when outliers are present, since the estimated weights are much more sensitive to squared errors than absolute errors in the presence of outliers.

The penalty method combats the tendency of neural networks to overfit the data by imposing a penalty on the estimated weights, or coefficients. Some suggestions for choosing penalties follow. For example, the squared method penalizes the square of the coefficients. This is the default and is a good choice if you think that most of your inputs contribute to predicting the output. The absolute method penalizes the absolute value of the coefficients, and this can be useful if you think that only some of your inputs contribute to predicting the output. The weight decay method can be useful if you think that only some of your inputs contribute to predicting the output. The no penalty option is much faster than the penalty methods, but it usually does not perform as well as the penalty methods because it tends to overfit.

As mentioned previously, to begin the iterative process of estimating the weights for the model, the initial weights are random numbers close to zero. Hence, the final set of weights is a function of the initial, random weights. It is this nature of neural networks to be prone to having multiple local optima that makes it easy for the minimization algorithm to find a local minimum for the sum of squared errors, rather than the global minimum. One set of initial weights can cause the algorithm to converge to one local optimum, but another set of initial weights might lead to another local optimum. Of course, you're seeking not local optima but the global optimum, and you hope that one set of initial weights might lead to the global optimum.

To guard against finding a local minimum instead of the global minimum, it is customary to restart the model several times using different sets of random initial weights, and then to choose the best of the several solutions. Using the Number of Tours option, JMP will do this automatically so that the user does not need to do the actual comparison by hand. Each "tour" is a start with a new set of random weights. A good number to use is 20 (Sall, Creighton, and Lehman, 2007, p. 468).

Complete the Data Preparation

Data with different scales can induce instability in neural networks (Weigend and Gershenfeld, 1994). Even if the network remains stable, having data with unequal scales can greatly increase the time necessary to find a solution. For example, if one variable is measured in thousands and another in units, the algorithm will spend more time adjusting for variation in the former rather than the latter. Two common scales for standardizing the data are (1) $x - \bar{y} \ / s$, where s is the sample standard deviation and (2) $x - \bar{y} / \max(x) \ - \min(x)$, although other methods exist.

Simply for ease, scale 1 is preferred because it is automated in JMP. Select **Analyze ▶ Distribution**. Then, after the distribution is plotted, click the red triangle next to the variable name and select **Save ▶ Standardized**. Another way is when creating the neural network model, check the box for **Transform Covariates** under **Fitting Options**.

In addition to scaling, the data must be scrubbed of outliers. Outliers are especially dangerous for neural networks because the network will model the outlier rather than the bulk of the data—much more so than, for example, with logistic regression. Naturally, outliers should be removed before the data are scaled.

A categorical variable with more than two levels can be converted to dummy variables. But this means adding variables to the model at the expense of making the network harder to train and needing more data.

It is not always the case that categorical variables should be turned into dummy variables. First, especially in the context of neural networks that cannot handle a large number of variables, converting a categorical variable with *k* categories creates more variables. Doing this conversion with a few categorical variables can easily make the neural network model too difficult for the algorithm to solve. Secondly, conversion to dummy variables can destroy an implicit ordering of the categories that, when maintained, prevents the number of variables from being needlessly multiplied (as happens when converting to dummy variables). Pyle (1999, p. 74) gives an example where a marital status variable with five categories (married, widowed, divorced, single, or never married), instead of being converted to dummy variables, is better modeled as a continuous variable in the [0,1] range as shown in Table 12.1.

This approach is most useful when the levels of the categorical variable embody some implicit order. For example, if the underlying concept is "marriedness," then someone who is divorced has been married more than someone who has never been married. A "single" person might be "never," "divorced," or "widowed," but you don't know which. Such a person is more likely to have experienced marriage than someone who has never been married. See Pyle (1999) for further discussion.

Neural networks are not like a tree or a logistic regression, both of which are useful in their own rights—the former as a description of a data set, the latter as a method of describing the effect of one variable on another. The only purpose of the neural network is for prediction. In the context of predictive analytics, you will generate predictions from a neural network and compare these predictions to those from trees and logistic regression. Then, you will use the model that predicts the best. The bases for making these comparisons are the confusion matrix, ROC and lift curves, and various measures of forecast accuracy for continuous variables. All these are explained in the Chapter 14.

Table 12.1: Converting an Ordered Categorical Variable to [0,1]

Marital Status	Value
Never Married	0
Single	0.1
Divorced	0.15
Widowed	0.65
Married	1.0

Use JMP on an Example Data Set

The Kuiper.jmp data set comes from Kuiper (2008). It contains the prices of 804 used cars and several variables thought to affect the price. The variable names are self-explanatory, and the interested reader can consult the article (available free and online) for additional details. To keep the analysis simple, you will focus on one continuous target variable (Price), two continuous independent variables (Mileage and Liter), and four binary variables (Doors, Cruise, Sound, and Leather).

Ignore the other variables (for example, Model and Trim). It will probably be easier to run the analyses if variables are defined as *y* or *x*:

1. In the Data Table, select a variable by highlighting its column.
2. Select **Cols** and then **Preselect Role**.
3. Select **Y** for **Price**.
4. Select **X** for **Mileage**, **Liter**, **Doors**, **Cruise**, **Sound**, and **Leather**.

Perform a Linear Regression as a Baseline

As a baseline for your neural network modeling efforts, first run a linear regression. Of course, before running a regression, you must first examine the data graphically. A scatterplot (select **Graph ▶ Scatterplot Matrix**) shows a clear group of observations near the top of most of the plots. Clicking them indicates that these are observations 151–160. Referring to the data set, you see that these are the Cadillac Hardtop Conv 2D cars. Since these cars appear to be outliers, exclude them from the analysis:

1. Select these rows, and then right-click and select **Exclude/Unexclude**.
2. Check the linearity of the relationship (select **Analyze ▶ Fit Y by X**).
3. Click the **Bivariate Fit of Price by Mileage** red triangle and select **Fit Line**. Do the same for **Bivariate Fit of Price by Liter**.
4. Linearity seems reasonable, so run the full regression. Select **Analyze ▶ Fit Model** and click **Run**.

The RSquare is 0.439881; call it 0.44.

Launch the neural network. With a baseline established, turn to the neural network approach. Since you have preselected roles for the relevant variables, they will automatically be assigned as dependent and independent variables. You do not have to select variables each time you run a model. Select **Analyze ▶ Predictive Modeling ▶ Neural** and get the object shown in Figure 12.7.

Figure 12.7: Neural Network Model Launch

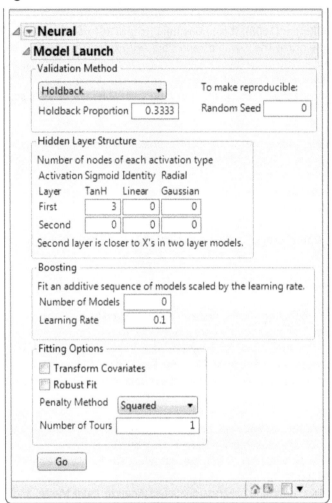

First notice the Random Seed box, which at default is set to 0. When this seed is set to 0, every time the model is run, it gets a brand-new sequence of random numbers. If you want to use the same sequence of random numbers, perhaps because you want someone else to reproduce your answers, set the random seed to a nonzero positive number. As long as the nonzero seed is the same, the same sequence of random numbers will be used, and the results will be the same. Now notice the default options. The validation method is Holdback with a holdback proportion of one-third. There is a single hidden layer with three nodes, each of which uses the tanh activation function. No boosting is performed, because the Number of Models is zero. Neither Transform Covariates nor Robust Fit is used, though the Penalty Method is applied with a particular type of method being Squared. The model will be run only once, because Number of Tours equals one. Click **Go**.

Figure 12.8: Results of Neural Network Using Default Options

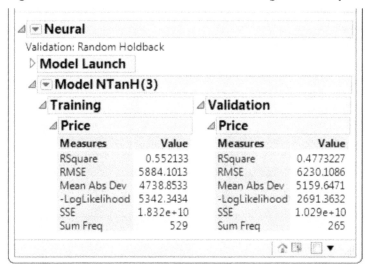

Your results will not be exactly like those in Figure 12.8 for two reasons. First, a random number generator is used to determine which one-third of the observations were used for the validation sample. Because your training and validation samples differ, so will your numerical results. Even if you had the same training and validation samples, your numerical results would still differ because your initial weights would be different. Remember that the neural network fitting of the weights is an iterative process that must begin somewhere, with some initial weights. These initial weights are random numbers near zero, produced by the JMP random number generator. Since your initial weights are different, your final weights will be different, too.

Perform the Neural Network Ten Times to Assess Default Performance

To get a feel for how much the results can vary, rerun the default neural network nine more times, keeping track of the training and validation RSquare each time:

1. Click the **Model NTanH(3)** red triangle and select **Remove Fit**. The Model Launch will reappear.
2. Click **Go**.

(You do not have to choose **Remove Fit**, but doing so reduces the number of results presented. Alternatively, you can click the drop-down menu for **Model Launch**, and the Model Launch dialog box will reappear.)

Table 12.2: Training and Validation RSquare Running the Default Model Ten Times

Run	Training	Validation
1	52	50
2	60	56
3	56	52
4	46	51
5	58	54
6	59	56
7	55	57
8	62	58
9	61	58
10	56	52

The results are presented in Table 12.2, but remember that your results will differ.

Notice that the Training RSquare varies substantially, from a low of 46 to a high of 62. These many different solutions are a manifestation of the "multiple local optima" problem that is common to neural networks. Because the model is so highly nonlinear, there often will be several local optima when you really want the unique global optimum. To guard against mistakenly settling for a suboptimal result (for example, the RSquare of 46 in Table 12.2), it is necessary to run the model several times. Since your goal is to get the best-fitting model on new data, you would naturally choose the model that has the RSquare of 62, as long as it was supported by the Validation RSquare. If the Validation RSquare was much lower than 58, you would take that to be evidence of overfitting and discard the model.

For this reason, JMP has the Number of Tours option that will automatically run the model several times and report only the model with the best RSquare. Typically, you expect to see a validation R^2 that is near the training R^2 if you have successfully modeled the data, or to see a validation R^2 that is much below the training R^2 if you have overfit the data. Occasionally, you can see a validation R^2 that is higher than the training R^2, as in the first column of Table 12.2 when the training R^2 is 46.

Boost the Default Model

Now that you have some idea of what the default performance is, you can try boosting the default model, setting the Number of Models option to 100. Results, shown in Table 12.3, are rather impressive. The average of the ten training Rsquared values in Table 12.2 is 56.5. The average of the ten training RSquare values in Table 12.3 is 67.4, an increase of more than 10 points.

Table 12.3: Training and Validation RSquare When Boosting the Default Model, Number of Models = 100

Run	Training	Validation
1	71	70
2	67	65
3	66	64
4	66	64
5	69	67
6	67	65
7	65	65
8	68	66
9	66	62
10	67	65

The downside is that boosting is designed to work with weak models, not strong models. It can turn a mediocre model into a good model, as you see, but it cannot turn a good model into a great model. Usually, you ought to be able to build a model good enough so that boosting won't help. When, however, the best that can be done is a weak model, it's nice to have the boosting method as a backup.

Compare Transformation of Variables and Methods of Validation

Perhaps other options might improve the performance of the model on the validation data. Tables 12.2 and 12.3 show run-to-run variation from changing initial coefficients for each run. After you click **Go**, the random draws that separate the data into training and validation for any particular run are fixed for the rest of the models that are run in the Neural report window. If this report window is closed and then the model is run again, the training and validation data will be different. To mitigate variation due to changing initial coefficients, you can select the Number of Tours option, which tries many different sets of initial coefficients and chooses the run with the best results. With respect to the difference between training and validation runs, you see that sometimes the R^2 is approximately the same, and other times one or the other is higher.

In what follows—and, indeed, in what you have done so far—it must be stressed that no firm conclusions can be drawn concerning the superiority of one set of options when the number of runs equals only 5 or 10. There is no reason to rerun the model 100 times in the hope of obtaining definitive conclusions because the conclusions would apply only to the data set being used. Hence, your conclusions are only tentative and conditional on the data being used.

Table 12.4: R^2 for Five Runs of Neural Networks

Run	K-Fold Train	K-Fold Validate	Holdback Train	Holdback Validate
Untransformed 1	73	62	67	68
Untransformed 2	64	59	60	57
Untransformed 3	75	76	73	76
Untransformed 4	68	52	54	56
Untransformed 5	74	66	56	55
Transformed 1	71	81	71	62
Transformed 2	75	67	71	73
Transformed 3	74	88	68	71
Transformed 4	73	73	70	73
Transformed 5	74	74	68	62

Next, compare transforming the variables as well as the method of validation. For this set of experiments, you will set the Number of Tours as 30. Results are presented in Table 12.4, where you use one hidden layer with three tanh functions, and compare 10-fold cross validation with one-third holdback sample on the car data, using the transform covariates option with Number of Tours = 30.

You tentatively conclude that transforming produces better results than not transforming, as evidenced by the higher training R^2. (Take care to remember that five runs are far too few to draw such a conclusion.) Look at the untransformed results. If you only ran the model once and happened to get 74/66 (74 for training, 66 for validation) or 73/62, you might think that the architecture that you chose overfit the data. Had you happened to get 75/76, you might think you had not overfit the data. This type of random variation in results must be guarded against, which means that the model must be run with many different architectures and many different options. And even then, the same architecture with the same options should be run several times to guard against aberrant results.

In the best scenario, when you finally have settled on a model and run it several times, all the training R^2 would be about the same, all the validation R^2 would be about the same, and the validation R^2 would be about the same as the training R^2 or perhaps a little lower. As for the present case in Table 12.4, you are far from the ideal situation. Between the training and validation data, sometimes the R^2 is approximately the same, sometimes it is higher for training, and sometimes it is higher for validation.

You have seen here situations in which the validation R^2 is noticeably higher than the training R^2. Two such cases occur in Table 12.4. In particular, look at the transformed/k-fold case for 74/88, which has 714 observations in the training data and 80 in the validation data. This situation is

Figure 12.9: Residual Plot for Training Data When R^2 = 74%

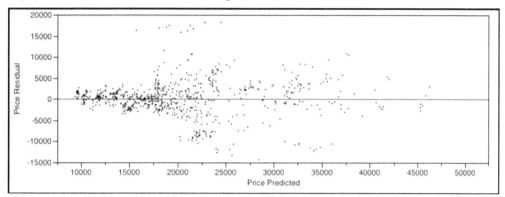

Figure 12.10: Residual Plot for Validation Data When R^2 = 88%

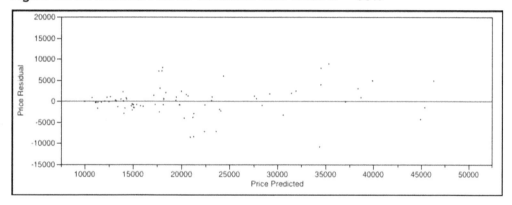

usually the result of some observations with large residuals (one hesitates to call them "outliers") that are in the training data not making it into the validation data. See the residuals plots for this case in Figures 12.9 (training data) and 12.10 (validation data). To make such plots, click the **Model NTanH(3)** red triangle and then select **Plot Residual by Predicted**.

A big difference between these residual plots lies in the 15,000–25,000 range on the X axis, and in the 15,000-20,000 range on the Y axis. The training data has residuals in this region that the validation data do not, and these are large residuals. Other such differences can be observed (for example, between 20,000 and 35,000 on the X axis, below the zero line). Hence, the big difference that you see in the R^2 between the two figures.

To be cautious, you should acknowledge that the Transform Covariates option might not satisfactorily handle outliers (you might have to remove them manually). Using a robust method of estimation might improve matters by making the estimates depend less on extreme values. For the validation methods, *k*-fold seems to have a higher R^2. This might be due to a deficient sample size, or it might be due to a faulty model.

In Table 12.5, the penalty varies. The Number of Tours option is set to 30, Transform Covariates is selected, and Holdback is set to one-third, with one hidden layer with three hidden nodes using the tanh activation function. Clearly, the Squared penalty produces the best results. So, moving forward, you will not use any other penalty for this data set.

Table 12.5: R^2 for Different Penalty Functions

Run	Train	Validate
No penalty 1	58	60
No penalty 2	61	62
No penalty 3	58	61
No penalty 4	58	57
No penalty 5	57	60
Squared 1	73	71
Squared 2	74	71
Squared 3	75	69
Squared 4	73	71
Squared 5	75	72
Absolute 1	58	62
Absolute 2	53	59
Absolute 3	53	58
Absolute 4	61	65
Absolute 5	58	62
Weight decay 1	56	60
Weight decay 2	58	60
Weight decay 3	60	62
Weight decay 4	60	62
Weight decay 5	58	61

Change the Architecture

Next, try changing the architecture as shown in Table 12.6. You use the Squared penalty, keep Number of Tours at 30, and select the Transform Covariates option. Increase the number of hidden nodes from three to four, five, and then ten. Finally, change the number of hidden layers to two, each with six hidden nodes. All of these use the tanh function. Using 4 nodes represents an improvement over 3 nodes; and using 5 nodes represents an improvement over 4 nodes. Changing the architecture further produces only marginal improvements.

Table 12.6: R^2 for Various Architectures

Architecture	Run	Train	Validate
1 Layer, 4 nodes	1	75	74
1 Layer, 4 nodes	2	79	78
1 Layer, 4 nodes	3	76	75
1 Layer, 4 nodes	4	75	75
1 Layer, 4 nodes	5	85	81
1 Layer, 5 nodes	1	87	83
1 Layer, 5 nodes	2	87	84
1 Layer, 5 nodes	3	78	77
1 Layer, 5 nodes	4	86	84
1 Layer, 5 nodes	5	88	85
1 Layer, 10 nodes	1	89	84
1 Layer, 10 nodes	2	86	84
1 Layer, 10 nodes	3	89	84
1 Layer, 10 nodes	4	89	85
1 Layer, 10 nodes	5	88	82
2 Layers, 6 nodes each	1	91	88
2 Layers, 6 nodes each	2	87	86
2 Layers, 6 nodes each	3	87	85
2 Layers,6 nodes each	4	89	84
2 Layers, 6 nodes each	5	89	85

Compared to linear regression (which had an R^2 of 0.44, you might recall), a neural network with one layer and five or ten nodes is quite impressive, as is the network with two layers and six nodes each.

Predict a Binary Dependent Variable

Predict a binary dependent variable. For the sake of completeness, you briefly consider using the neural network to predict a binary dependent variable. Create a binary variable that equals one if the price is above the median and equals zero otherwise. That the median equals 18205 can be found by selecting **Analyze ▶ Distributions**. To create the binary variable, complete the following steps:

1. Select **Cols ▶ New Column** and type **MedPrice** for the column name.
2. Click **Column Properties**, and select **Formula**.
3. Under the list of Functions on the left side, click **Conditional** and select **If**. The relevant part of the dialog box should look like Figure 12.11. Click **OK**.
4. Click **OK**.

Figure 12.11: Creating a Binary Variable for Median Price

$$\text{If}\begin{pmatrix} Price \geq 18025 \Rightarrow 1 \\ else \qquad\qquad \Rightarrow 0 \end{pmatrix}$$

Next, complete the following steps:

1. In the Data Table, highlight the column for **Price** and change its role to **No Role**.
2. Highlight **MedPrice**, select **Cols ▶ Preselect Role**, and select **Y**.
3. Click the blue triangle next to **MedPrice** and change its type to **Nominal**.
4. Select **Analyze ▶ Predictive Modeling ▶ Neural** and click **Go**.

The results including confusion matrices and confusion rates are displayed similarly to Figure 12.12. (Your results will be numerically different due to the use of the random number generator.)

Figure 12.12: Default Model for the Binary Dependent Variable, MedPrice

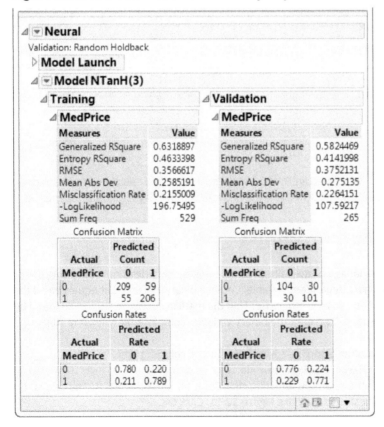

The correct predictions from the model, as shown in the Confusion Matrix, are in the upper left and lower right (for example, 209 and 206). Looking at the Confusion Rates, you can see that the correctly predicted proportions for zeros and ones are 0.78 and 0.789, respectively. These rates decline slightly in the validation sample (to 0.776 and 0.771), as is typical, because the model tends to overfit the training data.

Exercises

1. Investigate whether the **Robust** option makes a difference. For the Kuiper data that has been used in this chapter (don't forget to drop some observations that are outliers!), run a basic model 20 times (for example, the type in Table 12.4). Run it 20 more times with the **Robust** option invoked. Characterize any differences between the results. For example, is there less variability in the R^2? Is the difference between training R^2 and validation R^2 smaller? Now include the outliers, and redo the analysis. Has the effect of the **Robust** option changed?

2. For all the analyses of the Kuiper data in this chapter, ten observations were excluded because they were outliers. Include these observations and rerun the analysis that produced one of the tables in this chapter (for example, Table 12.4). What is the effect of including these outliers? You will have to set the seed for the random number generator and use the same seed twice: once when you run the model with the excluded observations, and again after you include the observations. If you don't do this, then you can't be sure whether the differences are due to the inclusion/exclusion of observations or the different random numbers!

3. For the neural net prediction of the binary variable MedPrice, try to find a suitable model by varying the architecture and changing the options.

4. Develop a neural network model for the Churn data.

5. In Chapter 10, you developed trees in two cases: a classification tree to predict whether students return and a regression tree to predict GPA. Develop a neural network model for each case.

6. As indicated in the text, sometimes rescaling variables can improve the performance of a neural network model. Rescale the variables for an analysis presented in the chapter (or in the exercises), and see whether the results improve.

Chapter 13: Bootstrap Forests and Boosted Trees

Introduction

Decision trees, discussed in Chapter 10, are easy to comprehend, easy to explain, can handle qualitative variables without the need for dummy variables, and (as long as the tree isn't too large) are easily interpreted. Despite all these advantages, trees suffer from one grievous problem: they are unstable.

In this context, unstable means that a small change in the input can cause a large change in the output. For example, if one variable is changed even a little, and if the variable is important, then it can cause a split high up in the tree to change and, in so doing, cause changes all the way down the tree. Trees can be very sensitive not just to changes in variables, but also to the inclusion or exclusion of variables.

Fortunately, there is a remedy for this unfortunate state of affairs. As shown in Figure 13.1, this chapter discusses two techniques, bootstrap forests and boosted trees, which overcome this instability and many times result in better models.

Figure 13.1: A Framework for Multivariate Analysis

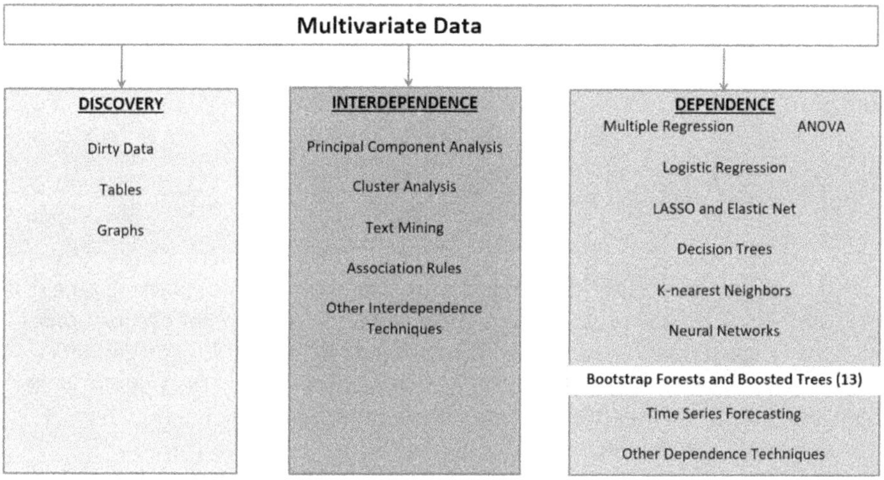

Multivariate Data		
DISCOVERY	**INTERDEPENDENCE**	**DEPENDENCE**
Dirty Data	Principal Component Analysis	Multiple Regression ANOVA
Tables	Cluster Analysis	Logistic Regression
Graphs	Text Mining	LASSO and Elastic Net
	Association Rules	Decision Trees
	Other Interdependence Techniques	K-nearest Neighbors
		Neural Networks
		Bootstrap Forests and Boosted Trees (13)
		Time Series Forecasting
		Other Dependence Techniques

Bootstrap Forests

The first step in constructing a remedy involves a statistical method known as "the bootstrap." The idea behind the bootstrap is to take a single sample and turn it into several "bootstrap samples," each of which has the same number of observations as the original sample. In particular, a bootstrap sample is produced by random sampling with replacement from the original sample. These several bootstrap samples are then used to build trees. The results for each observation for each tree are averaged to obtain a prediction or classification for each observation. This averaging process implies that the result will not be unstable. Thus, the bootstrap remedies the great deficiency of trees.

This chapter does not dwell on the intricacies of the bootstrap method. (If interested, see "The Bootstrap," an article written by Shalizi (2010) in *American Scientist*. Suffice it to say that bootstrap methods are very powerful and, in general, do no worse than traditional methods that analyze only the original sample, and very often (as in the present case) can do much better.

It seems obvious now that you should take your original sample, turn it into several bootstrap samples, and construct a tree for each bootstrap sample. You could then combine the results of these several trees. In the case of classification, you could grow each tree so that it classified each observation—knowing that each tree would not classify each observation the same way.

Bootstrap forests, also called *random forests* in the literature, are a very powerful method, probably the most powerful method, presented in this book. On any particular problem, some other method might perform better. In general, however, bootstrap forests will perform better than other methods. Beware, though, of this great power. On some data sets, bootstrap forests can fit the data perfectly or almost perfectly. However, such a model will not predict perfectly or almost perfectly on new data. This is the phenomenon of "overfitting" the data, which is discussed in detail in Chapter 14. For now, the important point is that there is no reason to try to fit the data as well as possible. Just try to fit it well enough. You might use other algorithms as benchmarks, and then see whether bootstrap forests can do better.

Understand Bagged Trees

Suppose you grew 101 bootstrap trees. Then you would have 101 classifications ("votes") for the first observation. If 63 of the votes were "yes" and 44 were "no," then you would classify the first observation as a "yes." Similarly, you could obtain classifications for all the other observations. This method is called "bagged trees," where "bag" is shorthand for "bootstrap aggregation"— bootstrap the many trees and then aggregate the individual answers from all the trees. A similar approach can obtain predictions for each observation in the case of regression trees. This method uses the same data to build the tree and to compute the classification error.

An alternative method of obtaining predictions from bootstrapped trees is the use of "in-bag" and "out-of-bag" observations. Some observations, say two-thirds, are used to build the tree (these are the "in-bag" observations) and then the remaining one-third out-of-bag observations are dropped down the tree to see how they are classified. The predictions are compared to the truth for the out-of-bag observations, and the error rate is calculated on the out-of-bag observations. The reasons for using out-of-bag observations will be discussed more fully in Chapter 14. Suffice it to say that using the same observations to build the tree and then also to compute the error rate results in an overly optimistic error rate that can be misleading.

There is a problem with bagged trees, and it is that they are all quite similar, so their structures are highly correlated. We could get better answers if the trees were not so correlated, if each of the trees was more of an independent solution to the classification problem at hand. The way to achieve this was discovered by Breiman (2001). Breiman's insight was to not use all the independent variables for making each split. Instead, for each split, a subset of the independent variables is used.

To see the advantage of this insight, consider a node that needs to be split. Suppose variable $X1$ would split this node into two child nodes. Each of the two child nodes contains about the same number of observations, and each of the observations is only moderately homogeneous. Perhaps variable $X2$ would split this into two child nodes. One of these child nodes is small but relatively pure; the other child node is much larger and moderately homogenous. If $X1$ and $X2$ have to compete against each other in this spot, and if $X1$ wins, then you would never uncover the small, homogeneous node. On the other hand, if $X1$ is excluded and $X2$ is included so that $X2$ does not have to compete against $X1$, then the small, homogeneous pocket will be uncovered. A large number of trees is created in this manner, producing a forest of bootstrap trees. Then, after each tree has classified all the observations, voting is conducted to obtain a classification for each observation. A similar approach is used for regression trees.

Perform a Bootstrap Forest

To demonstrate bootstrap forests, use the Titanic data set, TitanicPassengers.jmp, the variables of which are described below in Table 13.1. It has 1,309 observations.

You want to predict who will survive:

1. Open the TitanicPassengers.jmp data set.
2. In the course of due diligence, you will engage in exploratory data analysis before beginning any modeling. This exploratory data analysis will reveal that **Body** correlates perfectly with not surviving (**Survived**), as selecting **Analyze ▶ Tabulate** (or **Fit Y by X**), for these two variables will show. Also, **Lifeboat** correlates very highly with surviving (**Survived**), because very few of the people who got into a lifeboat failed to survive. So, use only the variables marked with an asterisk in Table 13.1.
3. Select **Analyze ▶ Predictive Modeling ▶ Partition**.

Table 13.1: Variables in the TitanicPassengers.jmp Data Set

Variable	Description
Passenger Class *	1 = first, 2 = second, 3 = third
Survived *	No, Yes
Name	Passenger name
Sex *	Male, female
Age *	Age in years
Siblings and Spouses *	Number of Siblings and Spouses aboard
Parents and Children *	Number of Parents and Children aboard
Ticket #	Ticket number
Fare *	Fare in British pounds
Cabin	Cabin number (known only for a few passengers)
Port *	Q = Queenstown, C = Cherbourg, S = Southampton
Lifeboat	16 lifeboats 1–16 and four inflatables A–D
Body	Body identification number for deceased
Home/Destination	Home or destination of traveler

4. Select **Survived** as **Y, response**. The other variables with asterisks in Table 13.1 are **X, Factor**.
5. For **Method**, choose **Bootstrap Forest**. **Validation Portion** is zero by default. **Validation** will be discussed in Chapter 14. For now, leave this at zero.
6. Click **OK**.

or

3. Select **Analyze ▶ Predictive Modeling ▶ Bootstrap Forest**.
4. Select **Survived** as **Y, response**. The other variables with asterisks in Table 13.1 are **X, Factor**.
5. **Validation Portion** is zero by default. Leave this at zero.
6. Click **OK**.

Understand the Options in the Dialog Box

Some of the options presented in the Bootstrap Forest dialog box, shown in Figure 13.2, are as follows:

- **Number of trees in the forest** is self-explanatory. There is no theoretical guidance on what this number should be. But empirical evidence suggests that there is no benefit to having a very large forest. 100 is the default. Try also 300 and 500. Setting the number of trees to be in the thousands probably will not be helpful.
- **Number of terms sampled per split** is the number of variables to use at each split. The default value is 6. If the original number of predictors is p, use $\sqrt{p}$ rounded down for

classification, and for regression use $p/3$ rounded down (Hastie et al. 2009, p. 592). These are only rough recommendations. After trying $\sqrt{p}$, try $2\sqrt{p}$ and $\sqrt{p}/2$, as well as other values, if necessary.

- **Bootstrap sample rate** is the proportion of the data set to resample with replacement. Just leave this at the default 1 so that the bootstrap samples have the same number of observations as the original data set.

  - **Minimum Splits Per Tree** and **Maximum Splits Per Tree** are self-explanatory.

  - **Minimum Size Split** is the minimum number of observations in a node that is a candidate for splitting. For classification problems, the minimum node size should be one. For regression problems, the minimum node size should be five as recommended by Hastie et al. (2009, page 592).

  - Do not check the box **Multiple Fits over number of terms**. The associated **Max Number of Terms** is only used when the box is checked. The interested reader is referred to the user guide for additional details.

For now, change the **Number of Terms Sampled per Split** to 1 and just click **OK**.

The output of the Bootstrap Forest should look like Figure 13.3.

Figure 13.2: The Bootstrap Forest Dialog Box

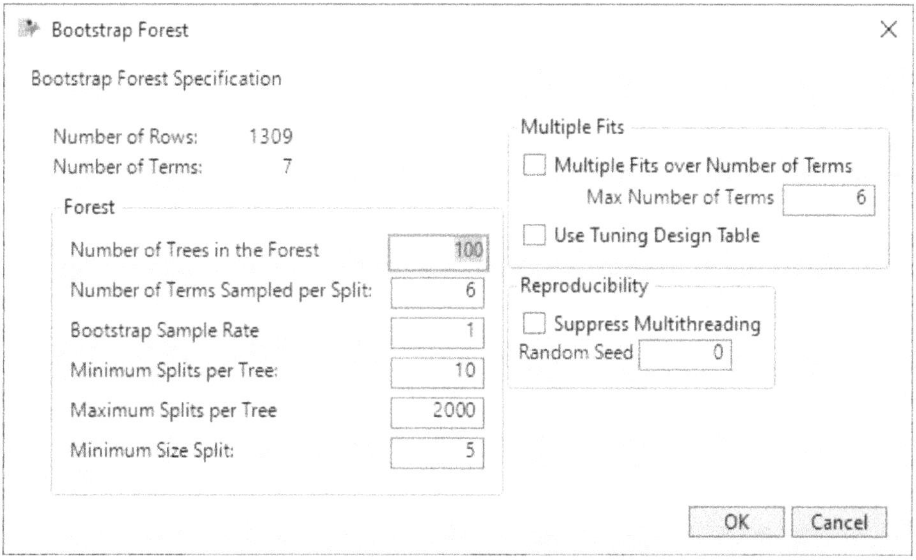

Figure 13.3: Bootstrap Forest Output for the TitanicPassengers.jmp Data Set

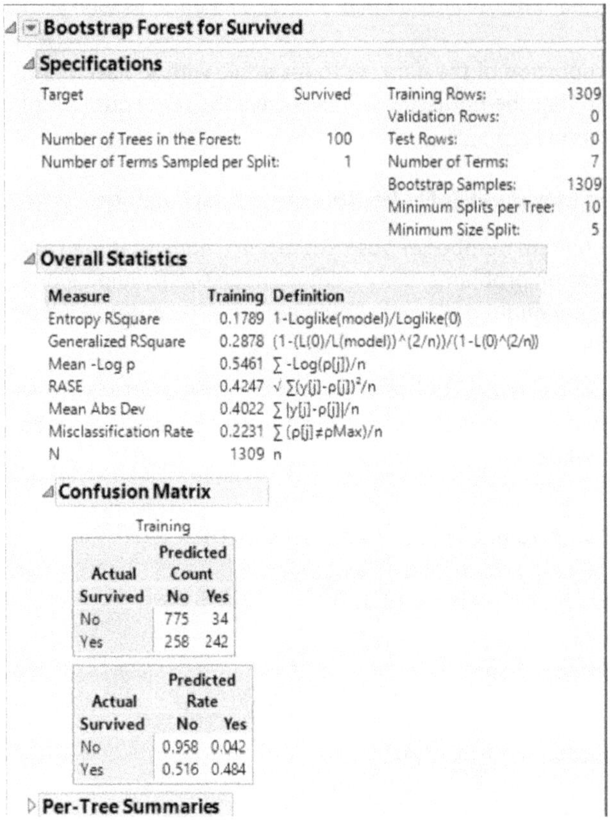

⊿ ⊡ **Bootstrap Forest for Survived**

⊿ **Specifications**

Target	Survived	Training Rows:	1309
		Validation Rows:	0
Number of Trees in the Forest:	100	Test Rows:	0
Number of Terms Sampled per Split:	1	Number of Terms:	7
		Bootstrap Samples:	1309
		Minimum Splits per Tree:	10
		Minimum Size Split:	5

⊿ **Overall Statistics**

Measure	Training	Definition
Entropy RSquare	0.1789	1-Loglike(model)/Loglike(0)
Generalized RSquare	0.2878	$(1-(L(0)/L(model))^{(2/n)})/(1-L(0)^{(2/n)})$
Mean -Log p	0.5461	$\sum -Log(p[j])/n$
RASE	0.4247	$\sqrt{\sum(y[j]-p[j])^2/n}$
Mean Abs Dev	0.4022	$\sum |y[j]-p[j]|/n$
Misclassification Rate	0.2231	$\sum (p[j] \neq pMax)/n$
N	1309	n

⊿ **Confusion Matrix**

Training

Actual	Predicted Count	
Survived	**No**	**Yes**
No	775	34
Yes	258	242

Actual	Predicted Rate	
Survived	**No**	**Yes**
No	0.958	0.042
Yes	0.516	0.484

▷ **Per-Tree Summaries**

Select Options and Relaunch

Your results will be slightly different because this algorithm uses a random number generator to select the bootstrap samples. The sample size is 1,309. The lower left value in the first column of the Confusion Matrix, 258, and the top right value in the right-most column, 34, are the classification errors (discussed further in Chapter 14). Added together, 258 + 34 = 292, they compose the numerator of the reported misclassification rate in Figure 13.3: 292/1309 = 22.31%. Now complete the following steps:

1. Click the **Bootstrap Forest for Survived** red triangle and select **Redo ▶ Relaunch Analysis**.
2. The Partition dialog box appears. Click **OK**.
3. Now you are back in the Bootstrap Forest dialog box, as in Figure 13.2. Click **OK**. This time, double **the Number of Terms Sampled Per Split** to **2**.
4. Click **OK**.

The Bootstrap Forest output should look similar to Figure 13.4.

Figure 13.4: Bootstrap Forest Output with the Number of Terms Sampled per Split to 2

⊿ ⊽ Bootstrap Forest for Survived

⊿ Specifications

Target	Survived	Training Rows:	1309
		Validation Rows:	0
Number of Trees in the Forest:	100	Test Rows:	0
Number of Terms Sampled per Split:	2	Number of Terms:	7
		Bootstrap Samples:	1309
		Minimum Splits per Tree:	10
		Minimum Size Split:	5

⊿ Overall Statistics

Measure	Training	Definition
Entropy RSquare	0.3645	1-Loglike(model)/Loglike(0)
Generalized RSquare	0.5223	$(1-(L(0)/L(model))^{(2/n)})/(1-L(0)^{(2/n)})$
Mean -Log p	0.4226	$\sum -Log(p[j])/n$
RASE	0.3606	$\sqrt{\sum(y[j]-p[j])^2/n}$
Mean Abs Dev	0.3030	$\sum |y[j]-p[j]|/n$
Misclassification Rate	0.1597	$\sum (p[j] \neq pMax)/n$
N	1309	n

⊿ Confusion Matrix

Training

Actual	Predicted Count	
Survived	No	Yes
No	761	48
Yes	161	339

Actual	Predicted Rate	
Survived	No	Yes
No	0.941	0.059
Yes	0.322	0.678

▷ **Per-Tree Summaries**

Examine the Improved Results

Notice the dramatic improvement. The error rate is now 15.97%. You could run the model again, this time increasing the **Number of Terms Sampled Per Split** to **3** and increasing the **Number of Trees** to **500**. These changes will again produce another dramatic improvement. Notice also that, although there are many missing values in the data set, Bootstrap Forest uses the full 1309 observations. Many other algorithms (for example, logistic regression) have to drop observations that have missing values.

An additional advantage of random forests is that, just like basic decision trees in Chapter 10 produced column contributions to show the important variables, random forests produce a similar ranking of variables. To get this list, click the **Bootstrap Forest for Survived** and select **Column Contributions**. This ranking can be especially useful in providing guidance for variable selection when later building logistic regressions or neural network models.

Perform a Bootstrap Forest for Regression Trees

Now briefly consider random forests for regression trees. Use the data set MassHousing.jmp in which the target variable is median value:

1. Select **Analyze ▶ Predictive Modeling ▶ Partition**.
2. Select **mvalue** for **Y, Response** and all the other variables as **X, Factor**.
3. For method, select **Bootstrap Forest**.
4. Click **OK**.
5. In the Bootstrap Forest dialog box, leave everything at default and click **OK**.

The Bootstrap Forest output should look similar to Figure 13.5.

Under **Overall Statistics**, see the In-Bag and Out-of-Bag RMSE. Notice that the Out-of-Bag RMSE is much larger than the In-Bag RMSE. This is to be expected because the algorithm is fitting on the In-Bag data. It then applies the estimated model to data that were not used to fit the model to obtain the Out-of-Bag RMSE. You will learn much more about this topic in Chapter 14. What's important for your purposes is that you obtained RSquare = 0.946 and RMSE = 1.863 for the full data set (remember that your results will be different because of the random number generator). These values compare quite favorably with the results from a linear regression: RSquare = 0.7406 and RMSE = 4.745. You can see that bootstrap forest regression can offer a substantial improvement over traditional linear regression. Additionally, bootstrap forest regression addresses nonlinearity better than ordinary least squares.

Figure 13.5: Bootstrap Forest Output for the MassHousing.jmp Data Set

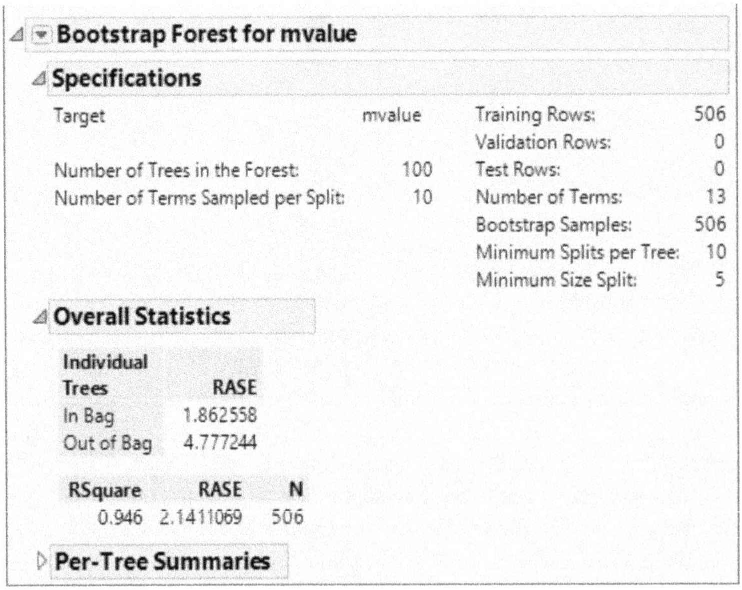

△ ▼ **Bootstrap Forest for mvalue**

△ **Specifications**

Target	mvalue	Training Rows:	506
		Validation Rows:	0
Number of Trees in the Forest:	100	Test Rows:	0
Number of Terms Sampled per Split:	10	Number of Terms:	13
		Bootstrap Samples:	506
		Minimum Splits per Tree:	10
		Minimum Size Split:	5

△ **Overall Statistics**

Individual Trees	RASE
In Bag	1.862558
Out of Bag	4.777244

RSquare	RASE	N
0.946	2.1411069	506

▷ **Per-Tree Summaries**

Boosted Trees

Boosting is a general approach to combining a sequence of models in which each successive model changes slightly in response to the errors from the preceding model.

Understand Boosting

Boosting starts with estimating a model and obtaining residuals. The observations with the biggest residuals (where the model did the worst job) are given additional weight, and then the model is re-estimated on this transformed data set. In the case of classification, the misclassified observations are given more weight. After several models have been constructed, the estimates from these models are averaged to produce a prediction or classification for each observation. As was the case with bootstrap forests, this averaging implies that the predictions or classifications from the boosted tree model will not be unstable. When boosting, there is often no need to build elaborate models; simple models often suffice. In the case of trees, there is no need to grow the tree completely out; a tree with just a few splits often will do the trick. Indeed, simply fitting "stumps" (trees with only a single split and two leaves) at each stage often produces good results.

A boosted tree builds a large tree by fitting a sequence of smaller trees. At each stage, a smaller tree is grown on the scaled residuals from the prior stage, and the magnitude of the scaling is governed by a tuning parameter called the learning rate. The essence of boosting is that, on the current tree, it gives more weight to the observations that were misclassified on the prior tree.

Perform Boosting

Use Boosted Trees on the data set TitanicPassengers.jmp:

1. Select **Analyze ▶ Predictive Modeling ▶ Partition**.
2. For **Method**, select **Boosted Tree**.
3. Use the same variables as you did with Bootstrap Forests. Select **Survived** as **Y, response**. The other variables with asterisks in Table 13.1 are **X, Factor.**
4. Click **OK**.

or

1. Select **Analyze ▶ Predictive Modeling ▶ Boosted Tree.**
2. Select **Survived** as **Y, response**. The other variables with asterisks in Table 13.1 are **X, Factor**.
3. Click **OK**.

The Boosted Tree dialog box will appear, as shown in Figure 13.6.

Figure 13.6: The Boosted Tree Dialog Box

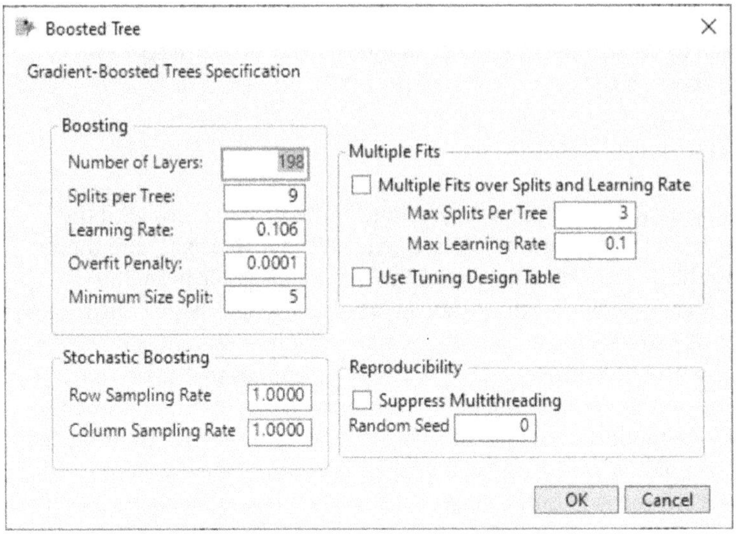

Understand the Options in the Dialog Box

The options are as follows:

- **Number of Layers** is the number of stages in the final tree. It is the number of trees to grow.
- **Splits Per Tree** is the number of splits for each stage (tree). If the number of splits is one, then "stumps" are being used.
- **Learning Rate** is a number between zero and one. A number close to one means faster learning, but at the risk of overfitting. Set this number close to one when the Number of Layers (trees) is small.
- **Overfit Penalty** helps protect against fitting probabilities equal to zero. It applies only to categorical targets.
- **Minimum Split Size** is the smallest number of observations to be in a node before it can be split.
- **Multiple Fits over splits and learning rate** will have JMP build a separate boosted tree for all combinations of splits and learning rate that the user chooses. Leave this box unchecked.

Select Options and Relaunch

For now, leave everything at default and click **OK**. The Bootstrap Tree output is shown in Figure 13.7. It shows a misclassification rate of 11.5%.

Figure 13.7: Boosted Tree Output for the TitanicPassengers.jmp Data Set

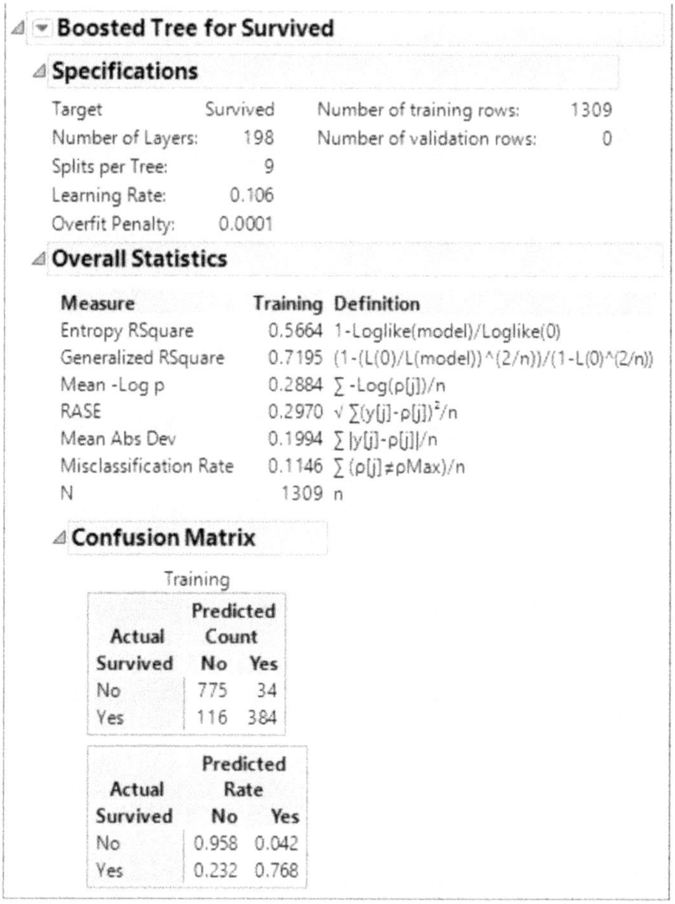

Boosted Tree for Survived

Specifications

Target	Survived	Number of training rows:	1309
Number of Layers:	198	Number of validation rows:	0
Splits per Tree:	9		
Learning Rate:	0.106		
Overfit Penalty:	0.0001		

Overall Statistics

Measure	Training	Definition
Entropy RSquare	0.5664	$1-\text{Loglike(model)}/\text{Loglike(0)}$
Generalized RSquare	0.7195	$(1-(L(0)/L(\text{model}))^{(2/n)})/(1-L(0)^{(2/n)})$
Mean -Log p	0.2884	$\sum -\text{Log}(p[j])/n$
RASE	0.2970	$\sqrt{\sum (y[j]-p[j])^2/n}$
Mean Abs Dev	0.1994	$\sum |y[j]-p[j]|/n$
Misclassification Rate	0.1146	$\sum (p[j] \neq p\text{Max})/n$
N	1309	n

Confusion Matrix

Training

Actual	Predicted Count	
Survived	No	Yes
No	775	34
Yes	116	384

Actual	Predicted Rate	
Survived	No	Yes
No	0.958	0.042
Yes	0.232	0.768

Using the guidance given about the options, set the **Learning rate** high, to 0.9.

1. Click the **Boosted Tree for Survived** red triangle and select **Redo**. Choose **Relaunch Analysis**. The Partition dialog box appears. Click **OK**.
2. The Boosted Tree dialog box appears. Change the **Learning rate** to **0.9**.
3. Click **OK**.

Examine the Improved Results

The Bootstrap Tree output will look like Figure 13.8, which has an error rate of 4.7%.

This is a substantial improvement over the default model and better than the Bootstrap Forest models. You could run the model again and this time change the **Number of Layers** to 250. Because this is bigger than the default, you could have chosen 200 or 400. Change the **Learning Rate** to 0.4. Because this is somewhere between 0.9 and 0.1, you could have chosen 0.3 or 0.6. Change the number of **Splits Per Tree** to **5** (again, there is nothing magic about this number).

Figure 13.8: Boosted Tree Output with a Learning Rate of 0.9

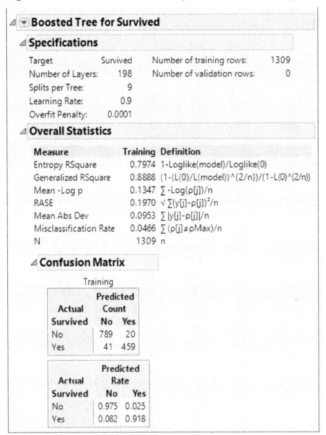

Boosted Trees is a very powerful method that also works for regression trees as you will see immediately below.

Perform a Boosted Tree for Regression Trees

Again, use the data set MassHousing.jmp.

1. Select **Analyze ▶ Predictive Modeling ▶ Partition**.
2. For **Method**, select **Boosted Tree**.
3. Select **mvalue** for the dependent variable, and all the other variables for independent variables.
4. Click **OK**.
5. Leave everything at default and click **OK**.

You should get the Boosted Tree output shown in Figure 13.9.

Figure 13.9: Boosted Tree Output for the MassHousing.jmp Data Set

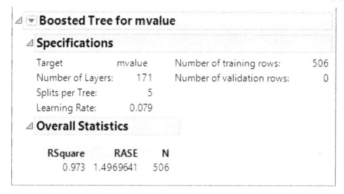

Boosting is better than the Bootstrap Forest in Figure 13.5 (look at RSquare and RMSE), to say nothing of the linear regression.

Next, relaunch the analysis and change the **Learning rate** to 0.9. This is a substantial improvement with a perfect fit with an RSquare of 1.0. This is not really surprising, because both Bootstrap Forests and Boosted Trees are so powerful and flexible that they often can fit a data set perfectly.

Use Validation and Training Samples

When using such powerful methods, you should not succumb to the temptation to the make the RSquared as high as possible because such models rarely predict well on new data. To gain some insight into this problem, you will consider one more example in this chapter in which you will use a manually selected holdout sample.

You will divide the data into two samples, a "training" sample that consists of, for example, 75% of the data, and a "validation" sample that consists of the remaining 25%. You will then rerun your three boosted tree models on the TitanicPassengers.jmp data set on the training sample. JMP will automatically use the estimated models to make predictions on the validation sample.

Create a Dummy Variable

To effect this division into training and validation samples, you will need a dummy variable that randomly splits the data into a 75% / 25% split:

1. Open TitanicPassengers.jmp.
2. Select **Analyze** ▶ **Predictive Modeling** ▶ **Make Validation Column**. Click **OK**.
3. The **Make Validation Column** report dialog box will appear, as shown in Figure 13.10.
4. Click **Go**.

Figure 13.10: The Make Validation Column Report Dialog Box

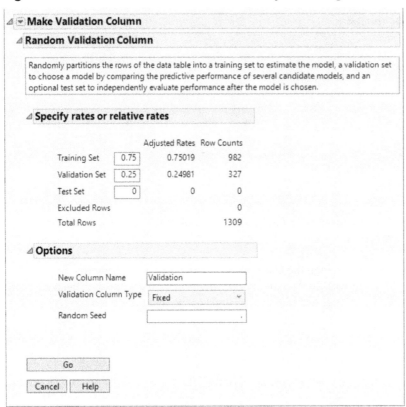

You will see that a new column called **Validation** has been added to the data table. You specified that the training set is to be 0.75 of the total rows, but this is really just a suggestion. The validation set will contain about 0.25 of the total rows.

Perform a Boosting at Default Settings

Run a Boosted Tree at default as before:

1. Select **Analyze ▶ Predictive Modeling ▶ Partition**.
2. As you did before, select **Survived** as **Y, response**. The other variables with asterisks in Table 13.1 are **X, Factor**.
3. Select the **Validation** column and then click **Validation**.
4. For Method, select **Boosted Tree**.
5. Click **OK.**
6. Click **OK** again for the options window. You are initially estimating this model with the defaults.

Examine Results and Relaunch

The results are presented in Figure 13.11. There are 982 observations in the training sample and 327 in the validation sample. Because 0.75 is just a suggestion and because the random number generator is used, your results will not agree exactly with the output in Figure 13.11. The error rate in the training sample is 15.1%, and the error rate in the validation sample is 21.4.

This strongly suggests that the model estimated on the training data predicts at least as well, if not better, on brand new data. The important point is that the model does not overfit the data (which can be detected when the performance on the training data is significantly better than the performance on new data). Now relaunch:

Figure 13.11: Boosted Tree Results for the TitanicPassengers.jmp Data Set with a Training and Validation Set

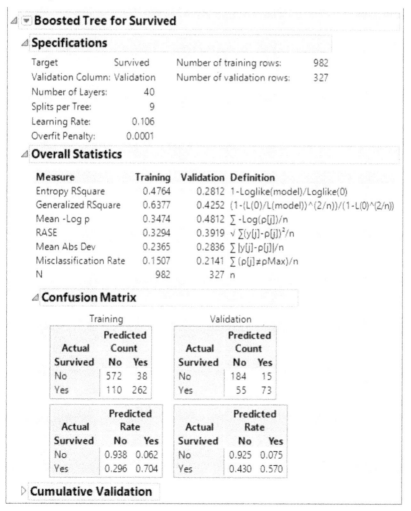

1. Click the **Boosted Tree for Survived** red triangle and select **Redo** and **Relaunch Analysis**.
2. Click **OK** to get the Boosted Trees dialog box for the options and change the learning rate to **0.9**.
3. Click **OK**.

Compare Results to Choose the Least Misleading Model

You should get results similar to Figure 13.12, where the training error rate is 11.7% and the validation error rate is 22.0%.

Now you see that the model does a better job of "predicting" on the sample data than on brand new data. This makes you think that perhaps you should prefer the default model because it does not mislead you into thinking you have more accuracy than you really do.

Figure 13.12: Boosted Tree Results with Learning Rate of 0.9

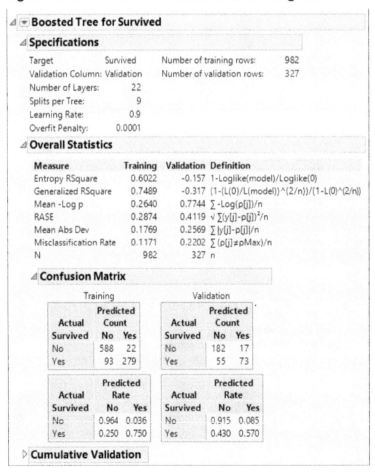

See if this pattern persists for the third model. Observe that the Number of Layers has decreased to 22, even though you specified it to be 198. This adjustment is automatically performed by JMP. As you did before, change the Learning Rate to 0.4. You should get similar results as shown in Figure 13.13, where the training error rate is 13.2% and the validation error rate is 21.4%. JMP again has changed the Number of Layers from the default 198 to 24.

It seems that no matter how you tweak the model to achieve better "in-sample" performance (that is, performance on the training sample), you always get about a 20% error rate on the brand-new data. So, which of the three models should you choose? The one that misleads you the least? The default model because its training sample performance is close to its validation sample performance? This idea of using "in-sample" and "out-of-sample" predictions to select the best model will be fully explored in the next chapter.

Figure 13.13: Boosted Tree Results with Learning Rate of 0.4

Boosted Tree for Survived

Specifications

Target	Survived	Number of training rows:	982
Validation Column: Validation		Number of validation rows:	327
Number of Layers:	24		
Splits per Tree:	9		
Learning Rate:	0.4		
Overfit Penalty:	0.0001		

Overall Statistics

Measure	Training	Validation	Definition
Entropy RSquare	0.5407	0.1132	1-Loglike(model)/Loglike(0)
Generalized RSquare	0.6969	0.1906	$(1-(L(0)/L(model))^{(2/n)})/(1-L(0)^{(2/n)})$
Mean -Log p	0.3047	0.5936	$\sum$ -Log(p[j])/n
RASE	0.3105	0.4122	$\sqrt{\sum (y[j]-p[j])^2/n}$
Mean Abs Dev	0.2082	0.2785	$\sum$ |y[j]-p[j]|/n
Misclassification Rate	0.1324	0.2141	$\sum$ (p[j]≠pMax)/n
N	982	327	n

Confusion Matrix

Training

Actual Survived	Predicted Count No	Yes
No	577	33
Yes	97	275

Validation

Actual Survived	Predicted Count No	Yes
No	177	22
Yes	48	80

Actual Survived	Predicted Rate No	Yes
No	0.946	0.054
Yes	0.261	0.739

Actual Survived	Predicted Rate No	Yes
No	0.889	0.111
Yes	0.375	0.625

Cumulative Validation

Predictions are created in the following way for both bootstrap forests and boosted trees. Suppose 38 trees are grown. The data for the new case is dropped down each tree (just as predictions were made for a single Decision Tree), and each tree makes a prediction. Then a "vote" is taken of all the trees, with a majority determining the winner. If, of the 38 trees, 20 predict "No" and the remaining 18 predict "Yes," then that observation is predicted to not survive.

Exercises

1. Without using a Validation column, run a logistic regression on the Titanic data and compare to the results in this chapter.

2. Can you improve on the results in Figure 13.3?

3. How high can you get the RSquare in the MassHousing example?

4. Without using a validation column, apply logistic regression, bootstrap forests, and boosted tree to the Churn data set.

5. Use a validation sample on boosted regression trees with MassHousing. How high can you get the RSquared on the validation sample? Compare this to your answer for Question 3.

6. Use a validation sample, and apply logistic regression, bootstrap forests, and boosted trees to the Churn data set. Compare this answer to your answer for Question 4.

Chapter 14: Model Comparison

Introduction

You know how to compare two linear regression models with the same number of independent variables: look at R^2. When the number of independent variables is different between the two regressions, look at adjusted R^2. What should you do, though, to compare a linear regression model with a nonlinear regression model, the latter of which really has no directly comparable definition for R^2? Suppose that you want to compare the results of the linear probability model (linear regression applied to a binary variable) to the results of a logistic regression. R^2 doesn't work in this case, either.

There is a definite need to compare different types of models so that the better model might be chosen, and that's the topic of this chapter. Because this chapter addresses model comparison, not a statistical technique, no technique is highlighted in the multivariate framework (Figure 14.1).

First, this chapter will examine the case of a continuous dependent variable, which is rather straightforward, if somewhat tedious. Subsequently, the binary dependent variable will be discussed. It permits many different types of comparisons, and its discussion will be quite lengthy.

Figure 14.1: A Framework for Multivariate Analysis

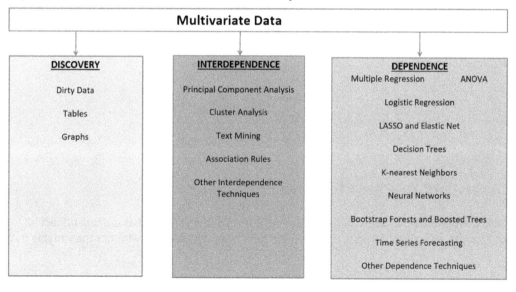

Perform a Model Comparison with Continuous Dependent Variable

Comparing models when the dependent variable is continuous relies largely on different ways of using the residuals to compute a measure of accuracy.

These performance measures are but a few of many such measures that can be used to distinguish between competing models. Others are the Akaike Information Criterion (AIC), which was discussed in Chapters 5 and 8, as well as the similar Bayesian Information Criterion (BIC).

Understand Absolute Measures

Three common measures used to compare predictions of a continuous variable are the mean square error (MSE), its square root (RMSE), and the mean absolute error (MAE). The last is less sensitive to outliers. All three of these become smaller as the quality of the prediction improves.

MSE is as follows:

$$\frac{\sum_{i=1}^{n}(\hat{y}_i - y_i)^2}{n}$$

RMSE is as follows:

$$\sqrt{\frac{\sum_{i=1}^{n}(\hat{y}_i - y_i)^2}{n}}$$

MAE is as follows:

$$\frac{\sum_{i=1}^{n}|\hat{y}_i - y|}{n}$$

Understand Relative Measures

These performance measures do not consider the level of the variable that is being predicted. For example, an error of 10 units is treated the same way, regardless of whether the variable has a level of 20 or 2,000. To account for the magnitude of the variable, relative measures can be used, as shown here.

The relative squared error is as follows:

$$\frac{\sum_{i=1}^{n}(\hat{y}_i - y_i)^2}{\sum_{i=1}^{n}(y_i - \bar{y})^2}$$

The relative absolute error is as follows:

$$\frac{\sum_{i=1}^{n}|\hat{y}_i - y_i|}{\sum_{i=1}^{n}|y_i - \bar{y}|}$$

The relative measures are particularly useful when comparing variables that have different levels.

Understand Correlation between Variable and Prediction

Another performance measure is the correlation between the variable and its prediction. Correlation values are constrained to be between −1 and +1 and to increase in absolute value as the quality of the prediction improves.

The correlation coefficient is as follows:

$$\frac{\sum_{i=1}^{n}(y_i - \bar{y})(\hat{y}_i - \bar{\hat{y}}_i)}{(n-1)s_y s_{\hat{y}}}$$

S_y and $S_{\hat{y}}$ are the standard deviations of y and ŷ, and $\bar{\hat{y}}_i$ is the average of the predicted values.

Explore the Uses of the Different Measures

In what follows, you will primarily use the absolute rather than the relative measures because you will be comparing variables that have the same levels.

Which measure should be used can be determined only by a careful study of the problem. Does the data set have outliers? If so, then absolute rather than squared error might be appropriate. If an error of 5 units when the prediction is 100 is the same as an error of 20 units when the prediction is 400 (5% error), then relative measures might be appropriate. Frequently, these measures all give the same answer. In that case, it is obvious that one model is not superior to another. On the other hand, there are cases where the measures contradict, and then careful thought is necessary to decide which model is superior.

To explore the uses of these measures, open the file McDonalds48.jmp, which gives monthly returns on McDonalds and the S&P 500 from January 2002 through December 2005. You will run a regression on the first 40 observations and use this regression to make out-of-sample predictions for the last eight observations. These eight observations can be called a *holdout sample*.

To exclude the last eight observations from the regression, select observations 41–48 (click in row 41, hold down the **Shift** key, and click in row 48). Then right-click and select **Exclude/ Unexclude**. Each of these rows should have a red circle with a slash through it.

Now run the regression:

1. Select **Analyze ▶ Fit Model**, click **Return on McDonalds**, and then click **Y**.
2. Select **Return on SP500** and click **Add**.
3. Click **Run**.
4. To place the predicted values in the Data Table, click the **Response Return on McDonalds** red triangle and select **Save Columns ▶ Predicted Values**.

Notice that JMP has made predictions for observations 41–48, even though these observations were not used to calculate the regression estimates. To calculate the desired measures:

1. On the top menu, select **Cols ▶ New Columns**.
2. In the New Column dialog box, in the Column name box, type **Sample** and click the drop arrow for Data Type. Change the type to **Character**. Click **OK**.
3. In Row 1 under Sample Column, type **In**. Click **Enter**.
4. Right-click the first cell under the Sample Column. Click **Fill ▶ Fill to row**. In the Repeat to row box, type **40**. Click **OK**.
5. Similarly, in row 41 of the Sample Column, type **Out** and click **Enter**. Right-click the 41st cell in the Sample Column. Click **Fill ▶ Fill to row**. In the Repeat to row box, type **48** and click **OK**. Now you should have a group variable called **Sample** that represents whether the observation is in or out of sample.
6. Now you need to create a new column called **Square Difference**. Click the drop arrow for Column Properties and choose **Formula**. In the Formula dialog box, click on x^y. In the formula rectangle, click on **Predicted Return on McDonalds**. Click -. Click on **Return on McDonalds** and in the power box, type **2**. Click **OK**. Click **OK**.
7. Similarly, you need to create a new column called **Abs Difference**. Click the drop arrow for Column Properties and choose **Formula**. In the Formula dialog box, under the function, click **Numeric ▶ Abs**. In the abs rectangle, click **Predicted Return on McDonalds**. Click - and click **Return on McDonalds**. Click **OK**. Click **OK**.

8. Unexclude rows 41-48. Click the red triangle on the Data Table for rows and click **Clear Row States**.
9. On the top menu, select **Tables ▶ Summary**. Choose **Sample** and click **Group**. Select **Square Difference** and **Abs Difference** and click the drop arrow for Statistics and click **Mean**.
10. To compute correlations, on the top menu, go to **Analyze ▶ Multivariate Methods ▶ Multivariate**. Select **Return on McDonalds** and **Predicted Return on McDonalds** and click **Y, Columns**. Select **Sample** and click **By**. Click **OK**.

The calculations and results are summarized in Table 14.1.

Table 14.1: Performance Measures for the McDonalds48.jmp File

	Mean Squared Error	Mean Absolute Error	Correlation
In-Sample	0.00338668	0.0473491805	.6834
Out-of-Sample	0.002849253	0.042934912	.7513

The in-sample and out-of-sample MSE and MAE are quite close, which leads you to think that the model is doing about as well at predicting out-of-sample as it is at predicting in-sample. The correlation confirms this notion. To gain some insight into this phenomenon, look at a graph of **Return on McDonalds** against **Predicted Return on McDonalds**:

1. Click the **Response Return on McDonalds** red triangle and select **Row Diagnostics ▶ Plot Actual by Predicted.**

or

1. Select **Graph ▶ Scatterplot Matrix (or select Graph ▶ Legacy ▶ Overlay Plot)**, select **Return on McDonalds**, and click **Y, Columns**.
2. Select **Predicted Return on McDonalds** and click **X**.
3. Click **OK**.

Alternatively, this graph could be made with Graph Builder.

In the Data Table, select observations 41–48, which will make them appear as bold dots on the graph. These can be a bit difficult to distinguish. To remedy the problem, while still in the data table, right-click on the selected observations, select **Markers**, and then choose the plus sign (**+**). (See Figure 14.2.)

These out-of-sample observations appear to be in agreement with the in-sample observations. This suggests that the relationship between **Y** and **X** that existed during the in-sample period continued through the out-of-sample period. Hence, the in-sample and out-of-sample correlations are approximately the same. If the relationship that existed during the in-sample

Figure 14.2: Scatterplot with Out-of-Sample Predictions as Plus Signs

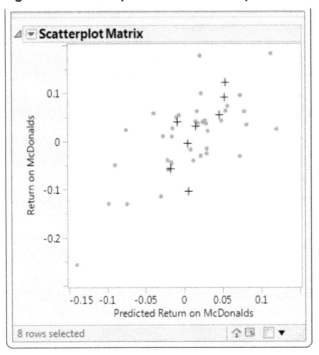

period had broken down and no longer existed during the out-of-sample period, then the correlations might not be approximately the same, or the out-of-sample points in the scatterplot would not be in agreement with the in-sample points.

Perform a Model Comparison with Binary Dependent Variable

Comparison measures for binary variables are based on the usual contingency table for binary variables.

Understand the Confusion Matrix and Its Limitations

When actual values are compared against predicted values for a binary variable, a contingency table is used. This table is often called an *error table* or a *confusion matrix*. It displays correct versus incorrect classifications, where 1 may be thought of as a "positive/successful" case and 0 might be thought of as a "negative/failure" case.

It is important to understand that the confusion matrix is a function of some threshold score. Imagine making binary predictions from a logistic regression. The logistic regression produces a probability. If the threshold is, for example, 0.50, then all observations with a score above 0.50

will be classified as positive, and all observations with a score below 0.50 will be classified as negative. Obviously, if the threshold changes to, for example, 0.55, so will the elements of the confusion matrix.

Table 14.2: An Error Table or Confusion Matrix

	Predicted 1	Predicted 0
Actual 1	True positive (TP)	False negative (FN)
Actual 0	False positive (FP)	True negative (TN)

A wide variety of statistics can be calculated from the elements of the confusion matrix, as labeled in Table 14.2. For example, the overall accuracy of the model is measured by the Accuracy:

$$\text{Accuracy} = \frac{TP + TN}{TP + FP + FN + TN} = \frac{\text{Number correctly classified}}{\text{Total number of observations}}$$

This is not a particularly useful measure because it gives equal weight to all components. Suppose that you are trying to predict a rare event—for example, cell phone churn—when only 1% of customers churn. If you simply predict that all customers do not churn, your accuracy rate will be 99%. (Since you are not predicting any churn, FP = 0 and TN = 0.) Clearly, better statistics that make better use of the elements of the confusion matrix are needed.

Understand True Positive Rate and False Positive Rate

One such measure is the sensitivity, or true positive rate, which is defined as follows:

$$\text{Sensitivity} = \frac{TP}{TP + FN} = \frac{\text{Number correctly classified as positive}}{\text{Number of positives}}$$

This is also known as *recall*. It answers the question, "If the model predicts a positive event, what is the probability that it really is positive?" Similarly, the true negative rate is also called the *specificity* and is given by the following:

$$\text{Specificity} = \frac{TN}{TN + FP} = \frac{\text{Number correctly classified as negative}}{\text{Number of negatives}}$$

It answers the question, "If the model predicts a negative event, what is the probability that it really is negative?" The false positive rate equals 1 − specificity and is given by the following:

$$\text{False positive rate}\left(\text{FPR}\right) = \frac{FP}{TN + FP} = \frac{\text{Number incorrectly classified as positive}}{\text{Number of negatives}}$$

It answers the question, "If the model predicts a negative event, what is the probability that it is making a mistake?"

Interpret Receiving Operator Characteristic Curves

When the FPR is plotted on the X axis, and the true positive rate (TPR) is plotted on the Y axis, the resulting graph is called a *receiver operating characteristic curve* (ROC curve); the name derives from the analysis of radar transmissions in World War II when this graph originated.

In order to draw the ROC curve, the classifier has to produce a continuous-valued output that can be used to sort the observations from most likely to least likely. The predicted probabilities from a logistic regression are a good example. In an ROC graph, such as that depicted in Figure 14.3, the vertical axis shows the proportion of 1s that are correctly identified, and the horizontal axis shows the proportion of zeros that are misidentified as 1s.

To interpret the ROC curve, first note that the point (0, 0) represents a classifier that never issues a positive classification: its FPR is zero, which is good. But it never correctly identifies a positive case, so its TPR is also zero, which is bad. The point (0, 1) represents the perfect classifier: it always correctly identifies positives and never misclassifies a negative as a positive.

Figure 14.3: An ROC Curve

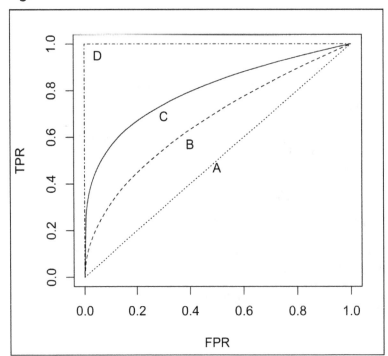

In order to understand the curve, you need to identify two extreme cases. First is the random classifier that simply guesses at whether a case is 0 or 1. The ROC for such a classifier is the dotted diagonal line A, from (0, 0) to (1, 1). To see this, suppose that a fair coin is flipped to determine classification. This method will correctly identify half of the positive cases and half of the negative cases and corresponds to the point (0.5, 0.5). To understand the point (0.8, 0.8), if the coin is biased so that it comes up heads 80% of the time (let "heads" signify "positive"), then it will correctly identify 80% of the positives and incorrectly identify 80% of the negatives. Any point beneath this 45° line is worse than random guessing.

The second extreme case is the perfect classifier, which correctly classifies all positive cases and has no false positives. It is represented by the dot-dash line D, from (0, 0) through (0, 1) to (1, 1). The closer an ROC curve gets to the perfect classifier, the better it is. Therefore, the classifier represented by the solid line C is better than the classifier represented by the dashed line B. Note that the line C is always above the line B; essentially, the lines do not cross. Remember that each point on an ROC curve corresponds to a particular confusion matrix that, in turn, depends on a specific threshold. This threshold is usually a percentage. For example, classify the observation as "1" if the probability of its being a "1" is 0.50 or greater. Therefore, any ROC curve represents various confusion matrices generated by a classifier as the threshold is changed. For an example of how to calculate an ROC curve, see Tan, Steinbach, and Kumar (2006, pp. 300–301).

Points in the lower left region of the ROC space identify "conservative" classifiers. They require strong evidence to classify a point as positive. So they have a low false positive rate; necessarily they also have low true positive rates. On the other hand, classifiers in the upper right region can be considered "liberal." They do not require much evidence to classify an event as positive. So, they have high true positive rates; necessarily, they also have high false positive rates.

When two ROC curves cross, as they do in Figure 14.3, neither is unambiguously better than the other. But it is possible to identify regions where one classifier is better than the other. Figure 14.4 shows the ROC curve as a dotted line for a classifier produced by Model 1—say, logistic regression. And the ROC curve is shown as a solid line for a classifier produced by Model 2—say, a classification tree. Suppose it is important to keep the FPR low at 0.2. Then, clearly, Model 2 would be preferred because when FPR is 0.2, it has a much higher TPR than Model 1. Conversely, if it was important to have a high TPR (for example, 0.9), then Model 1 would be preferable to Model 2 because when TPR = 0.9, Model 1 has an FPR of about 0.7, and Model 2 has an FPR of about 0.8.

The ROC can also be used to determine the point with optimal classification accuracy. Straight lines with equal classification accuracy can be drawn, and these lines will all be from the lower left to the upper right. The line that is tangent to an ROC curve marks the optimal point on that ROC curve. In Figure 14.4, the point marked A for Model 2, with an FPR of about 0.1 and a TPR of about 0.45, is an optimal point. Precise details for calculating the line of optimal classification can be found in Vuk and Curk (2006, Section 4.1).

Figure 14.4: ROC Curves and Line of Optimal Classification

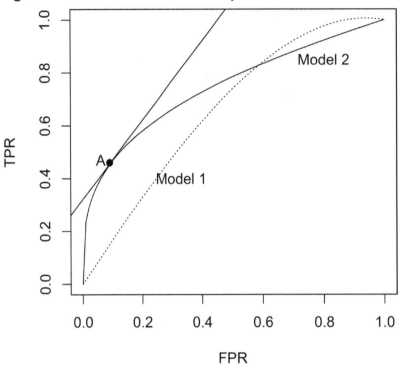

This point is optimal, assuming that the costs of misclassification are equal and that a false positive is just as harmful as a false negative. This assumption is not always true, as shown by misclassifying the issuance of credit cards. A good customer might charge $5,000 per year and carry a monthly balance of $200, resulting in a net profit of $100 to the credit card company. A bad customer might run up charges of $1,000 before his or her card is canceled. Clearly, the cost of refusing credit to a good customer is not the same as the cost of granting credit to a bad customer.

A popular method for comparing ROC curves is to calculate the *area under the curve* (AUC). Since both the X axis and Y axis are from zero to 1, and since the perfect classifier passes through the point (0, 1), the largest AUC is 1. The AUC for the random classifier (the diagonal line) is 0.5. In general, then, an ROC with a higher AUC is preferred to an ROC curve with a lower AUC. The AUC has a probabilistic interpretation. It can be shown that AUC = P (random positive example > random negative example). That is, this is the probability that the classifier will assign a higher score to a randomly chosen positive case than to a randomly chosen negative case.

Compare Two Example Models Predicting Churn

To illustrate the concepts discussed here, examine a pair of examples with real data. You will construct two simple models for predicting churn, and then compare them on the basis of ROC curves. Open churn.jmp (from Chapter 6), and fit a logistic regression:

1. Open churn.jmp.
2. **Select Analyze ▶ Fit Model. Churn** is the dependent variable (make sure that it is classified as *nominal*), where *true*, or 1, indicates that the customer switched carriers. For simplicity, choose **D_VMAIL_PLAN, VMail_Message, Day_Mins,** and **Day_Charge** as explanatory variables, and leave them as *continuous*. (If you don't recall what these variables are, refer to Chapter 6.)
3. Click **Run**.
4. Under the **Nominal Logistic Fit for Churn** red triangle, click **ROC Curve**.

Observe the ROC curve together with the line of optimal classification and the AUC is 0.65778 in Figure 14.5. The line of optimal classification appears to be tangent to the ROC at about 0.10 for 1-Specificity and about 0.45 for Sensitivity. At the bottom of the window, click the drop-down menu for the **ROC Table**. Expand it to see various statistics for the entire data set. Note that there is a column between Sens = (1 – Spec) and True Pos. Scroll down until Prob = 0.2284, and you will see an asterisk in the imagined column. This asterisk denotes the row with the highest value of Sensitivity = (1 – Specificity), which is the point of optimal classification accuracy. Should you happen to have 200,000 rows, right-click in the **ROC Table** and select **Make into Data Table**, which will be easy to manipulate to find the optimal point. Try it on the present example:

1. In the Logistic Table beneath the ROC Curve, click to expand **ROC Table**.
2. Right-click in the table itself and select **Make into Data Table.**

Figure 14.5: ROC Curves for Logistic (Left) and Partition (Right)

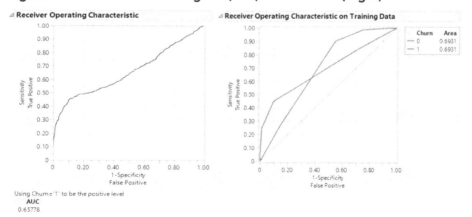

3. In the new Data Table that appears, **Column 5** is the imaginary column (JMP creates it for you). Select **Rows ▶ Data Filter**.
4. Select **Column 5** and click ⊞.
5. In the Data Filter that appears (see Figure 14.6), select the asterisk by clicking the box with the asterisk.
6. Close the data filter by clicking the **X** in the upper right corner.

In the Data Table that you have created, either scroll down to Row 377 or select **Rows ▶ Next Selected** to go to Row 377, which contains the asterisk in **Column 5**.

You want to see how JMP compares models, so go back to the churn data set and use the same variables to build a classification tree:

1. Select **Analyze ▶ Predictive Modeling ▶ Partition**.
2. Use the same Y and X variables as for the logistic regression (**Churn** versus **D_VMAIL_PLAN**, **VMail_Message**, **Day_Mins**, and **Day_Charge**).
3. Click **Split** five times so that RSquare equals 0.156.
4. Under the **Partition for Churn** red triangle, click **ROC Curve**.

You are shown two ROC Curves, one for *False* and one for *True*, as shown in the right ROC curve in Figure 14.5. They both have the same AUC because they represent the same information. Observe that one is a reflection of the other. Note that the AUC is 0.6920. The partition method does not produce a line of optimal classification because it does not produce an ROC Table. On the basis of AUC, the classification tree seems to be marginally better than the logistic regression.

Figure 14.6: Data Filter

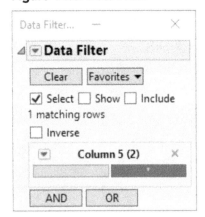

Perform a Model Comparison Using the Lift Chart

Now we show how to use the lift chart in practice.

Assess the Business Case. Suppose you intend to send out a direct mail advertisement to all 100,000 of your customers. On the basis of experience, you expect 1% of them to respond positively (for example, to buy the product). Suppose further that each positive response is worth $200 to your company. Direct mail is expensive; it will cost $1 to send out each advertisement. You expect $200,000 in revenue, and you have $100,000 in costs. Hence, you expect to make a profit of $100,000 for the direct mail campaign. Wouldn't it be nice if you could send out 40,000 advertisements from which you could expect 850 positive responses? You would save $60,000 in mailing costs and forego $150 * 200 = $30,000 in revenue for a profit of $170,000 − $40,000 = $130,000.

The key is to send the advertisement only to those customers most likely to respond positively, and not to send the advertisement to those customers who are not likely to respond positively. A logistic regression, for example, can be used to calculate the probability of a positive response for each customer. These probabilities can be used to rank the customers from most likely to least likely to respond positively. The only remaining question is how many of the most likely customers to target.

A standard lift chart is constructed by breaking the population into deciles and noting the expected number of positive responses for each decile. Continuing with the direct mail analogy, you might see lift values as shown in Table 14.3.

Table 14.3: Lift Values

Decile	Customer	Responses	Response Rate	Lift
1	10,000	280	2.80	2.80
2	10,000	235	2.35	2.35
3	10,000	205	2.05	2.05
4	10,000	130	1.30	1.30
5	10,000	45	0.45	0.45
6	10,000	35	0.35	0.35
7	10,000	25	0.25	0.25
8	10,000	20	0.20	0.20
9	10,000	15	0.15	0.15
10	10,000	10	0.10	0.10
Total	100,000	1,000	1.00	NA

Note: NA = not applicable.

Figure 14.7: Initial Lift Curves for Logistic (Left) and Classification Tree (Right)

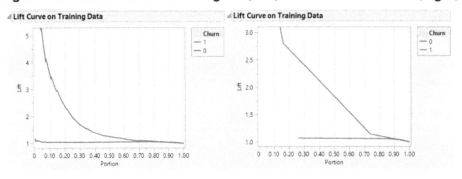

If mailing were random, then you would expect to see 100 positive responses in each decile. (The overall probability of "success" is 1,000/100,000 = 1%, and the expected number of successful mailings in a decile is 1% of 10,000 = 100.) However, since the customers were scored (had probabilities of positive response calculated for each of them), you can expect 280 responses from the first 10,000 customers. Compared to the 100 that would be achieved by random mailing, scoring gives a lift of 280/100 = 2.8 for the first decile. Similarly, the second decile has a lift of 2.35.

A lift chart does the same thing, except on a more finely graduated scale. Instead of showing the lift for each decile, it shows the lift for each percentile. Necessarily, the lift for the 100th percentile equals 1. Consequently, even a poor model lift is always equal to or greater than 1.

To create a lift chart, refer back to the previous section in this chapter, "Compare Two Example Models Predicting Churn," where you produced a simple logistic regression and a simple classification tree. This time, instead of selecting **ROC Curve**, select **Lift Curve**. It is difficult to compare graphs when they are not on the same scale. Furthermore, you cannot see the top of the lift curve for the classification tree. See Figure 14.7.

Figure 14.8: Lift Curves for Logistic (Left) and Classification Tree (Right)

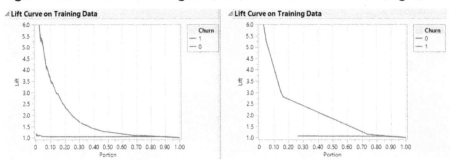

Extend the Y axis for both curves to 6.0:

1. Right-click inside the Lift Curve for the classification tree and select **Size/Scale ▶ Y Axis**.
2. Near the top of the pop-up box, change the Maximum from 3.25 to 6.
3. Click **OK**.
4. Do the same thing for the **Logistic Lift Curve**. (Alternatively, if you have one axis the way you like it, you can right-click it and select **Edit ▶ Copy Axis Settings**. Then go to the other graph, right-click on the axis, and select **Edit ▶ Paste Axis Settings**.)

Both lift curve graphs in Figure 14.8 show two curves, one for *False* and one for *True*. You are obviously concerned with *True*, since you are trying to identify churners. Suppose you wanted to launch a campaign to contact customers who are likely to churn, and you want to offer them incentives not to churn. Suppose further that, due to budgetary factors, you could contact only 40% of them. Clearly you would want to use the classification tree, because the lift is so much greater in the range 0 to 0.40.

Train, Validate, and Test

It is common in the social sciences and in some business settings to build a model and use it without checking whether the model actually works. In such situations, the model often overfits the data. That is, it is unrealistically optimistic because the analyst has fit not just the underlying model, but also the random errors. The underlying model might persist into the future, but the random errors will definitely be different in the future. In data mining, when real money is on the line, such an approach is a recipe for disaster.

Therefore, data miners typically divide their data into three sets: a training set, a validation set, and a test set. The training set is used to develop different types of models. For example, an analyst might estimate twenty different logistic models before settling on the one that works the best. Similarly, the analyst might build 30 different trees before finding the best one. In both cases, the model probably will be overly optimistic.

Rather than compare the best logistic and best tree based on the training data, the analyst should then compare them on the basis of the validation data set and choose the model that performs best. Even this will be somewhat overly optimistic. To get an unbiased assessment of the model's performance, the model that wins on the validation data set should be run on the test data set.

Perform Stepwise Regression

To illustrate these ideas, open **McDonalds72.jmp**, which contains the monthly returns on McDonald's stock, the monthly return on the S&P 500, and the monthly returns on 30 other stocks, for the period January 2000 through December 2005. You will analyze the first 60 observations, using the last 12 as a holdout sample:

1. As you did earlier in this chapter, select observations 61–72, right-click, and select **Exclude/Unexclude**.
2. Then select **Fit Y by X** and regress **Return on McDonalds (Y, response)** on the **Return on SP500 (X, factor)**.
3. Click **OK**.
4. Click the **Bivariate Fit of Return on McDonalds By Return on SP500** red triangle and click **Fit Line**.

Observe that **RSquared** is an anemic 0.271809, which, since this is a bivariate regression, implies that the correlation between y and $\hat{y}$ is $\sqrt{0.27189} = 0.52413$. This can easily be confirmed:

1. Select **Analyze ▶ Multivariate Methods ▶ Multivariate**.
2. Select **Return on McDonalds and Return on SP500**, click **Y, Columns**, and click **OK**.

Surely some of the other 30 stocks in the data set could help improve the prediction of McDonald's monthly returns. Rather than check each stock manually, use stepwise regression to automate the procedure:

1. Select **Analyze ▶ Fit Model**.
2. Click **Return on McDonalds** and click **Y**.
3. Click **Return on S&P 500** and each of the other thirty stocks. Then click **Add**.
4. Under **Personality**, click **Stepwise**.
5. Click **Run**. The Fit Stepwise page will open.
6. Under **Stepwise Regression Control**, for the **Stopping Rule**, select **P-value Threshold**. Observe that **Prob to enter** is 0.25 and **Prob to leave** is 0.1.
7. For **Direction**, select **Mixed**.
8. Note that **Prob to enter** is still 0.25, but **Prob to leave** is now 0.25. Change both **Prob to enter** and **Prob to leave** to 0.1.
9. Next to each variable are the options **Lock** and **Entered**. **Entered** will include a variable, but it might be dropped later. To keep it always, select **Lock** after selecting **Entered**. If you want a variable always omitted, then leave **Entered** blank and check **Lock**. You always want **Return on SP500** in the model, so check **Entered** and then **Lock** for this variable (Figure 14.9).
10. Click **Go.**
11. Observe that all the p-values (Prob > F) for the included variables (checked variables) in the stepwise output (not counting the intercept) are less than 0.05 except for Stock 21.

Figure 14.9: Control Panel for Stepwise Regression

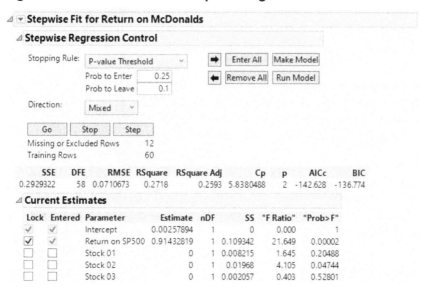

Figure 14.10: Regression Output for Model Chosen by Stepwise Regression

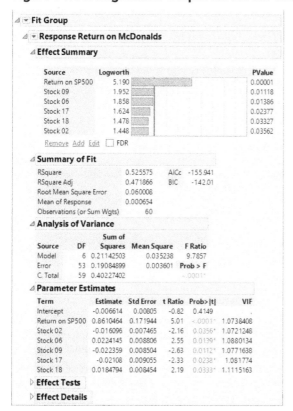

Uncheck the box next to **Stock 21** and click **Run Model** at the top of the Control Panel. The regression output for the selected model then appears (Figure 14.10).

Examine the Results of Stepwise Regression

You now have a much higher R^2 of .525575 and five stocks (in addition to S&P500) that contribute to explaining the variation in the Return on McDonalds. Stocks 02, 06, 09, 17, and 18 all have p-values of less than .05. In all, you have a very respectable regression model. You shouldn't expect to get an R^2 of .9 or .95 when trying to explain stock returns.

Indeed, this is where many such analyses stop—with a decent R^2 and high t statistics on the coefficients. Concerned as you are with prediction, you have to go further and ask, "How well does this model predict?" If you have correctly fitted the model, then you should expect to see an R^2 of about .53 on the holdout sample. This would correspond to a correlation between predicted and actual of $\sqrt{0.53} = 0.73$.

Compute the MSE, MAE, and Correlation

You can compute the MSE, MAE, and Correlation for both in-sample and out-of-sample as shown in Table 14.4:

1. In the Fit Model window, click the **Response Return on McDonalds** red triangle and select **Save Columns ▶ Predicted Values**.
2. Follow the same steps (outlined earlier in the chapter) that were used to create Table 14.1. An Excel spreadsheet for the calculations is McDonaldsMeasures72.xlsx.

You will find results matching Table 14.4.

Table 14.4: Performance Measures for the McDonalds72.jmp File

	Mean Squared Error	Mean Absolute Error	Correlation
In-Sample	0.00318082	0.04520731	0.72496528
Out-of-Sample	0.00307721	0.04416216	0.52530075

(If you have trouble reproducing Table 14.4, see the steps at the end of the exercises.)

Examine the Results for MSE, MAE, and Correlation

MSE and MAE are commonly used to compare in-sample and out-of-sample data sets, but they can be misleading. In this case, the MSE and MAE for both in-sample and out-of-sample appear to be about the same, but look at the correlations. The in-sample correlation of .725 compares with the RSquared of the model. Yet the out-of-sample correlation is the same as the original bivariate regression. What conclusion can you draw from this discrepancy? It is clear that the five additional stocks boost only the in-sample R^2 and have absolutely no effect on out-of-sample. How can this be?

The reason is that the additional stocks have absolutely no predictive power for McDonald's monthly returns. The in-sample regression is simply fitting the random noise in the 30 stocks, not the underlying relationship between the stocks and McDonalds. In fact, the 30 additional stock returns are not really stock returns but random numbers that were generated from a random normal distribution with mean zero and unit variance.[1] For other examples of this phenomenon, see Leinweber (2007).

Understand Overfitting from a Coin-Flip Example

Now take another look at this overfitting phenomenon, using coin flips. Suppose that you have forty coins, some of which might be biased. You have ten each of pennies, nickels, dimes, and quarters. You do not know the bias of each coin, but you want to find the coin of each type that most often comes up heads. You flip each coin fifty times and count the number of heads to get the results shown in Table 14.5.

Table 14.5: The Number of Heads Observed When Each Coin Was Tossed 50 Times

Coin Type	Coin 1	Coin 2	Coin 3	Coin 4	Coin 5	Coin 6	Coin 7	Coin 8	Coin 9	Coin 10
Penny	21	27	25	28	26	25	19	32	26	27
Nickel	22	29	25	17	31	22	25	23	29	20
Dime	28	23	24	23	33	18	22	19	29	28
Quarter	27	17	24	26	22	26	25	22	28	21

Apparently, none of the quarters is biased toward coming up heads. But one penny comes up heads 32 times (64% of the time); one nickel comes up heads 31 times (62%); and one dime comes up heads 33 times (66%). You are now well-equipped to flip coins for money with your friends, having three coins that come up heads much more often than random. As long as your friends are using fair coins, you will make quite a bit of money. Won't you?

Suppose you want to decide which coin is most biased. You flip each of the three coins 50 times and get the results shown in Table 14.6.

Table 14.6: The Number of Heads in 50 Tosses with the Three Coins That You Believe to Be Biased

Coin Type	Coin Toss	Number of Heads
Penny	No. 8	26
Nickel	No. 5	32
Dime	No. 5	28

[1] This example is based on Foster and Stine (2006). We thank them for providing the McDonalds and S&P 500 monthly returns

Maybe the penny and dime weren't really biased, but the nickel certainly is. Maybe you'd better use this nickel when you flip coins with your friends. You use the nickel to flip coins with your friends, and, to your great surprise, you don't win any money. You don't lose any money. You break even. What happened to your nickel? You take your special nickel home, flip it 100 times, and it comes up heads 51 times. What happened to your nickel?

In point of fact, each coin was fair, and what you observed in the trials was random fluctuation. When you flip ten separate pennies fifty times each, some pennies are going to come up heads more often. Similarly, when you flip a penny, a nickel, and a dime fifty times each, one of them is going to come up heads more often.

You know this is true for coins, but it's also true for statistical models. If you try 20 different specifications of a logistic regression on the same data set, one of them is going to appear better than the others if only by chance. If you try 20 different specifications of a classification tree on the same data set, one of them is going to appear better than the others. If you try 20 different specifications of other methods like discriminant analysis, neural networks, and nearest neighbors, you have five different types of coins, each of which has been flipped 20 times. If you take a new data set and apply it to each of these five methods, the best method probably will perform the best. But its success rate will be overestimated due to random chance. To get a good estimate of its success rate, you will need a third data set to use on this one model.

Thus, you have the train-validate-test paradigm for model evaluation to guard against overfitting. In data mining, you almost always have enough data to split it into three sets. (This is not true for traditional applied statistics, which frequently has small data sets.) For this reason, you split your data set into three parts: training, validating, and testing. For each statistical method (for example, linear regression and regression trees), you develop your best model on the training data set. Then you compare the best linear regression and the best regression tree on the validation data set. This comparison of models on the validation data set is often called a horse race. Finally, you take the winner (say, linear regression) and apply it to the test data set to get an unbiased estimate of its $R2$, or other measure of accuracy.

Use the Model Comparison Platform

In Chapter 9, you learned how to create a Validation variable to divide the data into Training and Validation sets. This feature also enables you to divide the data in Training, Validation, and Test sets if you want. In what follows, to keep things manageable, you will use only the Validation variable to define Training and Validation sets, although you could extend this to Test sets if desired. This section describes the model comparison process for continuous and discrete dependent variables.

Continuous Dependent Variable

Suppose you were concerned with predicting the variable mvalue in the MassHousing.jmp data set, MassHousing.jmp. In previous chapters, you have learned several methods for selecting a subset of variables. Now you will compare two of these methods, the LASSO and stepwise regression, using the Train-Validate-Test framework. To set the stage properly, first use both methods on the entire data set.

Perform the Stepwise Regression

First, run the forward selection version of stepwise regression:

1. Open the Mass Housing data set, **MassHousing.jmp**.
2. Select **Analyze ▶ Fit Model.**
3. Select **mvalue** as **Y**. Then, after selecting all the remaining variables, click **Add** under **Construct Model Effects**.
4. Under **Personality**, select **Generalized Regression** and click **Run**.
5. In the Generalized Regression window, under **Estimation Method**, choose **Forward Selection** and click **Go**. As you can see under **Parameter Estimates for Original Predictors**, only the variables **indus** and **age** have been zeroed out.

Perform the Linear Regression

Run the linear regression with only the nonzeroed variables:

1. Again, in the Generalized Regression output, click the **Forward Selection with AICc Validation** red triangle and choose **Select Nonzero Terms**.
2. Return to the Data Table, where you can see that the variables **indus** and **age** are not highlighted.

Figure 14.11: The Generalized Regression Output for the MassHousing.jmp Data Set with Nonzero Variables

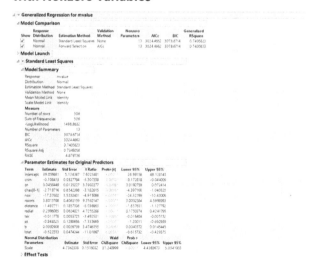

Figure 14.12: Solution Path Graphs and Parameter Estimates for Original Predictors

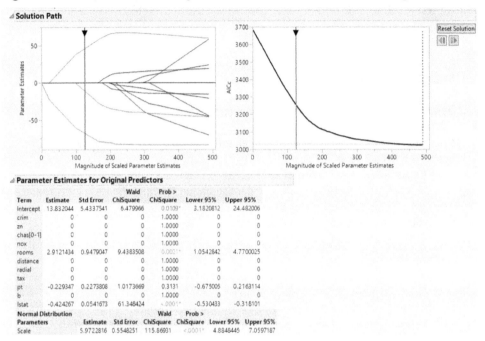

Parameter Estimates for Original Predictors

Term	Estimate	Std Error	Wald ChiSquare	Prob > ChiSquare	Lower 95%	Upper 95%
Intercept	13.832044	5.4337541	6.479966	0.0109*	3.1820812	24.482006
crim	0	0	0	1.0000	0	0
zn	0	0	0	1.0000	0	0
chas[0-1]	0	0	0	1.0000	0	0
nox	0	0	0	1.0000	0	0
rooms	2.9121434	0.9479047	9.4383508	0.0021*	1.0542842	4.7700025
distance	0	0	0	1.0000	0	0
radial	0	0	0	1.0000	0	0
tax	0	0	0	1.0000	0	0
pt	-0.229347	0.2273808	1.0173669	0.3131	-0.675005	0.2163114
b	0	0	0	1.0000	0	0
lstat	-0.424267	0.0541673	61.348424	<.0001*	-0.530433	-0.318101

Normal Distribution Parameters	Estimate	Std Error	Wald ChiSquare	Prob > ChiSquare	Lower 95%	Upper 95%
Scale	5.9722816	0.5548251	115.86931	<.0001*	4.8848445	7.0597187

3. Select **Analyze ▶ Fit Model** and click **Add** to move the nonzero variables to the **Construct Model Effects** space.
4. Select **mvalue** and click **Y**.
5. Under **Personality**, select **Generalized Regression** and click **Run**.
6. In the Generalized Regression window, under **Estimation Method**, choose **Forward Selection** and click **Go**. You can see that the Generalized RSquare is 0.740582 as showed in Figure 14.11.

Perform the LASSO

Next, run the LASSO:

1. As above, from the Data Table, select **Analyze ▶ Fit Model**, select **Recall**, and click **Run**.
2. In the Generalized Regression dialog box, under **Estimation Method**, choose **Lasso** and click **Go**.
3. In the rightmost graph, under **Solution Path**, move the solid red line until it is in the range of 130 to 150, as shown in Figure 14.12. Choose this value simply for ease of exposition. There is a very clear break in the data that makes it easy for the reader to reproduce what you do in the text.

In addition to the intercept, there are three nonzero variables: **rooms**, **pt**, and **lstat**. The coefficient on the intercept should be close to 13.8. It can be difficult to move the red line to exactly match a coefficient to several decimals. So if your intercept is close to 13.8, then you have moved the red line correctly.

Next, complete the following steps:

1. Click the **Normal Lasso with AICc Validation** red triangle and choose **Select Nonzero Terms**. You need to make sure that nothing is selected in the Data Table before doing so.
2. Now return to the Data Table, select **Analyze ▶ Fit Model**, and click **Add** to move the nonzero variables to the **Construct Model Effects** space.
3. Select **mvalue** and click **Y**.
4. Click **Run**, and click **OK**. See that the RSquare is 0.678624, substantially lower than that reported by Forward Model Selection.

Compare the Models Using the Training and Validation Sets

Now see how these models do when compared according to the Train-Validate-Test paradigm. (But obviously you are only using Training and Validation sets in this example.) First, you must create the Validation variable:

1. Select **Analyze ▶ Predictive Modeling ▶ Make Validation Column** and click **OK.** JMP defaults to 75% for the Training set and 25% for the Validation set.
2. Click **Go**. Note that the random number generator has been used to do this. Your random numbers will differ, so your results will not agree precisely with those in the book.

Next, you must exclude the validation set from your future calculations. To do so, complete the following steps:

1. Select **Rows ▶ Data Filter**. In the Data Filter dialog box, select the **Validation** variable and click ⊞. The dialog box changes slightly.
2. The Select box already is checked, but you want to also check the Include box. So, click the check box to **Include**. Near the bottom of the Data Filter window are two gray rectangles, **Training** and **Validation**. Click the **Training** rectangle.
3. Look at the Data Table. You can see that the Training data are selected and included, and the validation data are excluded.
4. Close the data filter by clicking the **X** in the upper right corner.

Perform Forward Selection and LASSO on the Training Set

Next, run Forward Selection and the LASSO on the Training set. You will then make predictions on both the Training and Validation sets and compare the predictions by using the **Model Comparison** Platform.

Figure 14.13: Forward Selection Generalized Regression for Training Data from the MassHousing.jmp Data Set

Generalized Regression for mvalue

Normal Forward Selection with AICc Validation

Model Summary

Response	mvalue
Distribution	Normal
Estimation Method	Forward Selection
Validation Method	AICc
Mean Model Link	Identity
Scale Model Link	Identity

Measure	
Number of rows	506
Sum of Frequencies	380
-LogLikelihood	1123.2569
Number of Parameters	13
BIC	2323.7361
AICc	2273.5084
RSquare	0.7508795
RSquare Adj	0.743433
RASE	4.6506211

Solution Path

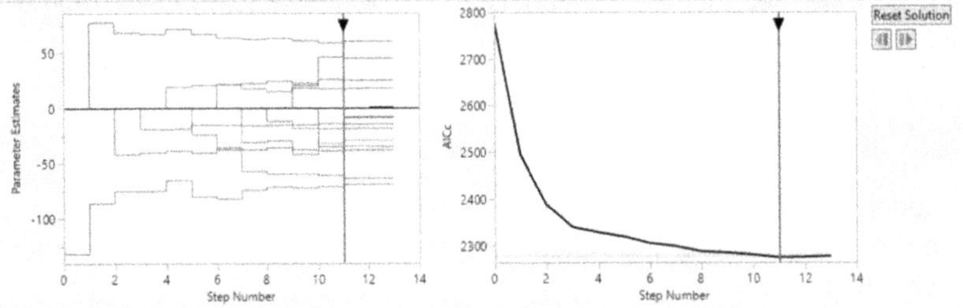

Parameter Estimates for Original Predictors

Term	Estimate	Std Error	t Ratio	Prob>|t|	Lower 95%	Upper 95%
Intercept	33.750508	5.9316388	5.6899128	<.0001*	22.086348	45.414668
crim	-0.117938	0.0388109	-3.038788	0.0025*	-0.194257	-0.041619
zn	0.0545352	0.015247	3.5767817	0.0004*	0.024553	0.0845173
indus	0	0	0	1.0000	0	0
chas[0-1]	-2.752992	0.9549952	-2.882729	0.0042*	-4.630925	-0.87506
nox	-14.43365	4.2031924	-3.433973	0.0007*	-22.69894	-6.168362
rooms	4.2380643	0.4648969	9.1161373	<.0001*	3.3238764	5.1522522
age	0	0	0	1.0000	0	0
distance	-1.446356	0.214789	-6.733847	<.0001*	-1.868724	-1.023989
radial	0.2716807	0.071174	3.8171316	0.0002*	0.1317218	0.4116396
tax	-0.010794	0.0038131	-2.830687	0.0049*	-0.018292	-0.003295
pt	-0.917353	0.1479899	-6.198754	<.0001*	-1.208365	-0.626341
b	0.0096125	0.0031249	3.0760615	0.0023*	0.0034675	0.0157574
lstat	-0.527264	0.0581876	-9.061445	<.0001*	-0.641686	-0.412842

Normal Distribution Parameters	Estimate	Std Error	Wald ChiSquare	Prob > ChiSquare	Lower 95%	Upper 95%
Scale	4.7258381	0.1756344	26.907248	<.0001*	4.3804652	5.0712111

Effect Tests

To run a Forward Selection, complete the following steps:

1. Select **Analyze ▶ Fit Model** and select **mvalue** as **Y**. After selecting all the remaining variables (not including **Validation**), click **Add** under **Construct Model Effects**. Under **Personality**, select **Generalized Regression** and click **Run**.
2. In the Generalized Regression dialog box, under **Estimation Method**, choose **Forward Selection** and click **Go**.

The Generalized Regression will look similar to Figure 14.13.

As can be seen, the **Number of rows** is 506, but the **Sum of Frequencies** is 380. (Your number might differ slightly because the number of Training records will be approximately 75%, which is the actual number of observations used in the estimation.) As before, only the variables **indus** and **age** are zero, so now run the linear regression with the nonzero variables:

1. Click the **Normal Forward Selection with AICc Validation** red triangle and choose **Select Nonzero Terms**.
2. Return to the Data Table and select **Analyze ▶ Fit Model**.
3. Click **Add**, select **mvalue**, and click **Y**. (Leave the Personality as Standard Least Squares.)
4. Click **Run**.

Figure 14.14: Regression Output for MassHousing.jmp Data Set, with Forward Selection

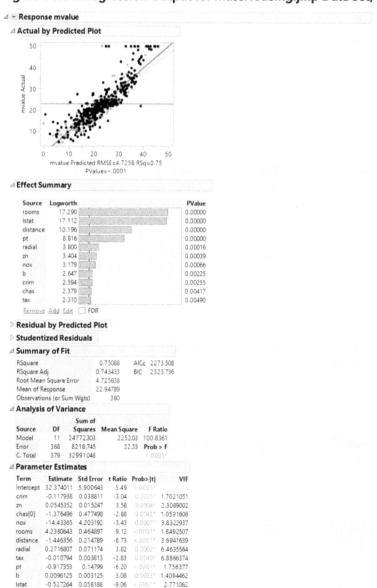

The RSquare is about 0.75 or so as shown in Figure 14.14. Remember that the use of the random number generator to select the training and validation sets means that you always have a different training data (and a different validation set) set every time you execute this procedure. Now make predictions from this model:

1. Click the **Response mvalue** red triangle and select **Save Columns ▶ Predicted Values**. A column **Predicted mvalue** appears in the data table with values for both Training and Validation observations.
2. Change the name of this new variable. Right-click at the top of the column **Predicted mvalue**, select **Column Info,** and insert **FS Predicted mvalue** (for **Forward Selection**) in the box for **Column Name**.
3. Click **OK**.

Perform LASSO on the Validation Set

Next, run the LASSO on the Validation set:

1. As before, from the Data Table, select **Analyze ▶ Fit Model**.
2. Select **mvalue** as **Y**. Then, after selecting all the original remaining variables, click **Add** under **Construct Model Effects**.
3. Under **Personality**, select **Generalized Regression** and click **Run**.
4. In the Generalized Regression dialog box, under **Estimation Method**, choose **Lasso** and click **Go**.
5. As before, move the red line in the Solution Path graphs to 130 -150 and the y-intercept is close to 13.8, so that three variables are nonzero: **rooms**, **pt** and **lstat**. Click the **Normal Lasso with AICc Validation** red triangle and choose **Select Nonzero Terms**.
6. In the Data Table, select **Analyze ▶ Fit Model**. Note that, for some reason, **FS Predicted mvalue** has been selected along with the three variables. Click **Add** and then double-click **FS Predicted mvalue** to remove it from the Construct Model Effects space.
7. Select **mvalue** and click **Y**.
8. Click **Run**.

The RSquare is about 0.69 as shown in Figure 14.15. Now make the predictions and save them:

Click the **Response mvalue** red triangle and select **Save Columns ▶ Predicted Values**. You have a new column of **Predicted mvalue** in the Data Table. As described earlier, change its name to **Lasso Predicted mvalue**.

This result does not necessarily compare unfavorably with the 0.75 RSquare from Forward Selection because they are both in-sample estimates. The real comparison will come on the Validation data.

First, you have to return to the Data Table and "unexclude" the validation data. In the data table at the top of the row numbers column, are two red triangles. The one at the top right is for the

Figure 14.15: Regression Output for MassHousing.jmp Data Set with Lasso

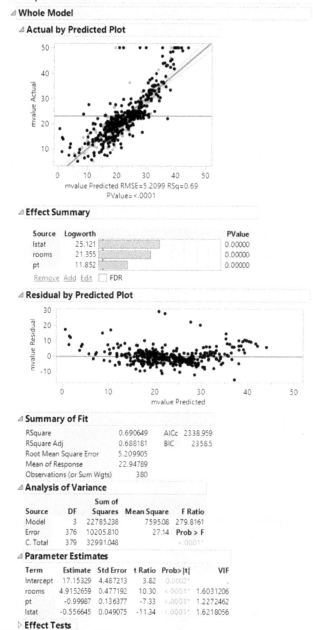

◢ ▾ Response mvalue

◢ Whole Model

◢ Actual by Predicted Plot

mvalue Predicted RMSE=5.2099 RSq=0.69
PValue=<.0001

◢ Effect Summary

Source	Logworth		PValue
lstat	25.121		0.00000
rooms	21.355		0.00000
pt	11.852		0.00000

Remove Add Edit ☐ FDR

◢ Residual by Predicted Plot

mvalue Predicted

◢ Summary of Fit

RSquare	0.690649	AICc	2338.959
RSquare Adj	0.688181	BIC	2358.5
Root Mean Square Error	5.209905		
Mean of Response	22.94789		
Observations (or Sum Wgts)	380		

◢ Analysis of Variance

Source	DF	Sum of Squares	Mean Square	F Ratio
Model	3	22785.238	7595.08	279.8161
Error	376	10205.810	27.14	Prob > F
C. Total	379	32991.048		<.0001*

◢ Parameter Estimates

Term	Estimate	Std Error	t Ratio	Prob>|t|	VIF
Intercept	17.15329	4.487213	3.82	0.0002*	
rooms	4.9152659	0.477192	10.30	<.0001*	1.6031206
pt	-0.99987	0.136377	-7.33	<.0001*	1.2272462
lstat	-0.556645	0.049075	-11.34	<.0001*	1.6218056

▷ Effect Tests

Figure 14.16: Model Comparison Dialog Box

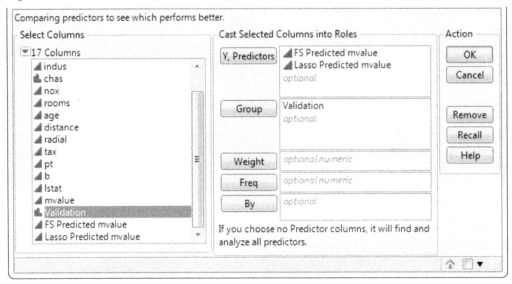

columns. The one at the bottom left is for the rows. Click the one at the bottom left and select **Clear Row States**. You should see that no rows are selected and no rows are excluded.

Compare Model Results for Training and Validation Observations

To compare the two models results for both the Training and Validation observations, complete the following steps:
1. Select **Analyze ▶ Predictive Modeling ▶ Model Comparison**.
2. In the Model Comparison dialog box, as shown in Figure 14.16, select **FS Predicted mvalue** and **Lasso Predicted mvalue**. Then click **Y, Predictors**.
3. Select the **Validation** variable and click **Group**.
4. Click **OK**.

The results are presented in Figure 14.17. It is a good thing that you changed the names of the predicted values to include **FS** and **Lasso**. Otherwise, you would have a difficult time comparing results.

You can see that the training and validation are approximately the same, so you can be sure that neither method is overfitting. You can also see that the **Forward Selection RSquare** is noticeably higher than that of the **Lasso**. So, you would prefer the former to the latter in this case. Hopefully, you can see how this method can be extended to Training, Validation, and Test sets if the need arises. For more details, see the Help files to learn about RASE and AAE.

Figure 14.17: Model Comparison of MassHousing.jmp Data Set Using Forward Selection and Lasso

▵ ▾ **Model Comparison**

▷ **Predictors**

▵ **Measures of Fit for mvalue**

Validation	Predictor	Creator	.2 .4 .6 .8	RSquare	RASE	AAE	Freq
Training	FS Predicted mvalue	Fit Least Squares		0.7509	4.6506	3.2624	380
Training	Lasso Predicted mvalue	Fit Least Squares		0.6906	5.1824	3.6172	380
Validation	FS Predicted mvalue	Fit Least Squares		0.6886	4.8362	3.3078	126
Validation	Lasso Predicted mvalue	Fit Least Squares		0.6228	5.3225	3.6827	126

Discrete Dependent Variable

The output for classification problems is a bit different, so let us try such a problem. Let us compare a logistic regression to a Bootstrap Forest. Let us use the logistic regression from Chapter 6 and the data set Churn.jmp. Churn is the dependent variable, and there are ten independent variables:

- State
- Intl_Plan
- D_VMAIL_PLAN (all three of which must be nominal)
- VMail_Message
- Day_Mins
- Even_Mins
- Night_Mins
- Intl_Mins
- Intl_Calls
- CustServ_Call

Create a validation variable and accept the defaults:

1. Select **Analyze ▶ Predictive Modeling ▶ Make Validation Column** and click **OK.**
2. JMP defaults to 75% for the Training set and 25% for the Validation set. Click **Go**.
3. Select **Rows ▶ Data Filter**. In the Data Filter dialog box, select the **Validation** variable and click ⊞. The dialog box changes slightly.
4. The Select box already is checked, but you want to also check the Include box. So, click the check box to **Include**. Near the bottom of the Data Filter window are two gray rectangles, **Training** and **Validation**. Click the **Training** rectangle.
5. Look at the Data Table. You can see that the Training data are selected and included, and the validation data are excluded.
6. Close the data filter by clicking the **X** in the upper right corner.

Run the logistic regression with the dependent and independent variables specified in the previous paragraph, and save the predicted values:

1. Click the **Nominal Logistic Fit for Churn** red triangle and select **Save Probability Formula**.
2. Four columns are added to the Data Table; change the name of all of these by adding **LR_** at the beginning.

Figure 14.18: Model Comparison Dialog Box

Run a Bootstrap Forest with Churn as the dependent variable and all the other variables (excluding the recently created ones like "Most Likely Churn"!) as independent variables. Save the predicted values:

1. Click the red triangle next to **Bootstrap Forest for Churn**, select **Save Columns ▶ Save Prediction Formula**.
2. Three columns are added to the data table. Change the name of all of these by adding **BF_** at the beginning.

Before you can use the Model Comparison Platform to compare these two sets of results across the Training and Validation sets, you must unexclude the validation data in the data table. Proceed with the model comparison.

Figure 14.19: Model Comparison Output Using the Churn.jmp Data Set

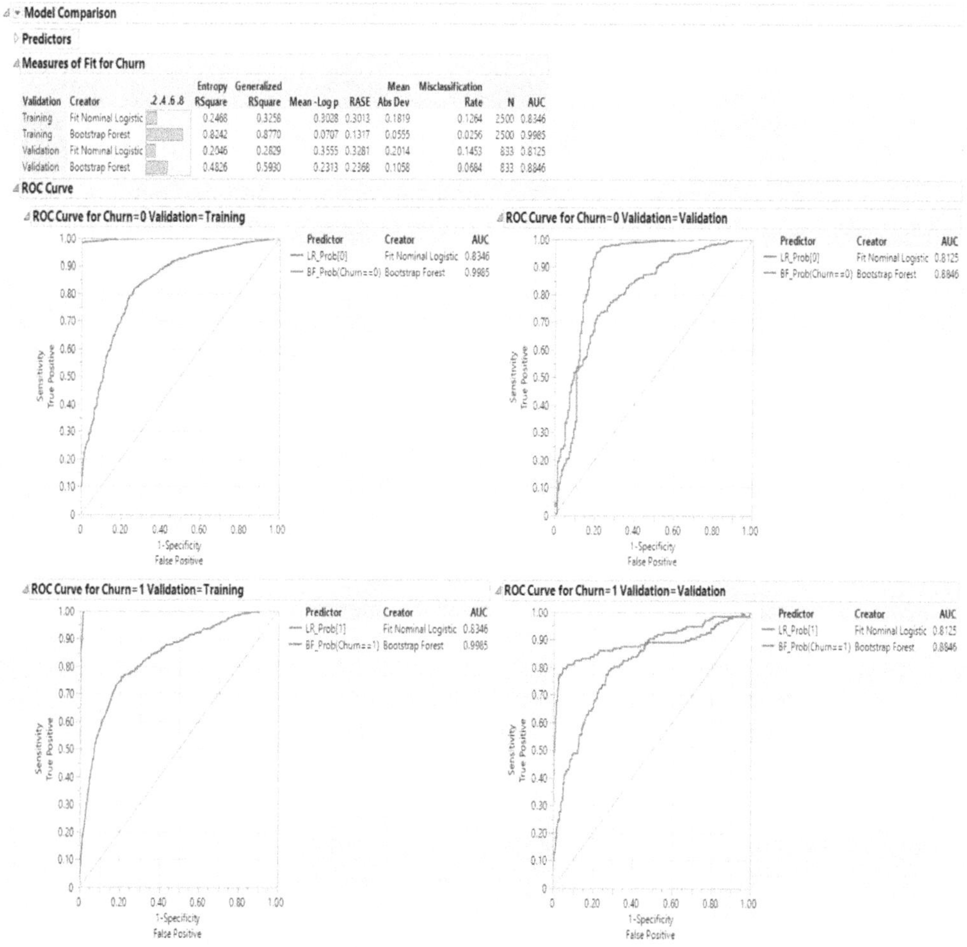

Select **Analyze ▶ Predictive Modeling ▶ Model Comparison**. For classification problems, for **Y, Predictors** it is necessary to enter the probabilities of both success and failure for each predictor. This will be represented by a sideways white triangle that can be clicked to show the variables that it contains. As seen in Figure 14.18, the first of these has been selected: **Prob for Churn (2/0)**. If you click it, you will see **LR_Prob(0)** and **LR_Prob(1)**. The predictor variables for the bootstrap forest can be seen already below **BF_Prob**.

Next complete the following steps:

1. Select **Prob for Churn (2/0)** and click **Y, Predictors**.
2. Select **BF_Prob(Churn==0)** and **BF_Prob(Churn==1)** and click **Y, Predictors**.
3. Select the variable **Validation** and click **Group**, as shown in Figure 14.18.
4. Click **OK**.

In the Model Comparison window, click the **Model Comparison** red triangle and select **ROC Curve**. The result is shown in Figure 14.19. (Remember, you will have different numbers due to the use of the random number generator.)

Look at the misclassification rate for the training set on the Bootstrap Forest: 0.0256. As remarked in the chapter on the Bootstrap Forest, you should not be surprised if your result is zero or near zero. The Bootstrap Forest is very flexible and capable of correctly classifying every observation in a training sample. It also seems like the Bootstrap Forest is overfitting, as the misclassification rate is significantly lower. If you were comparing Logistic and Bootstrap Forest models for this problem, you would choose the Bootstrap Forest. However, you would not expect as low of a misclassification rate. How could you get a better estimate of its performance on new data? You would have to use the Train-Validate-Test instead of just Train-Validate!

Exercises

1. Create 30 columns of random numbers and use stepwise regression to fit them (along with S&P500) to the McDonalds return data.

   To create the 30 columns of random normal, first copy the McDonalds72 data set to a new file (say, McDonalds72-A). Open the new file and delete the 30 columns of "stock" data. Select **Cols ▶ New Columns**. Leave the **Column prefix** as **Column**. Enter 30 for **How many columns to add?** Under **Initial Data Values**, select **Random**, and then select **Random Normal**, and click **OK**.

   After running the stepwise procedure, take note of the RSquared and the number of "significant" variables added to the regression. Repeat this process 10 times. What are the highest and lowest R^2 that you observe? What are the highest and lowest number of statistically significant random variables added to the regression?

   a. Use the Churn.jmp data set and run a logistic regression with three independent variables of your choosing. Create Lift and ROC charts, as well as a confusion matrix. Now do the same again, this time with six independent variables of your choosing. Compare the two sets of charts and confusion matrices.

b. Use the six independent variables from the previous exercise and develop a neural network for the churn data. Compare this model to the logistic regression that was developed in that exercise.

2. Use the Freshmen1.jmp data set. Use logistic regression and classification trees to model the decision for a freshman to return for the sophomore year. Compare the two models using Lift and ROC charts, as well as confusion matrices.

3. Reproduce Table 14.4. Open a new Excel spreadsheet and copy the variables **Return on McDonalds** and **Predicted Return on McDonalds** into columns A and B, respectively. In Excel, perform the following steps:

a. Create the residuals in column C as **Return on McDonalds – Predicted Return on McDonalds**.

b. Create the squared residuals in column D by squaring column C.

c. Create the absolute residuals in column E by taking the absolute value of column C.

d. Calculate the in-sample MSE by summing the first 60 squared residuals (which will be cells 2-61 in column D). Then divide the sum by 60.

e. Calculate the in-sample MAE by summing the first 60 absolute residuals (which will be cells 2-61 in column E). Then divide the sum by 60.

f. Calculate the out-of-sample MSE by summing the last 12 squared residuals (cells 62-73 in column D). Then divide the sum by 12.

g. Calculate the out-of-sample MAE by summing the last 12 absolute residuals (cells 62-73 in column E). Then divide the sum by 12.

h. Calculate the in-sample correlation between **Return on McDonalds** and **Predicted Return on McDonalds** for the first 60 observations using the Excel CORREL( ) function.

i. Calculate the out-of-sample correlation between **Return on McDonalds** and **Predicted Return on McDonalds** for the last 12 observations using the Excel CORREL( ) function.

4. Using the Churn.jmp data set, repeat the above exercise for Logistic, Bootstrap Forest, and Boosted Trees. Which model performs best? (Which does best on the validation data set?) What is the expected performance of this model on new data? (How does it perform on the test data set?)

5. Use salesperfdata.jmp data set. Run a stepwise regression with sales as the dependent variable. Build a regression tree to predict sales. Which model is better?

6. Use the Freshman1.jmp data set. Run a decision tree and logistic regression model with return as the dependent variable. Compare the models, which is best?

Chapter 15: Text Mining

Introduction

The growth of the amount of data available in digital form has been increasing exponentially. In his September 30, 2015, *Forbes Magazine* Tech post, Bernard Marr listed several "mind-boggling" facts (Marr):

- "The data volumes are exploding, [and] more data has been created in the past two years than in the entire previous history of the human race."
- "Data is growing faster than ever before and by the year 2020, about 1.7 megabytes of new information will be created every second for every human being on the planet."
- "By then, our accumulated digital universe of data will grow from 4.4 zettabytes today to around 44 zettabytes, or 44 *trillion* gigabytes."

Historical Perspective

To put this 44 trillion-gigabyte forecast into perspective, in 2011 the entire print collection of the Library of Congress was estimated to be 10 terabytes (Ashefelder). The projected 44 trillion gigabytes is approximately 4.4 billion Libraries of Congress.

Historically, because of high costs and storage, memory, and processing limitations, most of the data stored in databases were structured data. Structured data were organized in rows and columns so that they could be loadable into a spreadsheet and could be easily entered, stored, queried, and analyzed. Other data that could not fit into this organized structure were stored on paper and put in a file cabinet.

Today, with the cost and the limitation barriers pretty much removed, this other "file cabinet" data, in addition to more departments and more different types of databases within an organization, are being stored digitally. Further, so as to provide a bigger picture, organizations are also accessing and storing external data.

A significant portion of this digitally stored data is unstructured data. Unstructured data are not organized in a predefined matter. Some examples of types of unstructured data include responses to open-ended survey questions, comments and notes, social media, email, Word, PDF and other text files, HTML web pages, and messages. In 2015, IDC Research estimated that unstructured data account for 90% of all digital data (Vijayan).

Unstructured Data

With so much data being stored as unstructured data or as text (*unstructured data* will be considered to be synonymous with *text*), why not leverage the text, as you do with structured data, to improve decisions and predictions? This is where text mining comes in. Text mining and data mining are quite similar processes in that their goal is to extract useful information so as to improve decisions and predictions. The main difference is that text mining extracts information from text while data mining extracts information from structured data.

Both text mining and data mining initially rely on preprocessing routines. Since the data have already been stored in a structured format, the preprocessing routines in a data mining project focus on cleaning, normalizing the data, finding outliers, imputing missing values, and so on. Text mining projects also first require the data to be cleaned. However, differently, text mining projects use natural language processes (a field of study related to human-computer interaction) to transform the unstructured data into a more structured format. Subsequently, both text mining and data mining processes use visualization and descriptive tools to better understand the data and apply predictive techniques to develop models to improve decisions and provide predictions.

Text mining is categorized, as shown in our multivariate analysis framework in Figure 15.1, as one of the interdependence techniques, although text mining also includes the elements of discovery and possibly dependence techniques.

Text mining and the process of text mining have several definitions, extensions, and approaches. The text mining process consists of three major steps:

Figure 15.1: A Framework for Multivariate Analysis

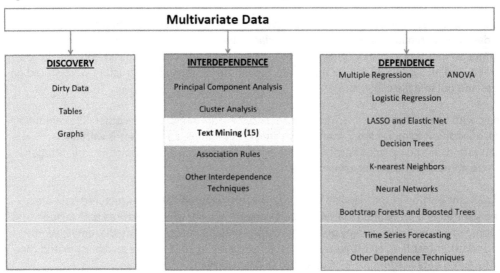

1. **Developing the document term matrix**. The document term matrix (DTM) is a set of zero and 1 variables (also called *indicator variables*) that represent the words in the text. Natural language processing techniques are used to initially develop the DTM. Subsequently, you explore the set of variables and curate the DTM, by grouping words or removing infrequent words, until you are satisfied.
2. **Using multivariate techniques.** Text visualization and the text multivariate techniques of clustering, principal components, and factor analysis (PCA/FA) (similar to the continuous multivariate techniques discussed in Chapters 4, 7, and 9) are used to understand the composition of the DTM.
3. **Using predictive techniques.** If a dependent variable exists, you can use the text multivariate analysis results (along with other structured data) as independent variables in a predictive technique.

More and more of today's digital data are unstructured data. In this chapter, how the text mining process can leverage information from this unstructured data or text to enhance your understanding of the text, as well as to improve your decisions and predictions, will be discussed.

Developing the Document Term Matrix

The Text Explorer platform in JMP uses a bag of words approach.[1] The order of words is ignored except for phrases, and the analysis is based on the count of words and phrases. The words are processed in three stages to develop the DTM as shown in Figure 15.2:

1. tokenizing
2. phrasing
3. terming

To understand this process of transforming the text into a structured format, open a small data set called toytext.jmp, which contains just one column of text in 14 rows as shown in Figure 15.3.

Each row of words in the variable **text** column is called a *document*. Hence, the toytext.jmp file has 14 documents. The entire set of these 14 documents is called a *corpus*.

Understand the Tokenizing Stage

To access the Text Explorer platform in JMP, complete the following steps:

1. Select **Analyze ▶ Text Explorer**. The Text Explorer dialog box appears as shown in Figure 15.4.
2. Under **1 Columns**, click **text** and click the box **Text Columns**, and the variable **text** will be listed.

---

[1] The author would like to thank Daniel Valente and Christopher Gotwalt for their guidance and insight in writing this chapter.

Figure 15.2: Flowchart of the Stages of Text Processing

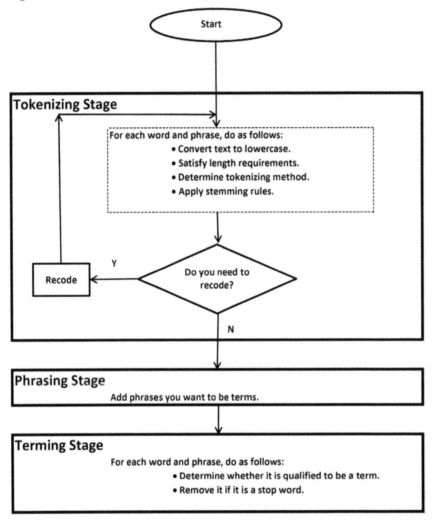

Select Options in the Text Explorer Dialog Box

The list of options offered in Figure 15.4 include the following:

- **Maximum Words per Phrase, Maximum Number of Phrases**, and **Maximum Characters per Word.** As you progress down the flowchart and curate the DTM, you will decide what these limits of words and phrases will be.
- **Stemming**. Stemming combines related terms with common suffixes, essentially combining words with identical beginnings (called *stems*), but different endings. The stemming process in JMP uses the Snowball string processing language, which is described at http://snowballstem.org. The drop-down arrow provides three options:

Figure 15.3: Data Table of Toytext.jmp File

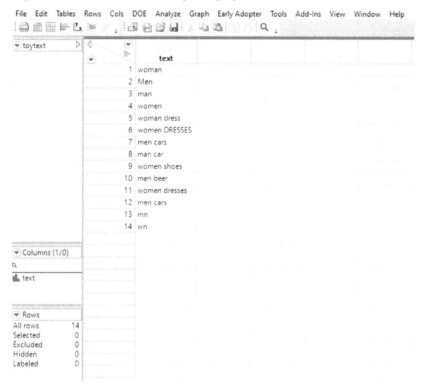

Figure 15.4: Text Explorer Dialog Box

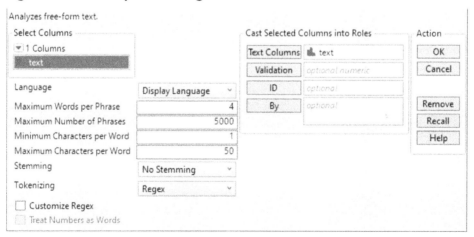

○ **No Stemming**. No terms are combined.
○ **Stem for Combining**. Terms are stemmed when two or more terms stem to the same term. For example, in your toytext.jmp data set, **dress**, **Dress**, and **dresses** would be stemmed to **dress·**. JMP uses a dot (·) to denote a word's being stemmed.
○ **Stem All Terms**. All terms are stemmed.

- **Tokenizing**. This is the method used to parse the body of text into terms or tokens. The drop-down arrow provides two options:

○ **Basic Words**. Text is parsed into terms by using a set of delimiters (such as white space, money, time, URLs, or phone numbers) that typically surround words. To view the default set of delimiters, click the red triangle, select **Display Options ▶ Show Delimiters**, and click **OK** after Text Explorer has been run.
○ **Regex** (short for *regular expression*). Text is decomposed using a set of built-in regular expressions. **Regex** is an advanced feature (beyond the scope of this book) and a very powerful tool for using regular expressions to identify patterns in the text. The **Regex** option is a superset of the **Basic Words** option. That is, when **Regex** is selected, in addition to the default regular expressions provided by the **Regex** option, the default delimiters included by the **Basic Words** option are also included. Furthermore, if **Regex** is selected and you want to add, delete, or edit this set of regular expressions, click the **Customize Regex** check box. Once you click **OK**, the **Regular Expression Editor** dialog box will appear. For more information about building your own **Regex**, see www.regular-expressions.info.

For this example, use the following options:

1. In terms of **Minimum Characters per Word**, to avoid words such as "a," "an," and so on, you would normally use at least 2 (and usually 2); but in this small example, leave it at the default value of **1**.
2. **Stem for Combining** is recommended; but, initially, with this small example, use **No Stemming**.
3. Select **Regex.**
4. Click **OK**.

These Text Explorer dialog box selections are the components in the dashed box within the Tokenizing Stage box in Figure 15.2.

The Text Explorer output box will appear as shown in Figure 15.5.

At the top of Text Explorer output (Figure 15.5), some summary statistics are provided.

Each document is broken into initial units of text called *tokens*. Usually, a token is a word, but it can be any sequence of non-whitespace characters. As shown in Figure 15.5, there are 22 total tokens.

Figure 15.5: Text Explorer Output Box

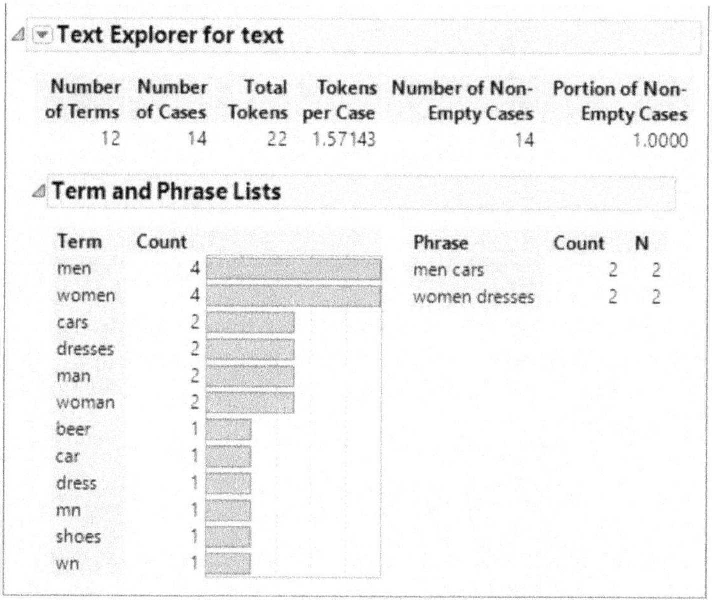

The basic unit of analysis for text mining is a *term*. Initially, the Text Explorer examines each of the tokens to determine a possible set of useful terms for analysis. As shown in Figure 15.5, the number of initial terms is 12; they are listed below on the left side and sorted by frequency. This number of terms will change as you transform the text.

On the right side of Figure 15.5, there is a list of phrases common to the corpus—the phrases "men cars" and "women dresses" occurred twice. A phrase is defined as a sequence of tokens that appear more than once. Each phrase will be considered as to whether it should be a term.

Terms are the units of analysis for text mining. Presently, since you have yet to do anything to the data set and if you want to analyze it, complete the following steps:

1. Click the **Text Explorer for text** red triangle, and select **Save Document Term Matrix**; accept all the default values.
2. Click **OK**.

The data table now has 12 new indicator variables, one for each term as shown in Figure 15.6. As you can see in Figure 15.6, one of the first steps that the Text Explorer module does is to convert all the terms to lowercase. In particular, note that **dresses** and **DRESSES** are considered as the same term. By default, the Text Explorer also treats the plural of terms, such as **dress** and **dresses** or **men** and **man**, as different terms or units.

Figure 15.6: Toytext.jmp Data Table with Initial Document Terms

	text	men Binary	women Binary	cars Binary	dresses Binary	man Binary	woman Binary	beer Binary	car Binary	dress Binary	mn Binary	shoes Binary	wn Binary
1	woman	0	0	0	0	0	1	0	0	0	0	0	0
2	Men	1	0	0	0	0	0	0	0	0	0	0	0
3	man	0	0	0	0	1	0	0	0	0	0	0	0
4	women	0	1	0	0	0	0	0	0	0	0	0	0
5	woman dress	0	0	0	0	0	1	0	0	1	0	0	0
6	women DRESSES	0	1	0	1	0	0	0	0	0	0	0	0
7	men cars	1	0	1	0	0	0	0	0	0	0	0	0
8	man car	0	0	0	0	1	0	0	1	0	0	0	0
9	women shoes	0	1	0	0	0	0	0	0	0	0	1	0
10	men beer	1	0	0	0	0	0	1	0	0	0	0	0
11	women dresses	0	1	0	1	0	0	0	0	0	0	0	0
12	men cars	1	0	1	0	0	0	0	0	0	0	0	0
13	mn	0	0	0	0	0	0	0	0	0	1	0	0
14	wn	0	0	0	0	0	0	0	0	0	0	0	1

The current number of 14 terms, or indicator variables, is probably more than what you want to work with. You most likely want to combine some of these terms as well as clean up the data before you proceed. (For now, to delete all 12 indicator variables, select all the indicator variable columns, right-click, and click **Delete Columns**.)

Recode to Correct Misspellings and Group Terms

Examining Figures 15.5 and 15.6 further, you can see that **women** and **woman** as well as **men** and **man** were not combined. You can also see that there are two misspellings: **mn** and **wn**.

To correct the misspelling of **mn**, click **mn** in the Text Explorer output, as shown in Figure 15.5:

1. Right-click the term **mn** in the **Text Explorer output box** and click **Recode**.
2. As shown in Figure 15.7, in the **New Values** box, enter **men.**
3. Click **Recode**.

Figure 15.7: Recode Dialog Box

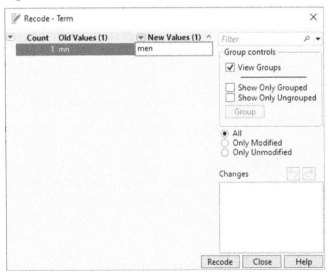

Figure 15.8: The Recode Dialog Box

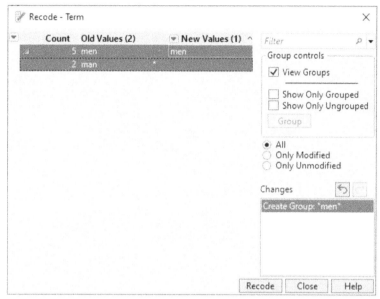

This misspelling is now included with the term **men**. The count for **men** should have increased by 1 to 5. Also, check the Data Table. Although **mn** is now included with **men** within the Text Explorer platform, it is still coded as **mn** in the Data Table.

To group together the terms **men** and **man**, complete the following steps:

1. Click the term **men** in the Text Explorer output box, hold down the **Ctrl** key and click **man**.
2. Right-click and click **Recode**. The Recode dialog box appears.
3. As shown in Figure 15.8, highlight **man** and **men** and right-click.
4. Click **Group To men** and click **Recode**. The count for **men** has increased by 2 to 7.

Similarly, recode **wn** to **women,** and group **women** and **woman**. The Text Explorer output box will look like Figure 15.9.

The process of combining related terms is called *stemming*. Stemming combines related terms with common suffixes—combining words with identical beginnings (called *stems*), but different endings. To accomplish this, complete the following steps:

1. Click the **Text Explorer for text** red triangle.
2. Select **Term Options ▶ Stemming ▶ Stem for Combining**.

Figure 15.9: Text Explorer Output Box

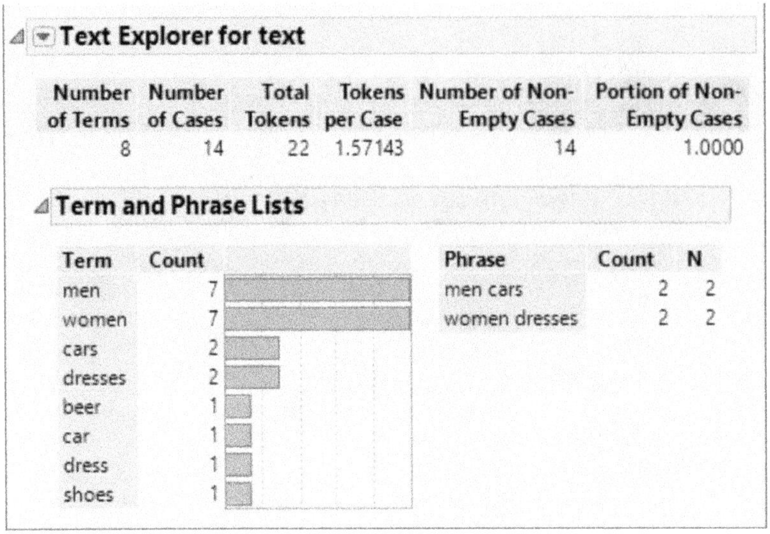

The Text Explorer output should look similar to Figure 15.10.

As shown in Figure 15.10, the terms **car** and **cars** have been combined into the one new term **car·** and similarly for **dress** and **dresses**. You can check this by clicking one of the stemmed terms **car·** or **dress·**, right-clicking, and then clicking **Show Text**.

The recoding of terms thus far completed applies only within the Text Explorer platform; that is, the data is not changed in the Data Table. To verify, click to open the Data Table and observe that **mn, man, wn**, and **woman** are still listed.

Figure 15.10: Text Explorer Output Box after Stemming

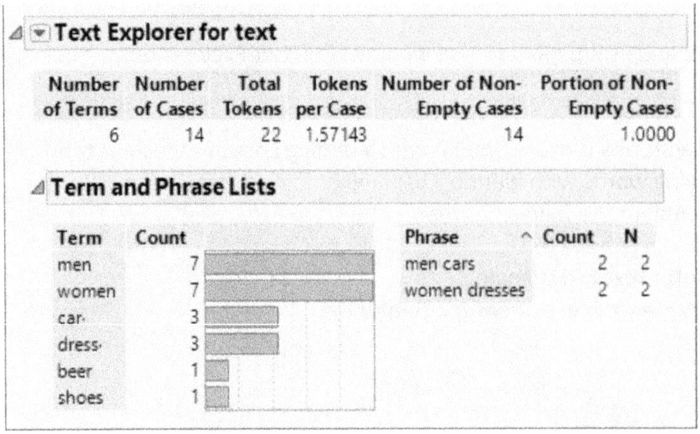

Additionally, to see the results of your Recoding, right-click somewhere in the Text Explorer output and select **Display Options ▶ Show Recodes.** Click the drop arrow for Recodes to see a list of all the recodes you made. Note if you accidentally made a mistake in your recoding, right-click the incorrect recode and click **Remove.**

Recoding does affect stemming and should occur before stemming. Hence, it is important that you should try to recode all misspelling and synonyms before executing the Text Explorer platform. Use the **Recode** procedure under the **Cols** option. The terms **woman dress** and **man car** will also need to be recoded.

Understand the Phrasing Stage

If you want any of the phrases to be analyzed as individual concepts and separated from their individual terms, then you can add these phrases to your term list. For example, to add the phrases **men cars** and **women dresses** to your term list, complete the following steps:

1. Click **men cars**, hold down the **Shift** key, and click **women dresses** under the list of Phrases.
2. Right-click, and then click **Add Phrase**.

The two phrases are now added to the list of terms. They were both stemmed with the plural phrase that appeared only once as shown in Figure 15.11. They are also dimmed in the phrase list, indicating that they are being treated as terms.

Similar to Recoding, if you do not want to keep one of the phrases that you added to the list of Terms and Phrase List, you would right-click that phrase listed under the Terms and Phrase Lists and click **Remove Phrase**. That phrase is removed from the list of Terms and Phrase Lists and added back to the Phrases (it is now not grayed out).

Figure 15.11: Text Explorer Output Box after Phrasing

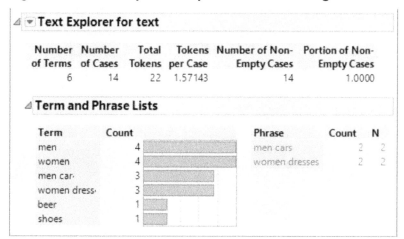

Examining Figure 15.11 further, you can see that the instances of the term **men** that were in the term **men car·** have been removed from the count of **men** and similarly for the term **women**. To clearly see what you have done so far, complete the following steps:

1. Click the **Text Explorer for text** red triangle.
2. Select **Save Document Term Matrix**.
3. Click **OK**.

Added to the Data Table are six indicator variables, down from your initial 12, one for each term in Figure 15.11, as shown in Figure 15.12.

Understand the Terming Stage

Stop words are words that can be characterized in one or more of the following ways:

- too common, such as "a,", "an," or "the";
- infrequent (their counts are low); or
- ignorable (not relevant to the analysis).

Create Stop Words

As shown in Figure 15.11, you have two terms with counts of 1. To make them into stop words, complete the following steps:

1. Click **beer** under the list of Terms.
2. Hold down the **Shift** key and click **shoes**.
3. Right-click and then click **Add Stop Word**.

Figure 15.12: Document Text Matrix

	text	men Binary	women Binary	men car· Binary	women dress· Binary	beer Binary	shoes Binary
1	woman	0	1	0	0	0	0
2	Men	1	0	0	0	0	0
3	man	1	0	0	0	0	0
4	women	0	1	0	0	0	0
5	woman dress	0	0	0	1	0	0
6	women DRESSES	0	0	0	1	0	0
7	men cars	0	0	1	0	0	0
8	man car	0	0	1	0	0	0
9	women shoes	0	1	0	0	0	1
10	men beer	1	0	0	0	1	0
11	women dresses	0	0	0	1	0	0
12	men cars	0	0	1	0	0	0
13	mn	1	0	0	0	0	0
14	wn	0	1	0	0	0	0

The list of terms now excludes the terms **beer** and **shoes** as shown in Figure 15.13. To see the list of stop words, click the **Text Explorer for text** red triangle, and select **Display Options ▶ Show Stop Words**.

Generate a Word Cloud

A visualization of the list of terms is called a *word cloud*. To produce the word cloud as shown in Figure 15.13, complete the following steps:

1. Click the **Text Explorer for text** red triangle.
2. Select **Display Options ▶ Show Word Cloud**.
3. Click the **Word Cloud** red triangle and select **Layout ▶ Centered**.
4. Again, click the **Word Cloud** red triangle and click **Coloring ▶ Arbitrary Colors**.

The word cloud is added to the Text Explorer output as in Figure 15.13. The size of each term in the word cloud is relative to its frequency.

Figure 15.13: Text Explorer Output Box after Terming

Observe the Order of Operations

The list of terms on the left side of Figure 15.13 shows the list of indicator variables that are used in creating the DTM. As you have worked your way through the flowchart (see Figure 15.2), your objective has been to examine and explore the list of terms and phrases to produce a final list of terms that you are satisfied with. There are no definitive approaches to take, particular words to focus on (depending on the objective of the study and domain expertise), nor a definitive measure to say that you have a good list of terms. This is also an iterative process. However, you should be aware that the order of operation in the creation of a list of terms can affect the resulting list of terms.

The following general steps are suggested:

1. Before executing the Text Explorer, recode all misspellings and synonyms in the Data Table.
2. In the Text Explorer dialog box, select these options:
   a. Minimum number of characters (use 2)
   b. Stemming (select **Stem for Combining**)
   c. Tokenizing (select **Regex** unless you have a custom Regex that you want to add)
3. In the Phrasing Stage, do the following:
   a. Examine the phrases.
   b. Specify which phrases you want to be included as terms; in particular, select the most frequent sequence of phrases.
4. In the Terming stage, do the following:
   a. Remove stop words.
   b. Remove least frequent terms.
   c. Remove too frequent terms (if any).

Developing the Document Term Matrix with a Larger Data Set

Now you will examine a larger and more realistic data set. The data set traffic_violations_dec2014.jmp contains all the electronic traffic violations that occurred in Montgomery County, Maryland, during December 2014 (Data Montgomery: "All electronic traffic violations"). The file contains 16,446 records and 35 columns. The 35 variables are as follows; their dictionary can be found at (Data Montgomery: "Variable dictionary"):

- Date of Stop
- Time of Stop
- Agency
- SubAgency
- Description
- Location
- Latitude

- Longitude
- Accident
- Belts
- Personal Injury
- Property Damage
- Fatal
- Commercial License
- Hazmat
- Commercial Vehicle
- Alcohol
- Work Zone
- State
- Vehicle Type
- Year
- Make
- Model
- Color
- Violation Type
- Charge
- Article
- Contributed to Accident
- Race
- Gender
- Driver City
- Driver State
- DL State
- Arrest Type
- Geolocation

Generate a Word Cloud and Examine the Text

Examine the text in the variable field **Description**:

1. Select **Analyze ▶ Text Explorer**.
2. In the Text Explorer dialog box under **35 Columns**, click **Description.**
3. Click the box **Text Columns**; change **the Minimum Characters per Word** to **2**.
4. Click the drop-down arrow for **Stemming** and choose **Stem for Combining**.
5. Click **OK**.
6. In the Text Explorer output, click the **Text Explorer for Description** red triangle.
7. Click **Display Options ▶ Show Word Cloud**.
8. Click the **Word Cloud** red triangle and click **Layout ▶ Centered,** and again click the **Word Cloud** red triangle and click **Coloring ▶ Arbitrary Colors**. The Text Explorer output box with the Word Cloud will appear as shown in Figure 15.14.

Figure 15.14: Text Explorer Output Box

Text Explorer for Description

Number of Terms	Number of Cases	Total Tokens	Tokens per Case	Number of Non-Empty Cases	Portion of Non-Empty Cases
733	16446	163221	9.92466	16446	1.0000

Term and Phrase Lists

Term	Count		Phrase	Count	N
veh	2217		driver failure	2260	2
speed	2035		vehicle on highway	2154	3
motor	1989		driving vehicle	1932	2
traffic	1925		motor vehicle	1578	2
license	1803		driver failure to obey	1501	4
devic·	1758		failure to obey	1501	3
control·	1715		traffic control	1487	2
suspended	1664		traffic control device	1419	3
obey	1504		control device	1419	2
proper·	1483		failure to obey properly	1376	4
posted	1454		obey properly placed traffic	1376	4
exceeding	1450		placed traffic control device	1376	4
place·	1382		properly placed traffic control	1376	4
instructions	1379		traffic control device instructions	1376	4
police	1376		control device instructions	1376	3
person·	1277		obey properly placed	1376	3
demand	1271		placed traffic control	1376	3
use·	1242		properly placed traffic	1376	3
light·	1237		device instructions	1376	2
plate·	1233		obey properly	1376	2
requir·	1170		placed traffic	1376	2
hwy	943		properly placed	1376	2
property	938		driving motor	1212	2
without	927		driving motor vehicle	1084	3
signal·	926		motor vehicle on highway	1064	4

Word Cloud

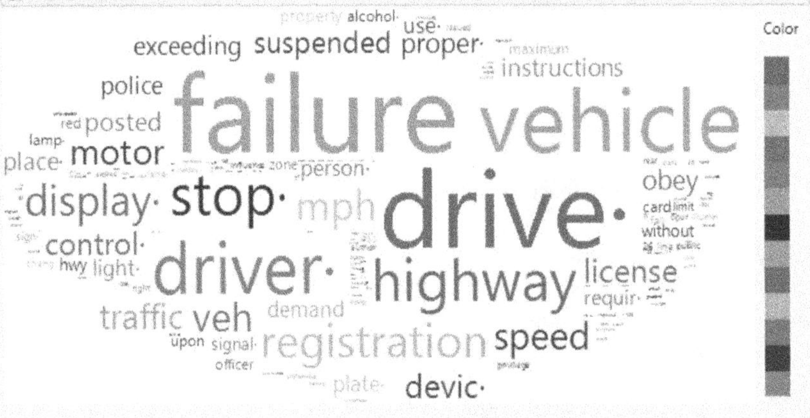

Examine and Group Terms

Under the list of phrases, find the phrase **motor vehicle** and complete the following steps:

1. Click the phrase **motor vehicle**.
2. Right-click and then click **Select Contains**. This option selects bigger phrases that contain this phrase. Scroll down the list of phrases on the right side of the Text Explorer output and you can see highlighted the other phrases that contain the phrase **motor vehicle**.

Similarly, under the list of phrases, scroll down until you find the phrase **driving vehicle on highway** and complete the following steps:

1. Click the phrase **driving vehicle on highway**.
2. Right-click and this time click **Select Contained**. Scroll up and down the list of phrases; highlighted are all the phrases that contain one or more of the terms in **driving vehicle on highway**.

As you can see in Figure 15.14, you initially have 733 terms with the terms **failure** and **drive·** appearing in a little more than one-third of the documents. (Sometimes, if a term occurs too often, it might not be that useful; you can make that term a stop word. This will not be considered to be the case here.) Continue with the following steps:

1. Right-click the term **failure**, and click **Show Text**. A new window appears, with all the text that contains **failure**, which appears to be only the term **failure**.
2. Right-click the term **failure**, but this time click **Containing Phrases**. This option selects small phrases that this phrase contains. All the phrases on the right side of Text Explorer output that contain the term **failure** (which you found to be just the term **failure**) will be highlighted.

Now examine the term **drive·** as follows:

1. Click the **Text Explorer for Description** red triangle.
2. Click **Display Options ▶ Show Stem Report**. Added to the Text Explorer output are two lists—on the left, a list of stemmed terms and their terms used in the stem and, on the right, the list of terms and the term that they are stemmed with.
3. Scroll down the left until you come to **drive·** (stemmed terms are in alphabetic order). You can see the terms associated with the stemmed term **drive·** are **drive** and **driving**.

(Note that if there is one or more stemmings that you do not like, it is probably best to exit the Text Explorer. Recode those undesired stemmings, and restart the Text Explorer.)

Add Frequent Phrases to List of Terms

Next add the most frequent phrases to your list of terms. Arbitrarily, you decide to include all the phrases occurring more than 500 times.

1. Click the first phrase under the list of phrases, which is **driver failure**.
2. Hold down the **Shift** key, scroll down, and click the phrase **influence of alcohol**. Notice that all the phrases above are now highlighted.
3. Right-click and click **Add Phrase**.

Several changes occur, and the Text Explorer output will look as shown in Figure 15.15.

Parse the List of Terms

Lastly, parse your list of terms:

1. Right-click anywhere under the list of terms and, in the list of options, click **Alphabetic Order**.
2. Click the first term -**103**; hold down the **Shift** key, and scroll down to and click **1971**.
3. Right-click and click **Add Stop Word**. All these number terms are now deleted from your list of terms.
4. Again, right-click under the list of terms and deselect **Alphabetic Order**. As before, the terms are now sorted by frequency.

Now delete all the terms that occur fewer than 100 times:

1. Scroll down the list of terms until you come to the term **secur·**, which occurs 97 times.
2. Click **secur·**; hold down the **Shift** key, scroll down to the end, and click **yellow**.
3. Right-click and click **Add Stop Word**.

The Text Explorer output will now look similar to Figure 15.16.

Using Multivariate Techniques

After you have curated the DTM to your satisfaction, you are ready to apply multivariate techniques to understand the underlying structure of the DTM.

These techniques are similar to principal components, factor analysis, and clustering techniques that are applied to continuous data that are discussed in other chapters in this textbook.

Figure 15.15: Text Explorer Output Box

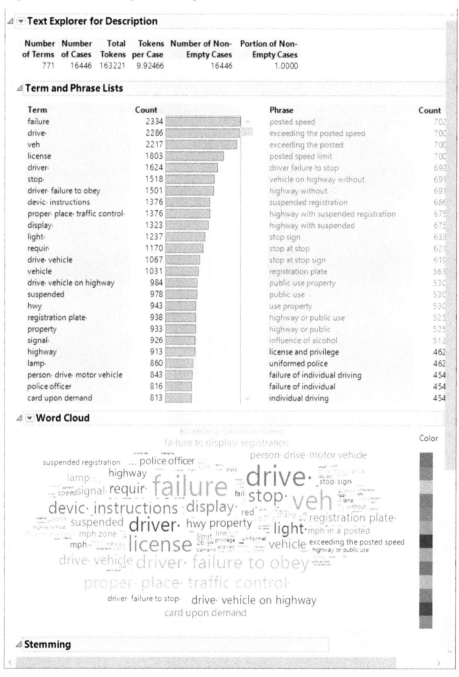

Figure 15.16: Text Explorer Output Box

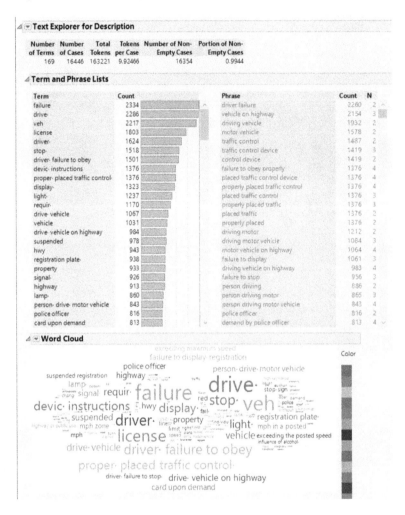

Perform Latent Semantic Analysis

Latent Semantic Analysis (LSA) is a family of mathematical and statistical techniques for extracting and representing the terms and phrases from a corpus. The DTM is reduced dimensionally to a manageable size, which makes the analyses go much faster. And the DTM is amenable to using other multivariate techniques by applying singular value decomposition (SVD).

Understanding SVD Matrices

SVD produces a set of orthogonal columns that are linear combinations of the rows and explains as much of the variation of the data as possible. SVD is an efficient approach to use with large, very sparse matrices, which the DTM typically tends to have. SVD decomposes the DTM into three other matrices:

$$DTM = D * S * T$$

These matrices are defined as follows:

- **D** is an orthogonal document-document matrix of eigenvectors.
- **T** is an orthogonal term-term matrix of eigenvectors.
- **S** is a diagonal matrix of singular values.

The singular vectors in **D** and **T** reveal document-document, document-term, and term-term similarities and other semantic relationships, which otherwise might be hidden.

Many of the singular values in the S matrix are "too small" and can be ignored. So they are assigned values of 0, leaving k nonzero singular values. The representation of the conceptual space of any large corpus requires more than a handful of underlying independent concepts. As a result, the number of orthogonal vectors that is needed is likely to be fairly large. So, k is often several hundred.

Similarities and relationships are now approximated by this reduced model. This process is analogous to using principal components in multivariate analysis. While principal components provide components for the columns, SVD simultaneously provides principal components for both the columns and rows (that is, for the documents and terms).

Plot the Documents or Terms

A common practice is to plot the documents or terms, these singular vectors, and especially the first two vectors, that result from the SVD. Similar documents or terms tend to be plotted closely together, and a rough interpretation can be assigned to the dimensions that appear in the plot. Complete the following steps:

1. Click the **Text Explorer for Description** red triangle and click **Latent Semantic Analysis, SVD**. The Latent Semantic Analysis Specifications dialog box will appear as shown in Figure 15.17.
2. Change the **Minimum Term Frequency** to **100**.
3. Click the drop-down arrow for **Weighting**.
4. The **TF IDF** weighting results are usually more interpretable than the **Binary**, so click the **TF IDF** option.

Regarding weighting options, various methods of the term-frequency counts have been found to be useful, with the **Binary** and **TF IDF** being the most popular:

- The **Binary** weighting option is the easiest to understand in that it assigns a zero or a 1 to indicate whether the term exists in the document. A disadvantage of the **Binary** option is that it does not consider how often the term occurs in the document.

Figure 15.17: Latent Semantic Analysis Specifications Dialog Box

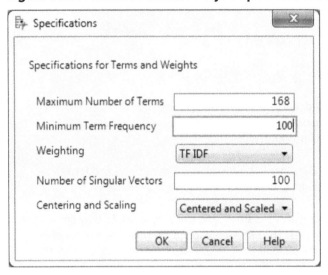

- The **TF IDF** weighting option, which is short for *term frequency–inverse document frequency,* does consider the tradeoff between the frequency of the term throughout the corpus and the frequency of the term in the document.

Next you will select one of three SVD approaches:

- **Uncentered**
- **Centered**
- **Centered and Scaled**

The benefits and drawbacks of each are as follows:

- Traditional latent semantic analysis uses an **Uncentered** approach. This approach can be problematic because frequent terms that do not contribute much meaning tend to score high in the singular vectors.
- The **Centered** approach reduces the impact of these frequent terms and reduces the need to use many stop words.
- The **Centered and Scaling** approach is essentially equivalent to doing principal components on the correlation matrix of the DTM. This option explains the variation in the data (not just the variation in the mean). Therefore, it tends to produce more useful results, whereas using just the **Centered** approach is comparable to doing principal components on the covariance matrix of the DTM.

Continue with the example as follows:

1. Click the drop-down arrow for **Centering and Scaling**. Select the **Centered and Scaling** approach.
2. Click **OK**.

The Latent Semantic Analysis output should look similar to Figure 15.18 (except for the highlighted regions).

The plot on the left displays the first two document singular vectors in matrix D. The plot on the right displays the first term singular vectors in T as shown in Figure 15.18. In each graph, the singular vectors have three branches or tendrils. In the document singular vector graph, the three tendrils are highlighted and labeled. To examine the text, complete the following steps:

1. Left-click the document singular vector graph, hold down the mouse button, and move to highlight the area labeled 1 in Figure 15.18.
2. Just below **SVD plots** and right above the plot, click **Show Text**. A window appears with a list of documents.

Examining the document list, you see that major themes are the **drive use handheld** and **failure of vehicle on highway to display lighted lamps**.

Similarly, highlight, the documents in the tendril labeled 2 and click **Show Text**. These documents appear to have several themes of **driving vehicle**, **person drive motor vehicle**, and **negligent driving**. Lastly, highlight the documents in Tendril 3, and you see the terms **driving vehicle on highway without current registration** and **failure of licensee to notify**. (Keep these documents in the third tendril highlighted.)

Figure 15.18: SVD Plots

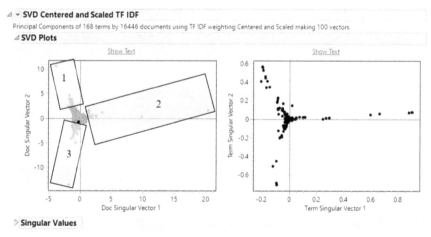

△ ▾ SVD Centered and Scaled TF IDF

Principal Components of 168 terms by 16446 documents using TF IDF weighting Centered and Scaled making 100 vectors

△ SVD Plots

▷ Singular Values

As you did with the document singular vectors, you can explore the term three tendrils in the term singular vector plot. In general, the document singular vector plot provides more insight than the term singular vector plot.

To examine more SVD plots, complete the following steps:

1. Click the **SVD Centered and Scaled TF IDF** red triangle.
2. Click **SVD Scatterplot Matrix**.
3. Enter **10** for the **Number** of singular vectors to plot.
4. Click **OK**.

Added to the Text Explorer output are scatterplots of the first 10 singular vectors for the documents and terms. Figure 15.19 shows the top part of this scatterplot.

The bottom diagonal plots are graphs of the document singular vectors. The upper diagonal plots are graphs of the term singular vectors. Highlighted in Figure 15.19 is the SVD plot of the first two document singular vectors, which is similar to the plot on the left in Figure 15.18. The highlighted documents in the third tendril are highlighted. And these documents are highlighted in the other

Figure 15.19: Top Portion of SVD Scatterplots of SVD Plots of 10 Singular Vectors

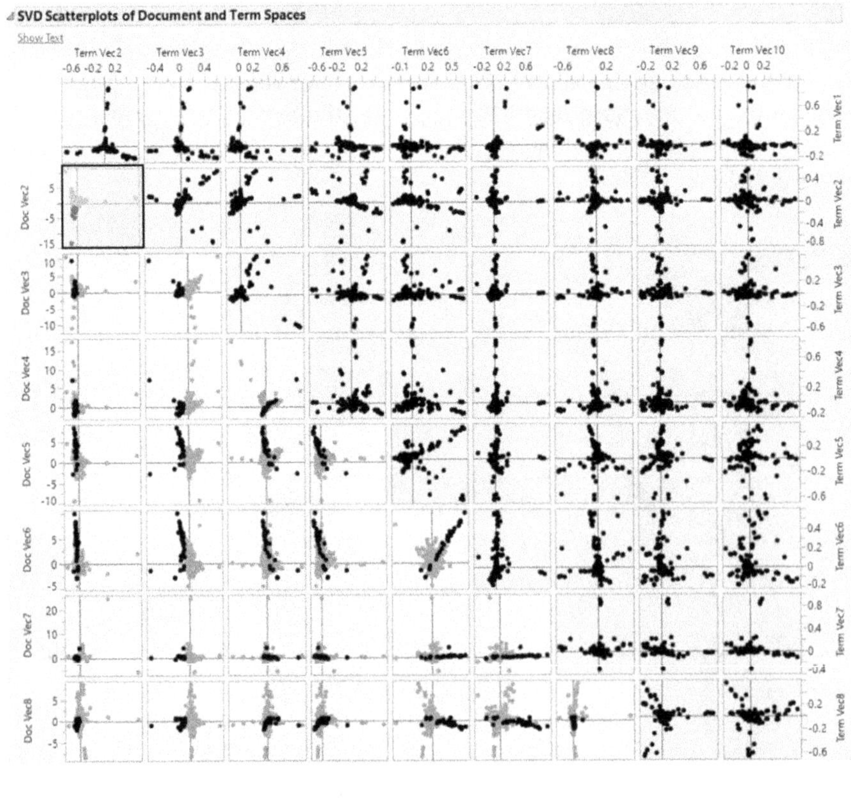

document singular vector plots. The term singular vector plot directly above the highlighted document singular vector plot in Figure 15.19 is the plot of the first two-term singular vectors, which is similar to the plot in Figure 15.18 but rotated 270°.

Perform Topic Analysis

Another way of observing these term themes in the documents is to perform topic analysis. Topic analysis performs a VARIMAX rotation, essentially a factor analysis, on the SVD of the DTM. Complete the following steps:

1. Click the **SVD Centered and Scaled TF IDF** red triangle and from the list options click **Topic Analysis, Rotated SVD**.
2. Click **OK**.

The Topic Analysis results are added to the Text Explorer output as shown Figure 15.20.

The scores represent the loading of the term in that topic. The larger a term's score, the stronger its contribution to the topic. Each topic can be examined for major themes or terms that contribute to that topic. In particular, when you examine the first topic in Figure 15.20, it appears that this topic deals with careless and negligent, somewhat like Tendril 2, which you identified in the SVD plots. And topic 2 seems to have similar terms as Tendril 1. If you choose to consider too few topics, then there can be significant overlap between competing information. But if you choose too many topics, then you will have some topics covering the same topics. Use trial and error to decide how many to consider.

Figure 15.20: Topic Analysis Output

Topic Analysis for 10 topics

Top Loadings by Topic

Topic 1		Topic 2		Topic 3		Topic 4		Topic 5	
Term	Loading	Term	Loading	Term	Loading	Term	Loading	Term	Loading
imprudent	0.97984	motion	0.97324	unfavorable	0.86596	days	0.96077	red	0.77442
life	0.97984	whilemotor	0.97324	cond	0.86596	address	0.95903	signal-	0.76755
endangering	0.97984	telephone	0.97251	visibl-	0.85471	notify	0.93949	traffic	0.71647
careless	0.97984	handheld	0.97251	devic-	0.85092	administration	0.93647	flashing	0.67076
manner	0.97547	hand	0.96655	illumin-	0.80838	licensee	0.93086	fail-	0.63428
negligent	0.97400	use-	0.94959	lamp-	0.70929	within	0.89091	stop-	0.62965
person-	0.79715	vehicle	0.60419	hwy	0.62510	chang-	0.72933	driver-	0.57673
drive-vehicle	0.51449	driver-	0.47064	light	0.56555			enter-	0.41279
property	0.48446			veh	0.54164			intersect-	0.40370
								turn-	0.39031
								line	0.35030
								right	0.34796

Topic 6		Topic 7		Topic 8		Topic 9		Topic 10	
Term	Loading	Term	Loading	Term	Loading	Term	Loading	Term	Loading
uniformed	0.7549	wanton	0.95205	speed	0.7143	registration plate	0.5936	learner's	0.7703
individu-	0.7542	disregard	0.95205	highway	0.6455	materi-	0.5413	holder	0.7678
demand	0.7526	reckless	0.94681	prudent	0.5549	vehicle on highway	0.5324	supervision	0.7339
police	0.7173	will-	0.89309	reason-	0.5496	valid-	0.5208	permit-	0.6704
display-	0.6594	safety	0.85785	excess-	0.5414	current	0.5141	req	0.6484
failure	0.5181	person-	0.46021	person- drive- motor vehicle	-0.5191	tint-	0.5107	drive-	0.3530
highway	0.4870	drive-vehicle	0.32486	highway or public use-	-0.5174	window	0.5099	highway or public use-	-0.3234
license	0.4142	property	0.30297	privilege	-0.4920	tab-	0.5032	person- drive- motor vehicle	-0.3191
drive-	0.3603			collision	0.4706	unauthorized	0.4968	vehicle on highway	-0.3174
driver failure to obey	-0.2862			control-	0.4653	without	0.4313	privilege	-0.3103
				suspended	-0.4470	license	-0.3751	tint-	-0.3057
				avoid-	0.4409	drive- vehicle on highway	0.3501	window	-0.3050
				property	-0.3848	person- drive- motor vehicle	-0.3408		
						highway or public use-	-0.3357		

Perform Cluster Analysis

Cluster analysis is used to further understand the singular vectors. The Text Explorer platform in JMP uses a customized latent class analysis methodology for cluster analysis. This is built just for text. This latent class analysis procedure is good for finding interesting patterns in the text, and because it is sparse matrix based, it is very fast.

Begin the Analysis

To begin, complete the following steps:

1. Click the **Text Explorer for Description** red triangle and click **Latent Class Analysis**.
2. In the Specifications dialog box, change the **Minimum Term Frequency** to **4** and the **Number of Clusters** to **10**.
3. Click **OK**.
4. Click the **Latent Class Analysis for 10 Clusters** red triangle and click **Color by Cluster**.

Figure 15.21: Top Portion of Latent Class Analysis for 10 Clusters Output Box

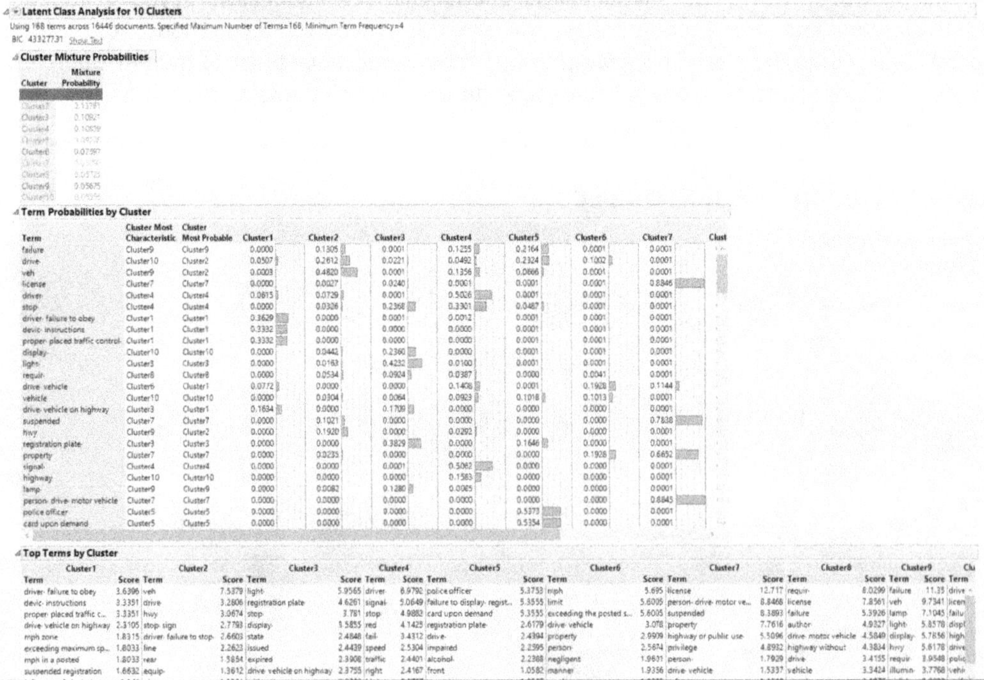

The cluster analysis results are shown in Figures 15.21 and 15.22. Because the latent class analysis procedure uses a random seed, your results will be slightly different.

Examine the Results

Scroll back up to the SVD scatterplots. The document SVD plots are now colored by cluster. Documents that tend to cluster together will appear near each other in their SVD plots. (You can increase the size of a plot by grabbing the border with the mouse while holding down the mouse key and dragging out wider.) For example, in Figure 15.23, the upper left portion of the SVD scatterplot is shown.

Figure 15.22: Lower Portion of Latent Class Analysis for 10 Clusters Output Box

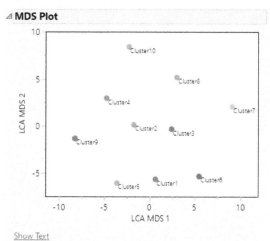

Show Text

◢ **Cluster Probabilities by Row**

Row	Most Likely Cluster	Cluster1	Cluster2	Cluster3	Cluster4	Cluster5	Cluster6	Cluster7	Cluster8	Cluster9	Cluster10
7	4				1.00000						
8	4				1.00000						
9	4				1.00000						
10	4				1.00000						
11	1	1.00000									
12	2		0.99974								
13	1	1.00000									
14	1	0.99998									
15	5					1.00000					
16	4				1.00000						
17								1.00000			
18	1	1.00000									
19	2		0.99974								
20	8								1.00000		
21	2		0.95786								
22	7							1.00000			
23								1.00000			
24	9									1.00000	
25	10										1.00000

Figure 15.23: Upper Leftmost Portion of SVD Scatterplots

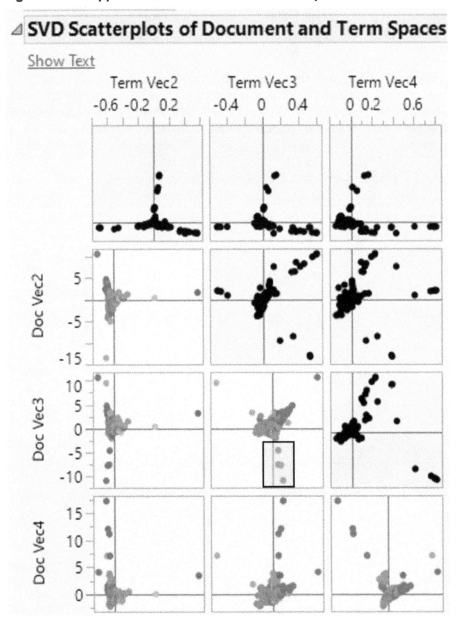

Look at the group of documents highlighted in **Doc Vec3**. All of these documents are in the same cluster and in other plots. You can see that they are close to each other. Match up the color of these documents with cluster colors as shown in Figure 15.21. Click that cluster number; in our case, it was Cluster 9. Now all the documents in Cluster 9 are highlighted in the SVD scatterplots.

Scroll farther up to **SVD Plots.** In the left document singular vector plot, the Cluster 9 documents are highlighted, which are mostly those documents in Tendril 3 (as shown in Figure 15.18). Click **Show Text**. You see phrases or terms similar to those that you found in Tendril 3. Similarly, you can highlight other clusters of the same colored documents and view the text.

Identify Dominant Terms

The **Term Probabilities by Cluster** report in Figure 15.21 has the term frequency in each cluster. You can examine the terms horizontally or the clusters vertically, focusing on the large frequencies. For example, look at the term **license**, which occurs most often in Cluster 7. Look at Cluster 7:

1. Right-click anywhere inside the report.
2. Select **Sort Column**.
3. In the new window, select **Cluster 7**.
4. Click **OK**.

The most frequent terms in Cluster 7 are toward the top of the report. It seems that the Cluster 7 theme addresses drivers who were driving with suspended licenses.

A scoring algorithm for identifying which terms are most dominant within a cluster is shown in the **Top Terms per Cluster report**. (See Figure 15.21.) The score is based on the term cluster frequency relative to its corpus frequency. Larger scores tend to occur more often in the cluster. Look at Clusters 7 and 9. You see the most frequent terms are the terms that you have identified earlier.

Occasionally, terms score negative numbers, which implies that those terms are less frequent (you do not have any negative scores in our example). Many times, when several terms have negative numbers, they occur in the same cluster. This is called a *junk cluster*. Most likely in this junk cluster are blank documents or simply documents that do not fit nicely in other clusters and just are adding noise to the analysis. If a junk cluster occurs, then it might be useful to identify those documents in this cluster and rerun latent class analysis to exclude these junk documents.

The multiple dimensional scaling (MDS) plot of the clusters in Figure 15.22 is produced by calculating the Kullback-Leibler distance between clusters. In natural language processing (NLP), a document is viewed as a probability distribution of terms. The Kullback-Leibler distance is

Figure 15.24: Singular Values

Number	Singular Value	Eigenvalue	Percent		Cum Percent
1	2.7438	7.5284	4.4812		4.4812
2	2.6076	6.7997	4.0474		8.5286
3	2.5115	6.3078	3.7546		12.2832
4	2.4914	6.2072	3.6948		15.9780
5	2.3811	5.6694	3.3747		19.3526
6	2.2789	5.1933	3.0912		22.4439
7	2.2050	4.8622	2.8942		25.3381
8	2.1305	4.5391	2.7018		28.0399
9	2.0856	4.3499	2.5892		30.6291
10	2.0805	4.3285	2.5765		33.2056
11	2.0679	4.2763	2.5454		35.7510
12	1.9827	3.9310	2.3399		38.0909
13	1.9648	3.8605	2.2979		40.3888
14	1.9374	3.7534	2.2342		42.6229
15	1.8480	3.4151	2.0328		44.6558
16	1.8185	3.3069	1.9684		46.6241
17	1.7905	3.2061	1.9084		48.5325
18	1.7763	3.1551	1.8780		50.4105
19	1.7700	3.1328	1.8648		52.2753
20	1.7601	3.0978	1.8440		54.1193
21	1.7406	3.0297	1.8034		55.9227
22	1.7305	2.9948	1.7826		57.7053
23	1.7014	2.8947	1.7230		59.4283
24	1.6897	2.8551	1.6994		61.1278
25	1.6512	2.7265	1.6229		62.7507
26	1.6364	2.6779	1.5940		64.3447
27	1.6085	2.5871	1.5400		65.8846
28	1.5796	2.4952	1.4852		67.3699
29	1.5343	2.3541	1.4013		68.7711
30	1.4995	2.2485	1.3384		70.1095
31	1.4843	2.2030	1.3113		71.4209
32	1.4739	2.1723	1.2931		72.7139
33	1.4283	2.0400	1.2143		73.9282
34	1.3859	1.9206	1.1432		75.0714
35	1.3721	1.8828	1.1207		76.1921
36	1.3546	1.8349	1.0922		77.2844
37	1.3352	1.7827	1.0611		78.3455
38	1.3068	1.7077	1.0165		79.3619
39	1.2926	1.6709	0.9946		80.3565
40	1.2907	1.6658	0.9915		81.3480
41	1.2153	1.4769	0.8791		82.2272
42	1.1819	1.3969	0.8315		83.0587

a widely used measure for calculating the distance between two documents or probability distributions (Bigi). An MDS is applied to these Kullback-Leibler distances to create coordinates for the clustering in two dimensions. You can explore the MDS plot to examine clusters that are near one another, as well as clusters that are far away from one another.

The clusters in your MDS plot are fairly well dispersed. Nonetheless, complete the following steps:

1. Click Cluster 1. You can see in the **Top Terms per Cluster** report that the main terms are **driver· failure to obey, devic· instructions**, and **proper· placed traffic control·**.
2. Scroll back up to the output. You can see where the Cluster 1 documents occur in the SVD plots.
3. Click **Show text**.

Most of the documents appear to have those terms that you detected.

Using Predictive Techniques

If the data set has a dependent variable and you want to do some predictive modeling instead of using the large DTM matrix, you can use the document singular vectors. To determine how many singular vectors to include, complete the following steps:

1. Scroll back up the output to find **Singular Values**. (It is just below the **SVD plots** and before the **SVD Scatterplots of Document and Term Spaces**.)
2. Click the down-arrow next to **Singular Values**.

In general, as in principal components and factor analysis, you are looking for the elbow in the data. Or another guideline is to include singular values until you reach a cumulative percentage of 80%. Many times with text data, the curve or percentages will only gradually decrease, so to reach 80% you might have to reach several hundred. As you will see, the default is 100. How many to include is a judgment call.

Figure 15.24 shows the first 42 singular values. In this case, the percentages quickly exceed 80%, and there is a sharp decrease. Thirty-eight singular document vectors are chosen:

1. Click the **SVD Centered and Scaled TF IDF** red triangle and click **Save Document Singular Vectors**.
2. In the input box in the new dialog box next to **Number of Singular Vectors to Save**, enter **38**.
3. Click **OK**.

Check the Data Table, and you can see 38 new singular vector variables.

Perform Primary Analysis

Before you perform any predictive modeling, do some primary analysis:

1. Click **Analyze ▶ Distribution**. The distribution dialog box will appear.
2. Click **Violation Type**; click **Y, Columns**.
3. Click **OK**.

As shown in the distribution output in Figure 15.25, you can see that most of the violations are equally distributed between **Warning** and **Citation**.

Figure 15.25: Distribution Output for Violation Type

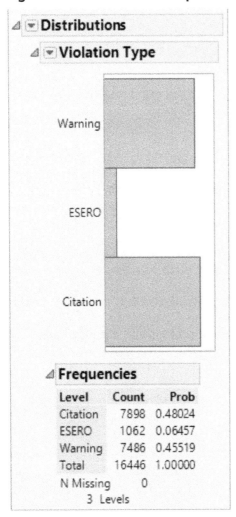

Perform Logistic Regressions

Now run a logistic regression, predicting **Violation Type** and using **Property Damage**, **Race**, and **Belts** as independent variables. The results are shown in Figures 15.26 and 15.27. You can see

Figure 15.26: Top Portion of Initial Logistic Regression Output

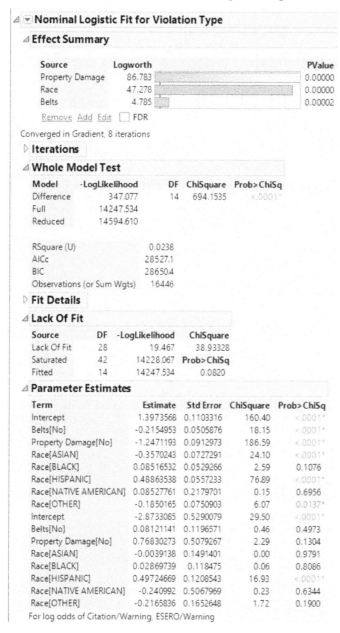

Source	Logworth	PValue
Property Damage	86.783	0.00000
Race	47.278	0.00000
Belts	4.785	0.00002

Remove Add Edit ☐ FDR

Converged in Gradient, 8 iterations

▷ **Iterations**

◢ **Whole Model Test**

Model	-LogLikelihood	DF	ChiSquare	Prob>ChiSq
Difference	347.077	14	694.1535	<.0001*
Full	14247.534			
Reduced	14594.610			

RSquare (U)	0.0238
AICc	28527.1
BIC	28650.4
Observations (or Sum Wgts)	16446

▷ **Fit Details**

◢ **Lack Of Fit**

Source	DF	-LogLikelihood	ChiSquare
Lack Of Fit	28	19.467	38.93328
Saturated	42	14228.067	Prob>ChiSq
Fitted	14	14247.534	0.0820

◢ **Parameter Estimates**

Term	Estimate	Std Error	ChiSquare	Prob>ChiSq
Intercept	1.3973568	0.1103316	160.40	<.0001*
Belts[No]	-0.2154953	0.0505876	18.15	<.0001*
Property Damage[No]	-1.2471193	0.0912973	186.59	<.0001*
Race[ASIAN]	-0.3570243	0.0727291	24.10	<.0001*
Race[BLACK]	0.08516532	0.0529266	2.59	0.1076
Race[HISPANIC]	0.48863538	0.0557233	76.89	<.0001*
Race[NATIVE AMERICAN]	0.08527761	0.2179701	0.15	0.6956
Race[OTHER]	-0.1850165	0.0750903	6.07	0.0137*
Intercept	-2.8733085	0.5290079	29.50	<.0001*
Belts[No]	0.08121141	0.1196571	0.46	0.4973
Property Damage[No]	0.76830273	0.5079267	2.29	0.1304
Race[ASIAN]	-0.0039138	0.1491401	0.00	0.9791
Race[BLACK]	0.02869739	0.118475	0.06	0.8086
Race[HISPANIC]	0.49724669	0.1208543	16.93	<.0001*
Race[NATIVE AMERICAN]	-0.240992	0.5067969	0.23	0.6344
Race[OTHER]	-0.2165836	0.1652648	1.72	0.1900

For log odds of Citation/Warning, ESERO/Warning

that the three variables are significant in predicting **Violation Type**. However, as the Confusion matrix in Figure 15.27 shows, the misclassification is rather high at 47.6%.

Rerun the logistic regression, now with only the 38 singular vectors. Figures 15.28 and 15.29 display the output. The model significantly improved and now has a misclassification rate of 24.4%, almost 50% less.

Figure 15.27: Lower Portion of Initial Logistic Regression Output

◢ Confusion Matrix

Training

Actual Violation Type	Predicted Count		
	Citation	ESERO	Warning
Citation	4859	0	3039
ESERO	596	0	466
Warning	3729	0	3757

Actual Violation Type	Predicted Rate		
	Citation	ESERO	Warning
Citation	0.615	0.000	0.385
ESERO	0.561	0.000	0.439
Warning	0.498	0.000	0.502

Figure 15.28: Top Portion with Singular Values Logistic Regression Output

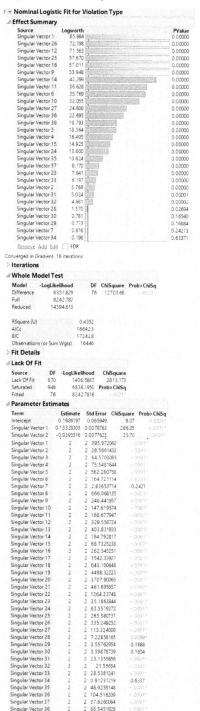

$\textdownarrow$ ▾ **Nominal Logistic Fit for Violation Type**

◢ **Effect Summary**

Source	Logworth		PValue
Singular Vector 1	85.984		0.00000
Singular Vector 26	72.798		0.00000
Singular Vector 12	71.563		0.00000
Singular Vector 25	57.670		0.00000
Singular Vector 16	57.011		0.00000
Singular Vector 9	53.948		0.00000
Singular Vector 14	42.299		0.00000
Singular Vector 11	36.628		0.00000
Singular Vector 6	35.769		0.00000
Singular Vector 10	32.055		0.00000
Singular Vector 27	24.608		0.00000
Singular Vector 36	22.695		0.00000
Singular Vector 38	18.793		0.00000
Singular Vector 3	18.364		0.00000
Singular Vector 4	16.405		0.00000
Singular Vector 15	14.925		0.00000
Singular Vector 24	13.600		0.00000
Singular Vector 35	10.624		0.00000
Singular Vector 37	8.170		0.00000
Singular Vector 23	7.641		0.00000
Singular Vector 33	6.197		0.00000
Singular Vector 2	5.768		0.00000
Singular Vector 31	5.024		0.00001
Singular Vector 32	4.661		0.00002
Singular Vector 28	1.570		0.02694
Singular Vector 30	0.781		0.16540
Singular Vector 29	0.773		0.16884
Singular Vector 7	0.616		0.24213
Singular Vector 34	0.198		0.63371

Remove Add Edit ☐ FDR

Converged in Gradient, 18 iterations

▷ **Iterations**

◢ **Whole Model Test**

Model	-LogLikelihood	DF	ChiSquare	Prob>ChiSq
Difference	6351.829	76	12703.66	<.0001*
Full	8242.782			
Reduced	14594.610			

RSquare (U)	0.4352
AICc	16642.3
BIC	17242.8
Observations (or Sum Wgts)	16446

▷ **Fit Details**

◢ **Lack Of Fit**

Source	DF	-LogLikelihood	ChiSquare
Lack Of Fit	870	1406.5867	2813.173
Saturated	946	6836.1950	Prob>ChiSq
Fitted	76	8242.7816	.0001*

◢ **Parameter Estimates**

Term	Estimate	Std Error	ChiSquare	Prob>ChiSq
Intercept	0.1986197	0.065949	9.07	0.0026*
Singular Vector 1	0.13328303	0.0078763	286.35	<.0001*
Singular Vector 2	-0.0393516	0.0077623	25.70	<.0001*
Singular Vector 1	2	2	395.972062	<.0001*
Singular Vector 2	2	2	26.5661432	<.0001*
Singular Vector 3	2	2	84.5703083	<.0001*
Singular Vector 4	2	2	75.5481644	<.0001*
Singular Vector 5	2	2	562.260758	<.0001*
Singular Vector 6	2	2	164.721114	<.0001*
Singular Vector 7	2	2	2.83653714	0.2421
Singular Vector 8	2	2	666.068135	<.0001*
Singular Vector 9	2	2	248.441957	<.0001*
Singular Vector 10	2	2	147.619574	<.0001*
Singular Vector 11	2	2	168.677947	<.0001*
Singular Vector 12	2	2	329.558724	<.0001*
Singular Vector 13	2	2	403.831933	<.0001*
Singular Vector 14	2	2	194.792817	<.0001*
Singular Vector 15	2	2	68.7325238	<.0001*
Singular Vector 16	2	2	262.545251	<.0001*
Singular Vector 17	2	2	3542.33921	<.0001*
Singular Vector 18	2	2	643.100648	<.0001*
Singular Vector 19	2	2	4498.32225	<.0001*
Singular Vector 20	2	2	3707.90065	<.0001*
Singular Vector 21	2	2	461.695857	<.0001*
Singular Vector 22	2	2	1264.23748	<.0001*
Singular Vector 23	2	2	35.1863844	<.0001*
Singular Vector 24	2	2	63.5519372	<.0001*
Singular Vector 25	2	2	265.580731	<.0001*
Singular Vector 26	2	2	335.249252	<.0001*
Singular Vector 27	2	2	113.324008	<.0001*
Singular Vector 28	2	2	7.22658165	0.0269*
Singular Vector 29	2	2	3.55762954	0.1688
Singular Vector 30	2	2	3.59878739	0.1654
Singular Vector 31	2	2	23.1355856	<.0001*
Singular Vector 32	2	2	21.55654	<.0001*
Singular Vector 33	2	2	28.5381241	<.0001*
Singular Vector 34	2	2	0.91231219	0.6337
Singular Vector 35	2	2	48.9239148	<.0001*
Singular Vector 36	2	2	104.516209	<.0001*
Singular Vector 37	2	2	37.6260064	<.0001*
Singular Vector 38	2	2	86.5451929	<.0001*

Figure 15.29: Lower Portion with Singular Values Logistic Regression Output

◢ **Confusion Matrix**

Training

Actual Violation Type	Predicted Count		
	Citation	ESERO	Warning
Citation	5422	3	2473
ESERO	10	1052	0
Warning	1488	35	5963

Actual Violation Type	Predicted Rate		
	Citation	ESERO	Warning
Citation	0.687	0.000	0.313
ESERO	0.009	0.991	0.000
Warning	0.199	0.005	0.797

Exercises

1. In the aircraft_incidents.jmp file is data for airline incidents that were retrieved on November 20th, 2015 from http://www.ntsb.gov/_layouts/ntsb.aviation/Index.aspx. For the Final Narrative variable, use the Text Explorer to produce a DTM by phrasing and terming. Create a Word Cloud.

2. Using the aircraft_incidents.jmp file from Problem 1, produce a DTM by phrasing and terming, and create a Word Cloud for the variable Narrative Cause.

3. In the file Nicardipine.jmp is data from adverse events from this drug. For the Reported Term for the Adverse Event variable, use the Text Explorer to produce a DTM by phrasing and terming. Create a Word Cloud.

4. In the Airplane_Crash_Reports.jmp file is one variable, NTSB Narrative, that summarizes the crash report. For this variable, use the Text Explorer to produce a DTM by phrasing and terming. Create a Word Cloud.

5. In the FDA_Enforcement_Actions.jmp file, the variable Citation Description describes the violation. For this variable, use the Text Explorer to produce a DTM by phrasing and terming. Create a Word Cloud.

6. The traffic-violation_jun2015.jmp is similar to the file used in the chapter except that the data is for June 2015 only. For the variable Description, use the Text Explorer to produce a DTM by phrasing and terming. Create a Word Cloud. How does this compare to data for December 2014?

7. Perform Latent Semantic Analytics, Topic Analysis, and Cluster Analysis on the DTM that you produced in Problem 1.

8. Perform Latent Semantic Analytics, Topic Analysis, and Cluster Analysis on the DTM that you produced in Problem 2.

9. Perform Latent Semantic Analytics, Topic Analysis, and Cluster Analysis on the DTM that you produced in Problem 3.

10. Perform Latent Semantic Analytics, Topic Analysis, and Cluster Analysis on the DTM that you produced in Problem 4.

11. Perform Latent Semantic Analytics, Topic Analysis, and Cluster Analysis on the DTM that you produced in Problem 5.

12. Perform Latent Semantic Analytics, Topic Analysis, and Cluster Analysis on the DTM that you produced in Problem 6. How does this compare to data for December 2014?

13. Similar to the predictive model that you did in the chapter, create a predictive model for violation type. How does this compare to data for December 2014?

Chapter 16: Market Basket Analysis

Introduction

Everybody is familiar with recommender systems like the one used by Amazon to offer you new books that you haven't read or the one by iTunes to offer new songs that you haven't heard. Perhaps you have checked out the table of contents and a few pages of a recommended book and decided to buy it. Or perhaps you have listened to a 30-second clip from a recommended song, thought to yourself, "I like this," and then bought the song. How did Amazon know that you might like that book, or how did Apple know that you might enjoy that song?

Association Analyses

Such recommendations come from *association analysis* (also called *affinity analysis*), the most common form of which is *market-basket analysis*. Association rules were first developed to analyze a one-time purchase of several items, such as the contents of a cart in a grocery store. The primary purpose is to determine which of the items are commonly sold together. Bread and milk commonly are sold together, but this is obvious. You are not interested in such trivial rules. The purpose of market-basket analysis is not to uncover the obvious, but to uncover relationships that were not previously known. As shown in Figure 16.1, association rules are in a method based on interdependence.

Figure 16.1: Framework for Multivariate Analysis

Multivariate Data		
DISCOVERY	**INTERDEPENDENCE**	**DEPENDENCE**
Dirty Data	Principal Component Analysis	Multiple Regression ANOVA
Tables	Cluster Analysis	Logistic Regression
Graphs	Text Mining	LASSO and Elastic Net
	Association Rules (16)	Decision Trees
	Other Interdependence Techniques	K-nearest Neighbors
		Neural Networks
		Bootstrap Forests and Boosted Trees
		Time Series Forecasting
		Other Dependence Techniques

Examples

A grocery store, for example, might sell very few jars of an exotic mustard, a fact which, in isolation, might lead the grocery manager to discontinue this product. But suppose that a market-basket analysis reveals that this particular brand of mustard almost always is purchased with a large number of exotic, expensive items that have large profit margins. The grocery manager might then figure that, if these customers no longer can buy the mustard at his or her store, then they might go elsewhere to buy this particular brand of mustard and, while there, also buy the large number of exotic, expensive items that have large profit margins. He or she might save a few pennies by discontinuing the mustard, but then lose the purchases that go with the mustard.

Market-basket analysis can be used to generate new business via coupons and by alerting customers to products that they don't know that they want or need. Suppose that a market-basket analysis shows that peanut butter and bread are commonly bought with jelly. A customer checks out, having purchased only peanut butter and bread. The customer can then be offered a coupon for jelly.

Of course, the method can be applied more generally. A bank might observe that many customers who have a checking account and a certificate of deposit also have a credit card. Thus, the bank might craft a special credit card offer for its customers who have only a checking account and a certificate of deposit.

There is an apocryphal story of which all practitioners of market-basket analysis should be aware: a convenience store discovered that beer and diapers were frequently sold together. The explanation was that married men with infant children would stop in to buy some diapers and also pick up a six-pack for themselves. No one ever would have guessed that this relationship existed, and the store was able to exploit it by moving the diapers closer to the beer cooler. The truth is much more mundane. In a nutshell, back in the early 1990s, a statistical analysis performed by Osco Pharmacies suggested that between 5:00 p.m. and 7:00 p.m., customers tended to buy beer and diapers together. But the store never attempted to verify the existence of the relationship or exploit it. For more detail, see Power (2002).

Understand Support, Confidence, and Lift

To motivate the basic ideas of market-basket analysis, Table 16.1 presents a toy data set that describes five hypothetical baskets comprising three or four items each.

Each row of Table 16.1 represents a purchase of some number of items. Note that Transaction 3 contains only three items, so the fourth item is a missing value. A subset of items is called an *itemset*. You search for rules of the following form: IF {*X*} THEN {*Y*} where *X* and *Y* are itemsets. *X* is called the *antecedent* or *condition*, and *Y* is called the *consequent*.

Table 16.1: Five Small Market Baskets

Transaction Number	Item 1	Item 2	Item 3	Item 4
1	Sugar	Diapers	Bread	Beer
2	Beer	Bread	Peanut butter	Jelly
3	Bread	Peanut butter	Jelly	
4	Mustard	Beer	Diapers	Jelly
5	Diapers	Peanut butter	Magazine	Beer

Association Rules

Inspection of Table 16.1 yields a pair of association rules: IF {Beer} THEN {diapers}; and IF {peanut butter, bread} THEN {jelly}. Of course, there are some useless rules in this data set: IF {sugar} THEN {beer} and IF {peanut butter} THEN {beer}. Clearly, any transaction data set can give rise to a seemingly countless number of rules, more than you can possibly use. So you will need some way to bring the number of rules down to a manageable level. You will see how to do so momentarily.

Support

The three primary measures of market-basket analysis are *support*, *confidence*, and *lift*. Support measures the proportion of transactions that satisfy a rule:

$$\text{Support}(X,Y) = \frac{\text{Number of transactions containing both } X \text{ and } Y}{\text{Total number of transactions}}$$

In Table 16.1, if X = {diapers} and Y = {beer}, then support(diapers,beer) = 3/5 = 0.6.

Confidence

Confidence measures how accurate a rule is likely to be:

$$\text{Confidence}(X,Y) = \frac{\text{Number of transactions containing both } X \text{ and } Y}{\text{Number of transaction containing } X}$$

In Table 16.1, if X = {diapers} and Y = {beer}, then confidence(diapers,beer) = 3/3 = 1.00. Every time you observe a transaction with diapers, that same transaction also contains beer. However, the converse is not true. If X = {beer} and Y = {diapers} then confidence(beer,diapers) = 3/4 = 0.75. So when you observe beer in a transaction, only 75% of the time does that transaction contain diapers.

For more complicated rules, the interpretation is similar. Consider the rule IF {a, b} THEN {c} where a, b, and c are individual items. If the confidence for this rule is 50%, then this means that every time a and b appear in a basket, there is a 50% chance that c is in the basket also.

Lift

A problem with confidence is that, if the Y item set is very common, then the rule is not very useful. For example, if confidence(X,Y) is 60%, but Y is in 70% of the transactions, then the rule IF {X} THEN {Y} is not very useful; the rule is worse than a random guess. The concept of *lift* addresses this problem.

Lift measures the strength of the rule by comparing the rule to random guesses.

$$\text{Lift}(X,Y) = \frac{\text{Support}(X,Y)}{\text{Support}(X,X) * \text{Support}(Y,Y)}$$

Here, support(X,X) is just the proportion all transactions that contain X, and support(Y,Y) is the proportion of all transactions that contain Y. If X = {diapers} and Y = {beer}, then lift(diapers, beer) = 0.6/(0.6 x 0.8) = 1.25. Clearly, lift(X,Y) = lift(Y,X). So only one of these needs to be computed. A lift of 1.0 means that the rule is just as good as guessing: X and Y are independent. A lift of less than 1.0 means that the rule is worse than random guessing. Rarely is there a reason to concern yourself with rules that have lift less than unity. Another way to think about lift is to realize that it is the ratio by which the actual confidence of the rule exceeds the confidence that would occur if the items were independent.

Similarly, you will not be interested in rules that don't have much support. Suppose you have a million transactions. If minimum support is 1%, then only rules supported by at least 10,000 transactions will be considered. This is the primary way that you cut down on the number of rules to analyze. Rules that fall below the minimum support threshold simply don't have enough observations to be worth considering. It is important to realize, and this is obvious from looking at the equation for lift, that when support gets smaller, lift gets larger. If minimum support is reduced from 0.01 to 0.001, lift can get very large. In general, rules with high lift have low support. Consider rules with a lift greater than 1 and approve a minimum support threshold.

Association analysis works best when items are equally prevalent across the baskets. That way an extremely common item doesn't dominate the results. It might be useful to limit a market-basket analysis to a subgroup, such as vegetables, rather than across groups, such as dairy and vegetables, where milk would be the dominant item and make it hard to uncover the relationships in the vegetables subgroup.

Use JMP to Calculate Confidence and Lift

Now you will apply JMP to Table 16.1 and try to reproduce a couple of the calculations from the previous section—specifically, confidence(diapers,beer) = 1.0, and lift(diapers,beer) = 1.25; and the converse, confidence(beer,diapers) = 0.75, and lift(beer,diapers) = 1.25.

The file ToyAssociation.jmp re-creates Table 16.1; open it. Remember that data are not always organized the way that the software wants, and here is a case in point. The association analysis procedure in JMP requires two columns of data: one for the ID (in this case, the transaction number), and another column of items. The data in Table 16.1 need to be stacked before you can use them:

1. Select **Tables** ▶ **Stack** and stack the items, omitting the Transaction Number.
2. Select **Items 1** through **4** and click **Stack Columns**. Click **OK**. The resulting new Data Table has three columns: Transaction Number, Label, and Data. You can ignore **Label**. Select **Analyze** ▶ **Screening** ▶ **Association Analysis**.
3. Select **Transaction Number** and click **ID**.
4. Select **Data** and click **Item**. Leave everything else at default. Click **OK**.

Look at the Association Analysis window for beer and diapers for similar results that you calculated above: confidence(beer,diapers) = 75%, confidence(diapers,beer) = 100%: lift(beer,diapers) = lift(diapers,beer) = 1.25.

Use the A Priori Algorithm for More Complex Data Sets

For this toy set, it was easy for the computer to generate all the possible itemsets and analyze them. Suppose, however, that your data set had $n = 5$ items. How many itemsets might there be? $(2 \wedge 5) - 1 = 31$. Why the "−1"? Imagine using 0 for *not buy* and 1 for *buy*. There are $2 \wedge 5 = 32$ possible sequences of zeros and 1s, including the sequence 0 0 0 0 0, which represents no purchases at all. So you have to subtract from that one sequence. If $n = 100$ then $(2 \wedge 100) - 1$. A typical grocery store has 40,000 items, and the number of possible itemsets is too large for any computer. You need some way to pare this number down to a manageable size so that a computer can handle it. There are many algorithms that do so, but the most popular is the *a priori* algorithm.

The a priori algorithm begins with the idea that you will only consider itemsets that have some minimum level of support. This might be 1%, it might be 10%. These are called *frequent itemsets*. Next, you generate all frequent itemsets that contain just one item. The key insight that drives the a priori algorithm is this: frequent itemsets with two items can contain only frequent itemsets that contain one item. Suppose drain cleaner appears in fewer than 1% of baskets. Not only can't it be in frequent itemsets that contain one item—it also necessarily cannot be in frequent itemsets that contain two items. Similarly, frequent itemsets with three items are derived from frequent itemsets with two items, and so on.

Form Rules and Calculate Confidence and Lift

Generating each level of frequent itemset requires only one pass through the data. Once all the frequent itemsets are generated, rules can be easily formed, and these rules can have confidence and lift calculated. Minimum levels of confidence and lift can be applied to filter out weak rules because you are really interested in strong rules that have high confidence and good lift.

Nonetheless, not all rules with high confidence and good lift will be useful. These rules will generally fall into one of three categories: actionable, trivial (useless), and inexplicable; with actionable rules being the rarest.

- An example of a useless rule is this: people who purchase maintenance agreements usually purchase large appliances.
- An example of an inexplicable rule is this: people who buy toilet cleaner also buy bread.
- An actionable rule might be this: people who buy bread and peanut butter also buy jelly.

You can then give jelly coupons with a recipe for peanut butter and jelly sandwiches on the back to people who buy just bread and peanut butter, in an attempt to convert them to regular jelly purchasers.

In practice, you need to play with the minimum support and confidence levels to find as many interesting rules as possible without including too many trivial or inexplicable rules.

Analyze a Real Data Set

Open the data file GroceryPurchases.jmp, which is due to the efforts of Brijs et al. (1999). Observe that it is already stacked. Each row contains a single purchased item and an ID indicating from which basket the item came. This file has 7007 rows, and the ID numbers run from zero to 1000, indicating 1001 baskets with an average of seven items per basket.

Perform Association Analysis with Default Settings

Run Association Analysis with the default settings:

1. Select **Analyze ▶ Screening ▶ Association Analysis**.
2. Select **Customer ID** and click **ID**.
3. Select **Product** and click **Item**. Leave everything else at default. Click **OK**.

Looking at the Rules in the output window, you see that the first thing to observe is that there are far too many rules for you to comprehend.

Reduce the Number of Rules and Sort Them

Reduce the size of the list of rules:

1. Click the red triangle next to Association Analysis at the top of the output window.
2. Select **Redo** ▶ **Relaunch Analysis.**
3. Change Minimum Confidence to 0.9 and Minimum Lift to 2.0.
4. Click **OK**.

The list is appreciably shorter. The next thing to observe is that the list of Rules is not sorted in any meaningful way. To remedy this, click the drop arrow next to **Confidence.** For follow-up visualization, you can also turn this list into a Data Table and then make a scatter plot:

1. Right-click over the text or numbers of the Rules, and select **Make Into Data Table**.
2. You can right-click the column name **Confidence**, select **Sort**, and then **Descending**. See that many rules have very high confidence.
3. Right-click the column name **Lift**, select **Sort** and then **Descending**. See that many rules have very high lift.

Examine Results

To view both Confidence and Lift at once, use a scatter plot:

1. In your new Data Table, select **Graph** ▶ **Graph Builder**.
2. Drag **Confidence** to **Y** and **Lift** to **X**.
3. The scatterplot might have a smoothing line through it. This is a distraction that is not appropriate for visualizing these data. If you see the smoothing line, click the second from left graph box at the top of the window to remove it and leave the points. (If the leftmost box is shaded, that means "show the points," and if the second box is shaded, that means "show the smoother.")

You see that about half the points have Confidence between 94% and 100% with a Lift between 2 and 3 as shown in Figure 16.2.

Return to the Association Analysis output window. Click the sideways triangle next to Frequent Item Sets. You see immediately that the customers of this store are quite fond of Heineken beer; it is in 60% of the baskets. You also see that the customers are fond of crackers, herring, and olives, as shown in Figure 16.3. Scanning down the list, you see that Coke has 30% support. Perhaps you are interested in increasing Coke sales. Two relevant questions are as follows:

1. What are customers likely to buy before buying Coke?
2. What are customers likely to buy if they purchase Coke?

Figure 16.2: Confidence versus Lift for the GroceriesPurchase.jmp Data

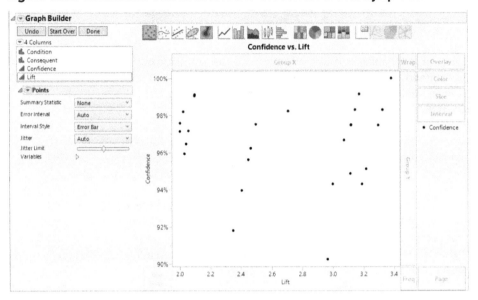

Looking at your list of Rules with a Minimum Confidence of 0.9, you see that there is not much scope for improvement. Everybody here who is already buying Coke or going to buy Coke is doing so with a very high probability.

Target Results to Take Business Actions

Rerun the analysis, this time with a Minimum Confidence of 0.6. You can see two opportunities, both with Confidence of about 70%: Coke => ice cream (74%) and ice cream => Coke (70%). There is a strong tendency for Coke and ice cream to be purchased together, but there are still plenty of people who buy one but not the other. So there are many potential customers. For people who already buy Coke but not ice cream, you can issue a coupon for ice cream at checkout. You can also place an advertisement for ice cream in the Coke aisle. For people who buy ice cream but not Coke, you issue coupons at checkout and place a Coke advertisement near the ice cream cooler.

The scope for association analysis is quite wide. In addition to analyzing market baskets, it has been used for the following:

- Analyzing a mailing list of donors to find out what characteristics lead to a donation
- Comparing different stores in a chain to uncover different selling patterns at different locations
- Conducting computer network forensics to detect and deter attacks by developing a signature pattern of an attack

Figure 16.3: Frequent Item Sets

Association Analysis

Frequent Item Sets

Item Set	Support	N Items
{Heineken}	60%	1
{crackers}	49%	1
{herring}	49%	1
{olives}	47%	1
{bourbon}	40%	1
{baguette}	39%	1
{corned beef}	39%	1
{crackers, Heineken}	37%	2
{avocado}	36%	1
{soda}	32%	1
{chicken}	31%	1
{apples}	31%	1
{ice cream}	31%	1
{artichoke}	30%	1
{ham}	30%	1
{Coke}	30%	1
{peppers}	30%	1
{sardines}	30%	1
{Heineken, herring}	29%	2
{turkey}	28%	1
{baguette, Heineken}	26%	2
{Heineken, soda}	26%	2

- Finding biologically important relationships between different genes
- Determining which customers of a health insurance company are at risk of developing diseases

Exercises

1. Identify other opportunities for increasing Coke sales, or for using Coke to spur sales of other goods.
2. For the data in Table 16.1, compute Confidence and Lift for *X* = {bread} and *Y* = {jelly, peanut butter} by hand. Then check your answer by using JMP.
3. Calculate the Support of *X* = {bread} and *Y* = {jelly, peanut butter}.
4. Analyze the GroceryPurchases.jmp data and find some actionable rules.

Chapter 17: Time Series Forecasting

Introduction

Forecasting is the act of predicting the future. For example, predicting the future demand for a product, future sales, future inventory levels, future energy prices, future ozone levels, and future water levels. The future is an upcoming time period: the next hour, tomorrow, next week, next month, next quarter, and so on. This chapter focuses on forecasting techniques in which historical data is available. Data that is collected sequentially over time is called time series data. Time series forecasting techniques capture the patterns of the data and based on these historical patterns, forecast the future. Alternatively, there are situations in which we desire to forecast the future, but we do not have any historical data, for example, the future sales of a new product or the effects of a new environmental policy on consumer consumption. These types of forecasting techniques are not the focus of this chapter and are not covered in this textbook. Time series forecasting techniques as shown in our multivariate analysis framework in Figure 17.1 are dependence techniques where the dependent variable is what we want to predict.

There are four historical time series patterns or components to consider: trend, seasonal, cyclical, and irregular. A trend is an overall increasing or decreasing of the values. Seasonal patterns are short-term changes in the data that repeat themselves. Cyclical patterns are similar to seasonal patterns, except cyclical patterns are long-term patterns in the data that repeat themselves. Cyclical patterns are usually assumed to be caused by economic factors, such as the business cycle. The major difference between a seasonal and cyclical component is that in general a seasonal pattern is of a constant length and occurs on a regular periodic basis, whereas a cyclical pattern varies in length and is usually longer than a seasonal component. In most cases, it is difficult to isolate the cycle effects because it requires a large amount of historical data, so, we will not address cyclical patterns in this text. The irregular component is the remaining variability after we remove the trend, seasonal, and cyclical patterns.

A basic assumption underlying these time series forecasting techniques is that what has happened in the past will happen in the future. That is, once we are able to capture these historical time series patterns, we can use them to develop forecasts. Once we are able to analytically describe these historical time series patterns, we can use them to develop forecasts.

Figure 17.1: A Framework for Multivariate Analysis

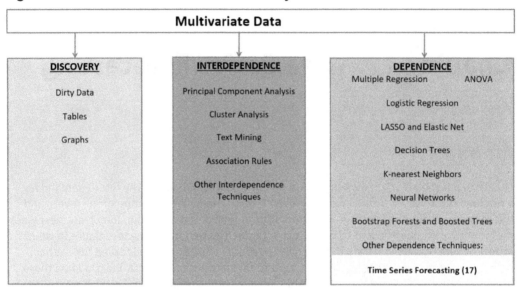

When conducting a forecasting project, an initial step should be ***discovery***. The objective of the discovery step is to develop a preliminary "feel" for the data and in particular take note of any trends or seasonal patterns. This step also includes the visualization of any patterns in the data through the use of graphs. The next step is to test for statistically significant trends and seasonal patterns in the data by calculating and interpreting the autocorrelation function. Autocorrelation is a measure of the similarity of the time series data values over time. Once these steps have been accomplished, we can use a number of different time series modeling techniques to fit the data. These techniques include: lagging, differencing, decomposition, and smoothing. These modeling approaches allow us to account for and "remove" the trend and seasonal patterns in the time series data; what remains should appear to be random. We present approaches to verify the randomness of the data. Following, the two most common smoothing techniques of moving average and exponential smoothing are reviewed. Next, we examine several performance measures used to evaluate the forecasting models. We subsequently examine several of the current more advanced time series models including advanced exponential smoothing, state space smoothing models, and autoregressive integrated moving average (ARIMA) models.

Discovery

One of the first discovery steps to do prior to developing a time series forecasting model is to produce a time series plot.

Time Series Plot

A graph of data versus time is called a time series plot. Our objective of generating this time series plot is to give us a visual tool to identifying possible patterns in the data, such as trend, seasonal, and perhaps cyclical patterns. To demonstrate, first:

1. Open Monthly_Sales.jmp. Select **Help ▶ Sample Index ▶ Times Series**. Click **Monthly Sales**. (Or you can find the Monthly Sales.jmp with other textbook files.)
2. Select **Cols ▶ New Columns** (or right-click on any column heading and select **New Column**). In the New Column dialog box, in Column Name box, type **TP**; click the drop arrow for **Column Properties ▶ Formula**.
3. In the Formula dialog box, click the arrow next to **Row** and click **Row**. Row() will appear in the formula area. Click **Apply**; click **OK**; click **OK**. A column name **TP** should appear with subsequent numbers for each row as shown in Figure 17.2.
4. Select **Cols ▶ New Columns**. In the New Column dialog box, in Column Name box, type **Month**; click the drop arrow for **Modeling Type** and click **Nominal**. Click the drop arrow for **Column Properties ▶ Formula**.
5. In the Formula dialog box, click the arrow next to **Date Time** and click **Month**. In the formula area inside the parentheses, click on the variable **Date**; click **Apply**; click **OK**; click **OK**. A column named **Month** should appear with the month number as shown in Figure 17.2.

Figure 17.2: The Monthly_Sales File

	Sales	Date	Month	TP
1	112	09/01/1978	9	1
2	118	10/01/1978	10	2
3	132	11/01/1978	11	3
4	129	12/01/1978	12	4
5	121	01/01/1979	1	5
6	135	02/01/1979	2	6
7	148	03/01/1979	3	7
8	148	04/01/1979	4	8
9	136	05/01/1979	5	9
10	119	06/01/1979	6	10
11	104	07/01/1979	7	11
12	118	08/01/1979	8	12
13	115	09/01/1979	9	13
14	126	10/01/1979	10	14
15	141	11/01/1979	11	15
16	135	12/01/1979	12	16
17	125	01/01/1980	1	17
18	149	02/01/1980	2	18
19	170	03/01/1980	3	19
20	170	04/01/1980	4	20
21	158	05/01/1980	5	21
22	133	06/01/1980	6	22

To produce a time series plot:

1. Click **Graph ▶ Graph Builder.** Select **Sales** and drag it to the **Y variable.** Select **TP** and drag it to the **X variable.**
2. Click on the third from the left graph icon; towards the top of the Graph Builder dialog box as shown below:

3. Right-click anywhere inside the graph. Click **Line of Fit**; click off the check mark for Fit.
4. On the left, under the Line of Fit, click the check box for R² and Equation.

Figure 17.3 shows the graph of Sales over time. The trend line shows a strong positive trend, and the regression equation is Sales = 87.65 + 2.657*TP with a high R^2 of 0.854.

5. On the Data Table, right-click the **Month** variable and click **Label/Unlabel.** From the top menu of options in the Data Table, click **Rows ▶ Color or Mark by Column.** Click the Month variable. Try various ways to visually see the seasonal pattern and hover your pointer over various points to see which month it is. For example:

   a. **Colors ▶ Teal to Brown.**
   b. **Markers ▶ Solid**

   Click **OK.**

Figure 17.3: The Trend and Graph of Monthly Sales Over Time

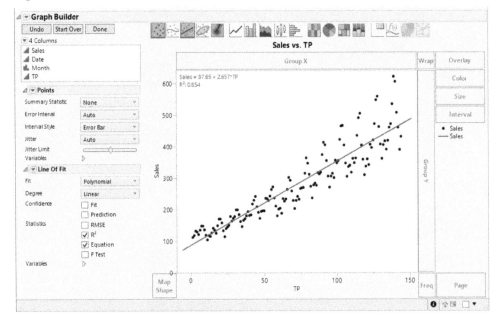

Figure 17.4: The Seasonal Pattern and Graph of Monthly Sales Over Time

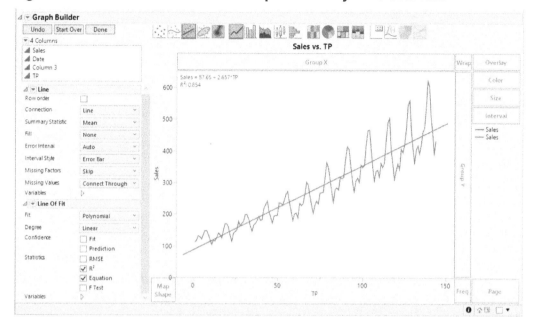

6. To further view the pattern of the Sales data over time, right-click anywhere inside the Graph Builder graph. Click **Points ▶ Change to ▶ Line**. The graph will now look like the graph shown in Figure 17.4.

Trend Analysis

One of our initial concentrations is to discover the overall tendency of the data. In most cases, a linear trend is considered, but the trend might be nonlinear. A linear trend and a nonlinear (exponential) trend are displayed in Figure 17.5. The direction and steepness (or rate of change) of the trend might also be of interest. The slope of the trend line measures the rate of change of a linear trend such that the larger the absolute value of the slope the greater the rate of change. The major focus in this chapter will be with data that is linear.

A commonly used approach to remove a nonlinear component of a variable is to take the log of that variable. For example, the variable GNP displays an exponential trend:

1. Open GNP.jmp. Select **Help ▶ Sample Index ▶ Times Series**. Click **GNP**. (Or you can find the GNP.jmp file with other textbook files.)
2. To graph the data, click **Graph ▶ Graph Builder** and select **gross national product ($billions)**. Drag it to the Y variable, and select **DATE** and drag it to the X variable. We can see that data has an exponential growth.

Figure 17.5: Example of Linear and Nonlinear Trends

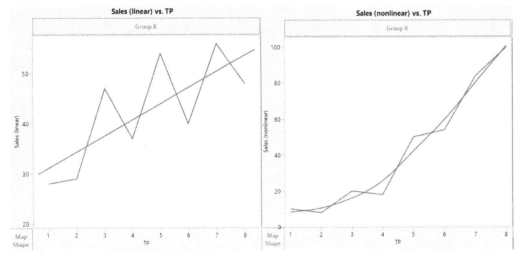

3. To remove this nonlinear component of the data, in the Graph Builder dialog box, move your pointer over the variable **gross national product ($billions)** in the Columns list and right-click. From the list of options, click **Log** and click **Log**.

4. A new variable is created and is included in the Columns list called **Log(gross national product ($billions))**. Click on this new variable **Log(gross national product ($billions))** and drag it right on top of the 5000 label on the Y axis and release it.

You can see the log variable has a linear trend. To include this log variable as part of your Data Table:

1. Create a new variable. Let's call it **Log_GNP**.

2. Select **Cols ▶ New Columns**. In the New Column dialog box, in Column Name box, type **Log_GNP**. Click the drop arrow for **Column Properties ▶ Formula**.

3. In the Formula dialog box, click the arrow next to **Transcendental** and click **Log**. Click **gross national product ($billions)** and click inside the parentheses in the **Log** formula. Click **Apply**; click **OK**; click **OK**.

Testing for Significant Linear Trend Component

A linear trend is an overall movement of the time series values. For example, is sales increasing or decreasing? All the values will not necessarily appear along a smooth curve or line. There will most likely be some variations—a little higher or lower. In a case in which data discovery shows the possible existence of a linear trend, we can be reasonably sure that the trend line fit to our data will have a nonzero slope coefficient. We should, however, test to see if the slope (coefficient) is statistically significant, that is, does it statistically differ from zero? We will use linear regression to assist us in making this determination. It is assumed that there is a theoretical regression line where:

$$Y_t = \beta_0 + \beta_1 t + \varepsilon.$$

β_0 is the y-intercept and β_1 is the slope. These model parameters, β_0 and β_1, are population parameters whose actual values are unknown. The least squares regression procedure, as discussed in Chapter 5, develops estimates, b_0 and b_1, of these population parameters, β_0 and β_1, respectively. The estimate b_1 is unlikely to equal β_1 exactly, but it is hoped that it is statistically close and the same is true for b_0 and β_0. We can conduct a statistical hypothesis test to test whether it can assume β_1 is equal to zero or not. If there is a significant trend and if the slope (trend) is positive, a significant positive trend exists, or if it is negative, a significant negative trend exists. The statistical hypothesis test determines whether our estimate of β_1, b_1 is statistically significantly close to 0 or whether it is statistically significantly far enough away so that it can be considered as not being equal to 0. On the other hand, if the test can conclude that there is not enough evidence to say there is a significant trend during subsequent forecasting modeling, it is unlikely to consider and find a significant trend component (although it is still possible). This statistical hypothesis test for linear trend is:

$$H_0: \beta_1 = 0$$

$$H_1: \beta_1 \neq 0$$

We have two possible conclusions:

(1) If H_0 is rejected, then there is a statistically significant trend, or

(2) If H_0 is not rejected, then there is no statistically significant trend

To determine whether or not to reject H_0, the p-value of the test is compared to a level of significance. The usual value of the level of significance or α is 0.01, 0.05, or 0.10 and is determined by the decision-maker or analyst. The p-value is based on the data and is reported as part of the statistical computer results. Therefore, if:

- the p-value $< \alpha$, then reject H_0,
- the p-value $\geq \alpha$, then do not reject H_0.

To perform the linear trend regression and the hypothesis test on our Monthly sales data:

1. Click **Analyze ▶ Fit Y by X**. Select **Sales** as the **Y, Response** variable and **TP** as the **X, Factor** variable.
2. Click **OK**.
3. Click the red triangle and click **Fit Line**.

Figure 17.6: Trend Line Using Linear Regression

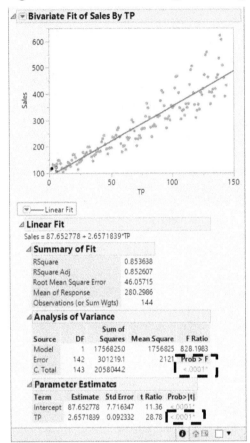

Figure 17.6 shows the trend line regression output. The p-value is significantly small for both the F test and t test, <.0001, so there is a significant trend, as highlighted in Figure 17.6. The trend line regression equation is Sales = 87.65 + 2.657*TP, which is the same equation that we found using the Graph Builder in Figure 17.3.

4. Click the **Bivariate Fit of Sales By TP** red triangle and click **Save Residuals**.

A new variable in the Data Table appears called **Residuals Sales**, which is the detrended Sales data: $(Y_t - \hat{Y}_t)$; (Actual value – Predicted value).

Seasonal Component

The seasonal component of a time series is a short-term pattern that repeats itself. What is considered to be short-term is relative to the time frame the time series data is collected. The time series data could be taken by the hour, day, week, month, year, or some other regular time interval. As a result, a seasonal influence could be time of day, day of the week, month of the year, quarter or whatever. For some reason(s), the data tends to be higher or lower during a particular season. For example, sales of skis are high in the winter and rather low during the summer, or restaurant sales are higher around meal times.

If no seasonal pattern is uncovered, further forecasting model development is not likely to consider any seasonal component. On the other hand, if a seasonal pattern is revealed, this seasonal pattern should definitely be considered in subsequent forecasting models.

Testing for Significant Seasonal Component

We will use regression to test for significant seasonal effects. However, before we can test whether or not there is a significant seasonal effect, we must first generate what is known as a set of indicator variables. Why? Seasonal components, whether they are weekly, monthly, quarterly, or hourly, are categorical variables. Measuring ratios and distances is not appropriate with categorical data. We therefore must transform these categorical seasonal components into continuous variables by using what is called *indicator* or *dummy variables*.

The appropriate set of indicator variables is defined by the number of indicator variables used and how their values are assigned. The number of indicator variables required is equal to c − 1, where c is the number of categories (or levels) of the categorical variable. For example, if we have monthly data, we will need 11 indicator variables. If we have quarterly data, we will need 3 indicator variables. Chapter 5 discusses further using indicator and dummy variables for categorical variables in a regression model.

There are several approaches to assigning values to these indicator variables. We will use the following approach:

1. Let the last category be the baseline indicator variable. So, with monthly data, it would be December. With quarterly data, it would be the fourth quarter.
2. Create c − 1 new variables or columns, starting with the first category until the second to last category. For example, if the category is monthly, the first new column would be January, and the last new column would be November. If the data is quarterly, the first new column would be quarter 1, and the last new column would be quarter 3.
3. Assign a value of 1 whenever the row name (that is what season the data is in) and the column name are the same.

To create these indicator variables in JMP:

1. Click the **Month** column heading in the Data Table.
2. Click **Cols** ▶ **Utilities** ▶ **Make Indicator Columns**. Click on the check box for **Append Column Name**. Click **OK**.

Although we only need 11 indicator variables, JMP creates 12 new month variables as shown in Figure 17.7.

Figure 17.7: Monthly Indicator Variables

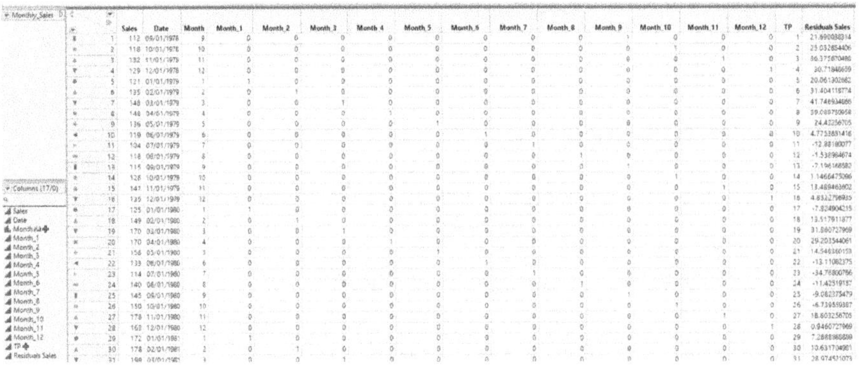

Once the indicator variables are created and assigned their values, we can now run the regression to test for seasonality. The seasonal component-only regression line for our monthly data is:

$$Seasonal_t = b_0 + b_1*Month\_1 + b_2*Month\_2 + b_3*Month\_3 + b_4*Month\_4 +$$

$$b_5*Month\_5 + b_6*Month\_6 + b_7*Month\_7 + b_8*Month\_8 +$$

$$b_9*Month\_9 + b_{10}*Month\_10 + b_{11}*Month\_11$$

To produce the seasonal component-only regression:

1. Click **Analyze ▶ Fit Model**.
2. In the Fit Model dialog box, click **Sales** and click **Y**. Click **Month_1** to **Month_11** and click **Add**. Click **Run**.

The p-value for the F test is 0.169, which is high, indicating no significant seasonal component. In observing the data, we believe there was some significant seasonal effect. What is probably happening is that the seasonal effect is being obscured by the trend. To control for the trend, add **TP** to the model:

$$Sales_t = b_0 + TP_t + b_1*Month\_1 + b_2*Month\_2 + b_3*Month\_3 + b_4*Month\_4 +$$

$$b_5*Month\_5 + b_6*Month\_6 + b_7*Month\_7 + b_8*Month\_8 +$$

$$b_9*Month\_9 + b_{10}*Month\_10 + b_{11}*Month\_11$$

Rerun the regression, now including **TP**. This new regression including **TP** and the seasonal components is called an additive regression forecasting model. Figure 17.8 shows the regression output. Now, the F test is quite significant, <0.0001, and the adjusted R^2 is 0.95. Most of the p-values for the months are <0.0001.

Figure 17.8: Additive Regression Model

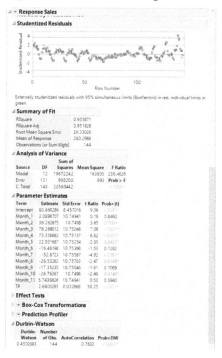

Externally studentized residuals with 95% simultaneous limits (Bonferroni) in red, individual limits in green.

Summary of Fit

RSquare	0.955871
RSquare Adj	0.951828
Root Mean Square Error	26.33026
Mean of Response	280.2986
Observations (or Sum Wgts)	144

Analysis of Variance

Source	DF	Sum of Squares	Mean Square	F Ratio
Model	12	19672242	163935	236.4626
Error	131	90820.0	693	Prob > F
C. Total	143	20580442		<.0001*

Parameter Estimates

Term	Estimate	Std Error	t Ratio	Prob>|t|
Intercept	80.860286	8.437016	9.58	<.0001*
Month_1	2.0896707	10.74941	0.19	0.8462
Month_2	39.262675	10.7498	3.65	0.0004*
Month_3	76.269012	10.75046	7.09	<.0001*
Month_4	73.358683	10.75137	6.82	<.0001*
Month_5	22.031687	10.75254	2.05	0.0425*
Month_6	-16.46198	10.75398	-1.53	0.1282
Month_7	-52.8723	10.75567	-4.92	<.0001*
Month_8	-26.53263	10.75763	-2.47	0.0149*
Month_9	-17.35235	10.75046	-1.61	0.1089
Month_10	-26.76267	10.7498	-2.49	0.0140*
Month_11	5.7436626	10.74941	0.53	0.5940
TP	2.6603293	0.052968	50.23	<.0001*

Effect Tests

Box-Cox Transformations

Prediction Profiler

Durbin-Watson

Durbin-Watson	Number of Obs.	AutoCorrelation	Prob<DW
0.4502383	144	0.7632	<.0001*

We can measure the seasonal effects for each month by sorting the regression coefficients for the appropriate indicator variables as shown in Table 17.1. Month_12, December, is our baseline; therefore, there would be no seasonal effects. December's seasonal index is 0 when using December as the baseline month. Months three and four have relatively high sales, and month 7 is significantly lower. This pattern is consistent with our initial visual inspection.

Cyclical Component

The cyclical component is a long-term pattern that repeats itself. In such a case, the data tends to stay above or below the trend line for long periods of time. Long-term is relative to how often the time series data is collected (for example, monthly data versus hourly data). Most of the time, cyclical patterns are assumed to be caused by economic factors such as the business cycle (hence a cycle is usually at least 12 months). An example of a cyclical pattern would be the effect on prices when you have periods of rapid inflation subsequently followed by modest inflation. The major difference between a seasonal and cyclical component is that the seasonal component is of a constant length and occurs on a regular periodic basis, whereas a cyclical component varies in length and is usually longer than a seasonal component.

Table 17.1: Sorted Seasonal Components Using December as the Baseline Month

Month	Coefficient
Month_3	76.269012
Month_4	73.358683
Month_2	39.262675
Month_5	22.031687
Month_11	5.7436626
Month_1	2.0896707
Month_12	0
Month_6	-16.46198
Month_9	-17.35235
Month_8	-26.53263
Month_10	-26.76267
Month_7	-52.8723

In many circumstances, it is difficult to isolate the cycle effects. The question is, should the cyclical component be addressed or not? To answer this question, three questions should be considered:

1. Are we forecasting short-term?
2. Does the data show a cyclical pattern?
3. Can we relate this pattern to some economic or business indicator?

The cyclical component should be considered if all three of the above questions are answered in the affirmative. Further, there is a hierarchy to these questions such that they should be asked in their order. That is, there is no need to ask a subsequent question if a preceding question is not satisfied.

Autocorrelation

Often, and especially with time series data, the data is correlated with itself. That is, it is correlated with its lagged values. A lagged value is the value of the data one or more prior time periods before the current time period. For example, sales in this time period are related to sales in the previous time period, or sales in this time period are related to sales three time periods earlier. The correlation between the lag values and itself is called autocorrelation. An additional discovery step is to examine the data's autocorrelation function (ACF). The formula to estimate the theoretical autocorrelation between observations k periods apart (or lagged k periods) is:

$$\rho_k = \frac{\sum\limits_{t=k+1}^{n} (Y_t - \overline{Y_k}^+)(Y_{t-k} - \overline{Y_k}^-)}{\sqrt{\sum\limits_{t=k+1}^{n} (Y_t - \overline{Y_k}^+)^2 \sum\limits_{t=k+1}^{n} (Y_{t-k} - \overline{Y_k}^-)^2}}$$

where :

ρ_k : theoretical estimate of autocorrelation coefficient for lag of k periods

Y_t : actual value in time period t

$$\overline{Y_k}^+ = \frac{\sum\limits_{t=k+1}^{n} Y_t}{n-k}$$

$$\overline{Y_k}^- = \frac{\sum\limits_{t=1}^{n-k} Y_t}{n-k}$$

n : total number of time periods.

For convenience, often in practice and in JMP, the mean of the entire series, $\overline{Y} = \dfrac{\sum\limits_{t=1}^{n} Y_t}{n}$, is used to estimate the partial means, $\overline{Y_k}^+$, $\overline{Y_k}^-$, and the sum of the square of the entire series is substituted for the partial sum of the squares. As a result, the equation to compute the sample autocorrelation coefficient of lag k is:

$$r_k = \frac{\sum\limits_{t=k+1}^{n} (Y_t - \overline{Y})(Y_{t-k} - \overline{Y})}{\sum\limits_{t=1}^{n} (Y_t - \overline{Y})^2}$$

where :

r_k : sample autocorrelation coefficient for lag of k periods

Y_t : actual value in time period t

$\overline{Y}$: average of the actual values

n : total number of time periods.

The difference between the theoretical estimate and the sample autocorrelation estimate is relatively small if the number of observations in the time series is large, compared to the number of periods lagged, k. For example, using the Monthy_sales data, the sample autocorrelation coefficient of lag 1 is calculated as:

$$r_1 = \frac{\sum_{t=2}^{20} (Y_t - \overline{Y})(Y_{t-1} - \overline{Y})}{\sum_{t=1}^{20}(Y_t - \overline{Y})^2} = \frac{\sum_{t=2}^{20} (Y_t - 280.30)(Y_{t-1} - 280.30)}{\sum_{t=1}^{20}(Y_t - 280.30)^2}$$

$$= \frac{1951123}{2058044}$$

$$= 0.9480$$

A graphical display of autocorrelations of various lags is called a correlogram (ACF). To produce the autocorrelations coefficients and correlogram:

1. Click **Analyze ▶ Specialized Modeling ▶ Time Series.**
2. Select **Sales** as the **Y, Time Series** and select **TP** as **X, Time ID. TP** is optional since the data is assumed to be sorted by time and equally spaced.
3. Click **OK.**

A time series plot and correlogram of autocorrelation of **Sales** similar to Figure 17.9 will appear. Observe the sample autocorrelation of lag 1 on the left side of Figure 17.9 is 0.9480, which is what we calculated above.

Like correlation, an autocorrelation coefficient can range from -1 to 1, and the closer the autocorrelation coefficient is to -1 or 1, the stronger the relationship. (Note that the autocorrelation coefficient of lag of 0 is equal to 1). Theoretically, each autocorrelation coefficient for a random series is equal to zero.

When time series data is analyzed using regression, as discussed earlier in this chapter with the additive regression, the Durbin-Watson test is used to test whether or not the error term in time period t is significantly related to the error term in time period t-1—that is, whether the first order autocorrelation is significant or not.

To compute the Durbin-Watson test after running the Fit Model, such as in Figure 17.8:

1. Click the red triangle next to **Response Sales**; click **Row Diagnostics** and click **Durbin-Watson Test**.

The results of the Durbin-Watson test will appear at the bottom of the Fit Model output as shown in Figure 17.8. The Durbin-Watson (DW) statistic is calculated as:

$$DW = \frac{\sum (e_t - e_{t-1})^2}{\sum e_t^2}$$

Figure 17.9: Time Series Output

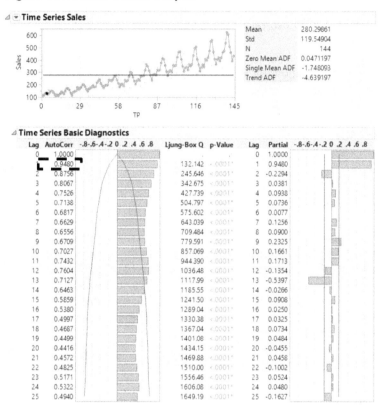

where e_t: error or residual in time period t.

The DW statistic can range from 0 to 4. If no significant autocorrelation exists, DW will be near 2; small values of DW (<2) indicate a positive first-order autocorrelation, and large values of DW (>2) imply a negative first-order autocorrelation. Positive first-order autocorrelation means that consecutive residuals tend to be similar.

The sampling distribution of autocorrelations is assumed to be approximately normal with a mean of zero and a standard deviation of $\frac{1}{\sqrt{n}}$. In the ACF correlogram in Figure 17.9, the blue lines represent ±2 standard errors for approximate 95% prediction limits. Autocorrelation coefficients outside these limits might be significantly different from zero. Statistically, when it is necessary to test whether one autocorrelation coefficient is equal to zero or not, there is a probability α of being incorrect. In determining the critical limits in the correlogram, a 95% prediction limit is used. So, there is a 5% chance of incorrectly deciding that an autocorrelation coefficient is nonzero. However, when this test is applied repeatedly to several autocorrelations, the likelihood of incorrectly deciding that at least one autocorrelation coefficient is nonzero can be rather significant. For example, if 20 autocorrelations are being tested, there is about a 64% chance of at least one false rejection.

A statistical test to test all the autocorrelations for all lags up to lag h is equal to zero (whether or not data values are random and independent up to a certain number of lags) is the Ljung-Box statistic. (Tests of this kind are known as portmanteau tests.) The equation for the Ljung-Box statistic is:

$$Q_h = n(n+2)\sum_{k=1}^{h}(n-k)^{-1}r_k^2$$

where h is the number of autocorrelation coefficients being tested.

The Ljung-Box statistic under its null hypothesis follows a χ^2 distribution with h degrees of freedom. If the Ljung-Box statistic is greater than the critical X^2 value or the p-value is less than 0.05, the conclusion is that one or more of the autocorrelations is nonzero (reject H_0). Otherwise, it can be assumed that all the autocorrelation coefficients up to lag h are not significantly different from zero. In our example in Figure 17.9, the Ljung-Box statistic is greater than the X^2 value, so it can be concluded that one or more of the first 25 autocorrelations is nonzero. A rule of thumb to determine the maximum number of lags to consider is:

non-seasonal data: h = min(10,n/5)

seasonal data: h = min(2m, n/5)

where m is the number of periods of the seasonality; n is the number of observations (Hyndman 2022).

Since the data is seasonal, h = min(2*12, 144/5) =24. So, with our monthly sales data, the maximum number of lags to consider should be 24.

The pattern and significance of the autocorrelation coefficients can be very useful in identifying significant components of the time series data. If the time series data is:

Random: All the autocorrelation coefficients are statistically equal to zero.

Stationary: The low-order autocorrelations (first several lags) are large, but higher-order lags decrease rapidly.

Trend: The low-order autocorrelations are large and decrease slowly as the lag increases.

Seasonal: A significant autocorrelation coefficient occurs at the appropriate time lag, for example, at lag 4, 8, 12, . . .; if there is a quarterly season or lag 12, 24, 36 . . .; if there is a monthly season.

On the right side of Figure 17.9 is a correlogram of the partial autocorrelations (PACFs) of the series. A partial autocorrelation measures the degree of association between Y_t and Y_{t-k}, after removing the effects of other earlier lags. Hence, it is called partial because we remove already found variations before we find the next correlation. Thus, the value for the autocorrelation and the partial autocorrelation at the first lag are the same because both measure the correlation between data points at time t with data points at time t – 1. However, at the second lag, the partial autocorrelation measures the correlation between data points at time t with data points at time t – 2 after controlling for the correlation between data points at time t with those at time t – 1. The PACF correlogram is on the right-hand side of Figure 17.9, and the approximate 95% prediction limits to determine whether the PACFs are significantly different from zero are drawn in blue. Partial autocorrelation coefficients outside these limits might be significantly different from zero.

For more complex models, the pattern and significance of both the ACF and PACF coefficients are useful in identifying significant factors in these models.

Lagging and Differencing

One of the common procedures to reduce the effects of autocorrelation is to lag or difference the data one or more periods.

Lagging

To lag a variable is to create a new variable whose values are lagged k periods behind the current period. That is, Y_{t-k}, would be a lag of k periods. We can lag for as many periods as we want. For example, we can lag by 1 period the Monthly sales by:

1. Click **Cols** ▶ **New Column**.
2. In the New Column dialog box, in **Column Name** type **Sales_lag1**. Click the drop arrow for **Column Properties** and click **Formula**.
3. Click the expand arrow next to **Row**; click **Lag**. In the formula, click **Sales**. Next to it, in the gray is <n=1>. Type **1** for a lag of 1 period.
4. Click **Apply**. Click **OK**. Click **OK**.

A new variable, **Sales_lag1**, with values equal to the previous period will appear in the Data Table. Note that with a lag variable, we lose up to the number of periods lagged (that is, with a lag of k, the 1st k periods will be blank).

Or,

1. Right-click the **Sales** column heading. Click **New Formula Column** ▶ **Row** ▶ **Lag**. A new variable **Lag(Sales)** is created.

Differencing

Another procedure that is quite similar to lagging is differencing, where you create a variable that is equal to the difference between the current value and the value k periods before, that is, $Y_t - Y_{t-k}$. Differencing is another approach to remove trend and seasonal components of the time series data. The k difference data measures the amount of change between the time t and time t – k, that is, $Y_t^k = Y_t - Y_{t-k}$.

The first difference, $Y_t^1 = Y_t - Y_{t-1}$, is one way to capture and remove the effect of the trend. To compute the first difference in the Time Series output box in Figure 17.9:

1. Click the **Time Series Sales** red triangle and click **Difference**.
2. In the **Specify Differencing** dialog box under Nonseasonal, click the drop arrow for Differencing Order and change it to 1; click **Estimate**.

The first difference output will be added to the Time Series output. Click the red triangle next to the Difference and click **Save**. A next column name **Difference** is added to the Data Table.

Differencing can also be applied to capture the seasonal component by performing a seasonal difference. In particular, for monthly data such as in the **Monthy_sales** data set, a monthly seasonal difference can be taken, yielding $Y_t^{12} = Y_t - Y_{t-12}$. If necessary, the trend and seasonal difference, that is the first and twelfth difference, can both be applied to the data. To compute the 12-period seasonal difference in the Time Series output box in Figure 17.9:

1. Click the **Time Series Sales** red triangle and click **Difference**.
2. In the **Difference Specification** dialog box under Seasonal, click the drop arrow for Differencing Order and change it to 12; click **Estimate**.

A helpful notation tool, especially when discussing differencing, is the backward shift operator B, which is defined as $BY_t = Y_{t-1}$. As such, the effect of B is to shift the data back one period. The first difference can then be expressed as:

$Y_t^1 = Y_t - Y_{t-1} = Y_t - BY_t = (1 - B)Y_t$. Shown in the JMP output as (1−B)^1.

Further, a seasonal difference can be written as $(1 - B^s)Y_t$. The monthly seasonal difference of 12 is shown as (1−B^12)^1. The backward shift operator B can also be useful in expressing the seasonal difference followed by a first difference that can be written as which is expressed as (1-B)^1(1-B^12)^1 in JMP.

Decomposition

The basic decomposition techniques develop forecasting models that separate and measure individually one or more time series component, such as trend or seasonal.

For example, to detrend the data, in the Time Series output box:

1. Click the **Time Series Sales** red triangle and click **Decomposition ▶ Remove Linear Trend**.

The detrended output is added to the Time Series output, as shown in Figure 17.10. At the top of the detrended output, under Linear Trend, the values of Beta0 and Beta1 are listed, 87.65278 and 2.657184, respectively. These are the same values when we fitted the regression line to the Monthly sales in Figures 17.4 and 17.6. The trend line is:

$$Trend_t = b_0 + b_1 TP$$

Figure 17.10: Detrended Monthly Sales

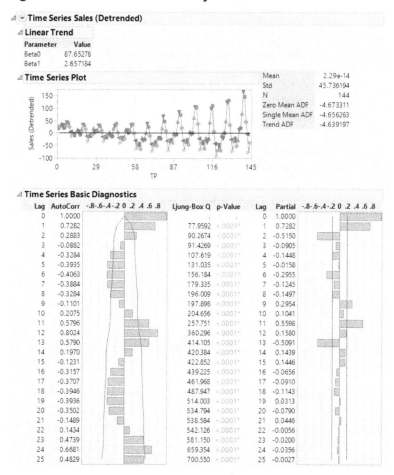

Further, the removal of the linear trend created a new variable in the Data Table called Sales(Detrended). The Sales(Detrended) series is equal to the Original values (t) – Trend(t), which is equal to the Residual (t). Earlier in the chapter in Figure 17.6, you created the residual variable. Examine your Data Table to see the same values for Residuals Sales and Sales(Detrended) variables.

To deseasonalize or decycle the data series under the **Decomposition**, there is option **Remove Cycle.** The cycle/seasonal component of the time series is estimated using a single cosine wave and then is removed from the original data series. A decycle/deseasonal report is added to the **Time Series report** along with a new decycle/deseasonal variable that is added to the Data Table.

The more comprehensive decomposition techniques in which the time series components, trend, seasonal, cyclical and irregular, are isolated and measured assume either an additive or multiplicative model (that is, the components are either multiplied by each other or they are additive). Many variations of the additive and multiplicative models are used. Earlier in the chapter, an additive decomposition model: $Y_t = T_t + S_t + I_t$ (where I_t = irregular component for time period t) using regression was discussed in the context of deseasonalizing the data (additive regression). One of the popular additive decomposition models, $Y_t = T_t + S_t + C_t + I_t$, and multiplicative models, $Y_t = T_t * S_t * C_t * I_t$, are the X-11 models developed by the Census Bureau. To create these X-11 models, in the **Time ID** the application needs to know the time period and season (note that X-11 modeling is available only for monthly or quarterly data):

1. Click **Analyze ▶ Specialized Modeling ▶ Time Series.**
2. Select **Sales** as the **Y, Time Series** and select **Date** as **X, Time ID.**
3. Click **OK.**
4. Click the **Time Series Sales** red triangle and click **Decomposition ▶ X11.**
5. Click on the button for either **Multiplicative** or **Additive**. Click **OK.**

Several graphs are added to the **Time Series** report. To get more information and a summary of results, click the red triangle next to **X11** and click **Show Tables.**

Stationarity

Most time series data are not stationary. A series of data is considered stationary if it satisfies the following criteria:

C.1: has no trend nor seasonality and

C.2: has a constant dispersion (equal variance is known as homoscedasticity).

Early in the chapter, we discussed approaches to detect and remove from the data any significant trend and seasonality. Removing any significant trend or seasonality from the data increases the likelihood that the remaining data is stationary. Homoscedastic implies that the data has a constant variance. Homoscedasticity implies that the dispersion of the data does not significantly change over time. For example, if for several periods the data does not vary much but then has a much higher range of fluctuation for several periods, the data would not be homoscedastic and would be called heteroscedastic. Although, there are formal statistical tests, in most cases a simple visual inspection of the time series plot is sufficient to tell if there are significant changes in the dispersion of the data. If there are no significant fluctuations in the size of the variation in the data, then the data is homoscedastic and C.2 is satisfied. On the other hand, if significant variations in the magnitude of the data are discovered, that is, the data appears to be heteroscedastic, whatever is causing these changes in variation should be removed. (By remove, we mean a model should be developed or a transformation of the data performed such that this variation is removed.)

Formal statistical tests for the stationarity of a time series are called unit root tests (a feature that changes over time). The Augmented Dickey Fuller (ADF) test is one of the most commonly used statistical tests to evaluate the stationary of a time series. The ADF test is preferred to the Dickey Fuller (DF) test since the ADF is more powerful and can handle more diverse models. The null hypothesis for the ADF test is that the time series is nonstationary.

Notice three tests towards the top right of Figure 17.10: Zero Mean ADF, Single Mean ADF, and Trend ADF. The Zero Mean ADF tests against a random walk with a mean of zero. The Single Mean ADF tests against a random walk with a nonzero mean. The Trend ADF tests against a random walk with a nonzero mean and a linear trend. Each of these metrics is associated with the distribution of the Tau statistic, and associated p-values are approximate, so JMP displays the ADF test statistic value. The ADF test produces a negative number. The more negative the number, the more likely the time series is stationary. The 5% critical value for the ADF test without a trend is -2.8 and with a trend for large sample is -3.41.

Randomness

Randomness implies that the data is unpredictable and has no pattern. If there is some pattern to the data, then a model can be developed to predict this pattern. Thus, if the forecast errors or irregular components are not random, a better model can be developed.

A series of data or the residuals from a model are considered to be random if they are stationary, that is, C.1 and C.2 are true, and in addition the following criteria are satisfied:

    C.3: Data points do not stay either above or below the trend line for a large number of consecutive periods, and

    C.4: Data points do not seem to oscillate rapidly above or below the trend line.

Runs Test

An informal test to check whether the data satisfies C.3 and C.4, again, is just a visual inspection of the time series plot. A formal statistical test is the Runs test, which is a hypothesis test that tests whether the data is meandering (C.3), and if the data is alternating back and forth too many times (C.4). In particular, the Runs test checks the number of values above or below a fixed value. This fixed value is usually the mean or median (when testing irregular components or residuals, this value is equal to zero). If the data is random, there should be approximately the same number of values above and below the fixed value. A run is the sequential occurrence of observations either above or below this fixed value. Further, if the data is random, the expected length of a run will be close to 2. Therefore, the expected number of total runs will be approximately equal to about one-half the number of observations.

For example, the mean of the 10 observations below is 4.4:

2 5 5 6 3 2 9 8 3 1

and there are five runs: (2) (5 5 6) (3 2) (9 8) (3 1).

Three of these runs are below the mean, (2), (3 2), and (3 1), and two runs are above the mean, (5 5 6) and (9 8).

There can be, and there will always be, two categories of runs: one above and one below the fixed value. In particular, n_1 is arbitrarily assigned to the above category and n_2 to the below category, where n_1 and n_2 are the number of values in each category. So, for the above example, $n_1 = 2$ and $n_2 = 3$.

If the data is random, it would be expected that:

- about the same number of values would appear above the mean as appear below the mean, that is, $n_1 \cong n_2$, and
- there will not be too many nor too few runs.

The null and alternative hypotheses for the Runs test are:

H_0: The data is random
H_1: The data is not random.

If n_1 and n_2 are greater than or equal to 10, the distribution of the number of runs is approximately normal, and the following statistic can be used:

$$Z = \frac{R - \mu_R}{\sigma_R}$$

where:

n_1 = # of values above fixed value

n_2 = # of values below fixed value

R = total number of runs

$$\mu_R = \frac{2n_1 n_2}{n_1 + n_2} + 1$$

$$\sigma_R = \sqrt{\frac{2n_1 n_2 (2n_1 n_2 - n_1 - n_2)}{(n_1 + n_2)^2 (n_1 + n_2 - 1)}}$$

If the p-value is small, that is, less than α, H_0 is rejected, and there is enough evidence to say that the data is not random. Otherwise, H_0 is not rejected, and the data can be assumed to be random.

With the **Sales** data, the mean is 280.299, n_1 = 64 and n_2 = 80. The calculated Z = -10.519 and its corresponding p-value is 0.

A JMP add-in is necessary to perform the Runs test:

1. Go to: https://community.jmp.com/t5/JMP-Add-Ins/Runs-Test-Wald-Wolfowitz-Test-and-JSL-Implementation-of-JMP/ta-p/23747
   This add-in can also be found with other textbook files on the author's page:
   http://support.sas.com/klimberg.
2. Download the **Runs Test.jmpaddin** file.
3. Find on your computer where you downloaded the file, double click the add-in file. Click **Install**.

To execute this Runs test add-in, on the top menu of the Data Table:

1. Click **Add-Ins ▶ Runs Test**.
2. In the Runs Test dialog box, select **Sales** and click **Y, Columns** and click **OK**.

Figure 17.11 shows the Runs test output and the graph of the data. As the graph obviously displays and with a small p-value of 0, H_0 is rejected, and the conclusion is that the data is not random.

(If n_1 or n_2 is less than 10, then the distribution of runs cannot be assumed to be normal, and the Runs test therefore should not be performed. In such a situation, it is necessary to graph the irregular components or residuals in the data and visually inspect the data for too many or too few runs; see C.3 and C.4)

Figure 17.11: Runs Test Output

Normality Test

To examine the distribution of values:

1. Click **Analyze ▶ Distribution**. In the Distribution dialog box, select **Sales** and click **Y, Columns**; click **OK**.

As shown in Figure 17.12, we visually see that the data approximately conforms to a bell-shaped curve with all the observations within the box plot. To further investigate:

2. In the Distribution report for **Sales**, click the **Sales** red triangle and click **Normal Quantile Plot**.

Points falling along the diagonal would indicate that the values are as far from the center of the distribution as would be expected if they were normally distributed. Points falling off the diagonal indicate that they are in a different location that would be expected if they were from a normal distribution. All the **Sales** data points are within the confidence limits of the normal quartile plot as shown in Figure 17.12, although several values are near the lower confidence limit bound.

To perform a formal hypothesis test:

3. Click the **Sales** red triangle in the Distribution output, as shown in Figure 17.12. Click **Continuous Fit ▶ Fit Normal**.

Figure 17.12: Distribution of Values and Normal Quantile Plot

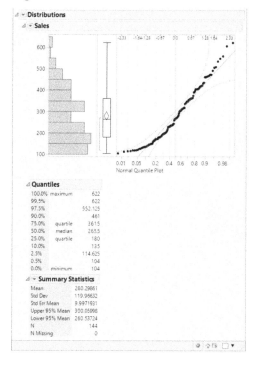

A normal distribution is fitted to the mean and standard deviation of the data. Toward the bottom of the Distribution output, a **Fitted Normal Distribution** report is provided, as shown in Figure 17.13.

> 4. Click the **Fitted Normal Distribution** red triangle and click **Goodness of Fit**.

The results of the Shapiro-Wilk W and Anderson-Darling (A-D) Goodness of Fit test will appear below the **Fitted Normal Distribution** output, as shown in Figure 17.13. The H_0 for these tests is that the data are normally distributed, so, if p-value < α, the H_0 that the data are normally distributed is rejected. If the p-value is greater than α, then the H_0 is not rejected. The Shapiro-Wilk W test has been shown to be more powerful than the A-D test for testing for normality. Thus, the Shapiro-Wilk W test is only used for testing normality. The p-values in Figure 17.13 are small, so we can assume that the data does not follow a normal distribution.

I-Chart

If the data is random and approximately normal (even though our **Sales** data cannot be assumed normal, we will assume that it is approximately normal), we can use a control chart

Figure 17.13: Shapiro-Wilk W and Anderson-Darling (A-D) Goodness of Fit Tests

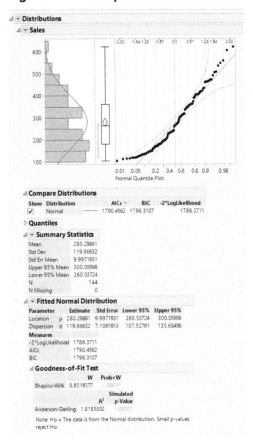

called an Individuals Measurement Chart (also called an I-Chart) to examine the variation in the data:

1. Click **Analyze ▶ Quality and Process ▶ Control Chart ▶ IMR Control Chart**.
2. Select **Sales** and click **Y**; click **OK**.
3. An Individual & Moving Range chart of **Sales** is produced, similar to Figure 17.14. Somewhere in the white space of the top I-Chart, right-click. From the list of options, select **Limits ▶ Zones**. Repeat, right-click and from the list of options, select **Limits ▶ Shade Zones**.

The zones in the I-Chart are defined relative to the distance from the mean:

Zone C: within one standard deviation of the mean (Green)
Zone B: between one and two standard deviations away from the mean (Yellow)
Zone A: between two and three standard deviations away from the mean (Yellow)
Beyond Zone A is shaded Red.

Figure 17.14: Individuals Measurement Chart

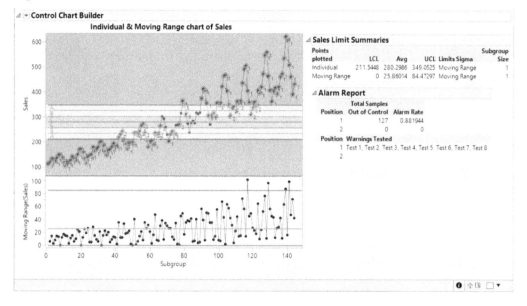

Nelson developed eight tests to identify special causes of possible non-random behavior in an I-chart (Nelson, 1984).

4. To perform these eight tests: right-click somewhere in the white space of the I-chart. From the list of options, select **Warnings ▶ Tests ▶ All Tests**.
5. To customize these eight tests (and to see what these tests are), right-click and from the list of options, select **Warnings ▶ Customize Tests.** The dialog box shown in Figure 17.15 will appear.
6. To see where the data violate these tests, click the **Control Chart Builder** red triangle and click **Show Alarm Report**.

For a set of data to be considered random, the data does not need to have no violations for all eight of Nelson's tests. These tests simply provide insight to some of the patterns of the data. The degree of randomness depends on which test is violated and the number of violations, and furthermore, the decision is left to the decision-maker or analyst to determine the magnitude of each violation. Also, the degree of concern about the violation will not only depend on the type of violation, but also will depend on when it occurs. For example, did it occur during one of the early time periods or toward the more recent values? In most situations, the decision-maker or analyst would be more concerned with recent violations because of their possible impact on forecasts.

Finally, it should be stated that randomness does not imply normality. Data is considered to be random if, by examining its time series plot, no pattern is observed (using the Runs test and I-Chart). Testing for normality is carried out by either performing a formal statistical test

Figure 17.15: Nelson's Eight Tests

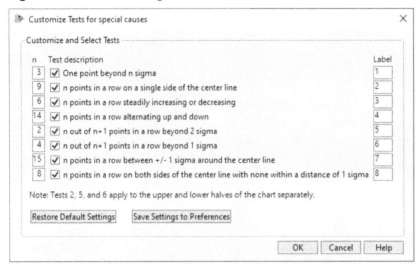

(Shapiro-Wilk W or A-D test) or simply by looking at the distribution of observations—the histogram—and finding that the data appear to be normal or symmetrical. Hence, data can be:

- random and normal,
- random and non-normal,
- non-random and normal, and
- non-random and non-normal.

This realization leads to an important result. If the data (error, irregular, or original data) can be considered to be random and approximately normal, then any other statistically significant variation in the data cannot be extracted. Thus, if the irregular component or residuals are being examined, all the significant time series components have been removed from the original data and no other statistically significant variation in the data can be extracted from the data—we cannot do better with what we got! (Or if the original data are being examined, and are found to be random and normal, then it can be concluded that there are no significant time series components in the data). The only way to improve the model is to bring in one or more variables to help predict the variable—this is called causal modeling, such as regression. On the other hand, if the data is random and not normal, the sources of variation are not acting independently and some time series forecasting technique might be used to remove the nonnormality.

In many instances, after extracting from the data the trend, cyclical, and seasonal components by applying a forecasting time series method, the remaining irregular component is random. Data that is random shows no pattern and must satisfy all four criteria (C.1–C.4). If the data violates C.1, a significant trend exists and should be removed. If the data displays a non-constant variance, that is, violates C.2, this suggests possibly that transforming the data using logarithms would help or using a causal forecasting technique (such as regression). If the data is stationary, that is, C.1 and C.2 are satisfied, but neither C.3 nor C.4 are satisfied, then one of the smoothing techniques (moving average, exponential, or State Space) or differencing, or the Box-Jenkins technique (discussed later in this Chapter) would be useful.

Simple Moving Average and Simple Exponential Smoothing Models

Let's return to the GNP.jmp data set and the variable **Log_GNP**. To produce the autocorrelations coefficients and correlogram:

1. Click **Analyze ▶ Specialized Modeling ▶ Time Series.**
2. Select **Log_GNP** as the **Y, Time Series** and select **DATE** as **X, Time ID.**
3. Click **OK.**

Note: If you know that your data is nonlinear prior to your time series modeling and you want to take the log, you do not have to create a new variable as we did earlier in the chapter, but you can:

1. Click **Analyze ▶ Specialized Modeling ▶ Time Series.**
2. Select **gross national product ($billions)** as the **Y, Time Series,** select **DATE** as **X, Time ID,** and check the box for **Use Box-Cox Transformation.** The default value in JMP for lambda is 0.
3. Click **OK.**

You get the same results.

We can see in the graph that there is a definite linear trend, the ADF values are not less than −3.4, and the confidence limits of the correlogram of the autocorrelation are bended out (if the confidence limits are in a straight line, that is an indication of the data being stationary). To remove the trend, let's take the first difference of the **Log_GNP**:

1. Click the **Time Series Log_GNP** red triangle and click **Difference.**
2. In the **Specify Differencing** dialog box under Nonseasonal, click the drop arrow for Differencing Order and change it to 1; click **Estimate.**
3. Click the **Difference: (1-B)^1** red triangle and click **Save.** A new column called **Difference** is added to the Data Table.

The first difference output will be added to the Time Series output. Note that the first observation of the Difference variable is blank, the linear trend is removed, the ADF values are less than -3.4, and the autocorrelation confidence limits are not bowing out as shown in Figure 17.16.

Figure 17.16: First Difference of Log_GNP Time Series Output

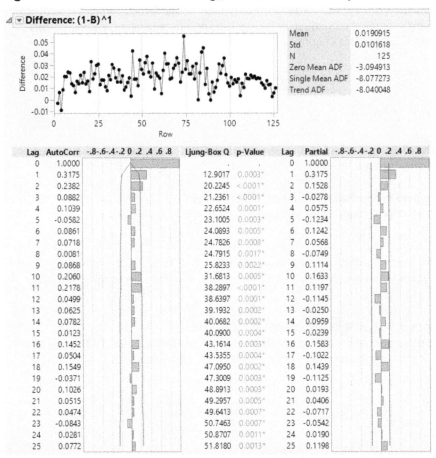

Given that the data is now stationary, we can develop forecasting models. We will discuss two popular smoothing approaches to forecast stationary data: the moving average and exponential smoothing techniques.

Simple Moving Average

The simple moving average smoothing method takes the average of the w most recent data values to predict the value of the series for the next period in the future. A moving average of order w, MA(w), is calculated as:

$$F_{t+1} = \frac{\sum_{i=t-w+1}^{t} Y_i}{w} = \frac{Y_t + Y_{t-1} + Y_{t-2} + \cdots + Y_{t-w+1}}{w} = L_t$$

where:

F_{t+1}: is the forecast for period t+1

$L_t = F_{t+1}$

Y_t: is the actual value for period t

w: is the order of the moving average

After the next time period that data comes available, t+1, the oldest value is removed from the equation and the most recent value is added to the equation to calculate the forecast of the next period.

The decision-maker or analyst must determine the order, w, of the moving average, that is, choose the number of periods to be used with the moving average method. The two extreme possible values of the order are 1 and n (where n is the total number of observations). A simple moving average of order 1, MA(1), simply uses the previous period's actual value to predict the value of the next period: $F_{t+1} = Y_t$. A MA(1) model implies that our best forecast for tomorrow is today's value and is commonly called a naive forecasting approach. On the other hand, a moving average of order n, MA(n), simply uses the average of all historical values to predict the value of the next period.

The larger the number of periods used, the more smoothed out or averaged out the forecasts are. Conversely, a smaller order puts more emphasize on recent values. If the data suddenly shifts, a high order simple moving average would take longer to respond to the change than a lower order moving average. Nevertheless, even a small order simple moving average will still lag behind the pattern by one or more periods. The decision-maker or analyst must use their understanding of the characteristics of the variable being predicted, their judgment in choosing the order, and the magnitude of various forecasting performance measurements.

To illustrate, let's use the **Difference** variable we just created from the **Log_GNP** and arbitrarily choose a moving average of order three, denoted as MA(3):

1. Click **Analyze ▶ Specialized Modeling ▶ Time Series.**
2. Select **Difference** as the **Y, Time Series** and select **DATE** as **X, Time ID.**
3. Click **OK.**
4. Click the **Time Series Difference** red triangle. From the list of options, click **Smoothing Model ▶ Simple Moving Average.**
5. The Simple Smoothing Average Specification dialog box will appear. In the smoothing window width enter **3** and then click **OK.**

Figure 17.17: Simple Moving Average of Three Periods MA(3) for Difference (Log_GNP (1-B)^1)

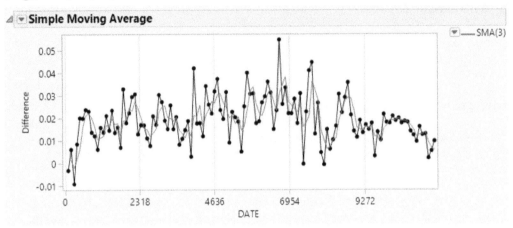

A graph of the actual and predicted (forecasted) values similar to Figure 17.17 will appear at the bottom of the Time Series Output window. To examine the actual forecast values:

1. Click the **Simple Moving Average** red triangle and click **Save to Data Table**.

A new Data Table similar to Figure 17.18 will appear. The forecast (for the log difference) for period 4, F_4, is:

$$F_4 = \frac{\sum_{i=2}^{4} Y_i}{3} = \frac{Y_2 + Y_3 + Y_4}{3} = \frac{-0.0031 + 0.0006 - 0.0091}{3} = -0.0020$$

Lastly, the next period forecast for a simple moving average of order w is equal to:

$$F_{t+1} = \frac{\sum_{i=t-w+1}^{t} Y_i}{w} = \frac{Y_t + Y_{t-1} + Y_{t-2} + \cdots + Y_{t=w+1}}{w} = L_t$$

and the two-period ahead forecast for a simple moving average of order k is equal to:

$$F_{t+2} = \frac{\sum_{i=t-w+2}^{t} Y_i}{w} = \frac{Y_{t+1} + Y_t + Y_{t-1} + Y_{t-2} + \cdots + Y_{t-w+2}}{w} = L_{t+1}$$

Figure 17.18: New Data Table from Simple Moving Average of 3, (MA(3))

Untitled 4

Columns (3/0)

Time Difference
Actual Difference
SMA(3)

Rows
All rows 126
Selected 0
Excluded 0
Hidden 0
Labeled 0

	Time Difference	Actual Difference	SMA(3)
1	0	•	
2	91	-0.00310499	
3	182	0.0062003686	0.001547689
4	274	-0.009120079	-0.00200823
5	366	0.0085404246	0.001873571
6	456	0.0200906021	0.006503649
7	547	0.0198806248	0.016170550
8	639	0.0238543421	0.021275189
9	731	0.0231213813	0.022285449
10	821	0.0137253606	0.020233694
11	912	0.0121592605	0.016335334
12	1004	0.0061962332	0.010693618
13	1096	0.0158314652	0.01139565
14	1186	0.0137539907	0.011927229
15	1277	0.0210985245	0.016894660
16	1369	0.0145727968	0.01647510
17	1461	0.0235118059	0.01972770
18	1552	0.0135674596	0.017217354
19	1643	0.015980672	0.017686645
20	1735	0.006987724	0.012178618
21	1827	0.0329070115	0.018625135
22	1917	0.0178563211	0.019250352
23	2008	0.0223385543	0.024367295
24	2100	0.0295301141	0.023241663
25	2192	0.0306722995	0.02751365
26	2282	0.0129000078	0.024367473
•			
•			
•			
110	9952	0.018052661	0.0166837114
111	10043	0.0177545031	0.0191712903
112	10135	0.0208501678	0.0188857773
113	10227	0.0187997096	0.0191347935
114	10318	0.0199856138	0.0198784971
115	10409	0.0177453294	0.0188435509
116	10501	0.018514384	0.0187484424
117	10593	0.0180994151	0.0181197095
118	10683	0.0141506746	0.0169214912
119	10774	0.0124082033	0.0148860976
120	10866	0.0096316249	0.0120635009
121	10958	0.0161470779	0.0127289687
122	11048	0.0125525047	0.0127770692
123	[illegible]	[illegible]	[illegible]

If the two-period ahead forecast is subtracted from the one-period ahead forecast, we get

$$F_{t+2} - F_{t+1} = \frac{\sum_{i=t-w+2}^{t} Y_i}{w} - \frac{\sum_{i=t-w+1}^{t} Y_i}{w} = L_{t+1} - L_t$$

$$= \frac{Y_{t+1} + Y_{t+1} + Y_{t-1} + Y_{t-2} + \cdots + Y_{t-w+2}}{w} - \frac{Y_t + Y_{t-1} + Y_{t-2} + \cdots + Y_{t-w+1}}{w}$$

$$= \frac{Y_{t+1} - Y_{t+w+1}}{w}.$$

The difference between Y_{t+1} and Y_{t-w+1} is assumed to be small. Even more so, if a high order of simple moving average is being used (that is a large w), this value will be even smaller.

Therefore, in practice this difference is assumed to be equal to zero. As a result, we can see that $F_{t+2} = F_{t+1} = L_{t+1} = L_t$. And all future forecasts using the moving average method are equal to the one-period ahead forecast. For our Log_GNP Difference variable: $F_{126} = F_{126+t} = 0.005871861$; $t \geq 0$.

Simple Exponential Smoothing

The simple exponential smoothing method takes a weighted average of past values. The equation for the simple exponential smoothing model is:

$$F_{t+1} = \alpha Y_t + (1 - \alpha)F_t =$$

$$L_t = \alpha Y_t + (1 - \alpha)L_{t-1}$$

where:

F_{t+1}: one-step ahead forecast

$L_t = F_{t+1}$

Y_t: actual value for period t

α: smoothing constant ($0 \leq \alpha \leq 1$).

This equation simply states that the forecast for the next period, t+1, that is the one-step ahead forecast, is equal to a weighted factor of this period's actual value, Y_t, plus a weighted factor of this period's forecast value, F_t.

To demonstrate how the simple exponential smoothing model is the weighted average of past values, we expand the simple exponential smoothing equation by repeatedly substituting F_t, then F_{t-1}, and then F_{t-2} and so on, we would get:

$$F_{t+1} = \alpha Y_t + (1 - \alpha)\, \alpha Y_{t-1} + (1 - \alpha)^2 \alpha Y_{t-2} + (1 - \alpha)^3 \alpha Y_{t-3} + (1 - \alpha)^4 \alpha Y_{t-4} + (1 - \alpha)^5 \alpha Y_{t-5} + \ldots$$

$$+ (1 - \alpha)^{t-1} \alpha Y_1 + (1 - \alpha)^t F_1 = L_t$$

This equation clearly shows that the next period's forecast using the simple exponential smoothing method is a weighted average of all past actual observations. Further, the sum of all these weights is equal to 1, that is:

$$\alpha + (1 - \alpha)\alpha + (1 - \alpha)^2\alpha + (1 - \alpha)^3\alpha + (1 - \alpha)^4\alpha + (1 - \alpha)^5\alpha + \ldots + (1 - \alpha)^{t-1}\alpha + (1 - \alpha)^t = 1.0$$

The value of the smoothing factor, α, has a significant impact on how much or how little each past observation is weighted. Table 17.2 lists and Figure 17.19 graphs the weights assigned to the

Table 17.2: Weights Assigned to Time Periods for α = 0.1, 0.5, and 0.9

		Time Period				
α	T	t-1	t-2	t-3	t-4	t-5
0.1	0.1	0.09	0.081	0.0729	0.06561	0.059049
0.5	0.5	0.25	0.125	0.0625	0.03125	0.015625
0.9	0.9	0.09	0.009	0.0009	9E-05	9E-06

current and the previous five observations for three different values of α—0.1, 0.5 and 0.9. With α = 0.1, each period's weight is approximately equal; actually, there is a slight decrease in weights as you go back further in time. In increasing α from 0.1 to 0.5 and from 0.5 to 0.9, more weight is given to recent observations with larger values of α. The weights assigned to past observations exponentially decrease as you go further back in time (hence, the name exponential smoothing), and the rate of decreasing weights is greater the larger the value of the smoothing factor, α.

To illustrate the simple exponential smoothing forecasting model, let's continue with the Log_GNP Difference variable and the Time Series Output in Figure 17.16 and arbitrary choose a smoothing constant of 0.1, (EXP(.1)):

1. Click the **Time Series Difference** red triangle and from the list of options, click **Smoothing Model ▶ Simple Exponential Smoothing**.
2. The Simple Exponential Smoothing dialog box will appear, and in the Constraints drop-down box, select **Custom**. The dialog box will expand. Under Custom Smoothing Weights in the Level drop-down box, select **Fixed** and in the Fixed Weight box type **0.1** and then click **Estimate**.

Figure 17.19: Graphically the Weighting Effect of Different αs

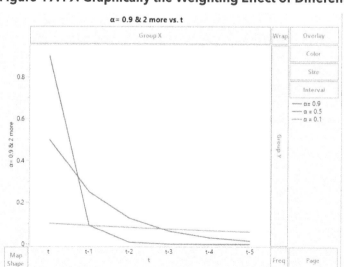

Figure 17.20: Simple Exponential Smoothing, EXP(.1) Output

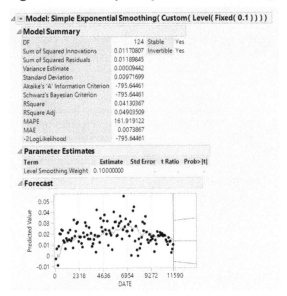

A model summary and a graph of the actual and predicted values similar to Figure 17.20 will appear at the bottom of the Time Series Output window. To examine the actual forecast values:

1. Click the **Model: Simple Exponential Smoothing** red triangle and click **Save Prediction Formula**.

A new Data Table similar to Figure 17.21 will appear.

In Figure 17.21, forecasts are calculated for each period using simple exponential smoothing with an α = 0.1 in column **Difference Prediction Formula**.

To initialize the simple exponential smoothing calculations, an assumption must be made as to what value to assign to F_1, t=0. The approach JMP takes to initialize the smooth process is obtained from a regression model containing a trend and seasonal components (Chatfield and Yar 1988). As the expanded exponential smoothing equation demonstrates, F_1 does have an impact on all subsequent forecasts. The size of impact depends on the smoothing factor chosen since F_1 is weighted by $(1-\alpha)^t$. The effect of the initial forecast is more significant with a small α than a larger α.

The first future forecast for time period 127 for our Log_GNP Difference variable in Figure 17.21 is:

$$F_{127} = F_{126+1} = .1Y_{126} + .9F_{126} = L_{126}$$

$$= .1(0.009794) + 0.9(0.013375)$$

$$= 0.013017$$

Figure 17.21: New Data Table from Simple Exponential Smoothing, EXP(.1)

	Actual Difference	Difference Prediction Formula	DATE	Predicted Difference
1	.	.	0	.
2	-0.00310499	.	91	.
3	0.0062003686	-0.00310499	182	-0.00310499
4	-0.009120079	0.0015733948	274	0.0015733948
5	0.0085404246	-0.002056428	366	-0.002056428
6	0.0200906021	0.0006941236	456	0.0006941236
7	0.0198806248	0.0048258879	547	0.0048258879
8	0.0238543421	0.0075822824	639	0.0075822824
9	0.0231213813	0.0102284637	731	0.0102284637
10	0.0137253606	0.0121368341	821	0.0121368341
11	0.0121592605	0.0123549111	912	0.0123549111
12	0.0061962332	0.0123296294	1004	0.0123296294
13	0.0158314652	0.0115748503	1096	0.0115748503
14	0.0137539907	0.0120784047	1186	0.0120784047
15	0.0210985245	0.0122703971	1277	0.0122703971
16	0.0145727968	0.0132561334	1369	0.0132561334
17	0.0235118059	0.0134001045	1461	0.0134001045
18	0.0135674596	0.0144871796	1552	0.0144871796
19	0.015980672	0.0143896528	1643	0.0143896528
120	0.0096316249	0.0169768849	10866	0.0169768849
121	0.0161470779	0.0162423589	10958	0.0162423589
122	0.0125525047	0.0162328308	11048	0.0162328308
123	0.012977358	0.0158647982	11139	0.0158647982
124	0.0023365978	0.0155760542	11231	0.0155760542
125	0.0054849032	0.0142521086	11323	0.0142521086
126	0.0097940619	0.013375388	11413	0.013375388
127	.	0.0130172574	11503	0.0130172574
128	.	0.0130172574	11593	0.0130172574
129	.	0.0130172574	11683	0.0130172574

The two-period ahead forecast for time period 128 is equal to:

$$F_{128} = .1Y_{127} + .9F_{127} = L_{127}.$$

We know F_{127} is equal to 0.013017; however, we do not know what Y_{127} is. (In real time, we are in time period 126, so we do not know the actual value one period ahead.) Our best estimate of Y_{127} is our forecast F_{127}. Substituting in F_{127} for Y_{127}, we get:

$$F_{128} = .1F_{127} + .9F_{127}$$

$$= F_{127} = 0.013017$$

In general, this implies all forecasts t+k periods ahead are equal to the forecast for period t+1:

$$F_{t+k} = F_{t+1} = L_{t+k-1} = L_t \quad k = 1, 2, \ldots, \infty$$

Another way of looking at the basic simple exponential smoothing model equation is to rearrange the right-hand side of the equation such that:

$$F_{t+1} = \alpha Y_t + (1 - \alpha)F_t$$
$$= \alpha Y_t + F_t - \alpha F_t$$
$$= F_t + \alpha(Y_t - F_t)$$

The expression $Y_t - F_t$ is simply the error for the last period. Therefore, simple exponential smoothing using this equation can be viewed as the forecast for next period is equal to last period's forecast plus a weighted adjustment of the error in the previous forecast. The larger the value of α, the more weight is given to this error adjustment.

Returning to the effect α has, Figure 17.19 clearly demonstrates that a large α would respond quicker to a change in the data than a small α (because significantly more weight is put on recent values). However, depending on the data, some or most of this changing in values might be simply due to random variation. So as not to overreact to random variation, a small α is preferred. Small αs tend to smooth out the random fluctuations. JMP determines an optimal α so as to minimize the sum of squared one-step-ahead prediction errors (SAS).

To produce a simple exponential smoothing model with this optimal α:

1. Click the **Time Series Difference** red triangle and from the list of options, click **Smoothing Model ▶ Simple Exponential Smoothing**.
2. The Simple Exponential Smoothing dialog box will appear. Click **Estimate**.

At the bottom of the Time Series Sales output, the optimal simple exponential smoothing model with its model summary and graph of actual and predicted values will appear. The optimal α with this data set ends up being 0.16367370.

Forecast Performance Measures

One of the major overall objectives of the forecasting process is to produce a forecast that minimizes the forecast error(s) of the future forecast(s): $\varepsilon_t = (Y_t - \widehat{Y}_t)$, where $\widehat{Y}_t$ is the predicted value for time period t. We do not know, however, the actual values of the variables being forecast in the future periods t+i because those periods have yet to occur. A surrogate measure for the accuracy of forecasts in future periods is the overall accuracy of the model forecasts for the possible historical (known) periods.[1]

There are several extant forecasting performance measures used to evaluate the magnitude of the forecast errors for time periods within which values are known.

---

[1] "Possible" because depending on the forecasting modeling technique used, we might not be able to calculate forecasts for one or more of those historical periods.

One popular measure of forecasting model overall performance is the mean absolute error (MAE) or mean absolute deviation (MAD). In summing the forecast errors, they tend to cancel each other out since some might be positive and some might be negative. To overcome this effect, MAE is the average of the absolute errors:

$$MAE = \frac{\sum |Y_t - F_t|}{n}$$

where:

t = time period t

n = number of periods forecasted

Y_t = actual value in time period t

F_t = forecast value in time period t

Another major forecasting performance measure of the size of the error is the mean square error (MSE). The MSE is calculated as the average of the square of forecast errors:

$$MSE = \frac{\sum (Y_t - F_t)^2}{n}$$

The square root of the MSE results in the standard deviation of the errors, which is sometimes called the standard error (s_e) or root mean square error (RMSE). The MSE or RMSE (s_e) is reported as part of regression model outputs (Chapter 5). The regression model calculates MSE and RMSE somewhat differently than the above forecasting MSE and should be adjusted in order to compare various time series forecasting models. The numerator in the regression models is (n-p-1), where p is the number of independent variables in the model and the numerator in the forecasting models as shown above is n. So, the regression MSE should be adjusted accordingly:

Adjusted MSE(Regression) = MSE(Regression)* $\frac{n-p-1}{n}$.

The smaller the MAE and RMSE (or MSE), the more accurate the forecasting method. Since the MSE squares the forecast errors, large forecast errors are penalized. As a result, the forecasting method that minimizes MSE will not necessary be the same forecasting method that minimizes MAE. The analyst that uses the approach to minimize MSE prefers several small forecasting errors to one possible large error.

A shortcoming of the MAE and MSE forecasting measures is that they do not take into consideration the magnitude of actual values. For example, imagine that we have two data sets, both with an RMSE = 10. In the first data set, the average value of the dependent variable being forecast is $\overline{Y}$ = 100. In the second data set, the average value is $\overline{Y}$ = 1000. The two data sets might have equal RMSEs, yet the second data set is relatively more accurate.

A widely used evaluation of forecasting methods that attempts to consider the effect of the magnitude of the actual values is the mean absolute percentage error (MAPE).

$$\text{MAPE} = \frac{\sum \frac{|Y_t - F_t|}{Y_t}}{n}$$

As with the other performance measures, the lower the MAPE, the more accurate the forecast. Listed in Table 17.3 is a scale to judge the accuracy of model based on the MAPE measure developed by Lewis (1982).

The smaller the MAE, RMSE, and MAPE values, the more accurate the forecasting model. A limitation of the MAD and RMSE measures is that we have no context to know when we have a "good" model or not. The MAPE and applying Lewis's scale provide us with some framework to judge the model.

As discussed in Chapter 5, two other criteria to assess model fit are the information criterion (AICc) approach developed by Akaike and the Bayesian information criterion (BIC or SBC) developed by Schwarz. Many statistical models in JMP use a technique called maximum likelihood to find the best fit. Rather than maximize the likelihood function, L(β), it is mathematically more convenient to work with the -2LogLikelihood (-2LL) function. The corrected AICc (the AICc corrects the AIC for small samples—similar to how the t distribution converges to the Z distribution) and Schwarz's BIC are information-based criteria that assess model fit, including regression models, and both are based on -2LL function. In practice, the two criteria often produce identical results. For both criteria, the lower the value the better. The two approaches have quite similar equations except that the BIC criterion imposes a greater penalty on the number of parameters than the AICc criterion, thus leading towards choosing more parsimonious models.

Returning to the Log_GNP Difference variable and the Time Series Output, right below the initial **Time Series Basic** Diagnostics output, there is a Model Comparison output similar to Figure

Table 17.3: A Scale of Judgment of Forecast Accuracy (Lewis)

MAPE	Judgment of Forecast Accuracy
Less than 10%	Highly accurate
11% to 20%	Good forecast
21% to 50%	Reasonable forecast
51% or more	Inaccurate forecast

Figure 17.22: Model Comparison Output

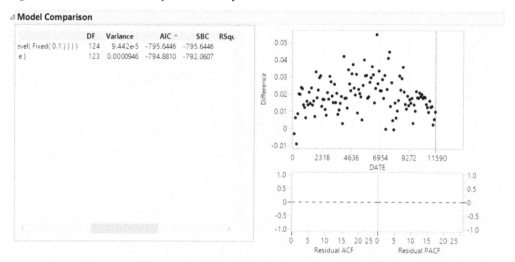

17.22. On the left is a report showing the two simple exponential smoothing models that we ran (α = 0.1 and when α is optimized). Toward the bottom, there is a scroll bar that you can slide to see various performance measures including MAE, MAPE, AIC, and SBC. (Note that there is no model comparison for the moving average model.)

When you have more than one model that you deemed to be adequate, some factors to consider to decide between the models are:

- Choose the model with the fewest parameters (principle of parsimony).
- Compare models with regard to statistics such as the RMSE, AIC, AICc, and SBC (BIC).

Autoregressive and Moving Average Models

Starting in Chapter 5, we introduced regression and further expanded our use of regression in this chapter when we discussed additive regression as a forecasting method. The general form of the regression equation is

$$Y_t = b_0 + b_1 X_1 + b_2 X_2 \ldots \ldots + b_p X_p + \varepsilon_t$$

where:

Y_t is the forecast variable

X_i is causal variable i

b_o, b_i are regression coefficients

ε_t is error term

Instead of using causal variables like GNP, advertising, or trend and seasonal, each explanatory variable or independent variable can be defined as a time lagged value, that is,

$$X_1 = Y_{t-1}$$
$$X_2 = Y_{t-2}$$
$$\cdot$$
$$\cdot$$
$$\cdot$$
$$X_p = Y_{t-p}$$

The previous general regression equation now becomes:

$$AR(p): Y_t = b_0 + b_1 Y_{t-1} + b_2 Y_{t-2} \cdots + b_p Y_{t-p} + \varepsilon_t.$$

Forecasting models such as this equation above, in which the forecast variable is a function of time lagged values, is called an autoregressive model of order p, AR(p).

Similarly, as lagged values of the time series are regressed, the lagged values of the errors can be used as explanatory variables:

$$MA(q): Y_t = b_0 + b_1 \varepsilon_{t-1} + b_2 \varepsilon_{t-2} \cdots + b_q \varepsilon_{t-q} + \varepsilon_t$$

This equation is called a moving average model of order q, MA(q).

The autoregressive model, AR(p), and the moving average model, MA(q), can be grouped together to form a family of models called autoregressive moving average (ARMA) models. The ARMA models are only useful if the data is stationary. When these ARMA models are extended to consider nonstationary data as well, they are called autoregressive integrated moving average (ARIMA) models. Differencing is used to reduce nonstationary issues. The success of a forecasting approach called the Box-Jenkins methodology is synonymous with general univariate ARIMA modeling.

One of the statistical assumptions of the regression techniques is statistical independence, meaning that any particular error term is statistically independent of any other error term. This independence assumption is often violated when time series data is analyzed. One significant advantage of the ARIMA or Box-Jenkins models is that autocorrelated residuals can be properly modeled. The Box-Jenkins approach has been shown to be a powerful forecasting tool and to be especially accurate for short range forecasting. As a rule of thumb, these ARIMA models should have at least 50 observations but preferably more than 100 observations. On the other hand, recent research has shown that the regression models using time series data provide accurate forecasts, even though the independence assumption is violated. Which approach provides a "better" model depends on the data, so the analyst should explore both approaches.

ARIMA Models

Standard notation to identify the type of ARIMA model is ARIMA(p, d, q), where:

p = order of autoregression

d = order of integration (differencing)

q = order of moving average

In their 1970 book, Box and Jenkins describe a three-stage iterative methodology of model selection, parameter estimation, and model checking to forecast univariate ARIMA models (Box and Jenkins, 1970). Extensions of their methodology have expanded Box-Jenkins' initial three-stage iterative process, which includes either an initial data preparation step and/or a final step of model forecasting. Our iterative ARIMA modeling process has the following four stages.

Step 1: Discovery

The first step in discovery stage, as we have discussed earlier in this chapter, is to generate graphs and statistics of the time series data. If the series is identified as being nonstationary, various transformations can be performed to convert the data into a stationary series. Often the process used to convert the data into a stationary process is to use differencing if the data has a trend or taking a log transformation as shown earlier in the chapter.

Step 2: Model Identification

Once a stationary series has been obtained, the form of the model to be used is identified by examining the autocorrelations (ACFs) and partial autocorrelations (PACFs) of the series. As discussed earlier in this chapter, the ACF plot shows the correlation of the series with itself at different lags. The PACF plots shows the amount of autocorrelation at lag k that is not explained by lower-order autocorrelations. The unique pattern of the data's ACFs and PACFs are compared with corresponding theoretical patterns of ARIMA models to identify the form of the model. In particular, Table 17.4 lists the expected patterns for the pure AR and MA models. An AR series usually has a positive autocorrelation at lag 1, and the corresponding ACF plot dies out gradually while the matching PACF cuts off sharply after a few lags. The PACF for an AR series helps identify the value of p that is likely needed.

For an MA series, the roles of the ACF and PACF are the reverse of that with an AR series. An MA series usually has a significant autocorrelation at lag 1, and the ACF plot cuts off sharply after

Table 17.4: Expected Patterns of ACF and PACF

Model	ACF	PACF
AR(p)	Exponential decay or damped sine-wave pattern	Significant spikes at lags 1 to p; greater than p significantly small
MA(q)	Significant spikes at lags 1 to q; greater than q significantly small	Exponential decay or damped sine-wave pattern

a few lags. The PACF dies out more gradually. The ACF tells you how the level of q that is likely to be needed.

Similarly, patterns of the ACFs and PACFs are used to identify the higher-order models. In practice, most models do not have both an AR and MA terms—usually it is sufficient to use only one type or the other. During this model identification process, an overarching theme should be the principle of parsimony, that is, in building a significant model with the least number of variables, simple models are preferred to complex ones.

If the data displays seasonality and has no trend, significant seasonality will appear in the ACF by tapering slowly at multiples of s. In such a case, take a difference of lag s. Another approach is to apply a seasonal ARIMA model that incorporates both non-seasonal and seasonal factors in a multiplicative model. The shorthand notation for the multiplicative ARIMA model is:

ARIMA (p,d,q)×(P,D,Q)s

with p = non-seasonal AR order, d = non-seasonal differencing, q = non seasonal MA order, P = seasonal AR order, D = seasonal differencing, Q = seasonal MA order, and s = time span of seasonality.

Step 3: Model Fit

After the model identification step, parameter estimates must be determined. JMP uses the method of maximum likelihood to fit the data to the specified ARIMA model and to estimate the model coefficients.

Step 4: Model checking

Given the estimation of the model parameters, the adequacy of the selected model is evaluated by performing various statistical tests on the residuals to see if they are random. In particular, a portmanteau test such as the Ljung-Box statistic, discussed earlier in this chapter, is performed. If the portmanteau test shows a lag less than the rule-of-thumb maximum number of lags to consider is significant, h, the model is deemed to be inadequate, and the analyst should go back to Step 2 and select a different model. For a good model, all autocorrelations up to lag h for the residuals should be non-significant. On the other hand, if the portmanteau test is not significant up to lag h, the model is viewed as adequate, and forecasts can be made.

ARIMA Modeling with Log Variable

Returning to the Log_GNP **Difference** variable and examining the ACF and PACF graphs in Figure 17.16 and under the Time Series Basic Diagnostics, the lag 1 in the PACF is significant (beyond the blue confidence interval blue line), suggesting an AR(1) model:

1. Click the **Time Series Difference** red triangle and from the list of options, click **ARIMA**.
2. The ARIMA Specification dialog box will appear. Change the Autoregressive Order to **1**. Click **Estimate**.

At the bottom of the Time Series Difference output, the AR(1) model of the Log_GNP **Difference** variable with its model summary and graph of actual and predicted values will appear. The AR(1) coefficient and intercept estimates are 0.3298 and 0.0190 respectively. So, the AR(1) model fit is:

$$Y(t) - 0.0190 = .3298*(Y(t-1) - 0.0190) + e(t) =$$

$$Y(t) = .3298*Y(t-1) + 0.0127 + e(t).$$

Click the expand arrow next to Residuals. A plot of the residuals will appear. ACF and PACF graphs will also appear, similar to Figure 17.23. A model with all the ACF and PACF lags up to the rule-of-thumb maximum number of lags to consider are insignificant, and all the Ljung-Box statistics up to this maximum number of lags are also insignificant, which indicate a good fit. The rule-of-thumb maximum number of lags to consider for non-seasonal data, h, is min(10, 126/5) = 10. As shown in Figure 17.23, all the lags and Ljung-Box statistics up to a lag of 10 are insignificant, so, we can consider this model to be adequate and forecasts can be made.

Scrolling back up the Time Series Difference output to the Model Comparison output, we can see that the AR(1) of Log_GNP difference variable is the best of the three models (AR(1), EXP(.1) and EXP(.163)).

It is noteworthy to mention that instead of returning to the **Log_GNP Difference** variable and creating the AR(1) model, we could have alternatively returned to the **Log_GNP** variable Time Series Output. In the ARIMA Specification dialog box, if we clicked on an Autoregressive Order of 1 and Differencing Order of 1, creating an ARI(1,1) model, we would get exactly the same results (except the MAPE would be different—because it uses a different scaled variable).

Figure 17.23: Residual Output of AR(1) Model of Log_GNP Difference

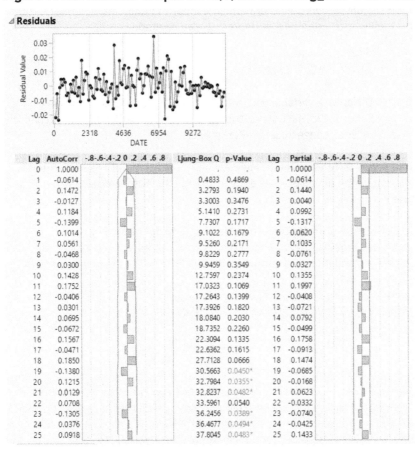

ARIMA Modeling with Seasonality

Let's examine another data set with some seasonality:

1. Open Steel Shipments.jmp: Select **Help ▶ Sample Index ▶ Times Series**. Click **Steel Shipments**. (Or you can find the Steel Shipments.jmp file with other textbook files on the author's page.)

Using the Graph Builder, as discussed earlier in the chapter during the Discovery step, we can observe some seasonal component and a possible slight trend as shown in Figure 17.24.

2. Click **Analyze ▶ Specialized Modeling ▶ Time Series**.
3. Select **Steel Shipments** as the **Y, Time Series** and select **DATE** as **X, Time ID**.
4. Click **OK**.

Figure 17.24: Time Series Graph of the Steel Shipments Data

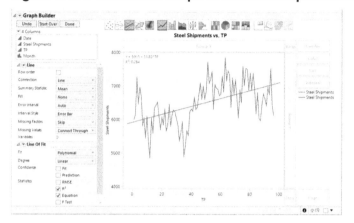

Figure 17.25 shows the time series output of the **Steel Shipments** data. Let's see if we need any differencing by taking the first difference:

1. Click the **Time Series Steel Shipments** red triangle and from the list of options, click **Difference**.
2. The **Difference Specification** dialog box will appear. On the left under the Nonseasonal in the Differencing Order, input **1**; click **Estimate**.

Figure 17.25: Time Series Output of the Steel Shipments data

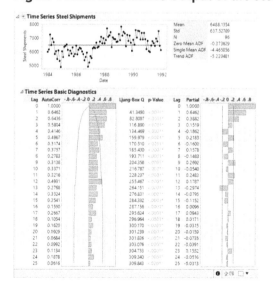

Figure 17.26: Time Series Output of the Difference (1-B)^1 of the Steel Shipments

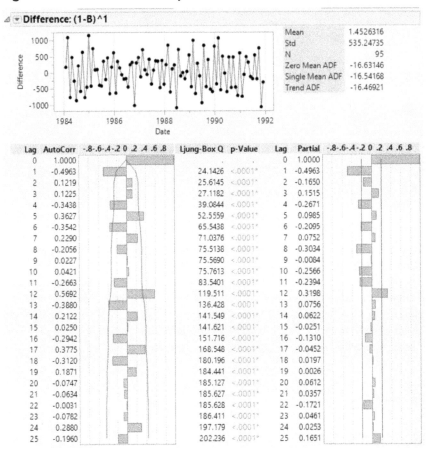

Difference: (1-B)^1

	Mean	1.4526316
	Std	535.24735
	N	95
	Zero Mean ADF	-16.63146
	Single Mean ADF	-16.54168
	Trend ADF	-16.46921

Lag	AutoCorr	-.8-.6-.4-.2 0 .2 .4 .6 .8	Ljung-Box Q	p-Value	Lag	Partial	-.8-.6-.4-.2 0 .2 .4 .6 .8
0	1.0000		.	.	0	1.0000	
1	-0.4963		24.1426	<.0001*	1	-0.4963	
2	0.1219		25.6145	<.0001*	2	-0.1650	
3	0.1225		27.1182	<.0001*	3	0.1515	
4	-0.3438		39.0844	<.0001*	4	-0.2671	
5	0.3627		52.5559	<.0001*	5	0.0985	
6	-0.3542		65.5438	<.0001*	6	-0.2095	
7	0.2290		71.0376	<.0001*	7	0.0752	
8	-0.2056		75.5138	<.0001*	8	-0.3034	
9	0.0227		75.5690	<.0001*	9	-0.0084	
10	0.0421		75.7613	<.0001*	10	-0.2566	
11	-0.2663		83.5401	<.0001*	11	-0.2394	
12	0.5692		119.511	<.0001*	12	0.3198	
13	-0.3880		136.428	<.0001*	13	0.0756	
14	0.2122		141.549	<.0001*	14	0.0622	
15	0.0250		141.621	<.0001*	15	-0.0251	
16	-0.2942		151.716	<.0001*	16	-0.1310	
17	0.3775		168.548	<.0001*	17	-0.0452	
18	-0.3120		180.196	<.0001*	18	0.0197	
19	0.1871		184.441	<.0001*	19	0.0026	
20	-0.0747		185.127	<.0001*	20	0.0612	
21	-0.0634		185.627	<.0001*	21	0.0357	
22	-0.0031		185.628	<.0001*	22	-0.1721	
23	-0.0782		186.411	<.0001*	23	0.0461	
24	0.2880		197.179	<.0001*	24	0.0253	
25	-0.1960		202.236	<.0001*	25	0.1651	

The autocorrelations and partial autocorrelations displayed in Figure 17.26 are more stationary, but there still appears to be significant yearly (12) seasonality in lag 12 for both the partial autocorrelation and autocorrelation. Now let's create a model with a nonseasonal and seasonal difference:

1. First, to keep our output somewhat neat, click the **Difference (1-B)^1** red triangle and click **Remove Fit**.
2. Click the **Time Series Steel Shipments** red triangle and from the list of options, click **Seasonal ARIMA**.
3. The Seasonal ARIMA Specification dialog box will appear. On the left under ARIMA in the Differencing Order, input **1**. On the right under the Seasonal ARIMA in the Differencing Order, input **1**. Click **Estimate**.

Figure 17.27 shows the residuals of the Seasonal ARIMA (0,1,0)(0,1,0)12 model.

The residuals appear to a certain degree stationary.

Figure 17.27: Residuals for Seasonal ARIMA(0,1,0)(0,1,0)12 Model

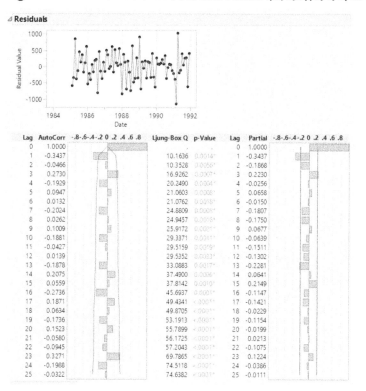

Lag	AutoCorr	-.8 -.6 -.4 -.2 0 .2 .4 .6 .8	Ljung-Box Q	p-Value	Lag	Partial	-.8 -.6 -.4 -.2 0 .2 .4 .6 .8
0	1.0000		.	.	0	1.0000	
1	-0.3437		10.1636	0.0014*	1	-0.3437	
2	-0.0466		10.3528	0.0056*	2	-0.1868	
3	0.2730		16.9262	0.0007*	3	0.2230	
4	-0.1929		20.2490	0.0004*	4	-0.0256	
5	0.0947		21.0603	0.0008*	5	0.0658	
6	0.0132		21.0762	0.0018*	6	-0.0150	
7	-0.2024		24.8809	0.0008*	7	-0.1807	
8	0.0262		24.9457	0.0016*	8	-0.1750	
9	0.1009		25.9172	0.0021*	9	0.0677	
10	-0.1881		29.3371	0.0011*	10	-0.0639	
11	-0.0427		29.5159	0.0019*	11	-0.1511	
12	0.0139		29.5352	0.0033*	12	-0.1302	
13	-0.1878		33.0883	0.0017*	13	-0.2281	
14	0.2075		37.4900	0.0006*	14	0.0641	
15	0.0559		37.8142	0.0010*	15	0.2149	
16	-0.2736		45.6937	0.0001*	16	-0.1147	
17	0.1871		49.4341	<.0001*	17	-0.1421	
18	0.0634		49.8705	<.0001*	18	-0.0229	
19	-0.1736		53.1913	<.0001*	19	-0.1154	
20	0.1523		55.7899	<.0001*	20	-0.0199	
21	-0.0580		56.1725	<.0001*	21	0.0213	
22	-0.0945		57.2043	<.0001*	22	-0.1075	
23	0.3271		69.7865	<.0001*	23	0.1224	
24	-0.1988		74.5118	<.0001*	24	-0.0386	
25	-0.0322		74.6382	<.0001*	25	-0.0111	

To explore a range of several ARIMA models, we can simultaneously fit a range of ARIMA and Seasonal ARIMA models by:

1. Click **Analyze ▶ Specialized Modeling ▶ Time Series.**
2. Select **Steel Shipments** as the **Y, Time Series** and select **DATE** as **X, Time ID.**
3. Click **OK.**
4. Click the **Time Series Steel Shipments** red triangle and from the list of options, click **ARIMA Model Group**.
5. The ARIMA Model Group dialog box will appear. We can specify a range for each of the terms in the different models. With this Steel Shipment data set, on the left side under the ARIMA in the Autoregressive Order, input **2** in the right box. In the Differencing Order on the left box, put **1** and in the right box put **1**. In the Moving Average Order, input **2** in the right box. On the right side under Seasonal ARIMA in the Autoregressive Order, input **1**. In the right box and in the Differencing Order, input **1** in the left and right box. In the Moving Average Order, input **1** in the right box similar to Figure 17.28.
6. As you can see in Figure 17.28, a total of 36 models will be produced and compared. Click **Estimate.**

Figure 17.28: ARIMA Model Group Dialog Box

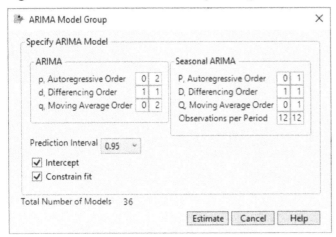

Examining the Model Comparison output, we can see that most of the new models are better than the Seasonal ARIMA (0,1,0)(0,1,0)12 model. Which model is the best depends on which criteria the decision-maker feels are the most important.

The models are initially ordered from lowest AIC to highest. If you click one of the performance measures' column headings, such as AIC, SBC, MAPE, or MAE in the Model Comparison box, the models are sorted according to that criterion.

Also, in the Model Comparison box, all the way to the left, first notice that Report is unchecked for each of the models. If you do want to see certain reports—the Model Summary, Parameter Estimates, Forecast and Residuals, for example—for one or more models just click the check for those models. Also, just to right of column for Report is a column entitled Graph. If you click the Graph box for a model, the model results are plotted in the graphs just to the right.

If you want to remove one or more of the models from the list in the Model Comparison box:

1. To remove all the models except the model Seasonal ARIMA (2,1,2)×(0,1,1)12, click off the report for all the models except the Seasonal ARIMA (2,1,2)×(0,1,1)12. Click one of the red triangles all the way to the left inside the Model Comparison box. Click **Remove Unselected**.

Advanced Exponential Smoothing Models

Earlier in this chapter, the simple moving average and simple exponential smoothing forecasting techniques for modeling stationary data that contained no trend or seasonal components were introduced and discussed. Historically, these two techniques have been good forecasting methods for stationary data.

One approach to forecasting data with a linear trend and some randomness uses exponential smoothing and is called double exponential smoothing (DES). Double exponential smoothing smooths the exponentially smoothed data. To apply exponential smoothing a smoothing factor, α, is needed, which can range from 0 to 1. The simple exponential smoothed value is:

$$F_{t+1} = \alpha Y_t + (1 - \alpha)F_t =$$

$$L_t = \alpha Y_t + (1 - \alpha)L_{t-1}$$

where:

F_{t+1}: 1-step ahead forecast
$L_t = F_{t+1}$
Y_t: actual value for period t
α: smoothing constant ($0 \leq \alpha \leq 1$).

Large values of α assign more weight to recent values, and small values of α assign more even weights to many recent values. Double exponential smoothing smooths the data twice, so it is necessary to estimate two αs. Two approaches are taken to estimate these αs. One approach uses the same α for both smoothing operations. This approach is called Brown's double exponential smoothing method. The smoothing equations for the double exponential smoothing (Brown's):

$$L_t = \alpha Y_t + (1-\alpha)\, L_{t-1}$$

$$T_t = \alpha(L_t - L_{t-1}) + (1-\alpha)\, T_{t-1}.$$

The second DES approach uses two different coefficients for the two smoothing operations, called α and γ. This two-coefficient approach is called Holt's double exponential smoothing method. The smoothing equations for the double exponential smoothing (Holt's) are:

$$L_t = \alpha Y_t + (1-\alpha)\, (L_{t-1} + T_{t-1})$$

$$T_t = \gamma(L_t - L_{t-1}) + (1-\gamma)\, T_{t-1}.$$

Gradually, these approaches were expanded to consider data not only with a trend but also a seasonal component. This expansion progressively no longer focused on the moving average approaches, which although easy to understand, were not as flexible nor as computationally efficient as the exponential smoothing approaches.

In addressing a trend or seasonal component, both additive and multiplicative models are considered. An additive model is most likely to be advantageous if the trend or seasonal factors are constantly the same above or below. For example, the first and third quarters might consistently be $1M higher, and the second and fourth quarters consistently $1M lower. On the other hand, with a multiplicative trend or seasonal model, the trend or seasonal effects are not a constant plus or minus. In this situation, the effects are a constant percentage above or below. For example, the first and third quarters might consistently be 10 percent higher and the second and fourth quarters consistently 10 percent lower. Generally, when should one or the other be used? Unless the graph of the data clearly illustrates a familiar pattern, both additive and multiplicative models should be run to see which one gives the best result.

In 1969, C. C. Pegels developed a general framework to classify exponential smoothing models with (additive or multiplicative) or without a trend and with (additive or multiplicative) or without seasonal components, as shown in Table 17.5 (Pegels 1969). Each model is denoted by two letters. The first letter is for the trend (row heading), and the second one is for the seasonality (column heading). For example, model (N,N) is the simple exponential smoothing and model (A,N) is Holt's double exponential smoothing.

Pegels also developed the following simplified set of equations for each of the nine exponential smoothing models:

$$L_t = \alpha P_t + (1-\alpha)\, Q_t$$

$$T_t = \gamma R_t + (1-\gamma)\, T_{t-1}$$

$$S_t = \delta X_t + (1-\delta)\, S_{t-p}$$

where P, Q, R and X vary according to which of the cells in Table 17.5 the method belongs to.

JMP has two additional exponential smoothing models: the (N,A) seasonal exponential model and the (A, A) Winters Additive model. Substituting the cell values for P, Q, and X into the above equations for L_t and S_t, the smoothing equations for the (N,A) model are:

$$L_t = \alpha\, (Y_t - S_{t-p}) + (1-\alpha)\, L_{t-1}$$

$$S_t = \delta(Y_t - L_t) + (1-\delta)\, S_{t-p}.$$

The smoothing equations for the (A, A) Winters Additive model are:

$$L_t = \alpha(Y_t - S_{t-p}) + (1-\alpha)\, (L_{t-1} + T_{t-1})$$

$$T_t = \gamma(L_t - L_{t-1}) + (1-\gamma)\, T_{t-1}$$

$$S_t = \delta(Y_t - L_t) + (1-\delta)\, S_{t-p}.$$

Table 17.5: Equations for Pegels' Nine Exponential Smoothing Models

(N, A, M; N, A, M)		Seasonal (S) Component		
		None (N)	Additive (A)	Multiplicative (M)
Trend (T) Component	**None (N)**	**(N,N)** $P_t = Y_t$ $Q_t = L_{t-1}$ $F_{t+m} = L_t$	**(N,A)** $P_t = Y_t - S_{t-p}$ $Q_t = L_{t-1}$ $X_t = Y_t - L_t$ $F_{t+m} = L_t + S_{t+m-p}$	**(N,M)** $P_t = Y_t/S_{t-p}$ $Q_t = L_{t-1}$ $X_t = Y_t/L_t$ $F_{t+m} = L_t S_{t+m-p}$
	Additive (A)	**(A,N)** $P_t = Y_t$ $Q_t = L_{t-1} + T_{t-1}$ $R_t = L_t - L_{t-1}$ $F_{t+m} = L_t + mT_t$	**(A,A)** $P_t = Y_t - S_{t-p}$ $Q_t = L_{t-1} + T_{t-1}$ $R_t = L_t - L_{t-1}$ $X_t = Y_t - L_t$ $F_{t+m} = L_t + mT_t + S_{t+m-p}$	**(A,M)** $P_t = Y_t/S_{t-p}$ $Q_t = L_{t-1} + T_{t-1}$ $R_t = L_t - L_{t-1}$ $X_t = Y_t/L_t$ $F_{t+m} = (L_t + mT_t)S_{t+m-p}$
	Multiplicative (M)	**(M,N)** $P_t = Y_t$ $Q_t = L_{t-1}T_{t-1}$ $R_t = L_t/L_{t-1}$ $F_{t+m} = (L_t T_t^m)$	**(M,A)** $P_t = Y_t - S_{t-p}$ $Q_t = L_{t-1}T_{t-1}$ $R_t = L_t/L_{t-1}$ $X_t = Y_t - L_t$ $F_{t+m} = (L_t T_t^m) + S_{t+m-p}$	**(M,M)** $P_t = Y_t/S_{t-p}$ $Q_t = L_{t-1}T_{t-1}$ $R_t = L_t/L_{t-1}$ $X_t = Y_t/L_t$ $F_{t+m} = (L_t T_t^m)S_{t+m-p}$

Other exponential smoothing models also have been developed to expand Table 17.5 by considering a damped trend effect which could be additive or multiplicative. Damped implies that the effect flattens over time. For example, the additive damped trend smoothing equations are:

$$L_t = \alpha Y_t + (1 - \alpha)(L_{t-1} + \varphi T_{t-1})$$

$$T_t = \gamma(L_t - L_{t-1}) + (1 - \gamma)\varphi T_{t-1}$$

As with simple exponential smoothing, these other exponential smoothing models also require that initial first period values be determined. Several alternative approaches can be used to decide on the initial values of L_1 and T_1, for example, assigning values, averaging values to more sophisticated approaches using least squares regression, decomposition, or backcasting. These initialization approaches are summarized by Gardner (1985). As with simple exponential smoothing models, the approach JMP takes to initialize the smooth process is obtained from a regression model containing a trend and seasonal components (Chatfield and Yar 1988). There is no real initialization standard. In general, the influence of the initial values has little effect on fits and forecasts after the first several periods. If there are more than 15 to 20 observations, the recent fits and forecasts should be relatively close regardless of the approach to estimating the initial values.

To apply one of the exponential smoothing techniques and in particular the additive Winters (N, A) method to the Steel Shipments data:

1. Click the **Time Series Steel Shipments** red triangle and from the list of options, click **Smoothing Model**. A list including Simple Moving Average, Simple Exponential Smoothing, and five advanced exponential smoothing models are displayed. Click **Winters Method**.
2. The Winters Method (Additive) Specification dialog box will appear. Click **Estimate**.

The Winters Method is added to the list of models in the Model Comparison box.

State Space Smoothing Models

During the time period from the mid-1980s until about the early 2000s there were two major criticisms of exponential smoothing models. One criticism was that exponential smoothing models lack any statistical rationale in determining model parameters except for fit, that is, they provide only a point estimate where there were no statistical criteria or testing to estimate their values. The other source of criticism was based on the belief that exponential smoothing models were just a special case of ARIMA modeling. Since Hyndman et al. introduced a general class of state space smoothing models, these criticisms have been reversed (Hyndman et al. 2002, 2008). In their framework, each exponential smoothing method has two corresponding state space smoothing models, each with an assumption of the error terms to calculate the prediction interval. One model has an additive error and the other has a multiplicative error.

We can view a time series consisting of three components: an error (E), a trend (T), and a seasonal component (S). These three time series components (E, T, S) can be combined in a number of ways. For example:

Purely Multiplicative: $Y = T * S * E$

Purely Additive: $Y = T + S + E$

Additive Trend and Seasonal, Multiplicative Error: $Y = (T + S) * E$

With two types of error (Additive, Multiplicative—A, M), five types of trend (None, Additive, Additive damped, Multiplicative, Multiplicative damped—N, A, Ad, M, Md), and three types of seasonality (None, Additive, Multiplicative—N, A, M), there are a total of 30 combinations (2x5x3). Below in Table 17.6 and 17.7 are the list of these combinations shown in state space smoothing model form by type of error.

where:

l_{t-1}: the level at t-1 b_{t-1}: the growth at t-1 φ: is a trend-damping factor

s_{t-m}: are the seasonal terms where m is the length of the seasonality (for example, 12 months, 4 quarters in a year)

Table 17.6: State Space Smoothing Models with Additive Error Models (A)

		Seasonal (S) Component		
		None (N)	Additive (A)	Multiplicative (M)
Trend Component (T)	None (N)	(A,N,N) $$Y_t = $$ $$l_{t-1} + \epsilon_t$$	(A,N,A) $$Y_t = $$ $$l_{t-1} + s_{t-m} + \epsilon_t$$	(A,N,M) $$Y_t = $$ $$l_{t-1}\, s_{t-m} + \epsilon_t$$
	Additive (A)	(A,A,N) $$Y_t = $$ $$l_{t-1} + b_{t-1} + \epsilon_t$$	(A,A,A) $$Y_t = $$ $$l_{t-1} + b_{t-1} + s_{t-m} + \epsilon_t$$	(A,A,M) $$Y_t = $$ $$(l_{t-1} + b_{t-1})\, s_{t-m} + \epsilon_t$$
	Additive Damped (Ad)	(A,Ad,N) $$Y_t = $$ $$l_{t-1} + \varphi b_{t-1} + \epsilon_t$$	(A,Ad,A) $$Y_t = $$ $$l_{t-1} + \varphi b_{t-1} + s_{t-m} + \epsilon_t$$	(A,Ad,M) $$Y_t = $$ $$(l_{t-1} + \varphi b_{t-1}) s_{t-m} + \epsilon_t$$
	Multiplicative (M)	(A,M,N) $$Y_t = $$ $$l_{t-1}\, b_{t-1} + \epsilon_t$$	(A,M,A) $$Y_t = $$ $$l_{t-1}\, b_{t-1} + s_{t-m} + \epsilon_t$$	(A,M,M) $$Y_t = $$ $$l_{t-1}\, b_{t-1}\, s_{t-m} + \epsilon_t$$
	Multiplicative Damped (Md)	(A,Md,N) $$Y_t = $$ $$l_{t-1}\, b_{t-1}^{\varphi} + \epsilon_t$$	(A,Md,A) $$Y_t = $$ $$l_{t-1}\, b_{t-1}^{\varphi} + s_{t-m} + \epsilon_t$$	(A,Md,M) $$Y_t = $$ $$l_{t-1}\, b_{t-1}^{\varphi}\, s_{t-m} + \epsilon_t$$

ϵ_t and ε_t are the additive and multiplicative forecast errors, respectively.

These state space smoothing models are identified by using a triplet by the type of E, T, S: Error (A, M), Trend (N, A, Ad, M, Md), and Seasonality (N, A, M). For example, an AAdN model has an additive error, additive damped trend and no seasonality.

To apply the state space smoothing models to the Steel Shipments data:

1. Click the **Time Series Steel Shipments** red triangle from the list of options, click **State Space Smoothing**.
2. The State Space Smoothing Models dialog box appears, as in Figure 17.29. JMP recommends 19 models and a Period of 12 since the data is monthly. Click **OK.**

Scrolling down to the Model Comparison box, we can see that JMP ran all 19 of the state space smoothing models. The models are sorted in ascending order of AIC values with our initial Seasonal ARIMA (2, 1, 2)(0, 1, 1)12 and Additive Winters model at the top. The best state space smoothing model with the lowest AIC has a multiplicative error, no trend, and multiplicative seasonality (MNM12).

Table 17.7: State Space Smoothing Models with Multiplicative Error Models

$$(\varepsilon_t = 1 + \epsilon_t)\ (M)$$

		Seasonal (S) Component	
	None (N)	**Additive (A)**	**Multiplicative (M)**
None (N)	(M,N,N) $Y_t = l_{t-1}\varepsilon_t$	(M,N,A) $Y_t = (l_{t-1} + s_{t-m})\varepsilon_t$	(M,N,M) $Y_t = l_{t-1} s_{t-m}\varepsilon_t$
Additive (A)	(M,A,N) $Y_t = (l_{t-1} + b_{t-1})\varepsilon_t$	(M,A,A) $Y_t = (l_{t-1} + b_{t-1} + s_{t-m})\varepsilon_t$	(M,A,M) $Y_t = (l_{t-1} + b_{t-1})s_{t-m}\varepsilon_t$
Additive Damped (Ad)	(M,Ad,N) $Y_t = (l_{t-1} + \varphi b_{t-1})\varepsilon_t$	(M,Ad,A) $Y_t = (l_{t-1} + \varphi b_{t-1} + s_{t-m})\varepsilon_t$	(M,Ad,M) $Y_t = (l_{t-1} + \varphi b_{t-1})s_{t-m}\varepsilon_t$
Multiplicative (M)	(M,M,N) $Y_t = (l_{t-1} b_{t-1})\varepsilon_t$	(M,M,A) $Y_t = (l_{t-1} b_{t-1} + s_{t-m})\varepsilon_t$	(M,M,M) $Y_t = l_{t-1} b_{t-1} s_{t-m}\varepsilon_t$
Multiplicative Damped (Md)	(M,Md,N) $Y_t = l_{t-1} b_{t-1}^{\varphi}\varepsilon_t$	(M,Md,A) $Y_t = (l_{t-1} b_{t-1}^{\varphi} + s_{t-m})\varepsilon_t$	(M,Md,M) $Y_t = l_{t-1} b_{t-1}^{\varphi} s_{t-m}\varepsilon_t$

Trend Component (T) is labeled along the left side of the table, spanning the row categories.

Clicking the report for this model and examining the model summary, this state space smoothing model seems a reasonable candidate to consider. (You should now have three models with their reports clicked).

1. Click one of the red triangles all the way to the left inside the Model Comparison box. Click **Remove Unselected**.

How do you choose which model is better? Note the red text warning that the Likelihood-based criteria are not comparable across ARIMA and State Space Smoothing modeling types. That means that we cannot scroll over to the right and use the various performance measures such as AIC to compare the models.

Figure 17.29: The State Space Smoothing Model Dialog Box

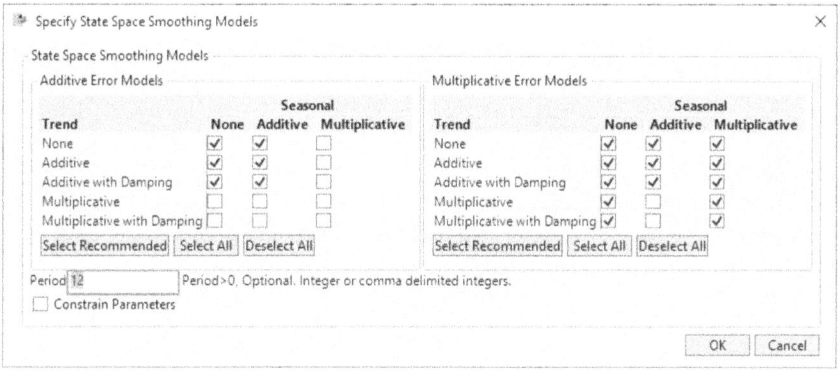

Holdback

One method to help us evaluate the models is to use the holdback option when launching the Time Series Platform. This holdback method excludes the last **Forecast Period** value number of observations at the end of the series to fit all of the time series models that you specify. The fit statistics shown in the Model Comparison box, including RMSE, MSE, MAPE and MAE, are now comparable between the ARIMA models and the state space smoothing models since they are evaluated on the holdback set. To apply this holdback option:

1. Click the **Time Series Steel Shipment** red triangle and click **Redo** and click **Relaunch Analysis**.
2. The Time Series dialog box will appear. Select **Steel Shipments** as the **Y, Time Series**; select **DATE** as **X, Time ID**; check on **Forecast on Holdback** and input **12** for the number of **Forecast Periods**. Click **OK**.
3. We need to rerun the state space smoothing models and the ARIMA models as we did before:
   a. Click the **Time Series Steel Shipment** red triangle and from the list of options, click **State Space Smoothing**. The State Space Smoothing Models dialog box appears. Click **OK.**
   b. Click the **Time Series Steel Shipment** red triangle and from the list of options, click **ARIMA Model Group**. The ARIMA Model Group dialog box will appear. On the left side under the ARIMA in the Autoregressive Order, input **2** in the right box. In the Differencing Order, on the left box put **1** and in the right box put **1**. In the Moving Average Order, input **2** in the right box. On the right side under Seasonal ARIMA in the Autoregressive Order, input **1.** In the right box and in the Differencing Order, input **1** in the left and right box. In the Moving Average Order, input **1** in the right box. As you can see, a total of 36 models will be produced and compared. Click **Estimate.**

Examining the Model Comparison box, Figure 17.30, where the models are initially sorted in ascending order by their RMSE, the best state space smoothing model has an additive error, damped trend, and no seasonality. The best ARIMA model is Seasonal ARIMA (1,1,2) (0,1,1)12.

The holdback method is good when the data set is relatively large such that the holdback set is reasonably large enough to produce accurate metrics. There are not any hard and fast rules of what is large enough. Another possible disadvantage with a time series data set when using a holdback set is that the most recent observations might contain a change or shift in the data, and this would not be captured in the model fitting.

Time Series Cross-Validation

A second method to assist us in determining which model or which approach to use is a technique called time series cross-validation (Hyndman and Athanasopoulos 2021). A JMP add-in developed by Jacob Rhyne of JMP is necessary to perform a time series cross-validation. To install the add-in:

1. Go to: https://community.jmp.com/t5/Discovery-Summit-Americas-2021/ Which-Forecasts-Should-I-Use-An-Add-in-for-Comparing-ARIMA-and/ta-p/398683

Figure 17.30: Model Comparison with Holdback Set

◢ **Model Comparison**

Report	Graph	Model Class	Model	RMSE ^	MSE	MAPE	MAE
		State Space Smoothing	AAdN	409.44835	167647.95	4.786613	317.11762
		State Space Smoothing	ANN	429.38158	184368.54	5.257269	339.92260
		State Space Smoothing	MNN	432.99508	187484.74	5.297416	341.96347
		State Space Smoothing	MMdN	433.44779	187876.98	5.302205	342.20685
		State Space Smoothing	MAdN	435.13150	189339.42	5.400721	347.38142
		State Space Smoothing	MAdM12	439.64529	193287.98	4.498887	287.36505
		State Space Smoothing	AAN	456.87426	208734.09	5.079778	335.51675
		State Space Smoothing	MAN	537.77216	289198.90	6.074821	408.42033
		ARIMA	Seasonal ARIMA(1, 1, 2)(0, 1, 1)12	571.33215	326420.43	6.688366	426.46609
		State Space Smoothing	MAM12	574.42480	329963.85	7.890032	521.28335
		ARIMA	Seasonal ARIMA(0, 1, 2)(0, 1, 1)12	592.71665	351313.03	7.050594	448.89076
		State Space Smoothing	MAA12	600.98093	361178.08	6.623848	422.55585
		State Space Smoothing	AAA12	618.83275	382953.97	7.063911	449.85211
		ARIMA	Seasonal ARIMA(1, 1, 0)(0, 1, 1)12	630.86325	397988.44	7.767428	494.48376
		State Space Smoothing	MAdA12	640.35277	410051.67	7.322160	466.74805
		State Space Smoothing	MNM12	643.50054	414092.95	7.702024	490.54849
		ARIMA	Seasonal ARIMA(1, 1, 2)(1, 1, 1)12	646.05070	417381.51	8.002108	509.81330
		State Space Smoothing	ANA12	658.31070	433372.97	7.648510	487.59680
		ARIMA	Seasonal ARIMA(2, 1, 2)(0, 1, 1)12	666.48295	444199.53	8.656942	549.74381

The Holdback Evaluation columns are: RMSE, MSE, MAPE, MAE.

This add-in can also be found with other textbook files. Download the **Time Series Cross-Validation.jmpaddin** file.

    2. Find on your computer where you downloaded the file, double click the add-in file. Click **Install**.

The time series cross-validation method iteratively subsets the data into training data sets and then tests models on each new training data set. Each subset is called a Group. With each successive Group, the training set is expanded by one more recent time period observation. This process continues until the last observation in the test set is the last period. The add-in default number of iterations or Groups is 6. For example, Figure 17.31 illustrates the six Groups for a data set with 25 observations, using the initial 14 observations in the first Group's training set and forecasting ahead (Forecast Length) of 6 periods (# of total observations = # of Initial Rows + Forecast Length + 6 (number of Groups) -1).

To execute this time series cross-validation add-in, on the top menu of the Data Table:

    1. Click **Add-Ins ▶ Times Series Model Selection**. The Disclaimer box will appear. Click **OK**.
    2. The Time Series – Model Class Selection dialog box similar to Figure 17.32 will appear. Click to select **Steel Shipments** as the **Y, Time Series** and select **DATE** as **X, Time ID.** Since

Figure 17.31: Example of Training and Testing Sets Using Time Series Cross-Validation

Time Period	Group 1	Group 2	Group 3	Group 4	Group 5	Group 6
1	◉	◉	◉	◉	◉	◉
2	◉	◉	◉	◉	◉	◉
3	◉	◉	◉	◉	◉	◉
4	◉	◉	◉	◉	◉	◉
5	◉	◉	◉	◉	◉	◉
6	◉	◉	◉	◉	◉	◉
7	◉	◉	◉	◉	◉	◉
8	◉	◉	◉	◉	◉	◉
9	◉	◉	◉	◉	◉	◉
10	◉	◉	◉	◉	◉	◉
11	◉	◉	◉	◉	◉	◉
12	◉	◉	◉	◉	◉	◉
13	◉	◉	◉	◉	◉	◉
14	◉	◉	◉	◉	◉	◉
15	●	◉	◉	◉	◉	◉
16	●	●	◉	◉	◉	◉
17	●	●	●	◉	◉	◉
18	●	●	●	●	◉	◉
19	●	●	●	●	●	◉
20	●	●	●	●	●	●
21		●	●	●	●	●
22			●	●	●	●
23				●	●	●
24					●	●
25						●

Figure 17.32: Time Series - Model Class Selection Dialog Box

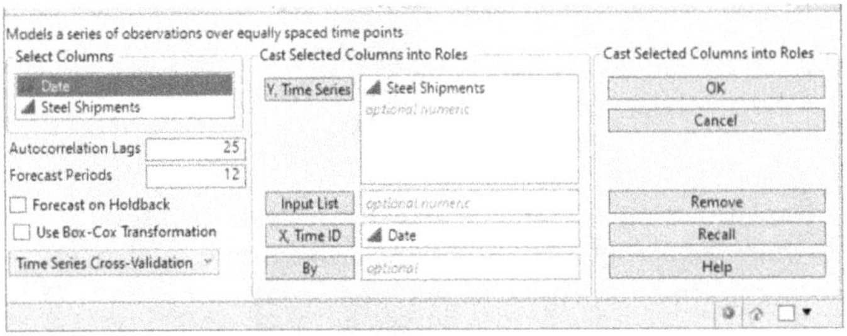

3. the data is monthly, change the default value of the number of Forecast Periods from 25 to **12**. Click **OK**.

3. The Time Series output similar to Figure 17.25 will appear with the addition of a Time Series Cross-Validation section at the bottom of the output. Click **Run**.

4. The ARIMA Model Group dialog box, similar to Figure 17.28, will appear. As before, on the left side under the ARIMA in the Autoregressive Order input **2** in the right box. In the Differencing Order on the left box, put **1** and in the right box put **1**. In the Moving Average Order, input **2** in the right box. On the right side under Seasonal ARIMA in the Autoregressive Order, input **1.** In the right box and in the Differencing Order, input **1** in the left and right box. In the Moving Average Order, input **1** in the right box.

5. Click **Estimate**.

The add-in expands the Steel Shipments data set into six time series cross-validation groups and fits, according to lowest AIC, the specified 36 ARIMA models and the recommended State Space Smoothing models to each training set. Then the add-in forecasts using the test set and stores the forecasting performance errors, RMSE, MAE, and MAPE. The routine returns a plot of the RMSE for each group and the average of each of the forecast error measurement, as shown in Figure 17.33. With this data set, the State Space Smoothing models consistently have smaller RMSEs in plot and lower average RMSE, MAE and MAPE. This analysis using the add-in would recommend using State Space Smoothing models to create forecasting for this Steel Shipment data instead of ARIMA models.

Time Series Forecast

The Time Series Forecast platform finds the best State Space Smoothing model automatically for each time series from a large set of time series. To illustrate the platform's functionality and capabilities, we will first demonstrate it with one time series and in particular the Steel Shipments data set:

1. Click **Analyze ▶ Specialized Modeling ▶ Time Series.**
2. Select **Steel Shipments** as the **Y, Time Series** and select **DATE** as **X, Time ID.**
3. Click **OK.**

Figure 17.33: Time Series Cross-Validation Output

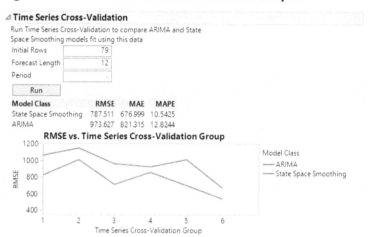

4. Click the **Time Series Steel Shipments** red triangle and from the list of options, click **State Space Smoothing**.
5. In the Specify State Space Smoothing Models dialog box, click **OK.**
6. Check the report box in the Model Comparison for the first model listed: MNM12.

Now, let's look at the time series model using the Time Series Forecast Platform:

7. Go back to the Steel Shipments data table and click **Analyze ▶ Specialized Modeling ▶ Time Series Forecast.**
8. The initial Time Series Forecast dialog box will appear. Select **Steel Shipments** as the **Y** and select **DATE** as **Time.** Click **OK.**
9. The second Time Series Forecast dialog box will appear, similar to Figure 17.34.

At the top of the dialog box are some summary statistics.

10. Under Modeling Specifications, click **Compete Specifications** and you can see that JMP is suggesting the same 19 State Space Smoothing models to run as it did when using the Time Series platform.
11. Click off the check in **Constrain Parameters**.
12. **NAhead** is the number of future forecasts to be made. Usually, **NAhead** and **Period** are equal to one season of the data. So, since we have monthly data, it is initially assigned a 12.
13. Click on the check box under **Other Options** for **Preserve Model Selection** Criterion. Click **Run**.

The best State Space Smoothing model using this platform is the same as before using the Time Series platform and is MNM12. Examining the two Model Reports, both platforms produced

Figure 17.34: Second Time Series Forecast Dialog Box

identical parameters and estimates. Click on the expand arrow next to **Information Criterion of All Models for All Series** and listed for each model will be its AIC value.

Similar to the holdback option in the Time Series platform, we can also perform holdback analysis under the Time Series Forecast platform. Click on the expand arrow next to **Modeling Specification** and click **Complete Specifications**. (You can also go back to the Data Table and start the analysis over; you will get identical Modeling Specification output.):

1. Under **Model Selection Strategy**, click **Complete Specifications**. Click the drop arrow for **Information Criteria** and click **Forecasting Performance**. The **Metric** changes to RMSE and **NHoldback** (number of holdback periods) to 12. Make sure **Constrain Parameters** is checked off and **Preserve Model Selection Criterion** is checked on.
2. Click **Run**.

The resulting new State Space Smoothing model is now AAdN as shown in Figure 17.35. This model is the holdback model that we found earlier shown in Figure 17.30 with the same RMSE; however, most parameters are slightly different.

Figure 17.35: Model Report Using a Holdback

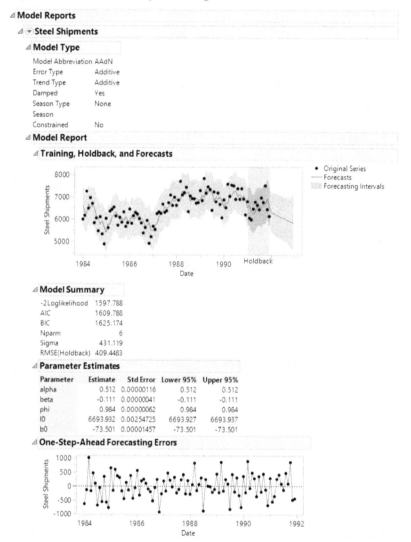

The Time Series and Times Series Forecast platforms each partition the data set into a training and holdback set and fit the selected models to the training set. Both platforms calculate the forecasting performance measures for the holdout set based on the model fitted with the training data set. At this point, the Time Series platform reports the results. On the other hand, the Times Series Forecast platform continues and refits the entire time series including the holdback using the selected type of error, trend, and seasonality. Thus, the different parameters.

To list the forecast values:

1. Click the **Time Series Forecast** red triangle and click Save **Results**.
2. In the Request Outputs dialog box, click **Save Original Series**; click **OK**.

A new Data Table is created with the Actual and Forecast values.

The Time Series Forecast platform is designed to find the best forecast model automatically for each time series from a large number of series. Let's use the data set M3C Quarterly Wide Format.jmp to demonstrate forecasting several time series all at once using the Time Series Forecast platform:

1. Open M3C Quarterly Wide Format.jmp: Select **Help ▶ Sample Index ▶ Times Series**. Click **M3C Quarterly Wide Format**. (Or you can find the M3C Quarterly Wide Format. jmp file with other textbook files.)
2. Click **Analyze ▶ Specialized Modeling ▶ Time Series Forecast.**
3. Select all 204 time series from **N 646** to **N849** as the **Y** and select **Time** as **Time.** Click **OK**.

Toward the top on the second Time Series Forecast dialog box, for each of the 204 times series there are some summary statistics.

4. Under Modeling Options, click off the check in Constrain Parameters.
5. Since the data is quarterly, **NAhead** and **Period** are equal to 4. Under **Other Options**, click **Preserve Model Selection Criterion**.
6. Click **Run**.

The best State Space Smoothing model is estimated for each of the 204 time series. One or more time series output can be added to the Model Report to examine. For example, as shown in Figure 17.36 for N648 to N650, their time series model report is added to the output.

In summary, in this time series forecasting chapter we have discussed many techniques and statistical tests. There is not one particular forecasting technique or methodology that is superior. Each data set presents a different challenge to develop a "good" or "best" model. This chapter provided the necessary statistical forecasting knowledge and explanation of JMP tools to assist you in seeking the "good" or "best" model.

Figure 17.36: Time Series N 648, N 649, and N 650 Model Output

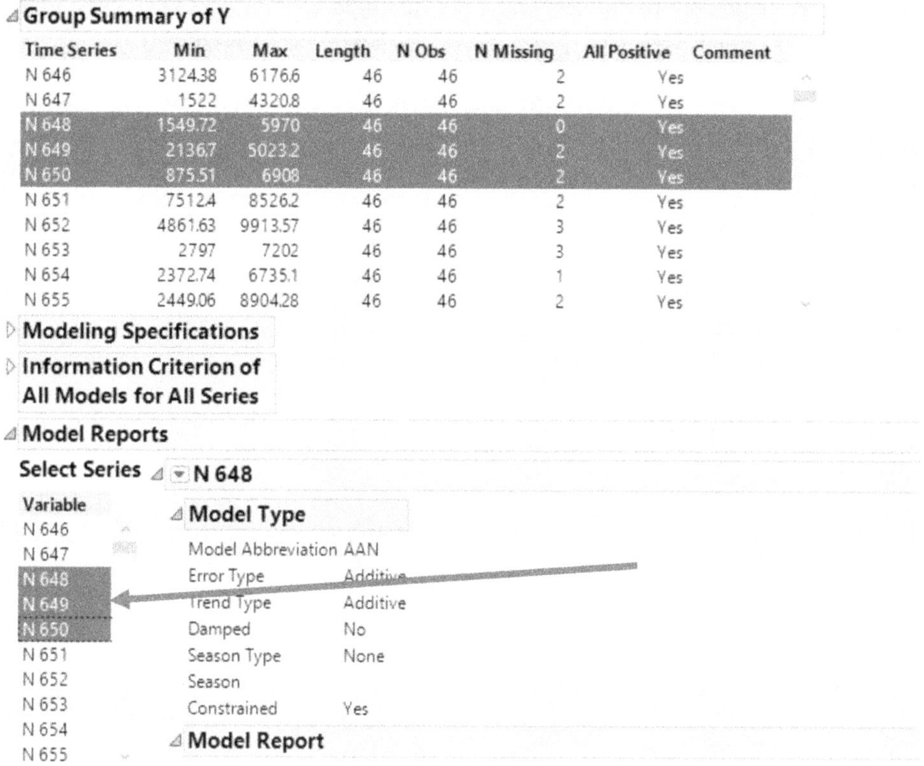

Group Summary of Y

Time Series	Min	Max	Length	N Obs	N Missing	All Positive	Comment
N 646	3124.38	6176.6	46	46	2	Yes	
N 647	1522	4320.8	46	46	2	Yes	
N 648	1549.72	5970	46	46	0	Yes	
N 649	2136.7	5023.2	46	46	2	Yes	
N 650	875.51	6908	46	46	2	Yes	
N 651	7512.4	8526.2	46	46	2	Yes	
N 652	4861.63	9913.57	46	46	3	Yes	
N 653	2797	7202	46	46	3	Yes	
N 654	2372.74	6735.1	46	46	1	Yes	
N 655	2449.06	8904.28	46	46	2	Yes	

▷ **Modeling Specifications**

▷ **Information Criterion of All Models for All Series**

◢ **Model Reports**

Select Series ◢ ▽ **N 648**

Variable	
N 646	◢ **Model Type**
N 647	
N 648	Model Abbreviation AAN
N 649	Error Type Additive
N 650	Trend Type Additive
N 651	Damped No
N 652	Season Type None
N 653	Season
N 654	Constrained Yes
N 655	◢ **Model Report**

Exercises

1. Use the Workers.jmp file. Find the best smoothing model. Explain why. What are the model's parameters and predict one period ahead.

2. Use the Raleigh Temps.jmp file. Using the variable Temperature, run an AR(1) model. Evaluate the model. Run a Seasonal model with an AR of 1 and seasonal differencing 1. Evaluate this seasonal model. Which model is best? Explain why.

3. Use the Lead Production.jmp file. Run ARIMA Model Group. Set the range for all parameters from 0 to 1. Which model is best? Explain why.

4. Use the Raleigh Temps.jmp file. Run the ARIMA Model Group. Which model is the best? Explain why. Is this model better than your best model in question 2?

5. Use the Lead Production.jmp file. Use the Holdback of 12 periods and run State Space Smoothing models (remember to deselect Constrain Parameters). Run ARIMA Model Group. Set the range for all parameters from 0 to 1. Which model is best? Explain why.

6. Use the Crates.xlsx file. Run an additive regression model. Evaluate it. Run other time series models. Which one is the best? Explain why.

7. Use the World_bank_life_expectancy.xlsx (USA) file. Find the best forecasting model. Explain why. Predict the next year.

8. Use the World_bank_life_expectancy.xlsx (World) file. Which country would you like to live in just in terms of life expectancy? Explain why.

Data from: https://data.worldbank.org/indicator/SP.DYN.LE00.IN

Chapter 18: Statistical Storytelling

The Path from Multivariate Data to the Modeling Process

As you have read the early chapters, you likely have come to realize that we feel strongly that before discussing predictive analytics or performing a modeling project, you need to understand how to deal with multivariate data. That is one of this book's main objectives. In particular, you need a foundation beyond the univariate and bivariate analysis taught and learned in a basic statistics course to understand some of the issues involved in addressing real-world—that is, multivariate—data. Hopefully, the previous chapters have achieved that goal. Now, you are better prepared to understand data mining (or predictive analytics and modeling) and to conduct a modeling project.

We conclude here with a basic overview of *data mining* (or *predictive analytics* or *predictive modeling*) and of the modeling process using JMP.

For the past 25 years, the big buzzword in the business analytics (BA) area has been *data mining*. The roots of data mining techniques run deep and can be traced back to three areas—statistics, artificial intelligence (AI), and machine learning. All data mining tools and techniques have a strong foundation in classical statistical analysis. In the 1970s and 1980s, AI techniques based on heuristics that attempted to simulate human thought processes were developed. Subsequently the field of machine learning, which is the union of statistics and AI, evolved. An example of machine learning is a computer program that learns more about the game of chess as it plays more and more games.

Early Applications of Data Mining

Two areas of early successful application of data mining have been credit card fraud detection and customer relationship management.

Credit Card Fraud Detection

On the basis of analyzing customers' historical buying patterns, data mining models identify potential credit card fraud in transactions that are out of the "norm." For example, suppose you have never traveled to South America, but you want to go to the World Cup in Brazil in 2014. So, you book a flight to Brazil and charge it on your credit card. While in Brazil, you think it would be nice to go on a few side trips—for example, to see Iguassu Falls. You then book a flight and accommodations and tour package with your credit card. Subsequently, you receive an email from your credit card company saying that your card transactions are temporarily suspended and to please contact it. The credit card company wants to make sure your card has not been stolen because you were making significant purchases outside your normal spending pattern. Data mining models are used to target such behavior.

Customer Relationship Management

The other area of early successful data mining applications is *customer relationship management* (CRM). CRM is a process or business strategy taken by companies to improve overall customer satisfaction, especially for their best customers. For example, large companies with multiple product offerings might have several customers that buy products across the company's product line. However, each division of the company might have separate sales and support staff as well as their own independent database. A CRM solution to this situation would be one company-wide database that allows everyone in the company to access the data on a particular customer, which improves customer satisfaction and promotes cross-selling opportunities.

Numerous JMP Customer Stories of Modern Applications

JMP provides numerous customer stories of successful data mining or statistical applications in several industry areas (aerospace, conservation, education, energy, genomics, government, health care, manufacturing, pharmaceuticals, and semiconductor) and by statistical application areas (see JMP Customer Stories: https://www.jmp.com/en_my/customer-stories/customer-listing/featured.html).

Definitions of Data Mining

Defined broadly, *data mining* is a process of finding patterns in data to help us make better decisions. Or more simply, as a good old friend of ours would say, it is mining data. In a nutshell, he is basically right. Furthermore, as Stuart Ewen wrote in the *New York Times,* "Probably at no time in the last decade has the actual knowledge of consumer buying habits been as vital to successful and profitable retailing as it is today" (1996, p. 184).

However, Ewen's statement was first written in 1931. So data mining is not new, and successful decision makers have always done it. Then why has the area of data mining grown so much recently? What has changed? The change has been the confluence of the three areas of data mining:

- Statistics, AI, and machine learning.
- The exponential increase in our computer power.
- The scale of data accumulation has amplified this new area called data mining.

Nonetheless, *data mining* is not the current buzzword anymore. It has been replaced by the terms *predictive analytics* and *predictive modeling*. What is the difference between these terms? As we discussed, with the many and evolving definitions of *business intelligence* in Chapter 1, these terms seem to have many different yet quite similar definitions. One SAS expert defines these terms as follows.

Data Mining

Data mining has been defined in a lot of ways, but at the heart of all of these definitions is a process for analyzing data that typically includes the following steps:

- Formulate the problem.
- Accumulate data.
- Transform and select data.
- Train models.
- Evaluate models.
- Deploy models.
- Monitor results.

Predictive Analytics

Predictive analytics is an umbrella term that encompasses both data mining and predictive modeling, as well as a number of other analytical techniques. We define *predictive analytics* as a collection of statistical and data mining techniques that analyze data to make predictions about future events.

Predictive modeling is one such technique that answers questions such as the following:

- Who's likely to respond to a campaign?
- How much do first-time purchasers usually spend?
- Which customers are likely to default?

Predictive analytics is a subset of analytics, which more broadly includes other areas of statistics like experimental design, time series forecasting, operations research, and text analytics.[1]

---

[1] http://www.sas.com/news/sascom/2010q1/column_tech.html

Figure 18.1: A Framework for Predictive Analytics Techniques

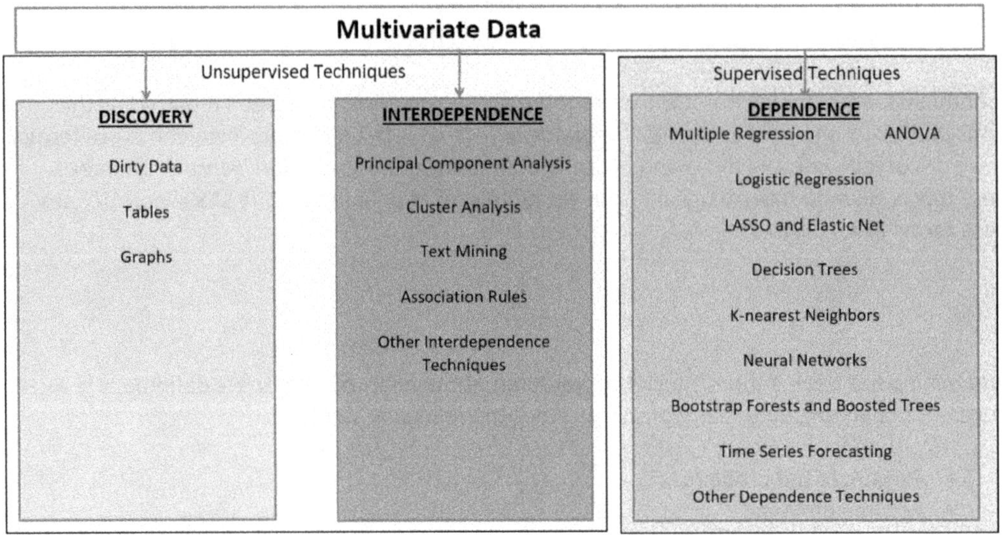

Multivariate Data	
Unsupervised Techniques	**Supervised Techniques**

DISCOVERY	INTERDEPENDENCE	DEPENDENCE
Dirty Data	Principal Component Analysis	Multiple Regression ANOVA
Tables	Cluster Analysis	Logistic Regression
Graphs	Text Mining	LASSO and Elastic Net
	Association Rules	Decision Trees
	Other Interdependence Techniques	K-nearest Neighbors
		Neural Networks
		Bootstrap Forests and Boosted Trees
		Time Series Forecasting
		Other Dependence Techniques

A Framework for Predictive Analytics Techniques

There appear to be two common major characterizations of the terms *data mining*, *predictive analytics*, and *predictive modeling*. You can view them as a collection of advanced statistical techniques. Or you can view them as a modeling process.

In terms of a collection of advanced statistical techniques, several approaches have been used to classify data mining, predictive analytics, and predictive modeling.[2] We categorize these predictive analytics techniques into supervised (directed) or unsupervised (undirected) learning techniques as shown in Figure 18.1.

With the unsupervised learning techniques, there is no target or dependent variable(s). An example of an unsupervised learning predictive analytics technique is association rules (or market basket analysis or affinity grouping). With the association rules technique, we try to identify which things (in most cases, products) go together. For example, when you go grocery shopping, which products are sold together? An example would be milk and cereal or the unexpected classic data mining example of diapers and beer.

With supervised learning techniques, the goal is to develop a model that describes what affects one variable of interest (and occasionally more than one). The variable of interest is called the *dependent variable*. The goal is to establish one or more significant relationships among the

---

[2] Remember that we use these terms interchangeably to mean the same thing.

other variables (called *independent variables*) and this dependent variable. We have examined several such supervised techniques in this book:

- regression
- logistic regression
- ANOVA
- decision trees
- *k*-nearest neighbors
- neural networks
- bootstrap forests
- boosted trees
- time series forecasting

The decision trees, *k*-nearest neighbors, neural networks, bootstrap forests, and boosted trees techniques are usually considered supervised learning predictive analytics techniques.

Another step found in many data mining and predictive analytics projects, especially when you have a large data set, is to compare the various models and divide the data set into training and validation, which was discussed in Chapter 14.

Finally, notice that in classifying and listing these predictive analytics techniques (see Figure 18.1), we do include the basic statistical tools and techniques that you learned in the introduction to statistics, as well as address dirty data and the multivariate techniques discussed in this book. These tools and techniques are also part of predictive analytics and the modeling process.

The Goal, Tasks, and Phases of Predictive Analytics

The goal of these advanced statistical techniques, whether supervised or unsupervised, is to extract information from the data. The six main tasks of predictive analytics with their associated activities are as follows:

Discovery

describes, summarizes, and visualizes the data and develops a basic understanding of their relationships.

Classification

places each object into a predefined set of classes or groups.

Estimation

is similar to classification but the dependent or target variable is continuous.

Clustering

segments each object into a number of subgroups or clusters where the difference between *classification* and *clustering* is that clustering the classes or groups is not predefined but is developed by the technique.

Association

determines which items go together (for example, which items are concurrently brought together).

Prediction

identifies variables that are related to one or more other variables so as to predict or estimate their future values.

The tasks of discovery, clustering, and association are all examples of unsupervised (undirected) learning. The other three tasks—classification, estimation, and prediction—are examples of supervised (directed) learning.

In this text, you have examined several of the fundamental-to-advanced statistical techniques:

- discovery tools
- clustering
- principal component analysis and factor analysis
- ANOVA
- regression
- logistic regression
- decision trees
- *k*-nearest neighbors
- neural networks
- bootstrap forests
- boosted trees
- time series forecasting
- model comparison

JMP is a comprehensive statistical and predictive analytics package. So, in addition to the JMP techniques and tools discussed in the text, JMP provides other predictive analytics and multivariate techniques such as conjoint analysis (in particular, discrete choice analysis), as well as several other statistical techniques.

The Difference between Statistics and Data Mining

So, what are the differences between statistics and data mining, predictive analytics, and predictive modeling? This question is difficult to answer. First, both disciplines share numerous similar tools and techniques. However, both disciplines are much more than several tools and techniques. The major differences seem to lie in their objectives and processes.

The broadening of the definition for *predictive analytics* from a collection of statistical techniques to a process is the second point of view of predictive analytics. This broadening of the definition reflects the maturity of the discipline

Berry and Linoff (2004) define *data mining* as "a business process for exploring a large amount of data to discover meaningful patterns and rules." The phases of the data mining process are listed in Table 18.1. This process is not necessarily linear. That is, you do not always proceed from one phase to the next listed phase. Many times, if not most of the time, depending on the phase's results, the data mining project might require you to go back one or more phases. The process is usually iterative.

As you can see from Table 18.1, what we have discussed in this book concerns only 20% of the time spent on a data mining project: model development and evaluation. While "data understanding" does require some use of statistics (scatterplots, univariate summary statistics, and the like), easily 50% of the analyst's time will be spent on the mundane and tedious tasks of data preparation and data understanding. You addressed some of these issues in Chapter 3. But note that little is written about data preparation and data understanding, which makes learning about these topics difficult. There is a notable exception, though—the excellent book by Pyle (1999). We recommend it to anyone who wishes to understand the basics of data collection and understanding.

Often in statistical studies, the study's objectives are well defined, so the project is well focused and directed. The data is collected to answer the study's specific questions. A major focus of most statistical studies and processes is to draw inferences about the population based on the sample.

Table 18.1: The Data Mining Process and the Percentage of Time Spent on Each Phase

Phase	Time (%)
Project definition	5
Data collection	20
Data preparation	30
Data understanding	20
Model development and evaluation	20
Implementation	5

By contrast, in many predictive analytics projects, besides having a significantly large data set, in many cases, the data is the entire population. This makes statistical inference a moot point. The data in a predictive analytics project is rarely collected with a well-defined objective of analysis. It is usually retrieved from several data sources, and it is most likely dirty data. As a result, unlike most statistical studies, the data must be integrated from these different sources and appropriately aggregated. Just like statistical studies, the data in a data mining project must be cleaned and prepared for analysis. However, due to the numerous sources of data and the usually larger number of variables, this phase of the process is much more labor intensive. Both processes share the same concern: to develop an understanding, description, and summary of the data.

SEMMA

The primary phase of the data mining or predictive analytics modeling process, which many people would define as data mining or predictive analytics (the first point of view), is the model development and evaluation phase. This phase might account for only about 20% of the project's overall efforts (mainly because of the large amount of effort to integrate and prepare the data).

SAS Institute Inc. developed a systematic approach to this phase of the data mining process called SEMMA (Azevedo and Santos, 2008):

S—Sample. If possible (that is, if you have a large enough data set), extract a sample that contains the significant information, yet is small enough to process quickly. The part of the data set that remains can be used to validate and test the model developed.

E—Explore. Use discovery tools and various data reduction tools to further understand data and search for hidden trends and relationships.

M—Modify. Create, transform, and group variables to enhance the analysis.

M—Model. Choose and apply one or more appropriate data mining techniques.

A—Assess. Build several models using multiple techniques, evaluate, assess the usefulness, and compare the models results. If a small portion of the large data set was set aside during the sample stage, validate and test the model.

Once the "best" model is identified, the model is deployed, and the ROI from the data mining process is realized.

The objective of the model development and evaluation phase is to uncover unsuspected but valuable relationships. So you search until you find a model that fits the data set arbitrarily well so that it is not overly complex and the model does not overfit the data. Statisticians become concerned with such a data-driven analysis approach to obtain a good fit because they are aware that such a search could lead to relationships that happen purely by chance. Unlike most statistical studies, predictive analytics projects are less focused on statistical significance and more on the practical importance—on obtaining answers that will improve decision making. Nevertheless, even though objectives and processes might differ, the bottom line of statistical studies and data mining projects is to learn from the data.

We hope this book has provided you with a foundation to conduct a statistical study (or a predictive analytics project) and planted the seeds on how to write a statistical story.

Happy storytelling!

References

Ashenfelder, Mike. (2011). "Transferring 'Libraries of Congress' of Data." *The Signal*, Library of Congress, July 11, 2011. https://blogs.loc.gov/thesignal/2011/07/transferring-libraries-of-congress-of-data/.

Azevedo, Ana, and Manuel Filipe Santos. (2008). "KDD, SEMMA and CRISP-DM: A Parallel Overview." *Proceedings of the IADIS European Conference on Data Mining*. Lisbon, Portugal: IADIS Press, 182–185.

Berk, Richard A. (2008). Statistical Learning from a Regression Perspective. New York: Springer.

Berry, Michael. J. A., and Gordon. S. Linoff. (2004). *Data Mining Techniques: For Marketing, Sales, and Customer Relationship Management.* 2nd ed. Indianapolis: Wiley.

Bigi, Brigitte. (2003, April). "Using Kullback-Leibler Distance for Text Categorization." *Advances in Information Retrieval*, 25th European Conference on IR Research, ECIR 2003, Pisa, Italy, Volume 2633 of the series Lecture Notes in Computer Science (Fabrizio Sebastiani, ed). Berlin: Springer-Verlag, 305–319.

Box, G.E.P. and G.M. Jenkins (1970). Time series analysis: Forecasting and control. San Francisco: Holden-Day.

Breiman, Leo. (2001, October). "Random Forests." *Machine Learning* 45(1), 5–32.

Brijs Tom, Gilbert Swinnen, Koen Vanhoof, and Geert Wets. (1999). "Using Association Rules for Product Assortment Decisions: A Case Study." *Proceedings of the Fifth International Conference on Knowledge Discovery and Data Mining*. New York: Association for Computing Machinery, 254–260.

Chatfield, C. and M. Yar (1988). "Holt-Winters Forecasting: Some Practical Issues," Journal of the Royal Statistical Society. Series D (The Statistician), Vol. 37, No. 2, pp. 129-140.

Cravens, David. W., Robert. B. Woodruff, and Joe. C. Stamper. (1972). "An Analytical Approach for Evaluating Sales Territory Performance." *Journal of Marketing*, 36(1), 31–37.

dataMontgomery, "Traffic Violations: Data." Montgomery County, Maryland. https://data.montgomerycountymd.gov/Public-Safety/Traffic-Violations/4mse-ku6q.

dataMontgomery. "Traffic Violations: API." Montgomery County, Maryland. http://www.opendatanetwork.com/dataset/data.montgomerycountymd.gov/4mse-ku6q.

Davenport, Thomas H., and Jeanne G. Harris. (2007). *Competing on Analytics: The New Science of Winning*. Boston: Harvard Business School Press.

Ewen, Stuart. (1996). *PR!: A Social History of Spin*. New York: Basic Books.

Eysenck, Michael. W. (1974). "Age differences in incidental learning." *Developmental Psychology*, 10(6), 936–941.

Few, Stephen. (2006). "Multivariate Analysis Using Parallel Coordinates." Manuscript. At https://www.perceptualedge.com/articles/b-eye/parallel_coordinates.pdf.

Foster, Dean P., and Robert A. Stine. (2006). "Honest Confidence Intervals for the Error Variance in Stepwise Regression." *Journal of Economic and Social Measurement*, 31(1–2), 89–102.

Gardner, E.S. (1985). "Exponential Smoothing: The state of the Art," Journal of Forecasting, Vol. 4, pp. 1-28.

Gorman, Michael. F., and Ronald. K. Klimberg. (2014). "Benchmarking Academic Programs in Business Analytics." *Interfaces*, 44(3), 329–341.

Hastie, Trevor, Robert Tibshirani, and Jerome Friedman. (2009). *The Elements of Statistical Learning: Data Mining, Inference, and Prediction.* 2nd ed. New York: Springer.

Hosmer, David. W., and Stanley. Lemeshow. (2000). *Applied Logistic Regression.* 2nd ed. New York: Wiley.

Humby, Clive, Terry Hunt, and Tim Phillips. (2007). *Scoring Points: How Tesco Continues to Win Customer Loyalty*. 2nd ed. Philadelphia: Kogan Page.

Hyndman, R. J. (2022). (https://robjhyndman.com/hyndsight/ljung-box-test/).

Hyndman, R. J. and G. Athanasopoulos (2021). Forecasting: Principles and Practice, 3rd edition. https://otexts.com/fpp3/.

Hyndman, R. J., Koehler, A. B., Snyder, R. D. and S. Grose (2002). "A state space framework for automatic forecasting using exponential smoothing methods," International Journal of Forecasting, 18, pp. 439-454.

Hyndman, R. J., Koehler, A. B., Ord, J. K. and R. D. Snyder (2008). "Forecasting with Exponential Smoothing: The State Space Approach," Springer.

JMP Customer Stories. https://www.jmp.com/en_us/customer-stories/customer-listing/featured.html.

Johnson, Richard A., and Dean W. Wichern. (2002). *Applied Multivariate Statistical Analysis.* 5th ed. Upper Saddle River, NJ: Prentice Hall.

Klimberg, Ronald K., and Virginia Miori. (2010). "Back in Business." *ORMS Today*, 37(5), 22–27.

Kuiper, Shonda. (2008). "Introduction to Multiple Regression: How Much Is Your Car Worth?" *Journal of Statistics Education*, 16(3), 1–14.

Lai, Eric. (2008, June 23). "The '640K' Quote Won't Go Away—But Did Gates Really Say It?" *Computerworld*. http://www.computerworld.com/article/2534312/operating-systems/the–640k–quote-won-t-go-away––but-did-gates-really-say-it-.html.

Leinweber, David J. (2007). "Stupid Data Miner Tricks: Overfitting the S&P 500." *Journal of Investing*, 16(1), 15–22.

Lewis, C. D. (1982). Industrial and business forecasting methods: A Radical guide to exponential smoothing and curve fitting. London; Boston: Butterworth Scientific.

Linoff, Gordon S., and Michael J. A. Berry. (2011). *Data Mining Techniques: For Marketing, Sales, and Customer Relationship Management*. 3rd ed. Indianapolis: Wiley.

Lomas, Natasha. (2008, November 19). "Q&A: Kurzweil on Tech as a Double-Edged Sword." *CNET News*. CBS Interactive. https://www.cnet.com/science/q-a-kurzweil-on-tech-as-a-double-edged-sword/.

Marquardt, Donald W. (1980). "You Should Standardize the Predictor Variables in Your Regression Models." Discussion of "A Critique of Some Ridge Regression Methods," by Gary Smith and Frank Campbell. *Journal of the American Statistical Association*, 75(369), 87–91.

Marr, Bernard. (2015, September 30). "Big Data: 20 Mind-Boggling Facts Everyone Must Read," *Forbes Magazine* Tech post.

Nelson, L. S., (1984). "The Shewhart Control Chart–Test for Special Causes," Journal of Quality Technology, 16, pp. 237-239.

Pegels, C. C. (1969). "Exponential Forecasting: Some New Variations," Management Science, Vol. 12, No. 5, pp. 311-315.

Pollack, Richard D. (2008). "Data Mining: Common Definitions, Applications, and Misunderstandings." *Data Mining Methods and Applications* (Discrete Mathematics & Its Applications), Boca Raton, FL: Auerbach Publications, 229–238.

Power, Dan. (2011). "What Is the 'True Story' about Using Data Mining to Identify a Relationship between Sales of Beer and Diapers?" DSS Resources.com.

Pyle, Dorian. (1999). *Data Preparation for Data Mining*. San Francisco: Morgan Kaufmann.

Rahman, Hakikur. (2009). Social and Political Implications of Data Mining: Knowledge Management in E-Government. Hershey, PA: IGI Global.

Sall, John, Lee Creighton, and Ann Lehman. (2007). *JMP Start Statistics: A Guide to Statistics and Data Analysis Using JMP.* 4th ed. Cary, NC: SAS Institute Inc.

SAS Institute Inc. (1983). *SAS Technical Report A-108: Cubic Clustering Criterion*. Cary, NC: SAS Institute Inc. Accessed December 16, 2015.

SAS, https://go.documentation.sas.com/doc/en/pgmsascdc/v_035/hpfug/hpfug_hpfdet_sect013.htm.

Shalizi, Cosma. (2010). "The Bootstrap." *American Scientist,* 98(3), 186–190.

Snee, Ronald D. (1973). "Some Aspects of Nonorthogonal Data Analysis: Part I. Developing Prediction Equations." *Journal of Quality Technology,* 5(2), 67–79.

Stathakis, D. (2009). "How Many Hidden Layers and Nodes?" *International Journal of Remote Sensing*, 30(8), 2133–2147.

Tan, Pang-Ning, Michael Steinbach, and Vipin Kumar. (2006). *Introduction to Data Mining.* Boston: Pearson Addison-Wesley.

Tuffery, Stephane. (2011). *Data Mining and Statistics for Decision Making (Wiley Series in Computational Statistics).* Chichester, West Sussex, UK: Wiley.

Vijayan, Jaikumar. (2015, June 25). "Solving the Unstructured Data Challenge." *CIO.* https://www.cio.com/article/244359/solving-the-unstructured-data-challenge.html.

Vuk, Miha, and Tomaz Curk. (2006). "ROC Curve, Lift Chart and Calibration Plot." *Metodoloski Zvezki,* 3(1), 89–108.

Weigend, Andreas S., and Neil A. Gershenfeld (Eds.). (1994). *Time Series Prediction: Forecasting the Future and Understanding the Past.* Proceedings of the NATO Advanced Research Workshop on Comparative Time Series Analysis, Santa Fe, New Mexico, May 14–17, 1992. Reading, MA: Addison-Wesley.

Ying, Li, and Wu Yuanyuan. (2010). "Application of Clustering on Credit Card Customer Segmentation Based on AHP." *International Conference on Logistics Systems and Intelligence Management*, 3, 1869–1873.

Yoon, Youngohc, Tor Guimaraes, and George Swales. (1994). "Integrating Artificial Neural Networks with Rule-Based Expert Systems." *Decision Support Systems*, 11(5), 497–507.

Index

Ready to take your SAS® and JMP® skills up a notch?

Be among the first to know about new books,
special events, and exclusive discounts.
support.sas.com/newbooks

Share your expertise. Write a book with SAS.
support.sas.com/publish

Continue your skills development with free online learning.
www.sas.com/free-training

sas.com/books
for additional books and resources.

THE POWER TO KNOW.